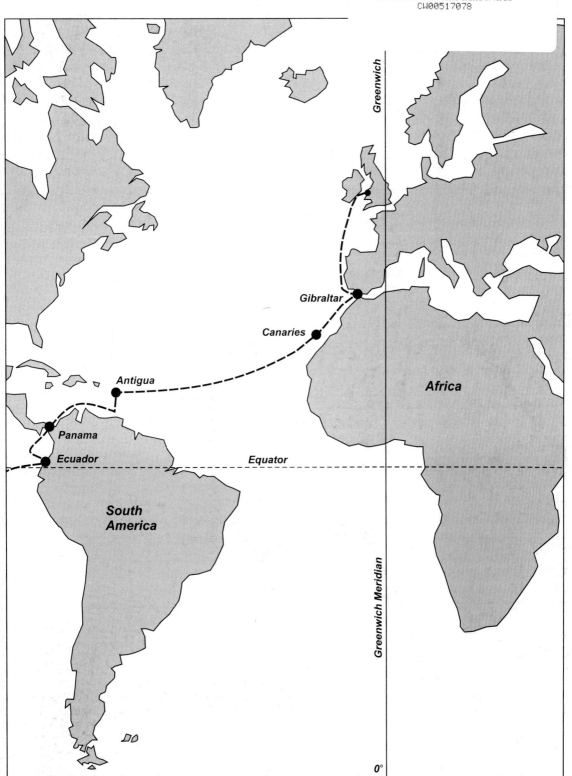

Published: 2002

Copyright©:   **Burke Publishing**
                  email: info@burkepublishing.com
                  email: promatec@xtra.co.nz
                  email: pacificvoyager@hotmail.com
                  website: bluewater-cruising.com
                  website: burkepublishing.com

Distributors: UK: Kelvin Hughes <southampton@kelvinhughes.co.uk>
                  UK: Kelvin Hughes <www.bookharbour.com>
                  UK: Sowester <sow@sowester.co.uk> <www.sowester.com>
                  UK:Gardners Books<sales@gardners.com>
                  UK: Gardners Books <www.gardners.com>
                  USA: Robert Hale <stacia@waggonerguide.com>
                  USA: Partners Book Distribution <partnersbk@aol.com>
                  SA: Technical Books <info@techbooks.co.za>
                  AUS: Kirby Books <orders@kirby.com.au>
                  NZ: Addenda <addenda@addenda.co.nz><www.addenda.co.nz>
                  HK: Publishers Assocites Ltd <pal@netvigator.com>
                  Singapore: Pansing Distribution <pansing@singnet.com.sg>

Mail order: www.bluewater-cruising.com
                  www.amazon.co.uk
                  www.amazon.com
                  www.flyingpig.co.nz

Production notes: Page size (168 x 240 mm), body text (Palatino Linotype, 10 point, 12 leading). Photograph captions (Arial, bold, italic, 9 point, leading 10.8). Chapter headline (Arial, bold, italic, 30 and 20 points, leading 20). Master pages (Arial Narrow, 11 point, leading 13). Pagemaker, Photoshop, CorelDRAW, Dell Inspiron notebook computer.

ISBN: 0-620-16557-X

Cover Design: Renegade, email: stormnz@ihug.co.nz
Printer: ABC Press, email: abcpress@iafrica.com

Greenwich to the Dateline

Bluewater Cruising to the Caribbean and Pacific

Rory Burke
Sandra Burke

.... dedicated to the explorers - their voyages of discovery inspired us to follow in their wake

Rory at Diaz's padrao in Namibia

Table of Contents

Appendices

Making landfall

Our bimini protects us from the sun

Foreword
by Ken Sheridan

Bluewater cruising around the world has become a popular challenge for cruising couples - so I was not surprised when Rory and Sandra embarked on such an enterprise. As we watched them depart, on their circumnavigation, from the old slate steps in front of the Madoc Yacht Club, we wondered what adventurers their bluewater cruise would have in store for them.

As an ex-RYA yachtmaster instructor I was particularly interested to see how Rory prepared for his cruise. Aside from starting out with a well-found and well-equipped yacht, Rory needed to team up with a sailing companion of complimentary skills and experience who shared his enthusiasm for adventure and the sea. Rory certainly succeeded in this regard when he met Sandra and persuaded her to join him. He had found an ideal mate in more senses than one - he found a wife too!!!

It is clear from this book that the bluewater cruiser requires a wide range of skills. Besides the traditional navigation and seamanship skills incorporated in the Yachtmaster Ocean syllabus, the bluewater cruiser should be street-wise when provisioning in foreign ports, diplomatic when dealing with bureaucracy, and have a wide range of trade skills to maintain and repair the yacht's equipment en route.

Greenwich to the Dateline is the perfect sequel to Rory and Sandra's first cruising book - *Managing Your Bluewater Cruise*. Here they tell their fascinating story of how they sailed from Porthmadog in North Wales, across the Atlantic Ocean, Caribbean Sea and Pacific Ocean, to New Zealand - at *the other end of the world*.

Their book is much more than just the story of their trip, it is full of useful information on *how to do it*, what you might experience along the way, and how to fulfil that dream and alternative lifestyle. I am sure it will inspire you to follow in their wake and lure you to many idyllic anchorages around the world.

Ken Sheridan
President
Madoc Yacht Club

Foreword
by Robert Burns

Chance encounters often lead to life-long friendships – we met Rory and Sandra during a close encounter with a shoal in beautiful Cook's Bay on Moorea [see page 219] and have shared more than a few bottles of rum with them over the better part of a decade since then.

When Judi and I set out to circumnavigate in 1992, we read everything we could get our hands on – narratives, cruising guides, how-to books, horror stories, and monthly letters from those who out there *'doing it'*- all in an attempt to avoid the mistakes of the past. We found the information helped us identify weather windows, catch water, avoid shoals, turn unused space into useful storage lockers, and learn many of the skills and customs of the accomplished cruisers. Now, more than 8 years and 20,000 miles later we feel we are almost *'old hands'* at the business of cruising. We have still made some mistakes, from lack of skill, or knowledge, or attention, but hopefully far fewer than if we had not been able to learn from those who lead the way. Like most cruisers, we have tried to share our information with those who are sailing with or behind us. The World Wide Web has provided us with an outlet where we share some of our exciting times and lessons learned at www.longpassages.org.

Fortunately, some people create bodies of knowledge with more longevity than the transient images on the Web, and Rory while becoming an *'old hand'* at cruising, is one of these people. As more baby-boomers reach retirement age and shed the shackles of 9-5 life, many will strike out for faraway places and some will do it on cruising yachts away from the beaten track of mainstream tourism. By narrating their experiences from the UK to the Antipodes, Rory and Sandra help to bring recent information and *'lessons-learned'* to those adventurous enough to follow in their wake. Sit back in front of a warm fire or under a shady tree and enjoy the adventures and misadventures of the crew of *'Pacific Voyager'*.

Robert Burns
S/V *Long Passages*
www.longpassages.org
Singapore

Acknowledgements

During the writing of this book we have re-lived our personal voyage of discovery from the Greenwich Meridian in Britain, to the International Dateline in the South Pacific - or more precisely from Porthmadog in North Wales, to Opua in New Zealand. Although it was just the two of us aboard *Pacific Voyager*, sailing the high seas together, we are indebted to many friends and family who supported our bluewater cruise and helped *'make it happen'*.

Our first challenge was to reorganise our lives in Cape Town, leave the security of employment, store our possessions and rent-out our house. At this stage, support was thin on the ground. In fact our friends thought we were mad, we must be having a mid-life crisis - this made us even more determined to pursue our dreams.

In Britain, our thanks go to Sandra's parents, Peggy and John, for looking after us while we scoured the South Coast for a yacht, and to our long standing friend, Nick Stanton, who checked over the Nicholson 35 and assured us we were making a good decision.

In Salcombe, thanks to Brian Watkins (yacht broker) who sold the Nicholson 35 to us, and for lending us his ladder so that we could climb up and live on board *Pacific Voyager* while she stood in the car park. Thanks to the local marine industry; boat stores and trades who provided us with the equipment and expertise to fit out our yacht. (This however, excludes the rigger who failed to fit a split-pin to the new forestay. We were lucky not to lose the rig on our first passage - see page 14.)

In Porthmadog, thanks to our friends at the Madoc Yacht Club, particularly Ken and Rosemary who organised a mooring for us beside their boat *Onaway*, Gareth the steward, Reg Sington for supplying the grog to rename our yacht *Pacific Voyager*, David Eastwood of Glaslyn Marine for suggesting where to stow our Bruce anchor, Dr. John for teaching us how to stitch oranges in his surgery, and Reg Maynard (Hong Kong) for giving us the inspiration to follow his lifestyle and take off on our circumnavigation.

In Portugal, thanks to Boris, a retired brain surgeon, for giving us our final immunisation injections and assuring us we were mentally okay. In Gibraltar and beyond, thanks to Westmarine for giving us the comfort of knowing that all their marine equipment was only a fax away.

Special thanks to all the yachties we met along the way who made our cruise a very special experience. Originally we thought bluewater cruising would be a sailing epic where we would spend long periods alone at sea - we were wrong. We have never lived in such a social environment, with a wonderful camaraderie between fellow cruisers.

Thanks to the volunteers who organised radio nets on the VHF, SSB and Ham - even in the remote anchorages there was always someone providing information. Special thanks to Herb (*Southbound 11*), Dave (*Misteen*), Arnold, and Jonathan and Roxanna (*Xaxero*) for providing accurate weather forecasts.

Thanks to the local people we met along the way who made our trip such a memorable experience; especially our friends in Tahaa for taking us to the local beauty contest (this made Rory's day!), Karla and her family in Tonga who invited us to their village church and into their home to partake in the most amazingly scrumptious Tongan feast.

In New Zealand, special thanks to Alan Taylor, Brian Farley and their team at AUT. They were always a phone call away to help Sandra set up the book in CorelDRAW, Photoshop and Pagemaker.

We are indebted to all the people who spent many hours proof reading our book as it developed progressively across the Atlantic and Pacific. Particular thanks to: John and Peggy (UK), Tony Shapiro (Cape Town), Ashley and Brenda (*Ashymakaihken*), Dale and Nigel (*Kieren*), Bob and Judy (*Long Passages*), Tim and Annabel (*Casimer*), Derek and Kath (*Neutrino*), David and Hazel (*Mon Tour*), Helen and Neil (*Alexandra Louise*), Kirk and Jenny, Russell and Laonie (*Aquachat*), Steve and Carol, Terry and Yvonne (*Silvergirl*), David and Susan (*Sloop de Jour*), and Terry and Lynn (*Irish Rover*).

Last but not least, special thanks to Jan Hamon and David Sadler who proof read the final draft, and Ken Sheridan and Bob Burns for writing their inspirational forewords.

Rory and Sandra
Pacific Voyager

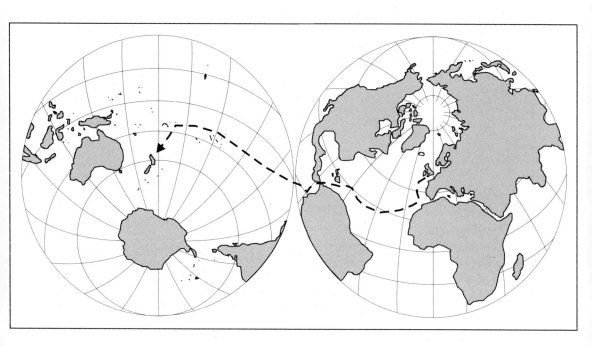

Author's Note

Greenwich to the Dateline tells the story of our bluewater cruise from the Greenwich Meridian in London to the International Dateline in the South Pacific. This is a sequel to our previous cruising book, Managing Your Bluewater Cruise, which is a preparation guide for those who want to go cruising. By contrast, this book is the personal story of our trip and experiences, together with a discussion about our yacht and its equipment.

Originally we thought cruising round the world would be a sailing epic where we would be pitched against mother nature and spend long periods alone at sea - we were wrong. Bluewater cruising turned out to be a unique cruising lifestyle which we shared with many other cruisers who were also out there doing it!!! Like a floating village we crossed the oceans together, and with SSB radio we kept in regular contact. And as for lonely, we had never had such a dynamic social diary.

We decided to call our book Greenwich to the Dateline because while we cruised, we were constantly referring to Greenwich; our longitude to Greenwich, our local hour angle to the Greenwich hour angle, and our time to GMT for celestial navigation, tide tables, cruiser's SSB nets and the BBC World service. Like Phileas Fogg in Round the World in 80 Days, we started our journey around the world from the Greenwich Meridian. In our case we stood on the zero degree prime meridian at the Royal Observatory at Greenwich, and later, we sailed across the International Dateline between American Samoa and Tonga.

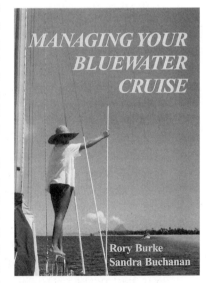

The importance of Greenwich was established in 1884 when an international conference of astronomers met in Washington DC and agreed to make Greenwich the prime meridian and Greenwich Mean Time (GMT) the "Time for all the world." On the other side of the world, 180 degrees east and west of the Greenwich Meridian is the International Dateline - where the date changes by one day. When Phileas Fogg travelled from east to west he gained a day. By contrast, we travelled from west to east and lost a day!!!

Greenwich to the Dateline is a sequel to our first cruising book, Managing Your Bluewater Cruise

Our interest in bluewater cruising evolved from reading about the adventures of the modern day pioneering sailors; Sir Francis Chichester, Sir Alec Rose, Sir Chay Blyth, Sir Robin Knox-Johnson and Bernard Moitessier. But their circumnavigations sounded like endurance epics. We felt there must be a more leisurely way to sail around the world and see all the places of interest along the route. Sure enough, we found the answer reading about the cruising adventures of the Hiscocks, the Smeetons, Tristan Jones and, the father of them all, Joshua Slocum. This seemed the logical way to cruise around the world and, like a snail, we could carry our worldly possessions with us.

This book is the story of how we converted our travelling dreams into a bluewater cruising reality. First we discuss the implications of bluewater cruising and the impact it had on our house, our possessions and our careers. Once we arrived back in Britain from working in Cape Town, it took us six

Rory on the Greenwich Meridian - zero degree longitude

months to find our perfect yacht, *Pacific Voyager* (a Nicholson 35), fit her out in Salcombe car park, and conduct sea trials around the coast of Britain, before departing from our home port of Porthmadog in North Wales.

We followed a well-established cruising route from Ireland to Spain, Portugal, Gibraltar and the Canaries, before making our first ocean passage following the sea route of Chistopher Columbus to the Caribbean, not in search of gold and spices, but sun and reggae. After cruising the Caribbean Islands we transitted the Panama Canal to follow in the footsteps of Charles Darwin to the Galapagos Archipelago, where we encountered his marine iguanas which looked like they were from the beginning of time itself. We explored the Pacific Islands, first charted by James Cook when he was looking for *Terra Australis Incognita*. Meanwhile we were searching for good snorkelling, fan coral, and hump-backed cowries.

Our experiences with nature were particularly memorable. Why did a shoal of tuna follow us for three days to the Canaries? Why did the sea lions in the Galapagos play with us? And why did the stingrays in Bora Bora feed from Sandra's hand? We had never come this close to nature before, not even in the game parks of Southern Africa.

Our experiences with history were also memorable. We never imagined bluewater cruising would be an extension of the History Channel where we would cross the

paths of so many influential people: Prince Henry the Navigator's School of Navigation at Sagres, Lord Nelson's famous battle off Cape Trafalgar, and Fletcher Christian's mutiny on the HMS *Bounty* off Tonga.

Our last chapter outlines how we have now achieved - *Sustainable Cruising* - through our writing and publishing. The book concludes with appendices on our budget, our yacht, and its equipment - the type of information we were looking for before we set off. If bluewater cruising is for you, this could be the most memorable period of your life.

Rory and Sandra Burke
Bay of Islands
email: rory@burkepublishing.com
email: sandra@burkepublishing.com
web site: www.bluewater-cruising.com

Further Reading:
Sobel, Dava., *Longitude*, Fourth Estate
Chichester, Sir Francis., *The Lonely Sea and the Sky*
Rose, Sir Alec., *My Lively Lady*
Blyth, Sir Chay., *The Impossible Voyage*
Knox-Johnson, Sir Robin., *A World of My Own*, Cassell
Moitessier, Bernard., *The Logical Way*
Hiscock, Eric., *Around the World in Wanderer 111*
Smeeton, Miles., *Once is Enough*
Jones, Tristan., *Yarns*, Adlard Coles Nautical
Slocum, Joshua., *Sailing Alone Around the World*
Aughton, Peter., *Endeavour*, Windrush Press
www.nmm.ac.uk (National Maritime Museum at Greenwich)

Implications of Bluewater Cruising

The thought of bluewater cruising kept me going through the stresses and strains of working life - cruising was the light at the end of the tunnel. Having read all the cruising books I could get my hands on further reinforced my desire to go cruising. Sailing round the world became my dream, but it took me twenty years to turn my dream into a reality.

I met Sandra in Cape Town where we were both working. Some months later, on our way back from a weekend viewing the spring flowers of Namaqualand, I asked Sandra if she would like to sail around the world with me. Thinking about the romantic side of cruising, she immediately said, *"YES!!!"*

Although Sandra flew overseas to the fashion shows twice a year she thought bluewater cruising seemed like an interesting way to travel. (However, she told me much later that she did not really think it would happen, but was prepared to play along with the idea.) But the idea never went away and when I started to consider the best time to leave to catch things called *weather windows*, Sandra started to realise this trip around the world was **going to happen**.

The desire to go bluewater cruising can be very impulsive, *"Let's just pack-up and go."* But we were concerned this short term adventure could have long term career consequences. So before running off into the blue yonder we wanted to strike a balance between the whims of cruising, with our education, career, and possessions, and map out a plan for our future.

In my 20s and 30s I enjoyed a number of overland backpacking expeditions using public transport - travelling up and down East Africa, trekking in Nepal, and journeying around China by train. But as I got older so the thought of bluewater cruising in my own yacht became more appealing. Like a tortoise Sandra and I could take our worldly belongings with us - this seemed the logical way to travel the world.

They say life begins at forty, this is when people start to go jogging!!! Instead of jogging we earnestly made our plans to sail around the world. We both felt we had come to an optimum time in our lives to go cruising.

Talking to a friend in Egypt
and Rory on the *Roof of Africa*

Career Implications: Our initial plan was to sail around the world in three years. Although three years sounded a long time to be away from work and contacts, we felt the adventure would be worth the risk and the experience could open up new career opportunities. We realised we had been defining our life around our careers and not our experiences - we wanted to change that. There were no plans to work en route, because we did not want to be away too long from our new home and friends, initially this was to be no more than a three year interlude.

Rory: My career in naval architecture had progressed from model testing submarines and frigates in the UK, to ship building in South Africa, to ship repair in Saudi Arabia. My subsequent career in project management had progressed from a MSc in Project Management at Henley Management College to project management consultancy, lecturing and writing. Having just completed a two year project management contract, this seemed like a good time to go.

Sandra: Sandra's decision to give up a career in fashion design for the sea also meant giving up Picasso perfumes for fresh sea air, Prada shoes for deck shoes and Gucci handbags for sailbags. Her career had progressed from a Master of Fashion

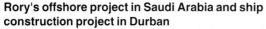

Rory's offshore project in Saudi Arabia and ship
construction project in Durban

Top left: Buying fashion magazines from Mr. Wong in Hong Kong. *"Have you got a fashion magazine in English please?"*

Top right: Sandra at Franks Book Shop - London's principal fashion book shop. "*Paul where will my fashion book be placed*?"

Left: Opening of the Hong Kong Fashion Exhibition - "*Gottle of gear, gottle of gear.*"

Right: Sandra using a light box to help her trace over her fashion drawing - another creation in the making

Design from the Royal College of Art in London to senior fashion designer. Sandra unfortunately had to resign from her position to embark on our bluewater cruise.

Route Planning: Deciding to sail around the world was one thing, but focusing on an interesting route was another. Through our reading and research we slowly built-up a picture of where we wanted to cruise, places of interest we wanted to see, and the best time to be there. This iterative process eventually converged on a logical route and an optimum chart portfolio.

Budget (see appendix 1): Developing our budget was another iterative process as we juggled the expenses to reflect our funds available. Finally we subdivided our expenses as follows:

The yacht	£30,000
Equipment	£10,000
Living/maintenance (for three years)	£40,000
Totals	£80,000

Having considered the living and maintenance costs first, we then subdivided the rest between the yacht and equipment. The budget allowed for a three year trip, which we considered (at the time) to be the minimum to make the most of the interesting places en route. It was possible to do it in less, the bluewater around the world rallies only take two years - but why rush?

Sponsor: Sandra suggested, *"Let's find a sponsor - someone who will help pay for our trip."* A few half-hearted attempts got us nowhere. Bluewater cruising was no longer a rare event, and if a sponsor had been found they would have wanted their pound of flesh, and we could have lost our sense of freedom. (However, we did meet a few cruisers who were sending back reports to their local newspapers and radio stations. Osman and Zuhal, for example, became the first Turkish couple to sail around the world, and their yacht *Uzaklar* a Nantuket Clipper 32, is now on display at the Maritime Museum in Istanbul!!!)

House and Possessions: Cruisers usually sell their house before they leave - we built ours! Shortly after starting to build our dream home in Cape Town, cruising around the world became our priority. Fortunately we had sufficient funds to do both projects. As we intended to return to Cape Town, we wanted to keep all our furniture and personal effects. To limit the cost of storage an additional room in the attic was built for all our belongings. We then rented our house through an agent while we were away.

Shipping: Deciding what personal possessions to take with us around the world meant it first had to be shipped from Cape Town to the UK, where we wanted to buy our boat. We balanced the cost of shipping against the cost of buying new items in the UK. We considered various methods of shipping: sea freight, air freight, excess baggage, unaccompanied baggage, parcel post and small packet post. Surprisingly for the 300 kgs we wanted to ship, small packet post turned out to be the most reasonable. Can you visualise the fun we had at the post office posting 150, two kilogram packets, and the poor postman in the UK as he delivered them on his push-bike!!!

Sandra reading *Pacific Odyssey*

Team Work: Sailing around the world had to be a team effort - it was therefore important that Sandra did not just live out my dream, but it was her dream as well. It was important that we shared the planning and preparations as any conflict here could have derailed all our plans and efforts. I gave Sandra a number of bluewater cruising books to read, fortunately the first book she read was *Pacific Odyssey* by Gwenda Cornell. This book described the fun of exploring tropical islands, but conveniently skipped the hardships of sailing to them.

Health and Fitness: At forty were we healthy and fit enough to go cruising? Although we did not partake in any particular sports we regularly walked on Table Mountain. But even with the latest yachting equipment we appreciated cruising would still be quite a physically demanding way of life. There were plenty of heavy weights to lift, like 20 kg jerry cans of water, and walking long distances with a fully laden rucksack of provisions. Besides being physically fit, being mentally alert was another requirement. Sailing in unfamiliar waters close to land, negotiating coral heads and crowded anchorages demanded a quick response to avoid unexpected dangers.

We were concerned about medical problems occurring while we were at sea or in a third world country, therefore before leaving the UK we had full medical and dental **checkups**, and all the recommended inoculations. Our budget included funds for basic medical attention from a doctor or dentist, but for all serious accidents and hospital operations we took out a hospital insurance policy.

Sailing Ability: In Britain there were no qualification requirements to go ocean cruising, we could simply buy a yacht and go wherever we liked having never set foot on a yacht before. However, the insurance companies we approached did request proof of sailing qualifications and experience. I learnt to sail in Porthmadog, sailing up and down the coast of Wales with the occasional trip across the Irish Sea to Ireland and Scotland. I supplemented this with a yachtmasters certificate, together with O' levels in Navigation, and Seamanship. Was that enough? The more we thought about bluewater cruising the more we realised that it included much more than just sailing and navigational skills. This was a whole new bluewater lifestyle that demanded a broader range of skills and competencies which included boat maintenance, snorkelling, exploring, to generally being street wise in foreign countries.

Languages: Having travelled extensively overseas we knew we could get by with English, but with Sandra's school level French and Spanish, this gave us the three main European languages of the cruising world. French was particularly useful when translating Radio France International's Atlantic weather forecast.

Living on Board: Moving from a house of 400 square metres to a boat of 20 square meters, was a major challenge. To bridge the gap between camping and living comfortably we port hoped along the coast of England, Wales, Ireland, Spain and Portugal before we made our first ocean passage across the Atlantic.

Cooking: When I first met Sandra, her flat in Camps Bay, in Cape Town had a very small kitchen, but our yacht's galley was even smaller - stowing provisions was a real challenge. We were not sure how much fresh produce and tinned food would be available along the way, so we stocked up for several months. (As it turned out we over stocked, and we should have taken books like *100 ways to Cook Coconuts and Bananas* as we consumed large amounts of in-season foods.)

Snorkelling: Although our cruising route passed through some of the best snorkelling areas in the world, when we set off we only had some average snorkelling gear. (However, we soon realised our mistake, and were fortunate to be able to buy good snorkelling gear at a reasonable price in the Free Zone in Panama, just-in-time for the crystal clear reefs in the Pacific.)

Bluewater Rallies: As we prepared to leave the UK it never occurred to us to join an organised rally. (However, having cruised the Caribbean and Pacific, we can now see the advantages and convenience of having a professional organisation smoothing the waves, particularly to battle with third world bureaucracy and organise the shipping of spare parts, not to mention the preparation seminars.)

Clubs and Societies: We were concerned that sailing into the blue horizon could very quickly turn into *out-of-sight, out-of-mind*. In an effort to keep in touch with our friends and professions our memberships included the following: Madoc Yacht Club, Ocean Cruising Club (OCC), the Royal Geographic Society (RGS), and the Association of Project Managers (APM).

Planning: Our time plan worked backwards from Jimmy Cornell's *World Cruising Routes,* which recommended leaving the Britain Isles between May and August. Returning to Britain in January gave us time to find a boat, fit her out and shakedown. (However, next time when we buy a larger yacht with more equipment we would rather give ourselves a longer procurement period.)

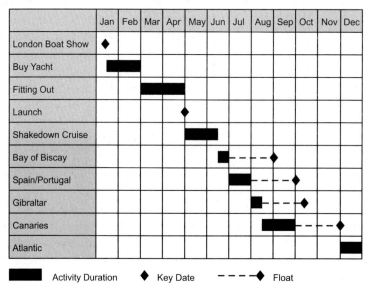

	Jan	Feb	Mar	Apr	May	Jun	Jul	Aug	Sep	Oct	Nov	Dec
London Boat Show	◆											
Buy Yacht		▬										
Fitting Out			▬									
Launch					◆							
Shakedown Cruise					▬							
Bay of Biscay						▬ - - - ◆						
Spain/Portugal							▬ - - - ◆					
Gibraltar								▬ - - ◆				
Canaries									▬ - - - ◆			
Atlantic											▬	

▬ Activity Duration   ◆ Key Date   - - - ◆ Float

Decision To Go: Having considered the implications of bluewater cruising we made our decision to embark on our bluewater challenge to explore the world in our own boat. While Sandra worked out her notice, I made arrangements to fly back to the UK for the London boat show.

Further Reading:

Burke, Rory and Sandra., *Managing Your Bluewater Cruise*
Cornell, Gwenda., *Pacific Odyssey*
Cornell, Jimmy., *World Cruising Routes*
Bluewater Rally <www.yachtrallies.co.uk>
The ARC <www.worldcruising.com>

2 Buying Our Yacht

16th January (Saturday): Approaching the ticket office at the London Boat Show I casually glance down at my Access credit card - it has expired!!! Having just walked off the plane from Cape Town with only £80 cash and £20 in sterling travellers cheques in my pocket, I curse myself for not checking the card before. Then curse Access for not renewing the card. Offering one of my travellers cheques to the cashier he says, *"Sorry mate we only take cash."* *"Some bloody international show,"* I think as I give him ten of my precious pounds.

With my ticket in hand I walk into the main hall. I have arrived back in England just in time to catch the last two days of the London Boat Show. Although sleeping was difficult on the 12 hour night flight from Cape Town my enthusiasm is keeping me going. The next two days will be spent looking at equipment for a yacht we have yet to buy - this is an important part of our procurement process.

Armed with a long equipment list, I want to look at anything and everything for our trip around the world. Boat shows are excellent venues to see a wide range of marine equipment, manufacturers, suppliers and yacht brokers all under one roof. Some areas of interest are clarified, while others become more confused. I can only absorb so much in such a short time before becoming totally mesmerised and saturated with information, to say nothing about being weary and footsore. If nothing else, I leave the boat show with many new contacts and a mountain of brochures to browse through later.

After the boat show I stay with Sandra's parents in Ringwood on the south coast of England. This means that I am ideally positioned near the centre of Britain's yachting industry. My hunt now starts in earnest with two months to find a yacht.

The first task is to develop a short list of suitable yacht types within our price range. This is where the yacht brokers are very helpful. Many of the brokers have become franchised with a worldwide computer network. They enter the basic yacht parameters and print out a list of yachts available in my price range. I also look for yachts in the classified adverts in all the key yachting magazines, particularly Yachting Monthly. To extend my search further I drive to most of the boatyards and marinas on the south coast - west to Poole, Salcombe and Plymouth, and east to Lymington, Buckler's Hard, Hythe, Southampton, Hamble, Portsmouth, and Chichester. This area is excellent for viewing a wide variety of yacht designs, thus speeding up my yacht selection process.

To help quantify and compare different boats I develop an equipment list (see appendix 2) which I send in response to a number of yacht adverts. After several replies to my equipment list its structure and contents are amended. Most yachts seem to have all the basic navigation equipment; compass, echo sounder, speed log, while others have some useful bluewater equipment; dinghy and outboard, self-steering gear, liferaft and wind generator. This is the transition period from Satnav to GPS, so all the old navigation systems are really worthless. From the information I gather there are three items which seem to make a financial difference:

- Dinghy and outboard (new £2,000)
- Liferaft (new £2,000)
- Self-steering (new £2,000)

If a yacht has unnecessary equipment, for example support legs, or a heater, I reduce its value accordingly, and am also tempted to devalue any equipment that will need replacing en route, such as the rigging and sails.

I prefer production built yachts to one-offs, because any design problems and arrangement compromises should have been ironed out, as the designs tend to be a development from previous successful designs. I am particularly keen to buy a well known yacht for ease of selling later when we have completed our circumnavigation.

The first week is stress free because there are no expectations about finding the right yacht straight away and I can enjoy the scenery; the old towns like Lymington with its cobbled streets, and the New Forest with ponies grazing at the sides of the roads, taking no notice of the cars driving past just inches away. Many of the towns and villages are steeped in naval history; Nelson's flagship the HMS *Victory* at Portsmouth and the bowling green at Plymouth Hoe where Sir Francis Drake finished his game while the Spanish Armada sailed up the English Channel.

By the end of the second week having seen most of the yacht types on my short list there is now a problem - they are all **too small**. It will be impossible to fit all our belongings into a Rival 31, 32 or 34, a Nicholson 32, or a Rustler 31. The Nicholson 35 would be ideal, but it is too expensive. I am particularly disappointed the Rivals are too small, because it was in a Rival 31 in 1969 that I made my first *long trip* across the Irish Sea from Porthmadog to Wicklow. I remember the Rival 31 as being a big boat, but 31 foot LOA and 9 foot beam is considered extremely small now.

Rory having a beer at the Jolly Sailor

So, relaxing in the Jolly Sailor, with a pint of the local brew I feel frustrated and confused, "*This was meant to be fun.*" Realising the dream of a teenager is definitely handicapped by the experience of a forty year old - I will have to review the budget.

Review Budget (see appendix 1): How can our yacht budget be increased so that we can buy a bigger yacht like a Nicholson 35? Not wanting to reduce the equipment budget, or living expenses, I finally move funds from our contingency to the yacht budget, and use our mortgage facility as our contingency. With an increased yacht budget our choice of yachts now includes three Nicholson 35s:

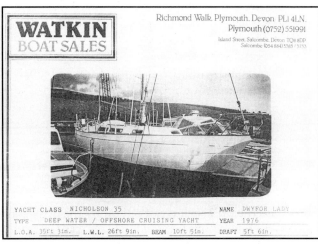

Advert for Nicholson 35 in Salcombe

- Nicholson 35, 1979, £42,000 Plymouth (private sale)
- Nicholson 35, 1976, £32,000 Salcombe (broker)
- Nicholson 35, 1973, £30,000 Balearics (private sale)

3rd February (Wednesday): By the time Sandra arrives at Heathrow at the beginning of February I have a short list of yachts ready for her to look at. In contrast to the blue sunny skies of the Cape Town she has just left, I drive her to a very damp, chilly, grey Port Solent to see a Nicholson 31. Sandra complains, "*It's a bit small.*" Then Port Hamble to see a Rival 32, "*No it doesn't feel like home.*" Then Lymington to see a Nicholson 35, which had just been sold, "*I like the space inside, and the shower and kitchen are great!!!*" Sandra agrees we should buy a Nicholson 35.

A few days later we drive to see two of the Nicholson 35s on my short list. The Plymouth yacht is owned by a doctor who is planning to live on a farm. The yacht looks beautiful, everything is clean and tidy, but he is asking a high price at £42,000.

The Nicholson 35 at Salcombe by contrast is in a sorry state. Sadly the owner had died and the boat has not been tidied up. We are surprised to see Geoff Pack (former editor of Yachting Monthly) on board. He is shaking his head as he looks through the equipment. The engine is covered in oil and rust, and the sails are damp and home to many flies. However, she is well equipped, with a Perkins 4108, RFD 6 man liferaft, Hydrovane self-steering, Decca, Autohelm instruments, Neco autopilot and an asking price of £32,000.

Leaving confused, we head back to Ringwood. At least we know the type of yacht we would like. The Nicholson 35 is a classic British yacht of the 1970s vintage, with an excellent reputation for good sailing performance and seakeeping. Camper and Nicholson are well known for building quality yachts which include the *'J' class* America's Cup yachts. Now we must make a choice between two yachts in contrasting condition and price.

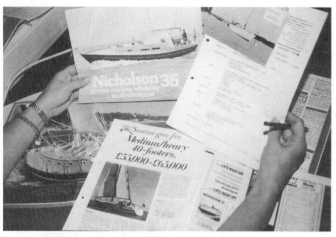

Sandra looking at yacht brochures

To help quantify the condition of the yachts I ask an old friend of mine, Nick Stanton, to give the boats a quick look over. Nick has been working as a boatbuilder for many years at Calshot Activity Centre near Southampton. Nick arrives with his little tool bag, pulls out a screwdriver and scrapes the skin fittings, taps the propeller, squeezes the water pipes and spends an hour or so accessing the condition of each yacht. Nick is not put off by the dirty condition of the Salcombe yacht - he can see how it will look with a bit of TLC and maintenance.

There is a third Nicholson 35 for sale in Mallorca, in the Mediterranean. The specifications and condition sound good, but the cost of travelling to Mallorca would add a couple of thousand pounds to our expenses. Then we would need to decide if we should sail the yacht back to the UK to get her ready or start our cruise from Mallorca. Sailing back to the UK could add a year to our trip which is not in our cruising budget.

After considering the three Nicholson 35s we decide to go for the yacht in the best condition as it is a sign the owner has looked after her. I ring the doctor in Plymouth and I am about to make an offer when he says, *"I'm afraid I've just accepted an offer from a Dutch buyer."*

This leaves the Salcombe and Mallorca yachts. They are both about the same age, condition and price, so we decide to go for the Salcombe yacht which is nearer. I ring the broker and make an offer subject to survey. The offer is too low and politely declined. We reconsider out budget and increase our offer, and wait anxiously while the broker contacts his client. This time he rings back positively, *"My client will accept your offer."* With great relief we celebrate having made one giant step nearer the Pacific.

Survey Cycle: In the UK we need a marine survey to ensure we are buying a sound yacht, and to satisfy the marine insurance underwriters. The insurance companies require a valuation by a surveyor who can provide professional indemnity through the Yacht Builders, Designers and Surveyors Association (YBDSA). Before a surveyor can become a member they must pre-qualify themselves, usually with a naval architecture or marine engineering qualification and previous marine surveying experience.

Although yacht surveyors may have many years of experience it is unlikely they will be an expert in all the marine fields, particularly as each discipline is moving towards specialist equipment. We address this limitation by subdividing our survey into four parts:

- Hull survey
- Engine survey
- Rigging survey
- Sail survey

Our hull structure and construction survey is to be carried out by a registered surveyor, which satisfies the insurance company's requirements. The engine survey is to be carried out by a diesel engine mechanic. The rigging survey is to be carried out by a rigging company with electronic rig testing equipment and the sail survey is to be carried out by a sailmaker. By subdividing the survey this way we feel the different areas are being addressed by the most qualified people, and the total cost will actually work out to be about the same as a full blown survey.

I discuss the format of the survey report with the surveyor and confirm it must comply with the insurance company's requirements. He is first to look at the key areas as they could abort the sale and therefore abort the survey. If the yacht has a costly problem, osmosis or a serious structural fault, there is no need for a full survey on the rest of the yacht. The hull and mechanical surveys are organised to be done on the same day as we want to be present.

22nd February (Monday): After a three hour drive from Ringwood to Salcombe we find the surveyor has already started scraping back the antifouling to the gelcoat in a number of places round the hull. By using a moisture meter the surveyor is able to build up a picture of the moisture content. The most serious finding is wicking caused by the chopped strand matt (CSM) taking in moisture and expanding. The expanded fibres can be seen as short white criss-crossing fibres and, if viewed from an angle, show as little bumps in the gelcoat. The surveyor feels that, as the Nicholsons of this period were heavily laid up, the presence of moisture in the hull does not indicate osmosis, or a reduction in strength.

The **mechanical survey** is performed in the afternoon. The mechanic attaches a hose pipe to the water intake to supply cooling water to the main engine and runs the engine for half an hour. Previously we had discussed the limitation of testing an engine which is not under load, but as the mechanic has been servicing this engine for the past few years, he is confident he can make an accurate assessment by listening and looking.

The surveys of the other equipment; rig, sails, electrical, anchoring, liferaft and LPG are to be done later as they do not influence the sale of the boat. The hull and mechanical surveys identify a number of small problems which can easily be fixed. After renegotiating the price we become the proud owners of a Nicholson 35. South Pacific here we come!

Further Reading:

Howard, Jim., *Handbook of Offshore Cruising*, Adlard Coles
Nicholson, Ian., *Surveying Small Craft*, Adlard Coles
ORC., *Category 1 Requirements*
Pack, Geoff., *Bluewater Countdown*, Yachting Monthly
Hammick, Anne., *Ocean Cruising on a Budget*, Adlard Coles
YBDSA., email: info@ybdsa.co.uk

3 Life In Salcombe Car Park

26th February (Friday): It takes us all day to drive to Salcombe, collect the bank guaranteed cheque and complete the brokerage paperwork. So it is late afternoon and the light is fading by the time we eventually arrive at our new home - Salcombe car park. This is to be our new address for the next few months as we prepare our Nicholson 35 for bluewater cruising.

We are now the proud owners of a yacht which is sitting on blocks in the middle of Salcombe's main car park - fortunately the parking meter has been switched off for the winter! As we climb up the ladder into the cockpit, there is a commanding view of our neighbouring yachts. It is cold and damp with the possibility of rain, a far cry from the warm sunny shores of Cape Town. Nevertheless the setting is still extremely attractive, with green rolling hills rising up behind us, a view of the quaint old town of Salcombe beside us, and the tranquil estuary wandering into the distance. Stepping down into the saloon it is damp, musty and unused - not very inviting. It certainly does not feel like home, but at least it is ours. *"Let's have a cup of tea."*

There is no shore power so we light a few meagre candles, a paraffin lamp, and a camping gas heater lent to us by Sandra's parents, and settle in for the first night in our new boat.

Salcombe experiences a huge influx of tourists during the summer months, but during the winter off-season it is quiet, which means the large car park is an excellent venue for the local council to turn it into a yacht park. Living and working on-board in cramped conditions will be a real test of life together; we are effectively eating and sleeping in a workshop.

Jobs: During the first few days I am like a dog chasing its tail. Everywhere I look there is another job and every job requires a tool or spare part I do not have. Eventually we sit down and discuss what we want to achieve, develop our scope of work and list the tools, equipment and materials required. The scope of work and procurement are then prioritised to identify all the critical jobs that must be done prior to launching, and when long lead items must be ordered. Service manuals and information are required for all the equipment on board - I write 60 letters to equipment manufacturers and suppliers.

My pocket notebook becomes our data base, my briefcase becomes our office, and the local telephone box becomes our link with the outside world. The post office staff in Salcombe have not heard of *poste restante* so our mail is directed to Watkins Marine, the yacht broker.

Typical Day: A routine soon develops. Our typical day starts by climbing down the ladder, dressed in endless layers of thermal clothing, old tracksuits, thick socks and boiler suits, walk around the car park and stretch our legs while planning our day. After a bowl of hot porridge for breakfast we work on our jobs until early afternoon trying to *do a job a day*. And then, in the late afternoon, we are ready to either drive to the supermarket in Kingsbridge followed by a beer in a country pub, or, walk along a coastal headland followed by a beer in a country pub!

Marine Facilities: Salcombe's marine facilities are quite impressive; all the main trades are represented, together with a couple of chandler shops selling new and used equipment. We try and support our local chandlers by giving them our business. I develop a long list of equipment we want to purchase, working on the principle that if they know they have our support they should be able to match other quotations and give us a good discount. This procurement process works up to a point, but in the end I feel priority should be given to the chandler who offers the best after sales service, particularly when we will be miles away on the other side of the world.

Engine: My first big job is to fix the exhaust which is fractured - an opportunity to redesign the old system which has the water inlet above the manifold, and is asking for trouble. After numerous trips to the mechanic's shop a few kilometres away, along the narrowest of country lanes, we eventually manufacture and install a new exhaust system.

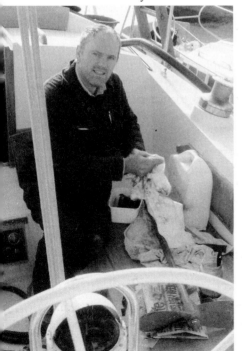

The next job is to withdraw the shaft and replace the cutlass bearing. Although the coupling splits relatively easily, removing the flange is a different matter. After squirting endless amounts of penetrating oil, it still will not budge a millimetre - defeated, I move on to the next job.

"*Let's do the seacocks instead, they should be easy.*" Starting with the easiest, the toilet inlet - success! However, the toilet outlet is not so forthcoming. The lever on the tapered Blake seacock is seized in the *on* position. I apply penetrating oil and leave it to soak in, while moving onto the next seacock.

Meanwhile, Sandra concentrates on making the boat habitable and comfortable. The inside of the boat has not been cleaned for months. She is surprised how a small boat can have so many compartments "*.... and you call this pleasure?*"

Rory working on the propshaft

Back to the seacocks. After two weeks of pouring penetrating oil on the toilet seacock and still no joy we seek advice. *"Give it a good whack."* But I am concerned about breaking the unit. *"Try heat!"* I buy a blow torch which does the trick and, as if the propshaft knew what was coming, its nuts ease off without any heat!

Jon Alsop fitting our new mainsail

Sails: Jon Alsop, the local sailmaker checks over all our sails in his sail loft. Jon feels the sails are generally in good condition, but the mainsail will not make it around the world. We decide to have a new main made now at a good price, instead of running the risk of endless repairs and then paying more for a replacement. This also has the additional advantage of Sandra being able to observe the sailmaking process, which should help her make sail repairs en route. Jon points out that the storm sails are in good condition which shows the boat has not been through many storms.

The roller furling is looking a bit tired and the foil sections are rotating at the joints, so we replace it with a new forestay and fit hanks to the genoa.

Rigging: Salcombe's local rigger replaces our forestay and rivets two mast steps near the top of the mast. (He must have been having a bad day because later, when the rigging is electronically tested in Southampton, the split pin at the mast head is missing, and we realise the mast steps are fitted too high to be a useful working platform).

The running rigging is mostly 12 mm braid-on-braid. We buy two 100 metre drums of 14 mm braid-on-braid, which is easier to grip, and replace the sheets and halyards progressively.

Electrical: Andy, the electrician, arrives with his own bosun's chair which consists of a plank of wood. "You're not going up on that??" I ask. "Yes this is the best - it's strong enough and no one will nick it." Andy wires up a Hella deck light on the mast, then a Sterling regulator to boost the alternator's output and an Aerogen wind generator.

Dinghy: Avon make Redstart, Redcrest and Redseal inflatable dinghies. The Redstart is too small for us, and the Redseal is perhaps too large, but after searching the boatyards for weeks we cannot find any second-hand Redcrests for sale, so reluctantly we settle for the Redseal.

Outboard: Initially we buy a second-hand outboard from Yacht Parts in Plymouth. The mechanic in Salcombe checks it over and condemns it. The seawater cooling is blocked and cannot easily be repaired. I notify Yacht Parts who accept responsibility and collect the outboard, and further, they pay the mechanic for his time. *"Maybe we should buy a new outboard as we will be using it as our wheels in the anchorages."* We buy a new 2 hp Suzuki.

Liferaft: The local testing station opens up our liferaft and leaves it inflated for 24 hours to see if it will hold pressure - it does. They check the material for perishing and deterioration, especially along the folds. The gas bottle is weighed and all the items in the emergency pack are replaced, together with the foot pump which had collapsed. To supplement the liferaft's emergency pack we buy a number of ex-MOD flare containers to use as panic bags (see appendix 4).

Liferaft stowed in the cockpit locker

Gas Oven: The old gas oven is condemned by Noyce's hardware store in Kingsbridge. So we replace it with a new Plastimo Neptune 2000 cooker from Sport Nautique, and use the attachments and fiddles from the old stove.

Calor Gas produce a booklet for bluewater cruisers and advise that it is better to carry propane (6.90 bar internal pressure) overseas, so we change all our blue butane (1.72 bar internal pressure) bottles for red propane. However, at the time, we did not appreciate that outside the UK they refill gas bottles instead of exchanging them, so we should have taken bottles with a long expiry date. This is not as easy as it sounds because Calor Gas, for some strange reason, stamp the date on a disk in code which only they can read! By luck our bottles turn out to have 3, 5 and 6 years before a re-test.

Buying Food: Should we buy our food all in one go as Robin Knox-Johnston did on his first trip round the world, or should we buy a little each time we go shopping? We opt for the progressive buying, and its subsequent progressive stowage. Sensibly we try out new brands before buying in bulk, but are always on the lookout for specials. My best buy is 150 tins of Heinz baked beans at a really good price!?!

As we drive back from our shopping expeditions, our car is usually full of supermarket bags. The drive back takes us over the rolling green hills with their complicated network of hedgerows criss-crossing the country side and the narrowest of country lanes where the brambles sometimes brush both sides of the car. Regularly we divert to one of the many quaint and irresistible country pubs to sup a couple of pints. While I am trying to get to know the locals, Sandra is more concerned about the meat defrosting in the back of the car.

Weather: The UK has a reputation of having cold, grey, bleak winters with a glimpse of sunshine in the summer. During our stay in Salcombe, the weather lives up to its reputation, with variable weather from beautifully fresh and sunny days to wet, windy and damp, not to mention frosty nights which gives us a slippery, icy deck the following morning. But we still manage to live comfortably on our yacht. Frequently we see rain squalls coming, which sets in motion a mad scramble to close our hatches and cockpit lockers, and put all our exposed tools away.

Walks: Most afternoons it is time for a long energetic walk. The exercise not only keeps us fit, but also motivates us to continue working on the boat. Our favourite trek is along the headland towards Bolt Head where the scenic cliffs look out to sea - a sea which will shortly be our highway to the world.

Salcombe: Salcombe has maintained much of its traditional maritime village atmosphere. The quaint narrow streets with old terrace houses are steeped in ancient maritime history. Exploring them feels like we have stepped back in time and we half expect Long John Silver to appear hobbling round the corner with a parrot on his shoulder. Salcombe was well known in the 1600s for prowling pirates coming ashore to forage, pilfer and strip the adjoining countryside of sheep. Not to mention the local smugglers returning from the Channel Islands laden with tobacco and spirits - some of our instincts have obviously not changed!

Salcombe in the off season is a quiet, sleepy little nook, just right to get to know the locals. One of our regular haunts is the Island Cruising Club which is only a few minutes walk from our car park. After a hard days work it is a great place to relax and sup a local brew while listening to the lifeboat crews' yarns.

4th April (Sunday) - Beaulieu Jumble: There are boat jumbles most weekends somewhere in the UK, where yachties can search for a few bargains. We decide to go to the Beaulieu boat jumble, the largest and most well known, held in the grounds of Beaulieu's National Motor Museum. On the day of the jumble I am dreading the heavy traffic, difficult parking, large crowds and long queues. However, we are pleasantly surprised by a highly organised boat jumble; we could not have parked

any quicker. After a day walking around and around three large fields full of stalls, we drive away with a car load of gear all at reasonable prices - our best buy being a new Plastimo clock for £1 - reduced from £20!

Charts: Buying our charts turns out to be one of the most expensive items in our budget. After studying the

Andy Hussey, manager at Kelvin Hughes

Admiralty Catalogue we have a rough idea of the charts to buy, but I want to have a look at them first. Armed with a list of charts we drive to Kelvin Hughes the Admiralty chart agent in Southampton. They organise a corner for us to set out the charts and finalise our route.

Sewing Machine: With Sandra's fashion background, she is keen to buy a sewing machine not only for making clothes, but also for repairing the sails, make canvas covers and courtesy flags etc. The famous **Read's Sailmaker** is the most well known marine sewing machine, so we drive to Southampton to see Mr. Read at his shop in Shirley High Street. The story goes like this - Mr. Read senior makes sewing machines and Mr. Read junior likes sailing. Seeing a gap in the market they marinised one of their robust sewing machines with stainless steel fittings for sailmaking in the marine environment. All went well until Lucas, the local supplier,

An invaluable crew member, Sandra's Reads sewing machine

stopped making electric motors and Mr. Read had to look to Japan for supplies. The Japanese wanted a large minimum order which Mr. Read could not justify and so the end of another great cottage industry. Mr. Read, an Irish charmer, talks Sandra into buying one of his refurbished machines.

VAT: With the UK's VAT rate at 17.5% it is worth claiming it back on the equipment we have purchased in the three months prior to departure. Surprisingly, most of the retailers are not particularly helpful and some are quite aghast that we are suggesting claiming the VAT back. To *make it happen* we go to the Customs office in Southampton. To our surprise they decline to give us the VAT 407 forms but, on our suggestion, they post them to the shops we intend to do business with - but only one form per shop!!!

16th April (Friday): After many weeks of scrubbing, antifouling, checking over all the equipment and fittings, we are now ready to launch. The big day eventually arrives almost two months after moving on board. We arrange to launch just after the Easter holidays using the resident mobile crane. This is quite an involved procedure as we are totally boxed-in by other yachts which were hauled out later.

Retail Export Scheme

VAT Refunds for Overseas Visitors to the United Kingdom

VAT 407 - OVERSEAS VISITORS

VAT form

Left: *Pacific Voyager* is lifted over the yachts which have boxed her in

Below: *Pacific Voyager* having her legs removed

The crane operators are not using spreaders on the slings so I pack the slings with pieces of old carpet below the capping rail, to prevent the slings damaging the rail. But, as the slings take the strain, they stretch more than I have allowed for and lift the rubbing strake on the port side. I later notice the capping rail has already been repaired in exactly the same place!!!

Apprehensively we watch the crane hoist her up high from behind a cluster of yachts, lift her carefully over them and gradually walk her to the edge of the quay where we remove the support legs. As she is lifted over the edge of the quay we naturally feel uneasy - what if the slings break (I saw this happen to another boat when I was working in the Middle East). With our hearts in our mouths our precious home is slowly lowered into the sea. Will she leak??? As she touches the water I instantly jump on board and check the underwater fittings before the slings are released - all okay. At last we are afloat and ready for our sea trials.

Further Reading:

Cornell, Jimmy., *World Cruising Routes*
Calor Gas., *LPG for the Bluewater Yachtsman*
www.salcombe.co.uk
www.boatjumbleassociation.co.uk

Shakedown Cruise

4

It seems odd but exhilarating to have our boat in the water at last. She looks outstanding with her white freeboard gleaming in the harbour lights. Our plan is to test the systems in the water while we port hop around the coast to our home port of Porthmadog in North Wales. The sea is to be her natural habitat for the next six years before she finds another car park in New Zealand on the other side of the world.

After all the excitement of the launch, with the noise of the crane and the throng of people milling around, it seems strangely quiet and lonesome. Our boat is on its own alongside the quay with only the gentle sound of wavelets lapping against her hull, and the muffled sound of sea gulls.

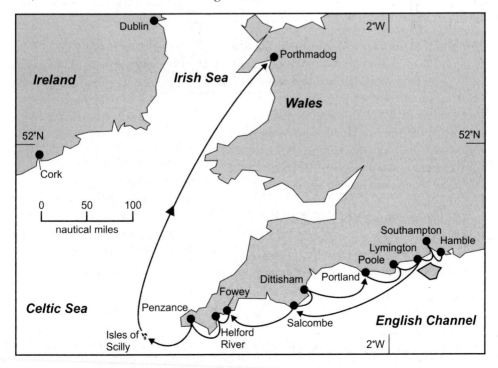

17th April (Saturday) - Perkins: The local mechanic arrives to start up our Perkins 4108, give her a service and check through the systems; fuel, air, oil, cooling, exhaust and transmission. I watch intently, looking over the mechanics shoulder as he changes the oil filter and bleeds the fuel system. Next time, 100 engine hours from now, it will be my turn.

Now for the sea trials. With the bow facing up river I battle to turn our boat around. The elements are against me - the tide is flooding and the wind is freshening from astern. This is to be the first of many clumsy manoeuvres in tight spaces. We soon realise the Nicholson, with all her sailing attributes, is a pig to manoeuvre in close quarters. After much revving, kick forward, kick astern, she finally starts to turn and point in the right direction.

Although we have been living on our boat for a couple of months with the instruments and equipment all around us, this is the first time we can actually authentically test them in action. We motor out into the main channel and head towards the *Bar*, passing the historic town of Salcombe to starboard and the Devon hills rising to port. The engine performs efficiently and is given the thumbs up by the mechanic - now for the sails.

18th April (Sunday) - Sail Trial: The next big event is to test the new mainsail, accompanied by Jon Alsop the sailmaker. With Jon aboard on this chilly, breezy day we sail out over the *Bar* again and tack between the headlands. The Nicholson handles well under-sail, pitching and rolling smoothly through the waves. After an hour or so we sail back up the estuary to the *Bag* where Jon is in his element tacking within inches of the moored yachts. We are somewhat relieved when Jon gives us a broad smile and shouts, *"She sails well. Let's go and have a beer."*

19th April (Monday) - Salcombe to Dartmouth: Log book: chart 442, Lizard Point to Berry Head (scale 1:150,000). We spend all the morning getting ready. The forecast is SW 3/4 which should be an ideal wind for our first passage to Dartmouth. Crossing once again Salcombe's famous *Bar*, we motor sail out past Prawle Point, passing the remains of a few shipwrecks strewn across the rocks - a scary reminder of just how cruel the sea can be. Five miles on from Salcombe we clear Start Point with no sign of the overfalls marked on the chart. Overdressed in our spanking new Henri Lloyd's heavy weather gear, the jackets soon get peeled off to let in some cool air. We have a pleasant sail in ideal conditions, just right to ease us slowly into the cruising life.

Job list: the speed log is not working; I need to check the impeller. And I also notice we are lacking a canvas pocket to stow our bits and pieces in the cockpit; a job for Sandra and her new Reads sewing machine.

After several hours of perfect sailing we arrive at the mouth of the River Dart, and drop the sails. We motor up the estuary, passing to port the impressive building of the famous Dartmouth Naval College and to starboard numerous marinas and boatyards. Two miles up river we finally reach the picturesque village of Dittisham, where we pick up a mooring buoy, turn off the motor and relax in the cockpit. In these pleasant surroundings, over a can of beer, we contemplate our first sail.

After a couple of sips, Sandra dives below and starts rummaging around - she reappears clutching her sketch pad and pencil. This is to be the first of many anchorage sketches for Sandra.

Anchored next to the picturesque setting of Dittisham

The British evenings are getting longer. Spring is in the air. After dinner, the evening is still light enough to encourage us to row to the pub overlooking the harbour. After a good drinking session with the publican listening to the details of our proposed trip, he actually ends up buying us drinks!!! Of course we are the last to leave (this is to become a habit, particularly in Ireland).

20th April (Tuesday) - Dartmouth to Portland: Log book: chart 3315, Berry Head to Portland (scale 1:75,000). Shipping forecast SW 3/4 occasionally 5 - still excellent sailing conditions. Slip the mooring early to give us time to reach Portland before dark, a journey of some 50 miles. As we leave Dartmouth I go forward to sort out the headsail. The bow is pitching violently in the choppy sea as we pass the headland. I am immediately seasick, not a good start to the day. We make good time with a following wind and sea (thinking about it now I am surprised we got away with towing the dinghy while reaching in 15 to 20 knots). We give Portland Bill an extra wide berth keeping away from the nasty looking overfalls indicated on the chart, and steer towards the lee of the headland, tucking ourselves in close as we motor into the protection of Portland harbour.

Log book: chart 2255, Approaches to Portland (scale 1:20,000). Motoring past the breakwater, the visibility rapidly reduces, as a bank of fog completely envelops us and a *Type 21* frigate preparing to leave. As we slowly motor on, we approach the naval dockyard where a large sign looms up out of the mist telling us to **Keep Away.** We ease over to starboard and pass some enormous pontoons before reaching the yacht moorings. Safely moored we settle down to a relaxing drink and our second dinner afloat. We have had enough excitement for one day, so we decide against going ashore. This is a sure sign we are starting to feel like cruisers, not just weekend sailors out for a day trip.

21st April (Wednesday) - Portland to Poole and the Firing Range: Depart at 08:00 we motor out in light airs - the fog lifted long ago. About two miles out with Sandra on the helm, a naval patrol boat motors up behind us on what looks like an interception course. I tell Sandra, *"They must be after their mooring fee."* The patrol boat comes alongside and shouts over to Sandra, *"Where are you going?"*

"Poole," Sandra shouts back.

"Please motor out of this area as quickly as you can as firing practice will commence

shortly." Unaware this area has a firing range, I check the chart and, sure enough, we are right beside the Lulworth firing range on the Purbeck Hills!!! I immediately increase our revs to hastily clear the area. Within the hour we hear the distant boom of exploding shells. *"We could have been their target!!!"*

As we sail past Swanage memories of my days as a Mod in the 60s come flooding back. I rode there on my Lambretta Li150 scooter, with its wing mirrors fashionably positioned all over the front like some silver-eyed bug.

The sea breeze picks up as the day unfolds and we end up having an exhilarating sail into Poole Harbour, reported to be the biggest harbour in the world (Sydney is second). Our plan is to spend a week or so there testing our gear in the protected harbour; however our plans are soon to change. Poole may have a big harbour, but its deep water is restricted to a surprisingly narrow channel, which feels even narrower when we share it with one of the enormous car ferries which come flying past on their journey to France.

As we approach the town I go forward to drop the sails. I shout back to Sandra, *"Turn her into the wind and go to the side of the channel."* Five seconds later we are aground!!! I did not expect the bottom to shelve so quickly outside the channel. Once again if I had checked the chart properly it would have been obvious - Log book: chart 2611, Poole Harbour (scale 1:12,5000). We try to motor off but the keel is stuck fast, so we launch the dinghy and position a kedge. A check of the tide tables indicates we are, fortunately, near the bottom of the tide. After an embarrassing hour and a half wait we float off and quietly motor up to Poole Quay.

But the fun is not over. The harbour wall is packed with yachts except for a small gap just big enough for us. We weigh up the situation as we motor past and circle around, my natural instinct is to come in against the wind but, in this case, there is also a strong flooding tide in the opposite direction - which is the stronger?

I manage to get the nose in and we tie the bow on securely, but we take too long and the stern swings out. Now we are at right angles to the quay. With a lot of pulling and heaving we eventually pull the stern in, to be faced with another problem - the piles are too widely spaced for our fenders. Looking at the other yachts the solution is obvious. They have positioned a plank of wood against the pile and two fenders against the hull. Our only problem is we do not have a plank of wood!!! Instead we make do with three fenders lashed together.

22nd April (Thursday) - Poole to Lymington: Log book: chart 2454, Start Point to the Needles (scale 1:150,000). Shipping forecast SW 3/4 - more ideal sailing conditions. After going aground yesterday we have second thoughts about staying in Poole Harbour to do our sea trials. A closer look at the chart reveals that we would run the risk of going aground again as we do not have local knowledge, and next time we may not be so lucky to go aground at the bottom of the tide - we decide to leave.

After a good start we motor sail up the channel, I casually glance at the instruments and am shocked to see the oil pressure dipping. *"Quick drop the sails we need to pick up a mooring."* Fortunately we are near some vacant mooring buoys.

Check the dip stick and, sure enough - no oil. "We must have an oil leak." The engine is totally covered in black oil. *"The rocker cover gasket must be blowing."* Or at

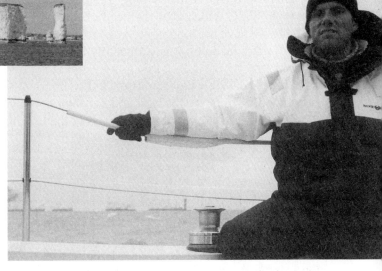

Sailing past the Needles off the Isle of Wight - note gloves and woollen hat - absolute necessity!

least I hope it is, because I can easily fix that. I start to take off the rocker cover. *"It won't come off."* As I lift it up it fouls the transverse bulkhead. I cannot believe the gasket has never been changed. If only it would rise a few more millimetres - out comes the pad saw to cut a notch in the bulkhead. Fit a new gasket, top up the oil and we are on our away again.

In the bay the wind is blowing a healthy 20 knots, *"Perfect - let's try the self-steering."* I set the Hydrovane's wind vane to the wind angle, and sit back with confident anticipation. For some reason the wind vane does not respond quickly enough and *Pacific Voyager* starts to sail an erratic "S" course. *"Perhaps I haven't set it right, but these machines are really straight forward and simple to use."* I had written to Hydrovane asking for a lubrication chart, but they recommended that their self-steering gear should not be lubricated as oil attracts salt crystals; rather it should be washed in fresh water. *"I'll have to look at that later."* I put it on my job list.

Log book: chart 2045, Outer Approaches to the Solent. As we approach the Needles off the Isle of Wight, in reducing visibility and building seas, we are accompanied by a high speed cross channel ferry. We continue past the 16th century Hurst Castle which marks the narrowest part of the channel. This is where King Charles was imprisoned in 1648.

Pacific Voyager **moored alongside Lymington town quay**

The oil problem has delayed our arrival in Lymington so it is getting dark when we arrive. It is true British sailing weather, windy and raining, as we motor up to the town quay, which is at the head of the navigable river by its bridging point. Initially we have the long pontoon all to ourselves for £10 a day. Although they do not offer any facilities, it is sufficiently less than the marina which charges £17.50 a day.

Over the next few days Sandra's family and friends who live near the New Forest start flooding in to see the boat and say their goodbyes. This is a delightful part of England, near to the Maritime Museum at the tiny hamlet of Bucklers Hard where Nelson's ship HMS *Agamemnon* was built in 1780.

Southampton's towing tank - where I studied naval architecture

27th April (Tuesday) - Lymington to Southampton: After several social days we leave Lymington early to ensure we reach Shamrock Quay by 10:00 for our rig test. As we motor past Calshot Point I recall seeing in 1979 the *Endeavour,* one of the famous 'J' class yachts, being refurbished there frame by frame by John Sager, after she had been bought from the National Maritime Trust for just £1.

Motor past Hythe where I used to work for the National Maritime Institute. This is where Christopher Cockerel developed the Hovercraft to reducing frictional and wave making resistance, by raising the vehicle on a cushion of air. We continue up the Southampton waters and pass the Southampton Institute where I studied Naval Architecture. A little further along we notice the ocean liner terminal where, in 1912 during her maiden voyage, the RMS *Titanic* departed on her way to Cobh. We pass under the Itchen Bridge, pass Vosper Thornycroft and Hovermarine where I used to build sidewall hovercrafts during my summer holidays. Next door is Rival's old yard, then Camper and Nicholson's yard. Finally we arrive at Shamrock Quay marina.

Electronic Rig Test: Rig maintenance presents a dilemma. I am advised there is almost no visual way of assessing the integrity of our stainless steel rigging. Wire and terminals can look as good as new up to the moment of failure. To address this dilemma insurance companies sometimes stipulate a *just-in-case* planned renewal period of around 10 to 15 years.

Solent Rigging test our rigging by measuring the internal resistance in the connections to 0.1 micro ohm. By comparative assessment the resistance readings are compared with average readings for our rigging size and type. A high reading indicates a fault of some kind within the terminal. This could be a broken strand, an incorrectly swaged terminal, movement inside the swaging, internal corrosion, or a crack. Our rigging passes the test except for the new forestay which was professionally fitted in Salcombe as there is no split pin at the masthead fitting. We were lucky not to loose the mast on our first trip!!!

28th April (Wednesday) - Southampton to Hamble: With the rigging test complete we now set off to cruise around the coast to Porthmadog in North Wales. Strong winds are forecast, but we feel we can sneak around the corner back to Lymington before the wind picks up - we are wrong. Just as we make Calshot Point the wind picks up to a steady 35 knots on the nose.

With three reefs in the main and the storm jib we tack between Calshot Spit and the Bramble Bank. This is *Pacific Voyager's* first test in strongish winds. The sea water has that hard iridescent shine of new-cut coal. It then dawns on me that Lymington's entrance will be open to these strong winds. So we take the safe option and tack back to the Hamble where we pick up a mooring and spend the rest of the day watching a group of sea cadets practice their safety drill. The rough weather makes me think of our conditions below, we need to fit strops to secure the washboards - another job!

Solent Rigging - electronic rig test

6th May (Thursday) - Salcombe to Fowey: After a brief stop over at Lymington and Salcombe we depart from Salcombe at 09:00. Our Nicholson handles well in fresh winds and a following sea, but the self-steering is still not right so we use the Neco autopilot which holds a perfect course, a much better course than we can hand steer. I practice my sun sight which seems to take me forever. I need to speed up my calculations. We initially steer 295 mag. to pass close to the mouth of the Plymouth Sound. *"This is where Drake completed his game of bowls while the Spanish Armada sailed up the channel, and where Francis Chichester finished his solo round the world trip in 1967 in Gipsy Moth."*

I throw our trailing Walker log over the side just to check it works okay. With a Decca navigation system (and now a GPS), the log is joining the sextant as a back-up in case of electronic failure.

After 36 miles we approach Fowey's entrance. The harbour master directs us to a mooring buoy which costs us £4 for the night (as we go to press I am shocked to find it now costs nearly £10 a night - eight times more than mooring in New Zealand!). After stowing our gear we row ashore and explore the picturesque town with its narrow streets winding up the hill side, giving commanding views of the harbour. Our sense of *old* is re-calibrated. Fowey is a hive of seaborne activity with the water taxi, a passenger ferry, a car ferry, and numerous sailing school yachts, which all scatter when a 10,000 tonne china clay bulk carrier turns around in the basin. This china clay is used to give magazines their glossy texture.

Cornish pasty tee-towel

Sandra finds a second-hand shop selling a wooden flag holder, just right for holding her cooking utensils. We also buy a tea towel with a print of a Cornish pasty recipe. *"While we're here we must try a traditional Cornish pasty."* They look wholesome and delicious, bulging with mouth watering filling wrapped in a beautifully baked golden pastry crust. With great expectations we bite into a potato and vegetable filling. *"Where are those mouth watering chunks of meat?"* I ask Sandra pointing at the recipe on the tea towel. We go back to the baker and ask if there is supposed to be any meat in them. Apologetically she replaces them with two more pasties also beautifully cooked but, as it turns out, with even less meat. We later read in the Times that this travesty had not gone unnoticed. An American restaurant critic compared the Cornish Pasty with a door stop. Sadly, instead of addressing the problem, the locals took the third world approach - they burnt the American Flag!!!

Fowey is different to the other tourist resorts on the Cornwall coast. What it lacks in sandy beaches and amusement arcades it makes up for with arts and literature festivals, which appeal to an older, more cerebral holidaymaker.

Fowey is also well known for its indigenous writers; Lucy Atwell who wrote children's books and Daphne Du Maurier who wrote novels based on her life's experiences and whose old home overlooks the river. The small town offers literary walks which are dotted with tributes of recognition to Daphne. One of Daphne's famous quotes reads: *"You will embark on a fair sea, and at times there will be fair weather and foul."* And on Daphne's wedding day at Lanteglos Church the priest said, *"Never lose courage. Safe harbour awaits you both in the end."* Very apt.

8th May (Saturday) - Fowey to Helford River: It is a toss-up between a stopover in Falmouth or Helford River. Falmouth has strong links with bluewater cruisers. This is where Robin Knox-Johnston became the first man to sail solo, nonstop around the world in *Suhaili* (now in the Greenwich Maritime Museum). However, we choose Helford River because it will be quieter. After a short sail we moor and row ashore to reward ourselves with a few beers in a traditional pub near the water's edge.

The following day we explore the estuary, pottering up to Porth Navas in our Avon Redseal, using our 2 hp Suzuki outboard. It is one of those lazy Sunday afternoons that you do not want to end because it is Monday tomorrow - but we do not have the Monday blues any more with our new cruising lifestyle.

9th May (Sunday) - Flat Batteries: In preparation to leave I switch on the starting battery and, to my horror, nothing happens when I turn the ignition key - all the batteries are flat. *"What's gone wrong?"* We religiously isolate the starting battery but, on closer inspection, find the Neco autopilot has been wired directly to the starting battery terminal, so we have managed to flatten all six of our 90 amp hour batteries. *"No problem, we have a petrol generator specially for this occasion."* I get the Clarke 600 watt petrol generator going and wire it directly to the starting battery and let it charge for an hour, then try the main engine again - nothing. I start the generator again, but this time check the current with my AVO only to find the generator has tripped. The trip indicator is so inconspicuously small that I do not notice it. After another hour charging the starting batteries we get the engine going. (Later in Gibraltar I fitted an ammeter in-line so I can always check the charging rate).

Helford River - preparing to leave

There is a certain satisfaction having all the wires labelled and organised. Nothing is more frustrating than an electrical problem and a mass of unknown wires. At the back of my mind there is a growing need for a comprehensive wiring diagram to complement the Nicholson's as-built drawings (Sandra later uses Coreldraw to develop a very useful wiring schematic). We are starting to find a need for log books to plan and control our activities - for example:

- Log book for passage making to plot our course and weather conditions
- Log book for maintenance and repairs
- Log book for ship's stores, fuel, water and LPG.

I particularly want to monitor our rate of water consumption. While coastal cruising it has been on average 28 litres a day - we will have to reduce this for the Atlantic ocean passage.

20th May (Thursday) - Porthmadog: After a brief stop at Penzance and the Isles of Scilly we are about to make our home port of Porthmadog just-in-time for the weekend. As we approach the Lleyn Peninsula I get out chart 1971 of Cardigan Bay (scale 1:75,000) - the chart of my youth. Ironically the chart number coincides with the year I was doing most of my sailing in this area. We sail around St Patrick's Causeway and make our landfall near Porth Ceiriad Bay where the hills end abruptly at a steep cliff and the sheep can be seen grazing precariously close to the edge.

Our route continues on through the passage between the mainland and St Tudwal's islands beside Abersoch. I remember with a chill how I had once sailed very close to Carreg-t-Trai in calm weather. If a gentle swell had not broken over the rock to warn me, the owner would have got a nasty fright - especially as he was sitting on the heads in the forepeak at the time!

The depth falls to 6 metres on the echo sounder, *"There must be a sand bank here."* I check the chart but it seems okay. *"I never realised it was so shallow."* When I sailed here before we used to measure the depth in feet and I suppose 18 feet sounds a lot more than 6 metres. In perfect sailing conditions we are creaming along at 7 knots in 22 knots of wind past Pen-y-Chain where the Butlins cable chairs run along the headland. Tack close to Criccieth Castle built several hundred years ago. In fact this corner of Wales has a wealth of castles; Harlech, Caernarvon, Conway and Penrhyn. As we motor into Porthmadog we are greeted by Ken and Rosemary holding up our mooring lines on the trots next to their yacht *Onaway, near* the Madoc Yacht Club (Ken kindly wrote the foreword).

THE COB
PORTHMADOG

Postcard of the Cob bringing the Ffestiniog railway to Porthmadog

Porthmadog used to be one of the busiest ports in Britain, shipping Welsh slate to all corners of the world; the Welsh know best how to keep rain out! The slate came from the nearby mountains, and was transported down the valleys on the narrow gauge Ffestiniog railway. The railway and some of the old slate mines, are now tourist attractions.

A tidal barrier called the Cob was constructed to provide a rail and road connection across the estuary. It incorporated sluice gates to give the estuary a good flush on the outgoing tide. The slate business spawned a wide range of supporting industries from ship building to sail making. In the 70s, Robin Kufin, my old boss, brought back one of Porthmadog's famous ships, the *Garlandstone,* for refurbishment and developed it into a local heritage museum.

Across the Cob, on the other side of the valley is Portmeirion, the pseudo Italian village built by Clough Williams-Ellis. Portmeirion became well known as the location of the TV programme, *The Prisoner.* Today it is better known for its beautifully decorated botanical painted pottery and a tourist village.

Prince Madoc: In the 12th Century Prince Madoc, a Welsh sailor, dreamt of a new continent beyond the western horizon, and sailed in search of it. This Welsh legend was given some credibility in the early 1800s when a tribe of Welsh speaking Indians, called Mandans, were found in America. The Mandans' appearance encouraged this romantic story; they were light skinned with chestnut hair and blue eyes. They built round, skin-covered boats (similar to the Welsh coracle), and muttered a few words which resembled the Welsh language. Are we now about to follow in the footsteps of Prince Madoc to a new continent?

Madoc Yacht Club: The Madoc yacht club was founded in 1970; I was still at Owestry boarding school. My father, a founding member, bought a Mirror

Postcard of Porthmadog - and my father's sailing boat *Ravioli* in the foreground

Offshore. What it lacked in sailing performance it made up for in accessibility - it only drew 18 inches. I was able to sneak in and out of all the shallow harbours in Cardigan Bay at almost any state of the tide. This was to lay the foundation for my present cruising aspirations.

17th May (Monday): Glaslyn Marine is our last chance to buy chandlery in Britain. We buy a few more shackles for the bosun's locker and a pair of Plastimo binoculars 7x50. David Eastwood is a mine of useful information, "*David what can we do with our Bruce anchor, it's always in the way*?" David suggests we hang it on the pushpit, lashed with a loop for quick release in an emergency. This turns out to be an excellent position.

27th May (Thursday) - Porthmadog: Over the next two days I work on the electrical wiring. I fit two, six-switch panels in the holes left by the old Baron instruments. I wire in the speakers to both radios, the gas detector, and fans over the galley and chart table.

1 June (Tuesday) - Medical: Dr. John gives us a crash course on how to give ourselves stitches and injections. He demonstrates the technique by stitching two bits of cardboard together, "*John you really make this look easy*." He then shows us how to give an injection. I try injecting myself against hepatitis, but I make the mistake of not pushing the needle in deep enough and some of the liquid squirts out. Dr. John suggests, "*Imagine the needle is a dart and jab it into your arm first, then press the syringe*." I do this on the next jab with a better result. However, Sandra does not share my confidence and politely declines my offer of giving her the first course of her inoculations.

"I name this yacht Pacific Voyager, may God bless her and all who sail on her"

5th June (Saturday) - The Naming Ceremony: My family and relations are in Porthmadog for the naming ceremony. Instead of breaking a bottle of champagne over the bow, Reg Sington (former vice commodore of MYC) gives us a bottle of Welsh whiskey, *Can Y Delyn* which means *Sound of the Harp*. Because it has a "*delicate silky smooth taste of honeyed perfume, from an ancient land of mystery and adventure, and is stored in cliff-top warehouses overlooking the sea*," we decide not to actually break the bottle over the bow, that would be a waste - never mind damaging the boat. Instead, we pour a healthy shot into a glass. We take a few slurps, "*.....I name this yacht* Pacific Voyager, *may God bless her and all who sail on her*." Back onshore, Deirdre my sister, then treats us to a Cadwalader ice cream, followed by a strenuous walk up Mole-y-Gest with cousins Alex and Louise.

After years of dreaming, months of planning, and weeks of preparation we are at the point of no-return. With *Pacific Voyager* tugging at the mooring lines, fully victualled and renamed we are finally ready to take our first step to Ireland, en route to the South Pacific.

Further Reading:

Hughes, Henry., *Immortal Sails*
Kittow, June., *Favourite Cornish Recipes*
Ryan, Rob., *Stay Healthy Abroad*, 1995
Calor Gas, *Guide to Bluewater Yachtsmen*
web.ukonline.co.uk/cornishlinks (traditional recipes and information)
www.cornwall-online.co.uk (Cornwall Tourist Board)
www.porthmadog.com

5 Ireland

Although Ireland is only an over night's sail away from Porthmadog, officially this is the beginning of our circumnavigation. Our plan is to sail to Wicklow and port hop, or rather pub hop, as one does in the land of Guinness and leprechauns, down the coast to Kinsale before making our passage across the Bay of Biscay to La Corona in Spain. Jimmy Cornell's *World Cruising Routes* recommends May to mid August as the best months to cross the Bay of Biscay.

4th June (Friday): After lunch with my mother in her chalet at Garreg Wen, we depart from the quay outside the Madoc Yacht Club. We are particularly keen on an inconspicuous start, just in case we have to return (we have read Sir Alec Rose's story). With a high spring tide and a good weather forecast we motor clear of Porthmadog and start our trip around the world. (It is with horror that we look back and see we started our trip on a Friday!!! Sailors are a superstitious bunch and they never start a long passage on a Friday - but perhaps a short over night hop to Ireland was okay).

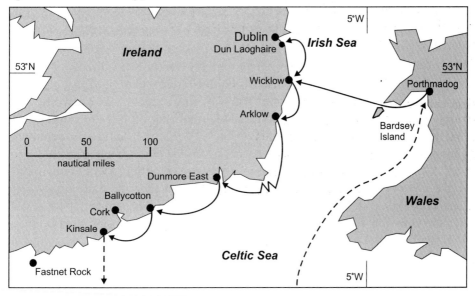

Phileas Fogg planned to travel around the world in 80 days - we thought we would do it in 3 years (as we go to print it looks more like 12 years!!!). He travelled with only a carpet bag containing two woollen shirts and three pairs of stocks, and his servant Passepartout. By contrast, we travel with a 35 foot yacht bulging with gear. Phileas Fogg left from the Reform Club at Charing Cross - we depart from the Madoc Yacht Club in Porthmadog.

5th June (Saturday): Six hours after departing from Porthmadog we have not yet left Cardigan Bay - Porthmadog is still in sight - there is no wind. A quick check on the tidal atlas indicates that we either start motoring or miss the favourable tide through Bardsey Sound. We start the Perkins.

This part of the Welsh coast is steeped in maritime history, particularly places like Hell's Mouth (Porth Neigwl), and Aberdaron with its 12th century church. Keeping close to the north side of Bardsey Sound, we sail inside Carreg Ddu to avoid the overfalls. Bardsey Island looks like a stranded humpback whale lying off the end of the Lleyn Peninsula. Bardsey has been an important place of pilgrimage for holy men since the 6th century. In medieval times, three visits to Bardsey would be equal to one visit to Rome. It is reputed to be the burial place of over 20,000 saints - this must give them a near monopoly. Sadly, Bardsey's early Celtic Monastery has not stood the test of time. There remains just a lighthouse and a few buildings for bird watching. It is said if you catch Bardsey Sound with a strong wind against a rip tide, the overfalls will make the Sound feel like hell itself.

Once through Bardsey Sound we enjoy excellent sailing conditions across the Irish Sea - at 18 knots the wind is just perfect to fill the sails. The visibility is the best I have ever known. When we are halfway across we can clearly see both the Welsh and Irish mountains at the same time.

A strange event occurs about two thirds across the Irish Sea when we notice a line of **breaking waves**. The depth is 80 metres which corresponds with the chart, so the waves must be caused by cross currents. But as we cautiously approach the depth reduces to 50 metres, then 25 metres, then 1.5 metres - with the depth alarm sounding I put the helm hard over and head back towards Wales. Totally puzzled, with my heart pounding, *"Surely we're not near the sand banks off the east coast of Ireland already?"* A quick check of the chart and a fix on the Sugar Loaf and Codling puts our position miles away from them. Tentatively we head for the breaking waves again - this time without any problem. The waves must have been caused by cross currents, and the depth sounder was probably bouncing off a water interface.

Wicklow: A few hours later as we approach Wicklow, I can see the prominent red brick building of my old boarding school up on the hill. At eight years old, even though I knew of the Pacific Islands from my stamp collection, I would never have thought that one day I would be sailing there. On reaching the harbour we moor alongside the sea wall by a rickety-looking ladder which has seen better days. With its top step missing, rock climbing skills come in useful. Before going for a Guinness in the yacht club we have a quick walk around the town and wander up to my old boarding school. I can clearly remember my dormitory and classrooms, but it has all changed. The boys have gone - it is a girls only school now and my old rugby field is a housing estate. We say a prayer in the church where I used to say the rosary everyday. It is amazing to think I used to know the mass in Latin!

Wicklow may not be internationally famous, but the fictitious TV town just up the road is - *Ballykissangel*. At the Wicklow yacht club we drink Guinness and Irish whiskey (Uisce Beatha) while we listen to live traditional Irish music played on a tin whistle, an accordion, a fiddle and a bodhrain. A local chap gives us some advice about our trip to Dun Laoghaire, *"There are three yacht clubs, the Royal Irish, the Royal St George and the Dublin Bay - which are known as the snobs, nobs, and yobs - I suggest you ask them on the VHF in that order if they have a visitor's mooring for you."*

6th June (Sunday) - Wicklow to Dublin: 06:00 the alarm goes off - where am I? I feel dead tired, I could easily just close my eyes and drift back into a deep sleep. But if we are to catch the favourable tide up the coast to Dublin we have to go now. Half awake with a very thick head I start the engine, cast off and motor out of the harbour. Sandra is still bopeep.

Early afternoon, as we approach **Dun Laoghaire** harbour, Sandra calls up the Royal

Irish Yacht Club on channel 22 and asks if they have a visitor's mooring. *"Yes we have - just let us know when you enter the harbour."* Thirty minutes later Andrew, an Australian, guides us to a visitor's mooring and organises temporary membership so that we can use their shower and bar facilities - great, we seem to have landed with our bum in Kerry Gold butter.

Royal Irish Logo

Later that evening while supping a glass of *Kilkenny* in the plush yacht club's bar with my cousins Lulu and Pat, they tell us that Dun Laoghaire used to be called Kingstown after King George. It is a port of refuge open to everyone during rough weather. However, the harbour wall had been mistakenly built short - someone obviously misread the drawings. Consequently the harbour is exposed to a narrow band of northerly winds, which we are shortly to experience.

Initially we thought we would only stay a couple of days, but thick fog, visibility down to 50 metres, and then gale force winds accompanied by heavy rain puts us off going anywhere. At least the wind generator is keeping our batteries topped up.

Rory leaving Wicklow after the night before

9th June (Wednesday): After a couple of days we venture ashore, secure the dinghy to the yacht club's pontoon and walk to the train station - a short train ride on the DART and we are in the centre of Dublin's fair city with its graceful Georgian buildings. We make straight for the book shops - Waterstones, Easons, Fred Hanna's and Hodges Figgis. In our rush to get the boat ready we had completely overlooked our reading material - shortly we will have long periods at sea with nothing to do but read. This is our opportunity to stock up on a few informative books on the lives of Columbus, Nelson, Livingstone, Drake, Darwin, and Cook.

We make a special trip to the Trinity College library to see the *Book of Kells* which is on permanent display. This is arguably one of the most beautiful manuscripts of the western world. It is thought to have been written in the St Columba monastery on the Hebridean island of Iona. We round off our cultural and shopping excursion with a late lunch at Bewleys. (It was only after we left Dublin, that we heard about James Joyce's 16th June Bloomsday celebrations, where people dress in Edwardian costume and wander around Dublin bearing a copy of *Ulysses*. It is a major event in literary tourism. We wish we had stayed a few more days. Particularly as my cousin, Val Joyce, in his foreword for my project management book, compared it on a scale of incomprehensibility with *Ulysses* and *Finnegan's Wake*.)

13th June (Sunday) - Wicklow to Arklow: After yesterday's day hop back to Wicklow we are up early to catch the tidal stream down the coast to Arklow. For lunch we have Irish Stew and Irish soda bread (recipes given to us by my cousins Hilda and Lulu in Dublin), and wash it down with a can of Guinness, while we read the Irish Times. Our fridge is not working so we are using a bucket of cold water to cool our cans of Guinness and cartons of milk. The weather deteriorates as we reach the protection of Arklow's inner harbour. We moor in 2.7 metres of water alongside a wooden boat which looks like it has not been used for years - there is even grass growing in-between the planking.

Soon after we berth, a Westerly Centaur from Aberystwyth moors alongside us. They have broken their tiller on the way over. It is now lashed to the rudder stock and reminds me of how Robin Knox-Johnston's gooseneck looked after his round the world trip. These chaps are over for a social evening with the Arklow Rowing Club. Apparently they often row across the Irish Sea for a social evening!!!

Sandra clearing the coast

Arklow has an interesting museum where we discover that Sir Francis Chichester's yacht Gipsy Moth III was built in the local shipyard (we are later to see her in Las Palmas). After dinner we walk to the nearest pub for a few pints of Guinness. Sandra cannot not believe the language - but then this is Ireland after all. We soon get chatting to a couple of local lads - Shamus and Ray - who entertain us with their Irish humour - it is good *'craic'* as they say in Ireland. And having encouraged us to try Guinness and blackcurrant, they suggest we should also try potato sandwiches for breakfast!!!

Arklow pub where the locals suggest we try potato sandwiches for breakfast

14th June (Monday) - Arklow to Dunmore East: 06:30 start - temperature is 10 degrees - is this summer or winter? Leaving Arklow with a favourable tide we make good progress down the coast, but do not quite make the Tuskar Rock before the tide turns against us. About the same time, Murphy's Law strikes and the wind freshens to 25 knots on the nose with visibility reduced to less than a mile. We tack out from the Tuskar for two hours, then back for another two hours. The Tuskar light is still in sight - in four hours we have only made a couple of miles in the right direction. Resolutely we repeat the tacking again and again like head-banging saltwater masochists, until the Decca eventually indicates the tide is weakening and finally we are making ground towards Dunmore East. I have to keep reminding myself that the purgatory of the Irish Sea is the flip-side of the tropical South Pacific.

15th June (Tuesday) - Dunmore East: We pass the Hook lighthouse, built around 1172 and named after an Anglo-Norman Knight - this is reputed to mark the site of the oldest lighthouse in Europe. The first warning light was a beacon lit by monks in the fifth century. These monks were also known for their Kilkenny beer which dates back to the 14th century, and can now be found in Irish pubs around the world.

Dunmore East - *Pacific Voyager* is moored alongside the pontoon on the left of the photograph

"*By Hook or by Crook,*" is a well known term, but we did not realise it originated from this area. Opposite Dunmore East is Hook Point and further up the river is a place called Crook. Apparently when Cromwell invaded Ireland he is reported to have said, "*We will land by Hook or by Crook.*"

We motor into Dunmore East and raft up - we are the eighth boat out from the quay! Although we were advised not to use the inner harbour because of all the fishing boats, we find the local fishermen very agreeable. Even though the fishermen have big boots and carry buckets overflowing with bait ready to drip over any exposed sail, they are extremely careful and light footed. The next day when we awake all the fishing boats have gone and we are safely moored against the quay.

After a lazy breakfast, we explore the village and find a local butcher whose name is Power. When I tell him my grandmother's maiden name was also Power, he reckons we are probably related and proceeds to give us an extra generous portion of meat for our Irish Stew. I always thought Irish stew was, "*Mash potatoes, boiled potatoes, fried potatoes and chips.*" Sandra corrects me, "*No it's lamb, potatoes, carrots and onions.*"

Back on board, I notice a well dressed jogger running purposefully along the harbour wall. As he approaches he pulls out a badge and introduces himself as a **customs officer**. Shocked - I try to visualise which TV cop programme this would fit into. He asks me where we have come from and where we are going, and asks to see the ship's log book and charts. Usually we do not plot our course down a clear coast in settled weather, but when we caught the foul tide and headwinds off the Tuskar Rock we felt it was sensible to do so. As he inspects our chart his head moves up and down with each tack between the Tuskar Rock and Coningbeg - this seems to prove our innocence. He thanks us and jogs on into the Irish mist.

Unsettled weather keeps us a day or so longer than planned - this is a good opportunity to catch up on our jobs. Sandra waterproofs the sprayhood and I work on the self-steering. With our departure for the Bay of Biscay only a few days away, "*I must fix the self-steering.*" I was hoping it might free up with the constant movement through the water - but it has not - so there must be something else causing the stiffness. Nothing for it but to dismantle the unit. So with the socket set in hand and Sandra positioning her umbrella underneath to catch any falling parts, I release the top bracket and to my surprise the whole unit suddenly frees up. The top bracket was pinching the top bearing. What a relief - I had visions of us hand steering across the oceans.

Dunmore East - Rory repairing the self-steering

19th June (Saturday) - Dunmore East to Ballycotton: Leave Dunmore East with a good forecast for the wind to ease and come round to a favourable direction. It is 60 miles to Ballycotton so we need to make good speed. The seas are still up as we head out - *Pacific Voyager* punches through them in 25 knots of wind with one reef in the main and no.2 jib set. Our Henri Lloyds are earning their keep protecting us from the elements. I consider going into Youghal, but we do not have a detailed chart and I do not fancy negotiating the estuary. It is tempting though as this is where they filmed Melville's *Moby Dick* in 1955. Herman Melville wrote this masterpiece in 1850, based on his own experiences aboard a whaling ship in the South Seas.

As we approach Ballycotton, I notice a fishing boat pottering around. When they see us they motor over frantically waving their arms in the air - which is just as well as we are motoring straight into their enormous salmon net blocking our course.

Ballycotton - Sandra up the mast

Ballycotton is a cute little port with just enough room for a few trawlers along the harbour wall. As we are mooring alongside one of the trawlers, the skipper introduces himself as the local publican and invites for a drink. In the evening we take up his offer and emerge a few hours later on first name terms with half the local community who were in the pub.

20th June (Sunday): We awake to a beautiful sunny morning just right for a traditional Irish breakfast of black pudding, bacon and eggs. Bursting with food, *"I need to walk off my breakfast."* We amble up the hill to the local church which is positioned on top of the ridge with commanding views of the bay and the diocese below. Outside the entrance there are two chaps smoking cigarettes. It would appear they have only come to accompany their family. They invite us into the packed church, *"No thank you, we only came for the view."* On the way back we buy the Sunday papers for a lazy reading session - this is, after all, what we like to do on Sundays.

Later in the day, we continue with our jobs which include repairing a tear in the top of our new mainsail, making lee cloths for our bookshelves and checking the rigging at the top of the mast. Afterwards, Sandra makes Irish tea brak (fruit cake) and an apple crumble for dessert.

We round off the evening with another visit to the pub. Shortly after the barmaid calls time, a local fisherman joins us for a pint of Guinness. The young barmaid declines to give him a drink, *"Sorry we are closed."* But the fisherman is quite adamant that he needs one more drink - the last drink for the week. The commotion attracts the attention of the landlady who sticks her head around the corner and enquires about the noise. With a wave of her arm she offers an Irish solution, *"Ah give him a drink and shut him up."*

21st June (Monday) - Ballycotton to Kinsale: We consider going into Cork and Cobh, but do not have the chart, and time is pushing on. We would have liked to have visited the Heritage Museum, especially as its exhibits include some interesting themes associated with this area. They are; the Irish immigrants departing during the potato famine, the sinking of the *Lusitania* off Kinsale, and the *Titanic's* last port of call.

  • The **potato famine** between 1845 and 1847 devastated the Irish population - as a single crop nation they were always at risk to the potato blight. The famine caused mass migration to America.

  • The **RMS** *Lusitania* was sunk on 7th May 1915 off the Old Man of Kinsale after she was torpedoed by a German *'U'* boat. The liner went down in only 20 minutes and 1200 people lost their lives.

  • On the *Titanic's* **maiden voyage** from Southampton to New York its last port of call was Cobh to collect mail. Built by Harland and Wolfe for the White Star shipping line, the *Titanic,* is probably the second most famous ship after Noah's Ark. The builders claimed she was unsinkable, but as we all know, a glancing blow with an iceberg tore a series of small holes below the waterline and the rest is history. The subsequent maritime enquiries encouraged far-reaching marine safety improvements - they increased the number of lifeboats to match the number of passengers, improved davit design, increased bulkhead design strength, introduced an international Mayday SOS signal, and required all ships to have a 24 hour radio watch.

This area is also well known for the St Brendan voyage. In 1977 Tim Severin sailed from Crosshaven (near Cork) across the Atlantic to Newfoundland in a reproduction of St Brendan's leather-covered currach. His year at sea showed that it was possible the Irish really did discover the New World before Columbus. And why not? St Brendan is after all the Patron Saint of sailors.

We consider making a detour to the Blarney Castle to kiss the famous stone that according to legend, endows those whose lips touch it with the ability to issue forth, *"A fine flow of eloquence with just a touch of good humour and exaggeration,"* in other words the gift of the gab - but Sandra already has that.

Continuing on the way to **Kinsale** the sea is like glass. We are hoping to see the QE2 leaving Cobh. Instead we meet plenty of fishermen patrolling more salmon nets, which extend on the surface for a mile or so, perpendicular from the coast out to sea. Their small floats bob on the surface as far as the eye can see. The fishermen escort us around their nets and advise us about the next lot further along the coast. The shoreline has no other obstructions so we are able to sail in close to the land and enjoy the *40 shades of green* as the rolling hills come down to the sea.

The old head of Kinsale is a steep rocky promontory jutting aggressively into the Atlantic from the south-west coast of Ireland. On its crest are a lighthouse, a coast guard station and the ruins of an early Celtic settlement. For two thousand years it has been a vantage point for those on shore and an essential landmark for

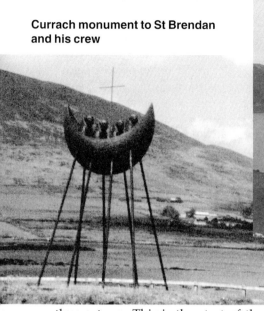

Currach monument to St Brendan and his crew

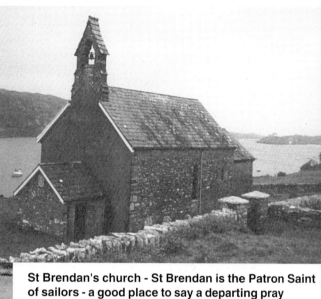

St Brendan's church - St Brendan is the Patron Saint of sailors - a good place to say a departing pray

those at sea. This is the start of the Blue Riband speed run across the Atlantic, a notional trophy for the fastest crossing - usually associated with passenger liners. The famous Fastnet Rock is only some 40 miles west of us.

As we motor up the long channel to Kinsale we pass Charles Fort to starboard. The fort is a good example of a 17th century star-shaped fort with two enormous bastions overlooking the estuary. Kinsale is a deep and secure harbour, once the shelter of the Spanish and British fleets, but now the old town of Kinsale is a sleepy fishing port.

There does not appear to be anywhere to anchor near the town so we tie up in a marina beside a diesel jetty. We want to be near the town to do our last shop in an English-speaking country, and also want to leave with full diesel tanks so that we have the option of motoring across the Bay of Biscay if necessary. I am amused to see the duty free marine diesel is stained green - why not! Fully victualled we are ready to leave Ireland. As a parting farewell gesture for us, Val Joyce, on his radio programme, plays Rod Stewart's *Sailing.* *"....we are sailing far away, across the sea......"*

Further Reading:

Cornell, Jimmy., *World Cruising Routes*
Hughes, Henry., *Immortal Sails*
Rose, Sir Alec Rose., *My Lively Lady*
Severin, Tim., *St Brendan Voyage*
Simpson, Colin., *Lusitania*, Penguin, 1983
Thomson, George., *Traditional Irish Recipes*
Hawthorn Series, *Irish Farmhouse Cooking*

6 Bay of Biscay

The Bay of Biscay is our first big hurdle before the Atlantic Ocean. (As we left Porthmadog we had three options; port hop down the coast of France and Spain, depart from Falmouth to Spain, or depart from Kinsale to Spain. We decided on the latter.) According to Jimmy Cornell's *Ocean Cruising Routes*, the best time of year for this passage is between May to August. An early departure in June will give us the opportunity to see more of Portugal and Spain. (As it turns out, our timing was just right because we had a good trip across the Bay of Biscay, while yachts that left a couple of months later encountered rough weather.)

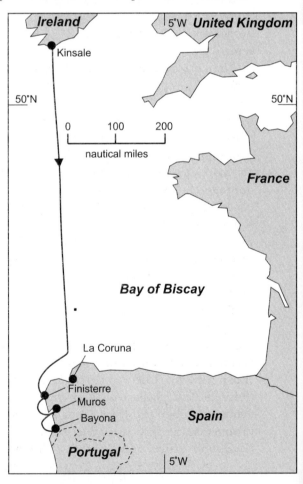

22nd June (Tuesday): Log book: Chart 1123, Saint George's Channel (scale 1:500,000). Although our departure from Kinsale is a quiet affair, and a natural progression after port hoping around the coast of Ireland, on our big plan it is a key milestone, because we are now leaving my home country. As we let go the mooring lines from the dock at Kinsale, we acknowledge that our dream of a three year circumnavigation has finally begun. It is a fantastic June morning, crisp and mild with a nip in the air and a few swirls of mist along the banks of the estuary.

As we leave Ireland it is flat calm - time to have lunch and catch up on the washing!!

Our yacht is laden to the hilt with provisions, clothing for all weather conditions, spares for every component that might fail, books to enlighten our adventure and exploration, and personal possessions that provide us with a strange perception that we are still at home.

The Bay of Biscay is flat calm. It is 20 centigrade, and we are motoring on a course of 195 magnetic heading for La Coruna in Spain. Sandra has been a bit rushed these past few days, so she now decides this is an ideal opportunity to catch up on her **washing**.

Breakfast is Weetabix and bananas, lunch is potato salad followed by raspberry yoghurt. In the afternoon we hear a loud bang, which brings back recent memories of the firing range near Portland. I check the chart to make sure we have not wandered into a naval testing area - we do not want a submarine surfacing beside us. The bang is probably **Concorde's** sonic boom.

The squawking of seagulls brings us into the cockpit. It sounds as though murder is being committed on the high seas - we watch helplessly as a large bird chases two smaller ones for their food. Later in the day we are visited by a school of porpoises who dart around *Pacific Voyager*. I am concerned they will damage the self-steering, while Sandra is concerned she will not get a good picture, as she jumps from side to side with her camera. Eventually she lies down flat on the deck and reaches out for them with her hand, they are only inches away. I am sure Sandra is dreaming of swimming with them.

Dolphins: More than 40 species of dolphins and porpoise thrive today, but several groups are dwindling, threatened by over fishing, accidental capture, pollution, and damage to their habitat. Closely related to whales, dolphins and porpoises are found in nearly every sea around the world. Generally dolphins have conical teeth, a defined beak, and a curved dorsal fin. Often confused with dolphins, the six species of porpoises usually have spade-

Porpoise leading the way just in front of our bow wave

shaped teeth, a rounded profile, and triangular dorsal. Virtually all dolphins and porpoises share a happy smile and are highly social. In the 1950s, scientists determined that the lower jawbone flares outwards and serves as an ultra-sensitive ear. They have also suggested that when porpoises jump in the air, they are looking for birds which may indicate a shoal of fish - they are more canny than we give them credit for. And even their highly efficient hydrodynamic shape has not escaped the notice of the naval architects who design the hunter killer submarines.

25th June (Friday): If we cannot make three knots under sail, on goes the engine and, for the first three days, the engine is on and off. The third day brings ideal sailing conditions and, on the fourth day, the wind continues to increase over 25 knots. In building seas we heave-to to steady the boat while we reef. Sandra hears a loud hiss and a whoosh as the shiny black body of a 30 foot whale appears alongside us, only a few feet away. *"It's as long as our boat!"* Our fascination and amazement soon turns to horror as we realise just how big it is; we feel minuscule beside him. Then another two whales appear in front of us - we are surrounded. They stay with us for a few minutes, probably puzzled why we have stopped. And then, as quietly as they came, they leave us.

The Bay of Biscay is my first real astro-navigation test. I take sun sights morning, noon and afternoon, together with the North Star in the evening. I am pleased to say my calculations generally agree with the Decca.

Collision Course: The BBC forecast SW6 for Finisterre; we are getting NE8. *Pacific Voyager* sails effectively under the self-steering, while we are below, popping up every so often to look out for shipping. The visibility is good, or so I thought until a Ro-Ro suddenly appears close on our port side. *"Where did that come from?"* I take bearings which are steady. Sandra calls them up a few times on channel 16 - no response. Too close for comfort, I tack away. Now we see the name BSC RO RO SERVICE in large letters on the side of the hull. Sandra calls them by name and makes contact. *"Can you see us?"* *"Yes"* a Spanish sounding voice responds. We feel like asking why they came so close, but decide to leave it. However, it certainly reinforces the need to keep a good look out. (We have since heard that other yachtsmen get a better response using *'Sécurité, Sécurité, Sécurité'* in this situation).

The wind remains gale force 35 knots gusting 40 for most of the day. The seas are now building up, but not causing *Pacific Voyager* any real difficulty except for the odd wave catching her awkwardly and the top of the wave splashing into the cockpit. I check the chart. At our present speed of 5 knots we will make landfall at La Coruna about 18:00. *"But La Coruna is open to this NE gale."* A quick decision is made to make our landfall at Cabo Finisterre. (Looking back on it now, it never occurred to us to heave-to and wait for the wind to ease).

Cabo Villano's light pierces through the haze, right where we expect it to be. The light fixes our position about five miles off the coast. During the night the wind and sea die down completely and next morning we end up motoring into Finisterre. We are relieved to have successfully completed the Bay of Biscay leg as this was the first opportunity mother nature had to express her power.

26th (Saturday) - Spain: Log book: chart 1111, Punta de La Estaca de Bares to Cabo Torinana (scale 1:200,000). Cabo Finisterre was dubbed

Finisterre Harbour - *Pacific Voyager* **in the background**

by the ancient pilgrims as 'Finis terrae' - the end of the earth. We decide to anchor off the entrance of the harbour behind the mole (breakwater) instead of trying to moor alongside the harbour wall. This turns out to be a good move because, apart from the swell in the harbour, which is quite alarming, we would be more likely to pick up some undesirable pests, and the risk of theft would be higher.

With *Pacific Voyager* safely anchored in 8 meters of water, we have a hot shower from the calorifier, followed by breakfast of toast with mashed bananas, washed down with a bottle of wine. Then we go to bed for a contented sleep, extremely tired after our five day crossing of the Bay of Biscay.

After a refreshing kip, we go ashore to explore the town we have heard mentioned so often on the BBC shipping forecasts. The harbour is packed with fishing boats ranging from rowing boats to small trawlers. The local design has a pronounced flared bow that maintains the beam all the way forward. I imagine they are dry boats, but would be prone to slamming in rough conditions.

Finisterre is a small fishing village of some 2000 people. As we walk around the streets we see many of them casually eating and drinking, and generally just hanging around with seemingly nothing much to do.

The buildings surrounding the harbour are quite impressive, with the original architecture of wrought iron railings decorating their balconies. The town seems to be between developments as some of the old architecture has beautifully cut stone that has stood the test of time, but many of the old windows have been replaced with aluminium. Sadly there is so much rubbish around that it detracts from the ambience of the place.

At a bank, we cash a Eurocheque. Now we can buy some cheap wine! No one speaks English or French. Looks like we are going to have to learn another language - Spanish. On the way back to the dinghy we visit a bar which overlooks the harbour, and Sandra has her first Spanish lesson while I try the local brew.

Back on board Sandra cooks dinner - tinned Spanish style chicken breasts in white sauce, with potato di Calabria, a recipe from Jane Gibb's book the *Reluctant Cook*. Quite good as a quick meal, but we are getting tired of potatoes after Ireland. Dessert is a tasty apple pie and tinned cream, I note we should buy more tinned cream as it really makes a dessert more interesting, regardless of the health factors!

Cornish Kestrel - they have just completed their circumnavigation

Visitor's book, *Pacific Voyager's* stamp

27th June (Sunday): We meet Jaakko and Ulla in town. "*Hi we're your neighbours on Cornish Kestrel.*" After a short chat they invite us over for dinner. They are from Finland, and are just completing their circumnavigation while we are beginning ours. After dinner we sign their **visitors' book** and they take a photograph of us all together. It is their way of recording their trip and those they enjoyed it with. They encourage us to also keep a visitors book, and to start now at the beginning of our trip.

We decide to use an A4 folder with separate plain A4 sheets of paper for each of our guests to write or draw on as they wish. Then we pop it into a plastic sleeve for protection and filing. Some cruisers keep a ready supply of photographs of themselves and their yacht, as well as a yacht stamp, a business card, a favourite cartoon or a rhyme. Ours is "*May you sail on the sea of tranquillity to reach the shores of inspiration.*"

30th June (Wednesday) - Finisterre to Muros: After three days in Finisterre, we are ready, mentally and physically to sail on to the next port - Muros. After a busy morning re-packing, we get away by 14:00. Leaving the shelter of Cabo Finisterre, the big Atlantic rollers come as an unexpected surprise. The wind freshens as we clear the headland and gives us an excellent reach. We stand off the coast to clear the sandbanks of Bajo de los Meixidos and Los Bruyos whose rocks litter this part of the coast. Rounding Punta Queixal we sail into the Ria de Muros ("*ria*" means "*estuary*" in Spanish). While I steer, Sandra is below cooking dinner - egg pasta with fresh pasta sauce.

The RCC Spanish pilot advises yachts to anchor outside Muros's harbour. As I let the chain out I am mentally multiplying the 18 meters depth by three. Rounding up I let out 60 metres of chain. If it blows up I can always let more out. As the chain runs out, the anchor tripping buoy goes a bit too early and starts to drift back along the side of the hull. With visions of it wrapping itself around the prop, I immediately grab the boat hook to retrieve it. But leaning over the side it is nowhere to be found, not on the port side, not on the starboard side, not ahead of us or behind us. Certain it is fouled, I pump up the Avon dinghy and make my way round the boat prodding with the boat hook and peering into the dark depths, but no buoy. (It is not until we leave Muros that the buoy reappears, for the simple reason that the 18 meter water depth is more than the length of the tripping line. The buoy had been floating a few meters below the surface all the time!)

1st July (Thursday) - Water: After breakfast of eggs and home-made Irish bread, we get ready to go ashore. As we motor past a Vancouver 32 anchored near by, Richard, the owner, calls us over for a chat. He shows us his internal buoyancy bags which are connected to an air bottle. There is a bag in the saloon and one in each quarter berth, *"I hope it doesn't go off when someone's in there!!!"* (Thinking about this interesting concept afterwards I feel the buoyancy bags may not be big enough. Unless the yacht has watertight bulkheads then the bags must displace a larger volume of water than the weight of the boat - about 6 tonnes therefore 6 m3.)

We motor on to the quay to fill our jerry cans. Although the fish market may not be the most salubrious quarter of town, it has a fresh water tap, and is only a short walk from the slipway. It takes two trips with seven 20 litre jerry cans to fill the fresh water tank. Our hunt for good fresh water is to become normal practice in every port we visit. Thankfully all the Spanish and Portuguese fishing ports have a good supply of fresh water. Since Kinsale we have almost used a full tank, which gives us an average of 25 litres per day. We will have to reduce our consumption on the ocean passages.

Muros has a population of 4000 people, double that of Finisterre, and the architecture is much smarter and well looked after. There is a distinctive charm about the narrow cobbled streets and the old stone buildings which seem to belong to another era. Nearly all the buildings that face the harbour have walk through arches, and the first floor windows have narrow balconies with iron railings. This picturesque Spanish architecture encourages Sandra to start designing her dream house. The central point of Muros is a square, which at this time of year, is used for amusements; the type of amusements that keep the kids happy but make a lot of noise into the night.

2nd July (Friday) - Muros to Bayona: A beautiful sunset last night is followed by a heavy dew this morning. Breakfast is potato puffs, a recipe from Sandra's Irish cook book - still using up Irish potatoes. Away by 09:00 to sail down the coast to Bayona, we stand out to clear the Ba. de Corrubedo banks. Good winds 15 knots NE, but poor visibility gives us a guessing game as to which islands we occasionally glimpse through the mist as we sail south. I have the external speaker working so we listen to Wimbledon on the BBC World service SW 12095 MHz, our link with the English speaking world during the day.

In the evening, when our reception is better, we listen to Radio 4's (LW 198) weather forecast during which the southerly sea area of Trafalgar is included. *"What are we going to do for weather forecasts in the Atlantic???"* Our Reeds Nautical Almanac suggests using Radio France International (SW 6175 Khz at 1130 GMT). This will certainly put Sandra's French to the test. However, Radio France International must have recently changed their weather forecast areas from the chart in Reeds, as the two do not agree. So we write to Radio France International for clarification, and they kindly send us a detailed booklet of their weather service.

The area around Bayona looks like an excellent cruising area, with plenty of islands and deep inlets with protected anchorages. (In hindsight we did not do the Rias justice; we should have spent a few days cruising these inlets and islands, but then, there will be another opportunity to explore them on the way back).

Bayona had the pleasure of experiencing Sir Francis Drake's company when his fleet anchored around the islands in search of fresh water. Drake would seize a few vessels and threaten to loot and burn them if they did not give him the victuals he required. Our reception is surprisingly friendly, considering past history.

After tacking up the inlet to Bayona we anchor near a smart looking yacht club between a French yacht, which looks like an overgrown dinghy, and a German yacht, which looks incredibly busy with all sorts of paraphernalia attached to the transom. It is 19:00 and we are exhausted so we devour dinner, washed down with a litre box of Spanish wine (locally called a brik of wine), and crash-out.

Next morning we pump up the dinghy and row across the anchorage towards the marina. We tie up on the pontoon behind a large British gin palace, where the lads are just having their first drink before the sun rises too much above the yard arm.

Our exercise today is to walk up and down Bayona's esplanade and watch the Spanish tourists. Bayona, with its bright lights and bars, is a weekend paradise and in complete contrast to the other traditional, quieter ports we have recently visited. I have to steer Sandra away from the expensive shops selling designer perfumes and clothes, and limit our shopping to fresh bread, cheese, vegetables, fruit, dried sausage and salami. It is really hot walking in the blistering sun, so we stop for ice cream and cokes to keep the metabolism going.

Bayona is our last port of call in northern Spain. We feel as if we have only just arrived and now we are off again. Tomorrow we will sail for Portugal and the Iberian Peninsula.

Further Reading:

Andrews, K. R., *Drake's Voyages*, Weidenfeld and Nicholson
Cornell, Jimmy., *Ocean Cruising Routes*
Gibb, Jane., *Reluctant Cook*
Radio France International, 42 Avenue Coriolis, 31057 Toulouse Cedex, France
Murdoch Books, *Step-by-Step Spanish Cooking*
Reed's Nautical Almanac, Thomas Reed

7 *Portugal*

Portugal is often referred to as the *balcony on the sea* - nestling between the Atlantic and the western mountain ranges of the Iberian Peninsula. Our plan is to continue port hopping down the Iberian Peninsula of Portugal and Spain, then on to Gibraltar and the Canaries.

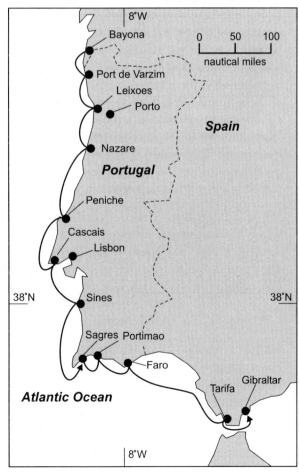

4th July (Sunday) - Bayona to Port de Varzim: Log book: chart 3633, Cabo Villano to Montedor (scale 1:200,000). Sail south, down an almost straight featureless coast, listening to Wimbledon's men's final day. The northerly Portuguese trades are still with us giving a healthy 15 to 20 knots, which enables us to make Port de Varzim as the men's final ends at 17:00.

Port de Varzim is our first taste of Portugal. We anchor in the middle of the fishing harbour as indicated in the RCC pilot, with five metres of dirty water under our keel. We are not sure what to expect as the immigration and custom rules within the EC have changed this year. There are now no borders, but I suspect this is a diplomatic agreement in Brussels which has not disseminated down to the officials in Port de Varzim.

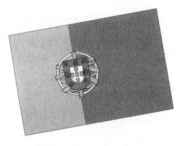

Sandra cooks chilli con carne using a packet of vegetarian bean feast, which we enjoy with a compulsory bottle of wine - so on top of a day's sea air we drift off into a carefree sleep, content that we have made our passage safely. An authoritative whistle disturbs me; I hear it again and again - am I dreaming? I stick my head through the forehatch to see a uniformed chap hanging off the harbour ladder frantically waving at us to come over.

We grab our passports and ship's papers, pump up the dinghy and row over to the quay. We do not speak Portuguese, he does not speak English, so we settle for French. He introduces himself as Jean as he leads us around the harbour towards his office. As we pass a restaurant, he suggests we should have a beer. *"A beer!!! - Yes thank you that would be great."* Perhaps this guy is not so bad after all. This is an interviewing technique the British officials should adopt, *"Please no more Whatney's, I'll tell you whatever you want to know."* Maybe they can make it compulsory within the EC.

After a couple of beers, during which time Jean tells us his life history and shows us his war wounds from Mozambique and Angola, we finally make it to his office to complete two simple forms. It takes ten slow minutes to fill out the form then another ten slower minutes to fill out a duplicate. It seems that carbon paper or a photocopier are not available. Right I thought, we are finished, but no, this is not the end. Now we have to accompany him to the police station which is two kilometres up the road in the town!

A beautiful old fort has been converted into the Chateau police station. It has a commanding view of the harbour with very distinctive sentry posts on each corner. We now have to see another officer and, believe it or not, are given more beers. Eventually an official takes one look at our forms, nods approval, we say our goodbyes and are off. This bureaucratic exercise although amusing, was all totally unnecessary and took all of two hours!

5th July (Monday) - Port de Varzim to Leixoes: The northerly Portuguese trade winds blow us the 12 miles down the coast to Leixoes. We anchor in 7 metres of water in a large outer harbour beside another British yacht *Ithaka* - a Vancouver 32. The yacht club is located in the inner harbour but is closed on Mondays, so, for our excursion ashore, we walk along the front and visit a beach bar where we have a *Super Broc*, the local beer. Back on board Sandra cooks chilli followed by bananas and tinned cream.

6th July (Tuesday) - Porto (Oporto): It is my birthday - I am 41. Up early to catch the bus to Oporto to have a look around and celebrate. The 6 km journey takes a very long 45 minutes but, once we reach Oporto, we are amazed by its beauty and architecture. Its north bank is a maze of steep dark alleyways, with outlandish baroque facades and shambling medieval buildings, with washing hanging from every tiny wooden balcony. Over cobbled streets we reach the centre of town with its ornate baroque tower, attached to the Clerigos church. The locals refer to this church as their Eiffel Tower, after the designer. Although Eiffel actually designed their D. Maria Pia Bridge! Even the old railway station is outstanding with a blue and white ceramic tiled facia and interior. The area is known as the Riberira and has been declared a United Nations World Heritage site but, with typical Portuguese nonchalance, it remains mainly unrestored. The Portuguese architect Alvaro Siza has designed many of the newer buildings here including the

Oporto's railway station with its outstanding blue and white ceramic tiles

Servales Museum of Contemporary Art, Oporto's version of Bilbao's Guggenheim.

My birthday lunch is traditional Portuguese sardines, bread and salad washed down with a bottle of Mateus Rose in one of the many restaurants on the north bank of the Douro. After lunch we go to the tourist information office to find some entertainment - they suggest port tasting!! Following the directions on our map, we stroll across Oporto's impressive bridge over the Douro River to the south bank and Sandeman's warehouse. The warehouse is situated beside the river amongst other well known names like Cockburn, Taylor's and Offley. Creaky port barges moored near the quays give an aura of authenticity and romance. At Sandeman's we join an *English language* tour which takes us through their cellars, before ending in the tasting room, where we are invited to quench our thirst.

Needless to say we arrive back in Leixoes some hours later happily intoxicated, but still have room for a beer in the yacht club where we meet David, the owner of *Ithaka* (Vancouver 32), who we are anchored beside. Later David joins us for dinner on *Pacific Voyager*.

Rory gazing at the port barges and wondering how much port we could carry on *Pacific Voyager*

7th July (Wednesday) - Drag Anchor: During the early hours of the morning the wind shifts and increases, tripping our anchor. A sixth sense wakes me up. It is not so much a noise that alerts my attention but maybe a slight motion change. Whatever it is, I poke my head through the hatch to see we are drifting sideways towards an unoccupied moored yacht. I quickly put out fenders, but the yacht is moored fore and aft at right angles to our drift. Our rudder fouls its stern line just as our anchor stops dragging, but now our anchor chain is at right angles to the bow roller which makes it almost impossible to pull in. We decide to kedge the stern away from the yacht, which works well and allows our stern to slip by. Thinking that our problems are now over we go to retrieve the kedge - oh dear it has also fouled something.

At this point David (*Ithaka*), seeing our predicament, rows over to help. We lead the kedge onto the cockpit sheet winch which is our most powerful winch, and inch by inch, haul the Bruce anchor up to reveal it has fouled a heavy mooring chain. We loop a rope around the heavy chain to take the weight, and then retrieve the Bruce anchor. Exhausted but relieved after this three hour ordeal I suggest, "*Let's move on before we foul something else.*"

8th July (Thursday) - Leixoes to Nazare: The northerly trades are still blowing a healthy 15 knots. We sail through the night outside the fisherman's pots, but inside the shipping lanes. In the morning we are engulfed by a fog bank, so we tack inshore to determine our position, then follow a line of sand dunes down the coast to Nazare.

At Nazare we decide to wait for the weather to improve, which gives us an opportunity to get a few more jobs done. We try to do *'a job a day'* to reduce what seems like an endless work list. I find some old planking which I cut into an outboard bracket for our second outboard while Sandra is sewing winch covers and mosquito netting for our hatches. Down to our last LPG gas bottle - we are not able to exchange the bottles as they do in the UK. I am not sure what to do, but I feel we should be able to exchange them in Gibraltar.

Moored beside us is Boris a retired surgeon. Boris has a nifty little motorbike which folds up to nothing, enabling him to see the local towns and villages. He is amused that people confuse him with Willy Nelson the musician. About this time

Left: Boris with his trolley to carry water bottles
Above: Bruce anchor fouled by a huge chain

we are due for our next Hepatitis jabs. I am not looking forward to repeating my last botch-up, so I ask Willy, sorry I mean Boris, if he will give us our injections. Although in his seventies, he still has a steady hand and gives us both a painless injection.

12th July (Tuesday) - Nazare to Peniche: Continue sailing down the coast with the Portuguese trades - these perfect sailing conditions encourage me to experiment with different sail arrangements. This time my focus is on our three headsail halyards; one is through the masthead sheave and the other two are through blocks at the masthead. While experimenting, I manage to wrap one halyard around the radar reflector which fouls the other two halyards. I cannot believe that in one go I can foul all my halyards. *"I'll leave it to the next port to sort out."* Later in Peniche we fit preventers from the radar reflector to the cap shrouds - a good lesson learnt.

Peniche is another secure harbour which we share with the local fishing fleet. For our daily exercise we row to a slipway beside the town, then walk around the town and buy a little more local produce. Back on board Sandra cooks a Portuguese dinner of chips, tomato salad, tinned sardines and grilled peppers, *"This is better than my birthday meal in Porto."* As we settle down to sleep, a chorus of howling dogs reverberates around the harbour. Every fishing boat seems to have a dog that continuously barks at all the other dogs all night.

Not feeling ready to leave, we decide to stay in Peniche another day to catch up with our jobs - Sandra finishes her windchute - a godsend in these hot anchorages.

14th July (Wednesday) - Peniche to Cascais: There is little wind as we set off for Cascais. We are making less than three knots so eventually we bang on the engine. The sails are flogging so we take down the main but leave the genny up. As we round Cabo de Rosa the wind suddenly increases to over 40 knots. Somewhat taken by surprise and with only two miles to go, we hold onto our genoa spilling most of the wind. Creaming along at seven knots, we roar into Cascais.

We anchor next to *Ithaka* again - thankfully no more anchor problems this time. In the burning heat of the afternoon we join David who has some chilled wine waiting for us. Cascais is not a harbour as such, more a protected anchorage, that is assuming the wind and swell are not coming from south-west through to south-east. While we are there the wind is offshore, but we are ready for a quick escape, either up the estuary to Lisboa or out to sea past Cabo Espichel. Boy it is hot - up with the awning and Sandra's new windchute.

We visit a singlehander who has just returned from an abortive start to his trip to Brazil. He broached his 24 footer off Cabo de Rosa and stoved in his port window. It sounds scary to come short while still in sight of land. We are developing a healthy respect for these Portuguese headlands.

The Cascais yacht club is one of those beautiful buildings that makes you wonder why other buildings which are also made from bricks and mortar cannot achieve the same level of aesthetic appeal. Our welcome is equally encouraging - the steward says visiting yachtsmen are offered a complimentary beer on the house (I must mention this to Gareth at our home yacht club in Porthmadog). We tell David of this unexpected bonus, but when he approaches the steward saying he has just arrived he has to pay for his beer!!

The yacht club is a stunningly luxurious gentlemen's club with leather-covered seats and lots of international yachting magazines scattered over ornately carved coffee tables. From the balcony there are outstanding views of the bay where we can watch people come ashore in their dinghies, while sipping a Super Broc draught for 120 Escudos.

15th July (Thursday) - Lisbon: Up early, dinghy ashore, take the train to Lisbon. In the days of Vasco da Gama, Lisbon was the centre of the Portuguese empire trading in spices and slaves. The ornate architecture speaks of prosperous times when the Portuguese explorers were pushing out the frontiers of human exploration. The church of Jeronimos was built to celebrate Vasco da Gama's voyage round the Cape of Good Hope in 1497-8 on his way to India and the land of spices - an inspiration for all bluewater cruisers.

Monument to the explorers

17th July (Saturday) - Cascais to Sines: After a bowl of hot porridge with milk and honey we leave early for Sines. No wind to start with so we motor for a couple of hours until the wind picks up as we pass Cabo Espichel. I foolishly sunburn my feet which were sticking out from under the awning - it now looks as if I have red socks.

Sines is the home of Vasco da Gama who is noted for his discoveries in Africa and the Far East. I can remember seeing his monument in Malindi, Kenya (see page 55) - Malindi was his departure point from Africa to India. Sines has a prominent statue of Vasco da Gama beside the fort which looks over our anchorage. We later have a closer look at the statue and the town's architecture.

Vasco da Gama

19th July (Monday) - Sines to Sagres: Up at 06:00, it is still dark. Scrambled eggs and toast for breakfast while I motor out of the harbour. We see many small boats out fishing and are greeted by a school of dolphins doing somersaults in front of us. The wind picks up as it usually does late morning and we are having a beautiful sail in 10 knots of breeze. By the time we reach Cabo St Vincent, which claims to have the brightest lighthouse in Europe, we are reefed and prepared for strong winds. But this time we not only get blasted by strong winds, we also get enormous mountainous waves rolling in from the Atlantic. Surfing down these brutes earns mother nature even more respect. Again these exceptional conditions are short lived and a few miles along the coast we anchor safely off **Sagres** beach. This corner of Portugal used to be considered the end of the world in the middle ages, for this is the most western tip of Europe, if you do not include Ireland.

The offshore winds build during the day to warrant an anchor watch. I keep reassuring myself that if we drag again, the worst that can happen is we will be blown out to sea. This is assuming the wind stays in the same direction, of course. Dinner is tinned chicken, rice, carrots and onions, followed by mashed bananas and custard.

21st July (Wednesday) - Henry the Navigator's School of Navigation: When the wind eases after two days of blustery conditions, we pump up the dinghy and row ashore with the intention of visiting Henry the Navigator's School of Navigation. This is the school that was responsible for promoting the Portuguese exploration down the west coast of Africa.

After dragging the dinghy halfway up the beach we are met by Portuguese officials who want to see our passports which, of course, we have left on board. They say we must check in at the next port which is actually a short walk over the hill but no, they want us to sail around. I explain that we have already checked into Portugal and as the UK is a member of the EC, and the EC now has no internal borders, there should be no need for further checking in, but to no avail. (Thinking about this event later, they probably thought we had just sailed over from the Azores and not down the coast of Portugal). Disappointed, we row back to our boat and sail on. (This was a mistake, because at the time we did not appreciate the importance of the School of Navigation, and should have made a greater effort to see it).

The Portuguese exploration and trade started in earnest after the fall of Ceuta in 1415. The Portuguese vaguely knew the position of India and its spices, and the position of China and its silks, from Marco Polo's travels (1254 - 1324), but they did not know if they could sail there around Africa. At the time the Indian spices were only available overland via Arab traders. It was Henry the Navigator's resolve to progressively explore further and further down the coast of Africa to find the logical sea route to India. And it was the School of Navigation at Sagres that provided the technology to achieve this objective.

The School of Navigation developed a maritime body of knowledge, and a culture of exploration. Captains and pilots were taught the art of seamanship, navigation, astronomy and cartography. The school developed the compass to steer by beyond the sight of land, and the astrolabe and declination tables to calculate their latitude from the sun.

They taught the naval architects and shipbuilders new design and construction techniques which developed the caravel into an ocean going craft. Up to the 15th century these vessels had been built for the coastal trade around the shores of Europe and the Mediterranean, but it was from the Iberian Peninsula that ocean going ships emerged.

Prince Henry was determined to find a sea route around Africa to the riches of India. He encouraged the ship builders to strengthen their caravels to face the mighty Atlantic ocean. And, year by year, the Portuguese explorers cautiously ventured further down the west coast of Africa, past Cape Nam, past Cape Bojador and the *Sea of Darkness*, inching ever closer to the Cape of Good Hope and the logical route to India and the spices. Consider the following chronological list of achievements.

Ocean going Caravel

1420: Henry inspired the rediscovery of Madeira.

1427: Henry discovered the Azores.

1434: Portuguese explorers reached Cape Bojador.

1471: Portuguese explorers reached the Gold Coast of Africa.

1474: Portuguese explorers reached the Equator.

1483: Angola - Diogo Cao (1450-1486) sighted the Congo River.

1485: Namibia - Diogo Cao placed a padrao at Cape Cross to mark their furthest distance south, and claim sovereignty for Portugal. These padraos (also spelt padroes) are carved from stone pillars bearing the date and Portugal's coat of arms. They were typically erected on prominent points to establish possession. The remains of the original padraos have been removed to various museums around the world, but have been replaced with replicas.

1487: Bartholomeu Dias (1455-1500) sailed around the Cape of all Torments (Cape of Storms), and Cape Agulhus, the most southern point of Africa. Dias made landfall in Mossel Bay and the mouth of the Great Fish River. There is now a museum at Mossel Bay to commemorate the place where he landed. A replica of his ship was built (original name unknown), to mark the 500th centenary, and sailed out from Portugal, retracing Dias' historic route.

1487: While Bartholomeu Dias was sailing around Africa's Southern Cape, **Pero da Covilhao** (1450-1545) another Portuguese explorer, was travelling overland down the east coast of Africa visiting Malindi, Mombasa and Mozambique. He observed the spice trade and the methods they were using to navigate across the Indian Ocean to Calicut. He also gained knowledge of the monsoon wind systems used by the Arab traders to cross the Indian Ocean. This invaluable information was given to the next Portuguese explorer - Vasco da Gama.

1492: Columbus (1451-1506): To bring these Portuguese achievements into perspective, 1492 is the year Columbus sailed west from Spain to discover the Caribbean. Columbus thought he had reached Asia, hence he named the islands the West Indies.

1494: Treaty of Tordesillas: Based on the reports from Dias and Columbus, the Pope decreed that all lands west of 100 leagues, west of the Azores and Cape Verde Islands, would belong to Spain. This unintentionally gave Portugal the Southern Atlantic, Brazil, and the logical route east to India.

1498: Vasco da Gama (1460-1524): Following the route of Bartholomeu Dias, and information from Pero da Covilhao, Vasco da Gama sailed to Malindi where he hired a Gujerti pilot to cross the Indian Ocean to Calicut in India. After two years, he returned with a rich cargo of spices and finally achieved Henry the Navigator's dream.

Southern Africa: (Since Sagres we have spent a few months, by car, touring Southern Africa where we visited many of the sites where the original Portuguese explorers left their padraos.) The padraos were erected on conspicuous headlands for navigation, sovereignty claims, and to mark the extent of their travels. The three most celebrated Portuguese explorers were Diogo Cao, Bartholomeu Dias and Vasco da Gama. In southern and east Africa they left padraos at Cape Cross (Cao), Luderitz (Dias), Cape of Good Hope (Dias and da Gama), Mossel Bay (Dias), East London (Dias) and Malindi (da Gama).

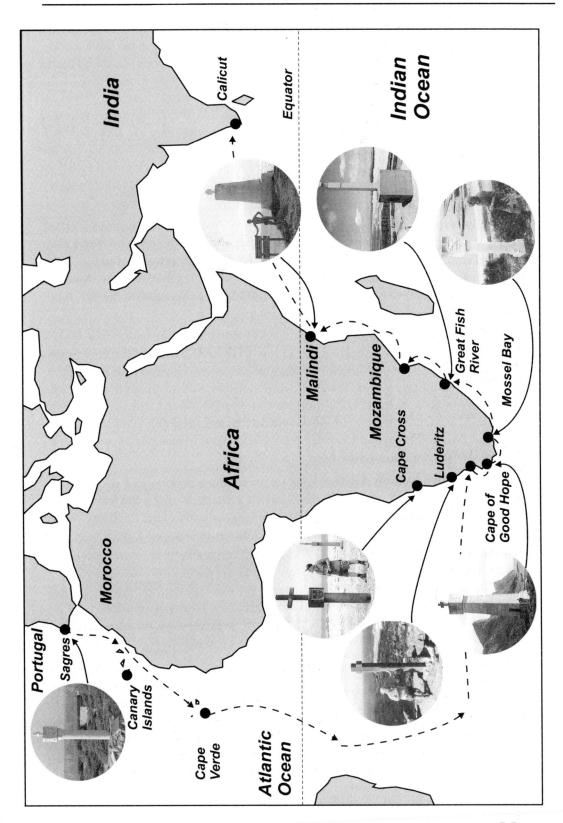

21st July (Wednesday) - Sagres to Portimao: There is virtually no wind as we quietly motor sail along the south coast of Portugal, gently gliding along in perfect visibility. Both of us have a lazy day with plenty of time to enjoy the glorious weather. I locate the entrance to Portimao from the aerial photographs in the RCC pilot.

In Portimao harbour we are anchored between two single-handers; David on *Ithaka* and Richard on *Blue Moves*. It surprises us that these two single-handers have not made the effort to talk to each other, even though they are anchored only inches apart and have the same type of boat - Vancouvers. They both join us for dinner one evening, to find they have been bottling up their need to talk. Once they get going it is impossible to get a word in edgeways, except to offer them another beer of course.

23rd July (Friday): The shore is far enough away from *Pacific Voyager* to warrant using our 2 hp Suzuki on our Avon dinghy. I notice our progress is no better than Richard rowing his rigid dinghy and, further, he can easily drag his dinghy up the beach on his own. Whereas we need both of us to half carry, half drag the Avon up the beach. If only we had a bigger boat we could have both an inflatable and rigid!

25th July (Sunday): It is blowing a healthy 25 knots the day we motor our Avon dinghy over to see Bob and Delores on *Summer Wind*. An hour later, while we are below having a chat, we receive a call on the VHF saying our dinghy has flipped over. It is all hands on deck to pull the dinghy and outboard alongside and right it. Fortunately nothing is lost; the oars were sensibly tied on but, of course, the outboard has been immersed. We limp back to *Pacific Voyager* to give our outboard first aid. The Suzuki manual outlines a recovery procedure to flush oil through the cylinder. (We are to have this capsizing problem a couple more times and an even greater disaster with the Avon dinghy in Antigua.)

28th July (Wednesday): Sandra has a busy morning making canvas bags and pockets, together with covers for the winches, outboards and wind vane. In the afternoon we walk into Ferragudo which is only 30 minutes along the beach. There is a good fresh produce market where we fill our rucksacks with fresh fish, fruit and vegetables.

Richard on *Blue Moves* invites us over for a dinner of liver and onions, with plenty of tinned Guinness to wash it down. It has taken Richard three years to build his Vancouver 28 from a hull and deck kit. Sandra is intrigued how it has been setup as a bachelor pad with a double bed.

5th August (Thursday) - Stowage: Our water containers have migrated from the cockpit lockers to the guard rails. The 20 litre container handles are level with the lower guard rail

Rory in the market laden down with fruit and veg

which makes them easy to tie on, but we also need a backing board in this exposed position. Moving the containers has made more room in the lockers which quickly gets filled with buckets and Sandra's stuff. My turn to cook lunch - we have beans on toast and a litre brik of red wine.

7th August (Saturday) - Portimao to Faro: With the anchor almost cemented in after three weeks in Portimao, we literally drag ourselves away from this easy going, social anchorage. Faro is a convenient distance from Portimao for a day sail. We anchor overnight just inside the breakwater as I do not fancy what appears to be a long motor up the estuary to the town of Faro.

8th August (Sunday) - Faro to Tarifa: Set off early for the long leg ahead of us. We consider sailing to Palos where Columbus departed with three caravels in 1492, and visit the monastery where he stayed while he was waiting for Queen Isabella of Castile to approve his ambitious plan to sail across the Atlantic. We also consider sailing to Cadiz, but are keen to push on and collect our mail in Gibraltar.

Our reading habits have changed somewhat. Sandra has not read a fashion magazine since Cape Town, but is now reading everything to do with sailing. And I have not read the *Economist* for weeks, partly because I seem to have an endless list of jobs to occupy my time, but mostly because it is not available in the newsagents.

9th August (Monday) - Cabo Trafalgar: Trafalgar Square with Nelson's Column is one of London's prominent landmarks and central to the British psyche of war and great fighting men. We have both read a couple of books about Nelson and the Battle of Trafalgar, and here we are passing the site of the battle, a far cry from Trafalgar Square!

As we cruise along the coast it is tempting to wander in and out of the harbours en route to see what they look like; we never know when we might need them for shelter. Motor into Barbate de Franco, but we do not feel like staying there so we push onto Gibraltar.

As we approach the Straits of Gibraltar we steer outside a wreck marked on the chart, "*We don't want to join it.*" In hindsight it would have been better to have taken the inside passage as we are greeted by a 30 knot head wind - *Pacific Voyager* does not like to motor into a head wind and building sea. Decide to cut our losses and pull into **Tarifa**. Anchor outside the harbour on a lee shore as close in as possible to the beach to reduce the offshore fetch. Tarifa is a windsurfers' paradise and, of course, *Pacific Voyager* makes a convenient turning mark for the surfboards to race past us within inches - swoosh. I am quite concerned about them hitting the self-steering. This must be a windy area because there are hundreds of wind generators lining the hillsides, all rotating like circus dancers.

Further Reading:

Andrews K.R., *Drake's Voyages*, Weidenfeld and Nicholson
Cornell, Jimmy., *Ocean Cruising Routes*
RCC Pilotage Foundation, *Atlantic, Spain and Portugal*
www.portugalinsite.pt (Tourist information office)

Gibraltar

In Greek mythology Gibraltar was one of the Pillars of Heracles (Greek spelling) (Hercules Roman spelling) marking the entrance to the Mediterranean, the other was Mount Acho in Ceuta. They both marked the limit of the known world. Our plan is to stopover in Gibraltar, an English speaking port, and catch up on our boat jobs before sailing to the Canaries and the Caribbean.

British naval history has always intrigued me, so I am excited at the prospect of exploring one of the last outposts of the British Empire. Gibraltar was captured by Sir George Rooke in 1704 and ceded to Britain in 1713 by the Treaty of Utrecht. The Spanish held Gibraltar under siege in 1727 and again during the great siege between 1779 to 1783. It was during the great siege that the upper gun gallery in *The Rock* was excavated. Gibraltar was Nelson's base port while he commanded the Mediterranean fleet which led to the Battle of the Nile in 1798, and later, in 1805 after the Battle of Trafalgar, both Nelson's body and HMS *Victory* were taken to Gibraltar, the nearest naval base.

Another famous vessel, the *Marie Celeste*, was also taken to Gibraltar. In 1872, she was found abandoned in mysterious circumstances, 400 miles east of the Azores on passage from New York with 1700 barrels of alcohol. A skeleton crew was put on board to sail her into Gibraltar.

Gibraltar with yacht anchorage this side of the runway, from tourist brochure

10th August (Tuesday): After the strong head winds blowing through the straits yesterday, there is now absolutely no wind. Quietly we motor sail with the constantly east flowing current - this is the Atlantic Ocean topping up the evaporation from the Mediterranean. Sandra is doing her jobs about the boat and I am steering. There is some shipping traffic around so a sharp lookout is required through the morning mist and haze which is slowly lifting. Then, out of the blue, our tranquillity is shattered by an RAF Buccaneer. He creeps up from behind us and comes in so low that the sudden deafening noise frightens the life out of us.

Checking into Gibraltar is a pleasure. They have sensibly built a long jetty outside the customs office, so it is easy to tie up alongside. All the officials are located together in the same hut; customs, immigration and the harbour master. The three officials fire questions at me and process our application simultaneously; it only takes a couple of minutes.

The anchorage is located near the end of the runway and can be clearly identified by all the yachts anchored there. As we motor around to find a suitable position we see flags from many nationalities - this is truly the cruising crossroads of the world. The anchorage is protected from all directions except the west, which is open to Algeciras Bay, a fetch of a few miles. A couple of weeks before we arrive there had been strong westerly winds and the yachts had to move to the main harbour where they were protected by the breakwater.

Soon after we anchor, Ann (*Peace* - 26 foot Shannon) motors over in her dinghy to say hi, and gives us a run down on the port, where to shop and what to see. Ann has sailed single handed across the Atlantic to Ireland, and is now making her way back to America.

For cruisers, Gibraltar's main disadvantage is finding a good place to moor a dinghy when going ashore. The options are either to tie up in-between the yachts in the marinas, or in a seedy corner of the harbour against a half floating pontoon, which looks like a scene out of Water World and Mad Max. In the end we use Sheppard's marina because we always seem to be going there to buy chandlery.

Pacific Voyager **anchored near the runway, with the Rock of Gibraltar in the background**

Reading the mail we have just collected from the *poste restante*

Mail: Gibraltar is our first mail stop since Porthmadog, so we are keen to collect our letters which have been sent to the harbour master.

"Which Harbour Master?" they ask.

"How many have you got?" I enquire.

"Three!" So we walk to the three harbour masters and find some mail at two of them. To prevent this sort of problem happening again we write to our friends asking them to use *poste restante* instead. The *poste restante* in Gibraltar is extremely well organised, and at present is being looked after by a pregnant young woman who looks as though the slightest strain would bring on child birth. Trying to advise friends of our constantly changing address is hopeless. It would be far better to have one agent where all our mail is posted, and then we only have to advise the agent of our next address.

Shopping: The town's buildings paint a fascinating picture of Gibraltar's past, with a mixture of Spanish and English Regency architecture on top of the original Moorish buildings. The old smoke filled pubs, tacky gift shops and Indian traders seem like a relic from the colonial days of the British Empire. You might mistakenly think you are in an English resort that slipped through a time warp back to the 1960s, when *Carry On* films were the pinnacle of British humour. Gibraltar's main street is a shopper's Mecca - the shops seem to sell everything and, if you believe their advertising, everything is a bargain. They are geared up for the day tourists who either come across the border from Spain, or from the visiting cruise ships. They must find us frustrating customers because we are not impulsive buyers. We have a procurement process which assesses our needs, gathers data, reassesses our needs, checks our budget, then negotiates. This way we buy only what we need and at a good price. Some of our best purchases include divers' watches, boots and an underwater camera.

Divers' Watches: On night watches we need an alarm to prompt us to have a look around every 15 minutes. We buy two Casio divers' watches which are waterproof to some incredible depth, with alarms which are just loud enough to be heard by the person on watch, but will not disturb the off-watch person.

Boots: When going ashore we always wear comfortable shoes to protect our feet. Some cruisers try to do everything in flip flops, a few even walk around bare foot! Although generally barefoot on board, when going ashore we always protect our feet. In Gibraltar we buy proper walking boots which give good ankle support.

We always seem to be walking long distances either exploring or shopping, so the extra support when carrying a heavy rucksack is sensible.

Underwater Camera: Sandra is keen to buy an underwater camera - I am sceptical. In the end after much bargaining we settle on a Minolta. It is certainly splash proof, so is ideal for taking photographs on deck and from the dinghy. (However, most of the underwater photographs we take are disappointing because of poor light. Even though the camera has a flash it is not powerful enough. However, we did get some excellent underwater photographs in the Galapagos swimming with the seals, and in Bora Bora of Sandra feeding the Stingrays. These were taken near the surface, and in Bora Bora's case there was good light being reflected off the sandy bottom, see page 232.)

Books: On the cruising route all the cruisers are exchanging books. The swap is generally on a book for book basis, or sometimes by the inch! But these are usually only novels, no one ever exchanges their quality books. We are concerned that, until we reach New Zealand, Gibraltar may be the last good source to buy quality books, so we stock up on some stimulating reading material about the places we intend to visit in the Caribbean and Pacific.

Charts: As our route firms up, so we consider buying more detailed charts. We are shocked to find they are £14 each in Gibraltar, yet we only paid £11 each in England - this seems an unnecessarily high mark-up. I know from our book printing that the cost to print a chart would only be a few pence. As they are a safety item I decide to write to the hydrographer of the Navy in Taunton, Somerset, expressing my concern.

Dear Sir, We are presently sailing round the world in our 35 foot yacht. One of the most expensive items on my budget is the procurement of charts. Since starting our cruise I have found that I can either buy copied American charts, or copy them legally myself (as the Americans do not claim copyright on a product the US tax payers have already paid for). This reduces the cost to a fraction of the Admiralty cost of 14 pounds per chart.

It seems to me that as the cheaper USA charts become known the Admiralty will lose market share, and as the printing cost per chart can be measured in pence I feel the Admiralty need to act.

May I suggest that the Admiralty charts should be sold in area packs at a greatly reduced unit cost and with reasonable production runs the unit price with profit should be kept below the cost of photocopying the full size chart. For the Admiralty to maintain (and increase) their market share they need to adopt a more proactive and innovative marketing approach."

Their reply was, *"There are of course numerous options and initiatives to consider during the formulation of our core product marketing strategy and we much appreciate you taking the trouble to submit your suggestion about packaging the charts."*

" *Correction contributor to **ALRS** "*

Admiralty List of Radio Signals
Hydrographic Office, Taunton, Somerset TA1 2DN, UK
(Tel: 0823 337900. Fax: 0823 284077. Telex 46274)

A neighbouring yacht comes to our rescue. There is a knock on our hull, "*Would you like to buy some charts? We have just come back from the Caribbean.*" "*Please come on board. Would you like a cup of tea?*" In the end we buy detailed charts for all the Leeward and Windward islands for £2.50 each.

Rory starting to write *'Managing Your Bluewater Cruise'* **on our prehistoric computer**

Library: Gibraltar has a small library with a wide collection of the British newspapers; Times, Sunday Times, Telegraph, Independent, Guardian and some of the easier reading papers. Although we regularly listen to the BBC World news, we enjoy reading about topical issues as well. The library also has an excellent source of reference material for our book writing.

Shopping in Spain: Across the runway in La Linea (Spain) there are some good supermarkets with a wider choice and better prices than Gibraltar. Our shopping expeditions are limited by what we can carry in our rucksacks. Besides general food shopping we also go mad buying plastic tool boxes at the equivalent of £1.50 each - they are ideal for subdividing our tools and spare parts. Also, over a number of trips, we buy 60 one litre briks of red wine. One day Sandra returns from the Spanish market carrying an enormous foam mattress that the customs make her pay duty on, even though we are a ship-in-transit.

Westmarine: While living in Britain we never thought about buying marine gear from the American mail order companies, but this is the best source for equipment while cruising. Westmarine's service is first class; I fax an order for a solar panel and GPS on a Thursday and, on the following Tuesday, I am carrying the couriered items onto *Pacific Voyager*. At the same time we order four ammeters from Maplin Electronics in England - they arrive three weeks later by snail mail! Reports from other cruisers indicate that Westmarine have an excellent policy about returning or replacing faulty equipment. One cruiser received a lamp with a chip on it - they told him to throw the damaged one away and a replacement lamp would be couriered.

11th September (Sunday): Our anchorage is literally a front row seat to watch the last RAF air display in Gibraltar. They have a collection of old planes; a Spitfire which was used in the Battle of Britain (which Biggles would have been proud of), a Dakota used in the invasion of North Africa, and a Catalina

flying boat which was the first aircraft to operate from Gibraltar. They also have a cross section of jet fighters; Tornado F-3's, Buccaneers, Jaguars, Hawks, together with four Harrier jump-jets which perform a hovering display over the runway.

There is always plenty of action around the runway, be it commercial flights or the daily Nimrod patrol. As the planes take off they actually fly over us if we happen to be passing the end of the runway in our dinghy. Conversation has to stop in the yacht basin when a jet takes off as the sound reverberates around the buildings. Apparently during the Gulf War, Gibraltar was a hive of military action as they monitored shipping in and out of the Mediterranean - an excellent venue for military enthusiasts and spies.

Winston Boys: Gibraltar has always been known for smuggling. Well the tradition is still alive and well. Every night high powered speed boats painted black with two 200 hp outboards race though the anchorage at 60 + knots. They do not show any lights so there is no chance of seeing them coming. In fact all we can see is the white wake after they have gone. One night, we are entertained by a high speed co-ordinated chase with police boats, helicopters and ground support. We feel like extras participating in a James Bond movie. The high speed boats are really scary especially when we are rowing back through the anchorage after dark. We have to quickly row from yacht to yacht and listen out for an engine noise. Naturally we complain to the authorities about these vessels racing through the anchorage at night without lights.

Dear Port Captain, We are a British yacht anchored north of the runway. We have experienced almost every night, for the past month, vessels racing through the anchorage without lights. We are concerned that:

1. A yacht will be hit in the anchorage.

2. At night slow moving tenders with lights proceeding to the anchorage may be run down.

Both of these situations may result in a serious injury or loss of life. Would you please advise what effective steps you will be taking to ensure the safety of visiting yachtsman.

The Port Captain points to a small notice indicating that we are located in a prohibited anchorage. This is not mentioned in any notice to mariners or on the charts. Further they declare the area is a disputed border. Does this mean we can pass from Gibraltar to Spain and back again without checking-in as the border does not exit?

Water: After numerous sieges, the people of Gibraltar know as well as any yachtsmen how valuable fresh water is - it is the water of life. Gibraltar is reported to have a large storage reservoir inside the mountain which is fed from a water catchment area on the east side (34 hectares of corrugated iron sheets). But now with modern technology, their fresh water is supplied by a desalination plant which can be heard in the evenings humming away.

Water catchment area on the side of 'The Rock', from a tourist brochure

The Great Siege Tunnel museum inside 'The Rock'

Mediterranean Steps: *"Today's a bit cooler, let's go for a walk."* Equipped with our new walking boots, rucksack, nibbles and water we are ready to climb up the Mediterranean Steps. It is hard going up the side of the mountain as it is covered in dense scrub, but we are rewarded with superb panoramic views along the ridge looking down on either side of the rock. It was with these commanding views and a few powerful guns that the British controlled the Gibraltar Straits. After a strenuous hike we are pleased to find a restaurant at the top. This enables us to have a couple of pints of lager to replace some of the fluids we lost on the way up. Meanwhile Sandra is trying to have a sensible conversation with Gibraltar's famous tailless Barbary apes who are cavorting around us, stopping every few minutes to groom each other.

On the way down, every hairpin bend on the coastal road affords another stunning view of the gorges and headlands directly below. We are lured into the *'great siege tunnels'* which were excavated by the British to provide a series of gun emplacements. Apparently the Spanish were so close during one of the sieges that the British had difficulty pointing their guns at such a low elevation. Sergeant Ince had the bright idea of tunnelling, and so the rock itself became a fortress.

My sister Deirdre and her university friend, Anita, join us for a couple of weeks. Deirdre has a doctorate in religious education so she is keen to research the religious sites of southern Spain. They stay for a few days on board *Pacific Voyager*, then hire a car and drive off to see the old city of Cadiz. On their return they are now keen to sail to Morocco to see the walled city of Tetouan.

Further Reading:

www.gibraltar.gi
www.westmarine.com

Pacific Voyager **moored alongside Sheppard's marina**

9   *Morocco*

From the ship of the sea to the ship of the desert, *"Let's go and the see the camels in Morocco."* Our plan is to sail across the straits of Gibraltar to Ceuta and M'diq in Morocco and stay for a couple of days. Deirdre particularly wants to see the walled city of Tetouan for its historical and cultural significance.

26th August (Thursday) - Morocco: Depart for Ceuta, Spain's equivalent to Gibraltar, and the other Pillar of Heracles. It is directly opposite Gibraltar on the isthmus of Africa's most northerly promontory, formed by the rock of Monte Hachp. Ceuta was captured by the Portuguese in 1415. From 1580 Portugal and Spain were under one crown for 70 years and, when they separated, Ceuta remained under Spanish rule. There is a Baroque church there called *Our Lady of Africa* which sounds interesting.

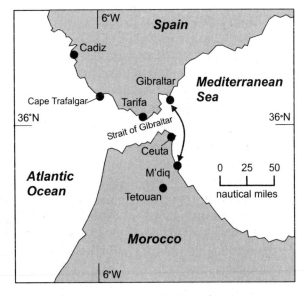

The wind is blowing a healthy 27 knots out of the west and the easterly current into the Mediterranean is an unbelievable 3 knots. I do not make sufficient allowance for the drift, so by the time we reach Morocco we have been pushed too far over to the east to make Ceuta. *"We can't make Ceuta - let's carry onto M'diq instead."*

Rounding the headland by Ceuta the sea settles, although the wind is still blowing a robust 25 knots. M'diq is not marked on our charts, but we have been given the latitude and longitude of the new marina in M'diq. As the light fades, we nearly sail into a large fish farming complex which is located a few miles offshore on the direct route to M'diq.

Marina Group Investments Ltd.
PORT MARINA SMIR
TETOUAN M'DIQ
Maroc
———

Pacific Voyager in M'diq's Marina -
surrounded by stunning buildings

We locate M'diq as per the coordinates. A green light at the end of the mole marks the entrance. Inside the mole there are a set of orange buoys which we assume are marking the channel, but are not sure which side to pass. As we ease up the left hand side of the channel, Deirdre is on the helm while I organise the fenders. A few moments later Deirdre screams to attract my attention - we are motoring into shallow water. I grab the wheel and back track into deeper water, then try the other side of the channel. At this point our attention is drawn to a power boat speeding towards us with shouts and waving arms encouraging us to follow them. Ten minutes later we are safely tied to the quay, and settle down for a peaceful night.

The next morning I enquire about checking-in. We are the only visiting yacht in a virtually empty, brand new, luxury yacht marina. Uniformed customs officers cluster round my documents like surgeons in an operation. They inspect the ship's papers and our passports in minute detail - this is, after all, their only job for today. Then the police, not to be outdone, do the same. At this point I discover a brilliant technique to speed up the process - I fall asleep - and when I wake up all the documents are complete!!!

**The Moroccan architecture
around the marina is superb**

***Pacific Voyager* in between luxurious yachts and beneath a towering Mosque**

The marina staff move us to a marina berth where their mooring ropes are too big for our fairlead. *"Do a rolling hitch,"* they instruct. My mind goes blank. I have since etched a rolling hitch in my mind, often using it to attach a snubber to the anchor chain.

The architecture around the marina is outstanding, with a blend of old and modern Moroccan arches and mosaics, together with mosques and palm trees piercing the skyline. The marina is ringed with apartments, whose narrow passageways and stairs lead up to roof gardens and terraces, with outstanding panoramic views over the marina and surrounding countryside. Inside the apartments, carpets are strewn across the tiled, terracotta floors, and more mosaic arches lead from the courtyards into inviting recesses where divans are piled high with Berber cushions.

The marina seems to have been developed as an up-market country club with facilities for the wealthy Moroccans to relax and play. However, with beers at £4 a pint at the Lord Nelson pub, it is too expensive for us.

27th August (Friday) - Tetouan: Deirdre organises a Mercedes taxi to drive us to the walled city of Tetouan. As we get in the car another chap appears from nowhere and surprisingly offers to be our guide for the day. *"No thank you we already have a guide."*

It is a 30 minute drive to Tetouan on a relatively quiet road. The origins of Tetouan lie in prehistory, in the Berber city of Tamuda, which was destroyed by the Romans in the first century AD. The Romans built a new city on the ruins which was later destroyed by Henry II of Castile. The present walled city of Tetouan has seven gates and a population of 400,000 people.

Shopping in Tetouan - Sandra please do not get tempted to buy something - we have no room on board

We change money in a safe looking bank (100 dinars = £7). Initially we are pestered endlessly by Moroccans offering to be our guide and children offering packets of cigarettes, but our driver, who stays with us, waves them away. The girls are constantly stared at by the locals - I wonder how many camels they would offer?

The streets are lined with cafes and tea rooms which serve tea in a glass - very hot, and very sweet with a sprig of mint leaves stuffed into the glass. These cafes are popular places to just sit and listen to the babble of strange languages, and watch the world pass by, although in Western terms time stopped long ago.

Once inside, the old town is a labyrinth of narrow alleys buzzing with activity. Our senses are assaulted by the dawn chorus cries of the muezzin, the scents of the souks, and the taste of spices. There are small stalls everywhere, bulging with produce to sell. There are craftsman working with their tools in their small shops mending this, fixing that; always seeming to be making something old and useless that we would have thrown away long ago, last for another few years. It makes me realise what a wasteful society we come from. There is even a dentist proudly displaying all the teeth he has pulled out. He sits amidst piles of extracted molars, awaiting another brave customer. There are stalls of food and drink offering everything from fresh oranges, to a tempting pig's head, and lamb brain samosas. I am assured the sheeps' eyes are very tasty.

Carpet: After a long day traipsing around the souks, we eventually succumb to the temptation of entering a carpet shop. A pot of fresh mint tea appears as we are invited to sit on a pile of rugs and Berber cushions - or rather collapse in our case. The carpet selling performance begins. One man sits with us and explains how the carpets are manufactured, and particularly their quality, while his two helpers run backwards and forwards with more carpets. (Looking back on the wonderful carpet display I think we might have been drugged because we each buy a £100 carpet - a bargain down from an asking price of £375 pounds). As we

Left: Carpet sales pitch in progress while we sip mint tea
Below: Camel park - *Ship of the Desert*

Rory holding our beautiful silk carpet before it goes into long-term storage

Rory loves couscous

leave with a carpet I ask Sandra, "*Why have we bought a carpet which is too big to fit on our boat?*" It must have been their excellent salesmanship and our gullibility. Deirdre kindly takes our carpet back to England for long term storage.

On the drive back to the marina the taxi stops in a lay-by beside a couple camels relaxing in the sun. Sandra is intrigued that people still use camels as a mode of transport. It feels as if we have stepped back in time, and Lawrence of Arabia may appear with his robes flowing in the dusty desert breeze. I steer Sandra away from the large clay pots; there is no way they would fit on board. Instead Sandra buys a bag of couscous - I hate couscous.

Back on board Sandra prepares a typical Moroccan dinner - vegetable couscous with chick peas. (I later find weevils in our bag of couscous. There is something about this food I have never liked, and seeing weevils in the bag confirms my feelings.)

28th August (Saturday) - Morocco to Gibraltar: Loaded with Moroccan magic carpets and treasures, two reefs in the mainsail and the no 2 jib, we beat back to Gibraltar into 25 knots of wind. This time I make sufficient allowance for the strong current, and reach Gibraltar without having to tack. This is the end of Deirdre and Anita's holiday. They fly home while we spend another month preparing *Pacific Voyager* for the Atlantic.

Further Reading:
Murdoch Books, *Step-by-Step Moroccan Cook*
Stanley, Stewart., *In the Empire of Genghis Khan*
www.arab.net

10 *Cadiz*

9th October (Saturday): Leave Gibraltar on one of those mornings when everything is peacefully calm and the early morning sun is making 'The Rock' glow a deep red. The only sound is the gentle throb of our Perkins 4108 powering us through the water. A marked change from the past few weeks when other yachts have battled to get through the Straits against head winds from the west and an easterly flowing current. This is, however, the lull before the storm.

Yesterday we obtained a weather forecast from the RAF Met Office in Gibraltar. They gave us a good forecast for the next 72 hours. The conditions are so calm that Sandra decides to start washing our clothes, *"The weather's perfect for drying."* I recall similar conditions when we started our passage across the Bay of Biscay. The wind starts to pick up in the late afternoon to give us perfect sailing conditions, and the wind direction is just right to set a course for Madeira if we want. I am tempted, as we have mail waiting for us there.

Later, in the evening, we cross the busy shipping lanes which turns out to be much easier than I thought it would be. The visibility is good and a line of ships can

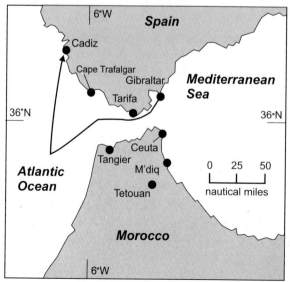

be seen stretching into the horizon. The ships are well spaced so it is relatively straight forward to take bearings and pick a gap, then quickly go for it.

10th October (Sunday): The wind continues to freshen as we make excellent progress in relatively calm seas. With intermittent reception I listen to the 00:33 BBC 4 shipping forecast. There is a great deal of crackle, then I hear, *".... Trafalgar severe gale south west force nine imminent."* I look at the radio in disbelief. Have I heard it correctly? This is the sort of shipping forecast that makes the hair on the back of my neck stand on end. What happened to the settled forecast for the next 72 hours???

Reluctant to engage horns with a severe gale, our option is to run for shelter. A quick check of the chart shows Gibraltar or Cadiz to be the most suitable ports to run into - Cadiz is the closest. But will we get there before the gale? Being caught on a lee shore could put us into a dangerous position. If that is the case it would be better to weather the gale and gain more sea room now.

The decision has to be made quickly. I check the RCC Cruising Pilot's charts of Cadiz harbour. It looks complicated, but at five knots we should be making a morning entrance, hopefully not with a gale behind us. *"Let's go for Cadiz otherwise we could be hove-to for a couple of days."* So we alter course for Cadiz and cross the shipping lanes again. The wind freshens to 25 knots during the night, but it is not gale force yet.

Cadiz: As we approach the entrance to Cadiz we are somewhat relieved to be sailing in before the gale. The entrance is slightly confusing with beacons and buoys to mark the shoals but, as we ease in, they all begin to make sense. We motor into the inner harbour and tie up alongside three trawlers and *Pen Duick*, Eric Tabarly's old racing yacht. Although we are in the inner harbour and protected from the elements, there is a constant swell which surges the boats backwards and forwards causing the mooring lines to chafe. Our first job ashore will be to buy short lengths of plastic pipe to protect our lines.

Cadiz is built on a peninsula joined to the mainland by a long causeway. The city is surrounded by massive walls and impressive fortifications. The castles and fortresses bear witness to blockades by Drake and Nelson. In April 1587, Drake made a pre-emptive strike and ransacked the city, destroying or capturing 24 Spanish ships, together with large amounts of food and stores destined for the Armada.

This delayed the Spanish Armada for a year and became known as *'Singeing the King of Spain's beard.'* And, in 1805, Nelson blockaded the Spanish and French fleets in Cadiz before they sailed out to do battle off Cabo Trafalgar.

Cadiz is an incredibly beautiful city, rich in its historic past. It is known as the most ancient city of all Western Europe. The inner part of the city is a maze of narrow streets and alleys, with buildings often constructed wider at the roof, leaning over, almost touching - resembling old men hunched over in deep conversation.

Our daily routine soon develops - the mornings we spend on board doing jobs, then a walk into town visiting the naval establishment for a weather report and looking at the local paper's weather synopsis. Each day we explore a different part of the city. Our

Cadiz harbour with *Pacific Voyager* in the background

Far left: Lion post box in the wall of Cadiz's Post Office

Left: Exquisite architecture in Cadiz

first impression is, *"This place needs a coat of paint. It looks really grubby."* But, after a few days this feeling is replaced with a more positive vibe. Despite the lack of paint the architecture is exquisite with detailed iron work, decorative balustrades and narrow cobbled streets. There are many churches; some look outstanding from the outside while others are part of a rather plain terrace of buildings but, inside, all of them are dripping with gold statues illuminated by thousands of flickering candles.

The old fishing harbour where we are moored seems miles away from the town at first, but after numerous trips the distance seems to get shorter. Our walk into town takes us past a slipway strewn with fishing nets laid out while they are being inspected and repaired.

On one shopping trip to the fresh fruit and vegetable market, we hear a group of South American musicians playing their ethnic mountain music. The melodic, mystic, staccato beat draws us in. This traditional Andean music has a distinctive haunting quality based on an unusual pentatonic scale. The sound of the contrasting instruments; percussion, bamboo panpipes and flutes, blends together to give a warm feeling of happiness. Their appearance is slightly rough and rugged in keeping with their long jet black hair, Peruvian hats and pony tails. Their exotic music fascinates me. It makes me want to immediately reappear in South America and go trekking with the lamas as we climb up to Machu Picchu. Instead I buy a beer and write up my notes as I listen to their music and Sandra goes shopping.

The market is well stocked with all types of quality fresh produce. I am intrigued by an olive seller, who only sells olives. My concern for his one product range is misguided as olives are big business here, and he is doing a roaring trade. His stall is surrounded by large glass jars of olives - I assume they are all different types because, when someone comes to buy, there is a lot of pointing at jars, then he delicately scoops one out for them to taste. With their nod of approval he makes up their order.

Charts: Our neighbours have a complete set of charts which they used to circumnavigate the world - they suggest we should copy any we need. They have 48

South American musicians playing their traditional Andean music

charts which could be useful depending how the wind takes us. In town we copy them for 225 pesetas each, which is less than a tenth of the Admiralty price, and the reproduction is excellent. However, I do miss the colours on the new charts, but am sure that on some lonely night watch with a blue and green pencil I can correct that. (When we use the charts some months later, it was a strange feeling to see our route following theirs - it was as if they are sailing beside us).

LPG: I have been monitoring our LPG consumption - a 3 kg cylinder lasts us 2 weeks of normal cooking, that is 1.5 kg per week. We buy another Camping Gas bottle which can be exchanged here, but they do not exchange UK Calor Gas bottles. We keep our three 4 kg Calor Gas bottles for the Atlantic trip as our gas locker is designed to securely carry the 4 kg bottles (see appendix 3).

13th October (Wednesday): Thought we would be off today, but another weather system bringing gales is forecast. For dinner Sandra buys 6 large prawns for 300 pesetas in the fish market. She grills them in lemon butter with a little garlic, and rice and onions on the side - they taste delicious.

Harbour Dues: During the rough weather a number of yachts seek shelter in the old harbour. Some tie-up alongside the harbour wall, while others anchor in the middle of the harbour. The harbour master appears one day and asks us to fill in a form with particulars of our yacht. The next day he reappears with an enormous mooring bill. He obviously thinks the port can charge yachts the same as the marinas do, although they do not offer any facilities. They have also misread our measurements - 35 feet has become 35 metres. Consequently he charges us as if we are a 35 metre (100 + foot) super yacht - part of the rich and famous. This is when Liz (*Aethelwyn*) comes to our rescue and, in reasonable Spanish she tells the harbour master that yachts do not pay harbour dues, that this is a port of refuge, etc., etc. After a few minutes the harbour master agrees to only charge us the equivalent of one pound a day.

15th October (Saturday) - Weather Forecast: The weather forecast looks good as we make our preparations to leave. This unplanned stopover has been extremely interesting - one of the pleasures of cruising - we never really know exactly where we will make our next landfall.

11 *Canary Islands*

After ten days stormbound in Cadiz a weather window appears and we are away. Over the past couple of weeks the unsettled weather was caused by the Azores high moving north which sent the Atlantic lows tracking south around it, bringing unsettled weather and south west winds. Now the Azores high has moved back south again, there is settled weather and northerly winds, ideal for a downwind sail to the Canaries.

Again, we consider sailing to Madeira where we have mail waiting for us but, with the unsettled weather and Funchal being a small harbour, we think it better to make straight for the Canaries.

18th October (Monday) - Set our course to keep clear of the Moroccan coast by a safe distance. This is also the first test for our new GPS as we plot our course on a large scale chart 1:1,000,000 of the Atlantic Ocean.

19th October (Tuesday) - Flying Fish: At first light on the second day, as I am checking over our sails and rigging, I glance down to see four succulent flying fish on the side deck. I can hardly believe my eyes, as I have always been a bit sceptical about stories of fish flying, and even more sceptical about finding them on the deck in the morning but, here they are. I quickly gather them in a bucket and bring them back to the cockpit. Sandra prepares them immediately and pops them in the frying pan. They are delicious, although a bit strong tasting. I find the concept of our breakfast waiting for us on the side deck in the morning intriguing.

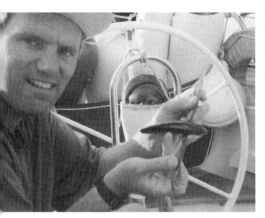

Rory holding our first flying fish and then preparing them in the cockpit

20th October (Wednesday) - Tuna: On my night watch I notice phosphorescence traces through the waves close to the hull. I am mesmerised. Something is following us!!! At first light I can see fish everywhere - even right up against the hull, especially on the shady side. *"Hey Sandra you won't believe this, there's a shoal of tuna following us."* It is fascinating to see this shoal of fish so close to the hull, but why are they following us? It is as if *Pacific Voyager* is their mother-ship. After watching them for hours, *"Why don't we catch one?"* If only I had a spear gun I could just lean over the side and zap - I could hardly miss. Instead of fresh fish for lunch today, we have bread rolls with cheese and pickle, followed by bread and butter pudding. The tuna continue to follow us for the next couple of days, nearly all the way to the Canaries. (I later bought a spear gun in Panama, but we were not to experience a shoal of tuna like this again).

Hydrovane: With following winds of 25 knots, gusting 30 knots, a steep sea is building up. This is the first real test for the Hydrovane self-steering gear. It manages well even though we tend to yaw +/- 15 degrees. In these conditions our most comfortable point of sailing is a reefed main with jib polled out on the other side. (In hindsight we would have been more comfortable with just the headsail pulling us along).

23rd October (Saturday) - La Graciosa: After a lively five day passage we make our landfall early in the morning. As the sun rises we can see the welcoming sight of Isla de la Graciosa, an *'Island of Your Dreams'*, lying to the north of Lanzarote. Coming from Britain this is our first experience of crystal clear water. We are amazed we can actually see our anchor chain snaking along the sand in ten metres of water! With only two other yachts in the whole of Bahia de Salado, and an extinct volcano in front of us, we settle down to enjoy the beautiful scenery and exotic ambience. Snug in our anchorage, we are safe away from the northerlies which are funnelling between the islands.

24th October (Sunday): Up early - row our dinghy ashore and set off to climb the volcano which is 172 metres above sea level - an ideal height for a short scramble. The climb takes us 30 minutes which includes two stops for Sandra's latest fad; flower pressing. I wondered why my pack was so heavy for such a short walk - it

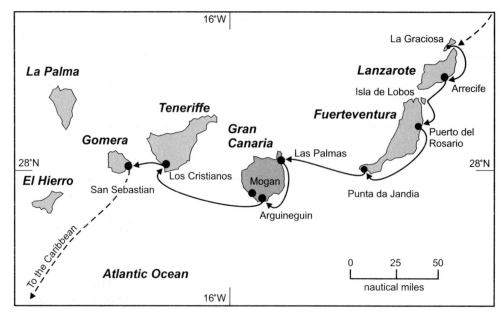

includes Sandra's flower pressing kit. The fauna is thinly covered scrub with a sparse covering of bush, no grass but plenty of sand on the black and purple volcanic rocks. From the sea the volcano has that classic conical shape, the type that makes you want to look over the rim into the crater. When we reach the crater rim and look into the heart of the volcano we are surprised to find the other side of the volcano is completely missing - it must have been blasted away in the eruption. This initial disappointment is soon forgotten as we savour the outstanding panoramic views of the whole island. There are plenty of small bays and inlets on the other side of the island and we wonder if they would provide safe anchorages.

After eating some fruit and nuts to sustain us, we walk along the crater's edge to the other side of the volcano and down through a ravine. We continue on a track to the town where a restaurant and bicycle hire shop are open. The other two shops, including the supermercado, are closed as it is Sunday. This is the unspoilt charm and absence of urban development.

Row our Avon dinghy ashore and prepare for our walk

View from the top of the volcano - *Pacific Voyager* is anchored in the bay below us

La Sociedad: The harbour is of particular interest as our idyllic anchorage is exposed to the south, and this is our nearest port with protection from southerly winds. A new pontoon has been built and there is plenty of room for us! However, the access to the pontoon through the harbour appears to be a minefield of swinging moorings. I view the harbour from different angles to work-out our best approach.

25th October (Monday) - Learning French: As we sailed away from Europe, so we sailed further away from Trafalgar, the last of the BBC shipping forecast areas. We have been trying to use the weather forecast booklet that Radio France International sent to us, but now we have another problem - the French terminology in their forecasts is difficult to translate. I suggest to Sandra that she needs to speak this through with a French person, so when a French yacht anchors near us I say to her, *"Go and ask him for a French lesson." "No I can't do that - he has only just arrived." "I have never known a Frenchman to refuse a woman's request."* Sandra motors over to the French yacht, and reappears some hours later, all smiles, having upgraded her French speaking skills and partaken in several glasses of French wine.

27th October (Wednesday) - Storm: After four gloriously, relaxing days in La Graciosa, better than any health farm, it all comes to a sudden end!!! Sandra translates the latest French weather forecast - a storm is approaching from the south. I look at my watch, then look at the chart. *"If we leave now we can make Arrecife before dark."* Sandra agrees. We promptly up anchor and make for Puerto de Naos (Arrecife) and anchor just as it is getting dark. Arrecife, which means *'reef'* in Spanish, is only 54 miles from Africa. Like bees to the honey pot, numerous other yachts have the same idea. The harbour is like one big happy family as most of us know one another from Gibraltar and Portugal. Before we have set the anchor, Richard, *Blue Moves*, is rowing over clutching a brik of wine between his knees.

28th October (Thursday): During the night the barometer starts falling at an alarming speed; the storm arrives at 04:00 with 40 knot winds from the South. In these blustery conditions, I regularly go on deck to check our anchor is holding securely - it must be well dug-in by now. I also keep a watchful eye on all the other equipment. During one inspection I notice we seem to be moving. *"Hey Sandra we're dragging."* I dash back to the cockpit to start the motor and check our position. It

seems okay. *"No it's not us - it's Richard*!!!" We shout and scream to try and attract his attention. We sound our fog horn - others join in - but Richard is fast asleep. Then we shine our powerful spotlight into *Blue Move's* cabin. That does the trick. Next thing Richard is running along the deck naked as the day he was born. Sandra is quite concerned he might stub his toe or catch something.

Blue Moves - **Richard's bachelor pad**

Checking over *Pacific Voyager* during the storm

PUERTOS DEL ESTADO EN LAS PALMAS
LA LUZ - ARRECIFE - EL ROSARIO
DARSENA DEPORTIVA

In the morning the wind is still blowing a blustery 40 knots from the south. All the yachts are now covered with a film of red sand which has blown over from the Sahara desert. This is followed by an electric storm and torrential rain which thankfully washes all the red dust away. With each strong gust I watch anxiously as *Pacific Voyager* almost swings broadside to the wind, until the anchor chain's catenary takes up the force and pulls the bow back. These alarming angles make me think we should have heavier chain if we are going to have a good night's sleep. *Pacific Voyager* has the recommended 5/16 (8 mm) but, with the increased displacement, it would be prudent to have 10 mm.

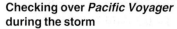 During this huge downpour and turbulence Sandra still manages to produce a superb meal of potato and leek soup, followed by a pizza with garlic and peppers, and a dessert of bananas and custard. After the storm we go to a trading store in Arrecife that supplies the trawlers and buy 60 metres of new 10 mm chain at a reasonable price.

29th October (Friday) - Dinghy: Today, one day after the storm revved-up, we hear Ann (*Peace* - Shannon 26) on the VHF radio requesting information on getting into Puerto de Naos. Over the breakwater we can see the heavy seas raging and do not envy anyone still out there while we are all safe and snug, sheltered inside the harbour. Then we spot *Peace* pitching and rolling as they make for the harbour entrance. The entrance to the channel has a hairpin bend. *Peace* has the wind behind her up to the hairpin and then they have to turn almost 180 degrees into the wind to motor up the channel. As they turn the corner in 40 knots, they appear to remain in the same spot for a couple of minutes. Later they tell us they could not make any headway even with the engine going full throttle and they feared they were going to be blown back into the corner but, very slowly, they inched their way forward into the harbour.

Their horror story started when they decided to stay another day at a beautiful anchorage near Playa Blanca, and were unaware of the forthcoming storm. They awoke in the middle of the night to find they were exposed on a lee shore. They immediately pulled-in their anchor and left with the dinghy in-tow. As they slowly made their way up the coast with the strong wind and growing, following seas, their dinghy was whipped over and the painter parted. They were not able to regain hold of the dinghy and eventually they lost sight of it. This unfortunately is the beginning of an unpleasant saga; they buy a second hand dinghy at a relatively high price from a local merchant, only to find the chambers are delaminating. The merchant would not take the dinghy back, so they spent a week patching it up. This unfortunate incident makes us appreciate how reliant we are on our dinghy - if only we could carry a spare.

3rd November (Wednesday) - Broken Mast: Mike and Marina (*Colombine* - Oholson 35) are one

Cruising down the coast of Fuerteventura with *Peace*

of the first yachts to leave after the storm but, to our surprise, they are back within a few hours - they have been dismasted in only 25 knots!!! As they motor up the channel their mast is strapped to the side of the hull. Once the word gets out there are offers of assistance from most of the cruisers in the anchorage. I am surprised to see that ten chaps lining the side deck are unable to lift the mast out of the water - what chance would a couple have at sea? Fortunately a mobile crane is on the quay and is able to lift the mast. At this time of the year this accident will probably delay their trip across the Atlantic until next season, but at least it will be a good opportunity for Mike and Marina to get to know the Canaries!!!

Puerto de Naos turns out to be the only harbour in the Canaries where we are asked to pay for anchoring - 350 pesetas per day. At the local supermarket, we try the local cheese, but it has very little taste, so we settle for Kerrygold at 160 pesetas per 100 gms (double UK price). We stock-up on brik wine at 49 pesetas a litre. Thankfully, not everything is expensive! Sandra makes liver and onions for lunch and cooks Irish stew in the pressure cooker for the next leg of our journey.

4th November (Thursday): A quick peep over the breakwater confirms the seas have settled down after the storm. We up anchor and join a few other departing yachts to buddy sail down the coast of Lanzarote, exploring the bays and harbours along the way. As we sail down the coast, Lanzarote looks very bleak. Its explosive geology has shaped the landscape. There are no trees or vegetation. Apparently this is where the American astronauts came to see what the moon could look like.

As we approach Isla de Lobos, named after the seals who used to frequent this area, we consider anchoring, but the conditions look a bit hairy. We continue down the coast of Isla de Fuerteventura to Puerto Rosario, arriving just as it is getting dark at 18:30. Fuerteventura is the second largest, but least populated island. It is treeless, greenless, thirsty scrub and stone with only the occasional oasis of palm trees adding colour to the khaki scene.

We anchor in an open space in the middle of the harbour beside *Peace*. The anchorage looks safe and well protected. A trumpet sounds ashore - we think at first it might be another cruiser, but it is actually a military school sounding the last post. After a relaxing dinner on *Peace* and a couple briks of wine we retire to *Pacific Voyager* for a good night's sleep.

5th November (Friday): At 07:30 I notice a boatman approaching *Peace*. "*This is a bit early to collect the mooring fees!*" Then I realise he is pointing out to sea. I follow his direction to see a large Ro-Ro ship coming our way - we are in its turning space. It is amazing how quickly we can up anchor and leave when we need to. An hour later as we sail down the coast, "*I haven't had breakfast yet - and I've still got my pyjamas on!*"

Acceleration Zones: The cruising pilots advise cruisers to be aware of the *wind acceleration zones*. This is the first time we have heard of such a thing but, with the combination of the high mountains, high ambient temperature and the geometry of the treeless ravines, this gives rise to sudden increases in wind strength from 15 to 30 knots, in narrow areas and without any real warning. The wind literally rolls down the valleys. White horses on the water are our only clue. A keen lookout must be kept and, for this reason, night sailing in acceleration zone areas is not advised.

Ahead of us, *Peace* is reefing their headsail as they enter an acceleration zone. As we approach the same area we also experience stronger winds. I ease the sheets to see if we can get away with it - no it is too strong - we have to reef.

Punta de Jandia - Rory doing foredeck jobs

7th November (Sunday) - Punta de Jandia: Anchor for the night off the Jandia peninsula with two other yachts. After a good night's kip there is a mad scramble to leave at the crack of dawn to cross to Las Palmas, on Gran Canaria, in daylight. To avoid an area of shallow water and overfalls marked on the chart, we have to sail a little south (downwind). But, as we head up into the wind, the seas are still quite steep and we are not as organised as we should be. At one point we sail over the top of a wave which literately leaves the bow airborne. The bow whips down and throws us forwards. We feel as if we are about to be catapulted out of the cockpit, but Nicholson's have a beautifully designed 'V' shaped hull section which cushions the fall. "*I think we should wait for the sea to ease. Why should we punish ourselves like weekend sailors?*"

Back at the anchorage Sandra sets to work on a pen and ink drawing of *Pacific Voyager* for our Christmas cards, then starts making our courtesy flags for the Caribbean Islands. Meanwhile I find the odd job to do about the boat. It rains on and off all day, but we are warm and cosy inside while we bob around in strong offshore winds. Dinner on our own tonight - the other yachts that sailed onto Las Palmas have missed out on Thai lemon grass soup and courgette souffle.

11th November (Thursday) - Las Palmas: With two reefs in the main and the no.2 jib we have an exhilarating sail across to Las Palmas, broad reaching all the way in 25 knots of wind. The bow cuts comfortably and speedily through the breaking seas, ensuring we make Las Palmas before night fall. Las Palmas is at the northern tip of Grand Canaria. It was founded in 1478 and named after the palm stockade the Spanish built to protect themselves from attack.

The Canaries are named after a pack of dogs - not a little yellow bird!

I always thought the Canaries were named after a little yellow bird - not so! They were actually named after large dogs which were originally found roaming one of the islands. Hence the name Canary, which has its root in *canis*, the Latin name for dog. Statues of these majestic black dogs stand guard opposite the cathedral in Las Palmas - an impressive sight.

22nd November (Monday) - Anchor Chain: I fit the 10 mm anchor chain we bought in Arrecife - we can sleep easy now. But a few hours later we start dragging in only 15 knots of wind!!! Fortunately we are on-board as we drift slowly through the anchorage. Our attention is drawn to our plight by shouts from the other cruisers as we drift past. As we pull in the chain I know what to expect - no anchor. Fortunately we have buoyed the anchor which we retrieve. There is no evidence of why the chain parted. I now check every link but cannot see any damage. (Later we wrote both in English and Spanish, to the merchant who supplied the chain, but he never replied. We also wrote to Mastercard who claimed to have some type of buying protection, but their response stated it was limited to purchases in the UK only).

17th November (Wednesday) - Oil Spill: Las Palmas is a working port with commercial shipping constantly on the move. Little do we suspect that one of these vessels will discharge its oil into the harbour. At first light we notice dark brown marks on the neighbouring yachts. It does not take long to realise the oil is covering our hull as well. The oil gets absolutely everywhere; on the dinghy, on the anchor chain, on any ropes that are in the water and, with the dinghy covered in oil, it needs to be cleaned before being lifted on board, otherwise the deck will get covered as well. No apologies from the port - it is a disgrace.

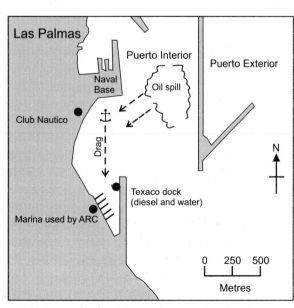

Las Palmas harbour plan, showing oil spill and where the anchor dragged

Sandra cleaning oil off the dinghy   *Pacific Voyager's* **hull is covered in oil**

It appears Las Palmas is well known for oil spills. We later meet cruisers in Arguineguin who avoided Las Palmas for this reason. It takes days working from the dinghy with rags and paraffin to slowly remove the oil. In discussion with other yachts, it is felt that if a hull has a good coat of wax this helps. This is where cruising organisations like the Bluewater Rallies and the ARC, which represent about a fifth of the cruisers crossing the Atlantic, can help by threatening to move to another port unless Las Palmas cleans up their act.

Oil-slicks are reported to kill over 250,000 birds a year, and animal conservationists are very concerned as there is a spill somewhere around the world every three days. Accidents account for only 10% of the oil spills; the rest are from activities like washing out oil tanks. This has a great impact on the environment. About 60% of the birds washed up on the beaches in the UK are covered in oil. Mammals like whales and seals may be able to avoid the oil slicks, but could starve from the lack of fish.

The commercial ferries also pose another problem as they speed into the harbour creating standing waves which radiate across the anchorage. When the wave catches us broadside and the wave period is close to our natural roll period, *Pacific Voyager* rocks violently. I am sure we lost two water containers this way. Needless to say, they should have been lashed them down. With all these problems I mentally cross Las Palmas off our cruising route.

ARC: We are intrigued by all the ARC yachts moored together in the marina - the crews are all wearing ARC tee-shirts. I remember in 1987, while I was studying for my MSc in Project Management at Henley, trying to organise a berth on a yacht sailing in the ARC. This would have been the second rally. I was due to fly out to Gibraltar to meet the chap but, unfortunately, he blew-out his sails crossing the Bay of Biscay and decided to wait a year.

ARC

TRANSATLANTIC RALLY

Joining organised rallies does reduce cruising hassles: particularly checking-in, shipping spares and organising tours. As we watch the ARC leave for St Lucia in the Caribbean we would like to have joined them, but we still have a few jobs to do.

CASA DE COLON

🏴󠁧󠁢󠁥󠁮󠁧󠁿

The Columbus museum

Oyster Yachts are using this opportunity for some marketing footage - we listen to them on the VHF as they try to line up a few Oyster yachts for that *'perfect shot.'*

Shopping: The supermarkets in Las Palmas are well stocked with food and drink, but we are surprised to find they only take Visa cards, and of course, we only have Mastercard. Next time we will carry both credit cards. (Later, in Panama, we had a major problem with our Mastercard.)

Fireworks: The local yacht club, Club Nautico, is celebrating a special event with fireworks. Initially we are entertained by a colourful pyrotechnics display, but our enjoyment soon turns to horror as parachute flares start landing in-between the yachts in our anchorage. *"We're under attack. They're getting their own back for Drake!"* Fortunately no flares score a direct hit, but there are enough near misses to raise our concern.

Columbus' House: Sailing across the Atlantic is all about following in the footsteps of Columbus, so the museum, Casa de Colon, is part of our pilgrimage. We suspect every second tourist must go there because, as we stop to ask directions, they are given before we ask the question! The museum is located in the house where Columbus presented his credentials in 1492. He stopped at the island to have repair work done to one of his ships, before sailing onto Gomera, his departure point. The museum displays old maps and charts, models of Columbus' three ships, nautical flags and old navigation instruments. The historical ambience envelops us, making us feel we are also taking part in the quest for a route west - not for gold and spices, but tropical beaches and snorkelling!!!

25th November (Thursday) - Arguineguin: *Pacific Voyager* enjoys a lively sail, flexing her bulkheads, down the coast to Arguineguin where we meet up with friends last seen in Gibraltar (they have successfully avoided the oil spill in Las Palmas). The old fishing village, with small houses and narrow streets, surrounds the picturesque

harbour of Arguineguin and, in contrast, just around the next headland there is an enormous development of time-share accommodation and recreational facilities. *"Where are the time-share salesmen?"* We jest, but the ironic thing is, in this idyllic setting, the time-share buildings are threating to engulf the very beauty they have persuaded tourists to come and see in the first place.

Pacific Voyager anchored off Arguineguin

28th November (Sunday) - Tenerife: Delay our departure from Arguineguin until the late afternoon, to give us an overnight trip to Los Cristianos. As we cruise along the coast we are able to get a close look at Puerto Rico and Puerto de Mogan. There are several yachts anchored off Puerto de Mogan, but it does not look as inviting as Arguineguin. As we pass Puerto de Mogan, the wind dies completely. It is peacefully calm, so we motor for an hour until the wind freshens. Initially we beat south of the direct course but, as the wind shifts, we go with it and make the northing we need. It is the most perfect sail across to Tenerife in 10 to 15 knots of wind, little swell and a mild comfortable night. The type of passage when we do not mind being up all night because we want to savour every moment of it. I wish our friends could be here to enjoy these perfect sailing conditions - these treasured moments are always worth waiting for. There are very few clouds in the sky which is lit up by a beaming full moon to guide us. The moonbeams are sending down shafts of light through the hatch and, to cap this extraordinary night, there is a partial **eclipse** of the moon. Yes, the alignment of the sun, earth and moon! I thought the earth's shadow on the moon was a cloud at first. I call Sandra from her slumber to look at this unique event, *"Come and have a look at this - there's a lunar eclipse."*

If we were on terra firma looking through a powerful telescope we might be able to see the shadow begin to cover the moon's finely etched mountain peaks, descend into its valleys and advance across the craters and plains. This inspiring night ends with an incredible sunrise which lights up Tenerife's snow covered peak of Pico de Teide.

We follow the early morning high speed ferry into Los Cristianos and anchor in company with several other yachts. The anchorage is open to an unpleasant swell which we have to live with - fortunately *Pacific Voyager* is naturally lying most of the time into the swell. This is our last opportunity to provision for the Atlantic passage. Ashore we buy fresh fruit and vegetables, plus a huge chunk of jambon serano (dried venison), which keeps forever and tastes wonderful, especially as a substitute for bacon sarnies.

Water: Water is free if we collect it in our jerry cans, but we have to pay if we bring our boat alongside to fill up the tanks. By taking a few cans with us on each trip ashore, we soon top up our tanks. Our main tank holds 275 litres, and with ten 20 litre jerry cans lining the deck, our total capacity is 475 litres. In addition, on our last trip ashore, we also fill up our six 20 litre ice-cream container buckets with water, and leave them in the cockpit well, giving us an even larger capacity of 595 litres.

Tenerife - beaching the Avon dinghy to fill up the water cans

29th November (Monday): Los Cristianos *poste restante* is to be our last mail stop in the Canaries - we are very impressed with their postal service as we receive all our mail which has been forwarded from Madeira's *poste restante*. We spend a couple of days writing our Christmas post. This is our last chance and, as usual, we have left it to the last minute. In the post office we hear an Australian cruiser ask, "*We have been waiting two weeks for mail from our correspondence course for our children - we have to leave now - can you forward it to Antigua?*" Collecting mail is always a problem - thankfully the internet and email is coming to our rescue. Many cruisers use their boat's name for their address - ours is <pacificvoyager@hotmail.com>.

1st December (Wednesday) - Gomera: It is a short day hop over to San Sebastian in Gomera the last island we are to visit in the Canaries. After breakfast we up anchor and follow one of the whale watcher boats, but no whales make an appearance while we are around. About halfway across, a light northerly wind develops, so we turn the engine off and start sailing. This light breeze quickly builds and heads us as we approach the coast. For the last few miles

Our Lady of the Assumption **where Columbus said his last prayer before crossing the Atlantic**

we are punching into a very steep choppy sea, that sends waves and spray all over the boat. After an hour of pounding we eventually make San Sebastian and anchor in 9 metres of water between two other yachts. We use them as reference points as we tug on the anchor.

San Sebastian's breakwater is being extended to offer more harbour facilities and protection. The marine and civil construction equipment is strewn along the harbour wall. Inside the harbour a black sandy beach fringes the bay.

All the cruisers are here for the same reason; to anchor in the same harbour as Columbus, say a prayer in the same church as Columbus (*Our Lady of the Assumption*), and depart from the same port as Columbus did on the 6th September 1492. Columbus' departure would be a tad early by today's accepted weather windows, as he would run the risk of catching a late hurricane, but at least he would be in the New World for Christmas!!!

Further Reading:

Martin, Colin and **Parker**, Geoffrey., *The Spanish Armada*, Penguin, 1988
Cornell, Jimmy., *Canary Islands Cruising Guide*, World Cruising Publishing
Hammick, Anne and **Heath**, Nicholas., Atlantic Islands, RCC

12 Atlantic Crossing

After port hopping down the coast of Portugal, Spain and the Canaries we now face the same challenge as Columbus, "*Is the world round*?" Our plan is to sail from San Sebastian in Gomera to the Caribbean, and visit as many of the Caribbean Islands as possible before transiting the Panama Canal in April or May. We have reduced our landfall options to either Antigua (Leeward Islands) or Barbados (Windward Islands). Barbados is the nearest island to the Canaries, but it is in the middle of the Windward Islands, while Antigua is at the northern end of the Leeward Islands. It seems sensible to start at the top and sail southwards with the prevailing wind - we decide to make for Antigua.

2nd December (Thursday): With healthy northerly winds we cream down the coast of Gomera. *"If this keeps up we will have a quick passage,"* but the winds do not last and soon after clearing Gomera we are becalmed. We motor for a few hours to clear the coast as we are concerned about the current setting us north during the night. And sure enough, by next morning we have actually drifted back towards Gomera. But not for long - the wind comes first as a flutter, then steadily builds up to 20 knots northerly, *"Great we are on our way to the Caribbean."*

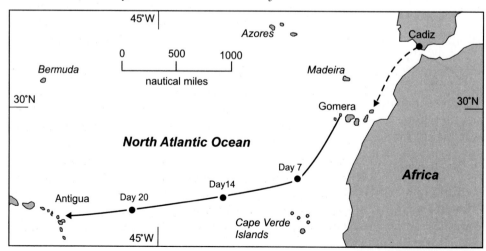

Log book: chart 4012 (scale 1:10,000,000): Out comes our chart for the southern part of the Atlantic Ocean. Crossing this vast expanse of ocean from the Canaries to the Caribbean seems a daunting task at an average speed of 4 miles per hour - walking speed! We take a more southerly route than the rhumb line partly to have the option of stopping over in the Cape Verde Islands, but mostly to catch the tradewinds. (However, this year the tradewinds are further north than normal and therefore we could have taken the rhumb line directly to Antigua). As we near the Cape Verde Islands we calculate that the detour to the Verdes will add at least a week to our arrival in Antigua, and as we will probably already miss Christmas ashore we would at least like to celebrate the New Year there.

Atlantic Ocean - Typical Day: A daily rhythm soon develops of sail inspection, eating, SSB, reading, sleeping and watch-keeping - it is the best way to kill time on a long passage. Our typical day starts by inspecting our gear looking for damage and chafe (any two items rubbing together).

Typical Breakfast usually starts with cereals with long life milk or powdered milk. Powdered milk is our best option as we become used to its taste. It also takes up less space, and we only use what we need. Fresh bread will only last a day or two, but we have been given a tip to wrap bread in tea-towels or muslin lightly soaked in vinegar. Vinegar tasting bread is not my favourite, but the bread does last longer, even if it makes me think we are sailing in the days of Horatio Hornblower. Sandra often makes Scotch pancakes which are easy to make and even easier to eat. She mixes an egg, flour, milk, and a pinch of salt, to make a thick batter, and then adds a heaped tablespoon of the batter to a greased frying pan and cooks for a minute each side or until golden brown. I eat them on their own, or with butter and marmalade, washed down with a hot cup of tea - just the way to start the day.

Typical Lunch is usually a sandwich in a plastic *'dog bowl'* - Sandra keeps the china for best! Grovelling around in my Tupperware bowl makes me feel like a convict having his daily ration. I am conditioned to expect food on a china plate, but a plastic bowl on a rocking boat is more sensible. Tinned corned beef sandwiches were my favourite for a long time - my mouth would salivate at the thought of a corned beef roll with fresh bread and crunchy salad, but at some point I went off corned beef just as Sandra stocked up with a locker full of it. Now I can only eat it as a curry with rice.

Having a tender tummy at sea I have to eat what I look forward to which surprisingly is Sandra's home made fruit cake. I say surprisingly, not because Sandra makes it but because it is rich and heavy. It consists of dried fruit, flour, sugar and eggs, but no butter so is excellent for our digestion, health and cholesterol. About halfway across the Atlantic I develop a craving for tinned peaches - yes, tinned peaches of all things. Fortunately we are well stocked up - I start to eat two tins of peaches a day. (As you can imagine we are well stocked with tinned peaches for the Pacific leg, but I do not get the craving again - such is life!)

Typical Dinner is similar to what we would eat at home - why should we change now? So meat and two veg is generally on the menu. Our choice of food is obviously influenced by our ability to store and preserve food. Our fridge is not working so we have to resort to the traditional ways of storing that our grandparents would have been more familiar with. We discuss this in detail in our book *Managing Your Bluewater Cruise* (see page 66).

Reading is a great time killer, and we certainly have plenty of time to kill. We have both found comfortable reading positions snug in the cockpit against the bulkhead. The long passages gives us time for in depth reading - we can get into the books we would like to read but are always putting off. For example, we read Churchill's four volumes of the *English Speaking Nations* on this passage. Each place we visit encourages us to become more interested in its history.

Music: When it is really noisy with the wind screaming, the spars banging, the timber creaking and the waves crashing against the hull, we often put our headphones on and listen to our favourite music. Being a product of the sixties I love to drift away to the sound of the Beatles, Rolling Stones or Queen which often tends to be louder than the racket outside. Meanwhile Sandra prefers to listen to the more mellow tones of Vivaldi, Enya or Phil Collins.

Radio: For news and entertainment we listen to the radio (SW, AM, FM, LW, MW). BBC World is good for keeping us up to date on world events. If the off watch person is asleep we put on the headphones. We often record interesting programmes to listen to later. All the BBC World programmes are announced in GMT - another reason for our GMT clock on the bulkhead.

SSB: 08:00 GMT listen to the SSB cruisers net on 4483 Khz on our Roberts radio. As our radio is only a receiver we have to bite our lips as we listen to the other yachts giving their positions and discussing weather faxes. Every blip on their weather faxes is discussed in detail - one day they are recommending everyone to go north a bit, the next day south a bit. On our chart we note the GPS positions of our friends, and plot their tracks - our chart soon becomes a mass of dots. As the fleet moves across the Atlantic Ocean we are in the middle of the pack. Our list of radio schedules is growing - it now includes:

Pacific Voyager's **route overlaid on the Radio France International sea areas chart**

08:00 GMT: 4483 Khz - Cruisers net
09:00 GMT: 7070 Khz - Alec (Canaries)
11:30 GMT: 15300 Khz - Radio France International weather forecast in French
13:30 GMT: 21400 Khz - Repeat of the Radio France International weather forecast in English by a Ham called Trudy from Barbados
17:00 GMT: 4483 Khz - Cruisers net
00:30 GMT: 6224 Khz - Herb from Bermuda weather forecast.

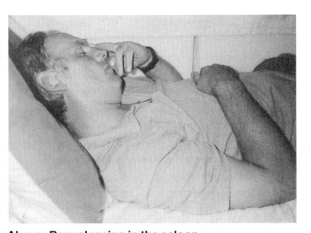

Above: Rory sleeping in the saloon
Right: Rory washing from a bowl of fresh water

Washing Ourselves: Yes we do wash at sea! We like to wash before dinner after a hard day reading in the sun. Sandra's washing procedure starts with a bucket of sea water to wet herself down, then she lathers up using an inexpensive shampoo, followed by a rinse in fresh water. I prefer to start with an electric shave. (I charge the shaver through the inverter when we run the engine.) Then I do the whole of my wash in a bowl of fresh water. By keeping my hair short I use less water.

Sundowner: While sailing we rarely drink alcohol. I recall one relatively calm evening we both have a glass of wine from a one litre brik, with the intention of finishing the box the following day. But, come the following evening the seas have built up and drinking wine is the last thought on our minds. Consequently by the time we have another calm evening the wine tastes like vinegar - well it tasted pretty close to vinegar in the first place, but now it is awful. What a waste! From now on if we feel like a drink we will have a tot of whiskey.

Watches: Keeping a good lookout day and night is essential to limit our risk of collision and check on our gear. If we are travelling at 5 knots and an approaching vessel is travelling at 15 knots, then our closing speed will be 20 knots, or a mile every 3 minutes. So if the visibility is about 5 miles, we should lookout every 15 minutes. Even though the risk of being rundown mid ocean is minimal, we sleep better knowing someone is keeping a good lookout. Watches during the day are relaxed - usually one of us is reading in the cockpit and keeps a lookout as we turn the page, or every other page if it is a good book. During the night our watches are flexible - they could be two, three even four hours depending on how we feel. We try and give the person below a good long sleep in line with their REM cycles. However, there is the odd night when both of us feel like zombies - we could easily crash out and be completely oblivious to the outside world. (It surprises us to find out that some cruisers do just that - although they do set their radar to do an automatic sweep every few minutes, which will warn them if a vessel enters their safety box.)

There are occasions when we need to shorten the time between our lookouts due to heavy weather, poor visibility and shipping lanes. And, by contrast, in mid ocean when we have not seen any shipping for weeks we are tempted to increase the time between lookouts to 30 minutes. At night we always keep our 5 watt anchor light on which draws less power than the 25 watt masthead tricolour. Some nights when we are wide awake, we can read, we can write and the time passes really quickly, while other nights we are dead tired and battle to stay awake - it is an endurance test. This is when we cat nap between the 15 minute alarms. But there have been occasions when we are both so exhausted that we actually sleep through the alarm.

Day 5: It is Sandra's birthday. I make Sandra breakfast for a change, while Sandra lies in bed videoing this rare event. I then give Sandra her birthday present I bought in Portugal many weeks ago - a Portuguese linen tea towel - taking her out for dinner will come later!

Day 7: Check food condition - the cabbage should have been wrapped in newspaper as it is starting to go yellow on the edges. Sandra successfully grows mung beans in a jam jar - these are a great source of vitamins. Lemon squash is a must to make our water drinkable (we really need a water filter). As a change from tea and coffee we try hot blackcurrant. Our cheddar cheese is lasting well wrapped in muslin - even in the heat. However, I notice the butter is going a bit runny.

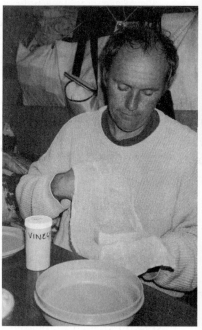

Rory wrapping cheese in muslin

I write in the logbook: First cloudy night since leaving Gomera. Sandra's star gazing has come to a standstill - it is pitch black. Pleased with the 130 mile run today which brings us to a quarter of the way across the ocean. Celebrate with Captain Morgan's grog. Sandra puts on lipstick, perfume and earrings for the occasion and devours half a bar of chocolate.

Day 8: Another rocky night - it is a continuous succession of gusts and calms. Three reefs in the main and the no.2 jib is polled out to balance the sails and give the Hydrovane self-steering a better chance to steer in the 35 knot gusts.

Day 9: Listen to Herb's (South Bound 11) weather forecast - amazingly he does this for fun!!! Wind easing - no need to reef - no ships sighted, moon in last phase. Boat very rocky - even difficult to write the log book. Great night star gazing, there is a wonderfully clear sky - not a speck of industrial pollution.

Day 10: Find an extra large flying fish on the deck this morning - we must have had babies so far. I open it up and find a few milky eggs along the spine - we decide to give it a miss. Feeling tired most of the time from the constant rocking - there is no relief. Everything takes so long to do and it is awkward having to constantly grab with one hand to keep our balance.

Sandra repairing the sail

Day 11: Good tradewinds so far - but they are eluding us now - we are becalmed. Our dilemma is; should we leave the sails up to catch the occasional zephyr, or take the sails down to protect them from flogging??? By first light we have the answer - we should have taken them down. There is a rip along the bottom seam which takes Sandra three hours to repair with her sewing machine. Every locker is open below - thankfully it is calm. The message should be clear to us now - do not let the sails flog. I suppose we should motor - everyone else seems to.

While Sandra repairs the genny I go through our panic bags. I find a tin of Turkey, *"We should keep this for Christmas dinner."* I remove a packet of digestive biscuits which are nearly out of date and remove items I would not fancy eating cold, like the tin of Irish Stew!!! I also remove a tin of chicken curry which we have for lunch with a can of beer.

Checking through the food lockers I find some food is already past its use by date - cherries, powdered eggs, coconut, sosamix - amazing how quickly the year has gone by. In hindsight we really over stocked in the UK - fresh produce and tinned food has been readily available - we are not sailing in the days of Columbus any more. Sandra makes some flapjacks to use up the cherries and coconut.

Discuss our life again - this is an ideal time to reflect. Of all the places we have visited, Ireland is the place we would like to go back to - we really enjoyed the *'craic.'* Not being able to talk to the locals in Portugal and Spain may be part of the reason. Certainly the weather has improved as we move south. Meanwhile Sandra is longing for the Pacific Islands.

Day 12: Where have the tradewinds gone? Are they a myth? Have they been privatised and I must pay? Or nationalised and on strike? *Pacific Voyager* is wallowing about on a sea of glass which emphasises the emptiness of a vast ocean. When hundreds of jellyfish overtake us we know we are not going anywhere fast.

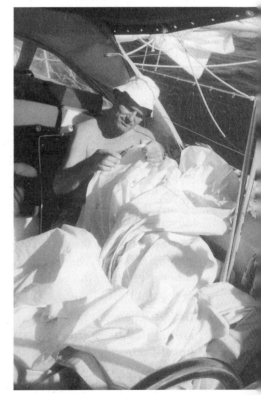

Rory sealing the raw sail edges with our portable gas Portasol

Calms are very frustrating. As I lie in my bunk trying to get some relief. It is hot - there is no refreshing breeze. And as we roll every few seconds from the constant swell, the rigging clangs and there is the annoying sound of a pen rolling in a locker somewhere. I feel helpless - there is nothing we can do but wait for wind like the old sailing ships used to do.

With each whisper of wind we look at each other in hope, only daring to peep out occasionally in fear that we will scare the zephyrs away, but the zephyrs continue to build and after two days of calm we are sailing again.

Day 13: The BBC announce there are only 10 more shopping days to Christmas - no problem for us, because we had to do our shopping weeks ago. We are both feeling really tired and lethargic today. Because we have not seen any ships for days, we decide to extend our watches to every 30 minutes.

Day 14: According to the GPS we are halfway, "*Let's celebrate.*" I write in the logbook, '*Halfway - seas quite lumpy and large - have not seen another ship for days - both of us feeling a bit queasy - feel okay to read but nothing else - if only the seas would ease a little life would be fantastic.*' Now we can visualise how big the Atlantic Ocean really is as we are only halfway across. Sandra tries to make bread which turns out to be a disaster as it does not rise - but I still have to eat it!! As we move west the time of sunrise and sunset are changing. We alter our clocks an hour every 15 degrees to keep them on local time.

Day 15: No ships, no fish, no birds - we could be the only people on the planet except for the cruisers on 4483 Khz and the BBC World service. Sandra makes oat crunchies and flap jacks using a recipe from Jane Gibb's cook book, making twice the amount this time as the last batch did not last very long. Both of us have constant back ache from the rolling motion - there is no relief. *Pacific Voyager* is rocking excessively in the following sea. Sandra is reading about David Livingstone searching for the source of the Nile, and I am reading about the problems facing the Spanish Armada after Drake's fire ships scattered the fleet. We share a tot of whiskey in the evening - it sort of rounds off the day.

Day 16: SSB and GPS, items of new technology for the bluewater cruiser, are making cruising much safer. For example, we hear on the SSB of an Australian having difficulties. Not only is his wife threatening to leave him if he does not come straight home to Australia, but he has also blown out a few sails and now his rudder has fallen off mid Atlantic - not sure which is the most serious. Every morning, on the SSB, we listen to his latest update. Yachts have altered course to offer assistance and diesel. With the accuracy of the GPS a mid-ocean rendezvous is relatively straight forward. After an attempt to fix the rudder fails, they trail warps from the side deck to steer the yacht, and are now making between 50 and 75 miles per day in the right direction.

Day 18: The radio nets are becoming more comical and light hearted - the cruisers are telling jokes, quoting poetry, playing games, and even playing musical instruments - a bagpipe and a didgeridoo no less. Rain squalls lurk on the horizon - eventually one of them gets us. We dash up on deck to let the genoa out, then we sit in the cockpit in the rain - it is wonderfully refreshing. I am amazed to see the end of a rainbow by our stern. "*All we need is the pot of gold to go with it.*"

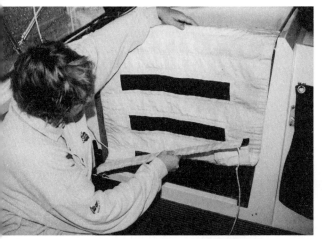

Our new companionway cover works brilliantly

Companion Cover: The cockpit and spray hood are designed to protect the galley and navigation area from the rain and spray while sailing into the wind. However, when ocean cruising in the tradewinds, the rain and spray comes from behind - right through the companionway. In the Canaries, Sandra made a companionway cover from our old mainsail which includes a number of clear plastic windows, so she can now keep an eye on me steering through the squalls.

Day 20: During my morning inspection I notice the pole is chafing on the inner shroud. I reposition the pole and whip the contact area. I also notice the genoa has two small holes where it has chafed against the anchor - Sandra repairs this before breakfast - consequently breakfast is at 14:30. Out comes the small fresh water hand spray to cool us down as we start to feel the heat, and we discuss how we can make a cockpit awning to protect us from the sun. We are experiencing wonderful sunrises and sunsets in the pollution free atmosphere. A storm petrel circles the boat for ten minutes - we must be getting closer to land. Not sure if it wants to land - in the end it flies off.

Sandra finishes reading about the ex-British prime minister McMillan. She is now reading my project management book which must be really heavy going. A lot of noise on the foredeck has us racing up on deck - the sheet has come off the genoa and the sail wraps itself round the forestay.

Three quarters across - Sandra makes serano sandwiches to celebrate. They taste just like the bacon butties we used to have every Saturday morning in Cape Town. With plenty of fresh water left we can now increase our daily ration (overall on this Atlantic crossing we are averaging 5 litres per day). Nearly all our vegetables and fruit are used up except for potatoes, onions and oranges - we have thrown very little food away. Obviously our storage methods are working - wrapping all citrus in foil, and everything else in newspaper, placing them in a box under the forepeak berth where it is cool and dark, and turning them occasionally has done the trick.

We change the gas bottle - our consumption is down from 1.5 kg per week ashore, to 1 kg per week sailing. Although we are only having one cooked meal a day, Sandra has been baking bread and cakes. Job list: The switch for the spot light over the galley has corroded - this also happened to our friends on *Summer Wind* - there must be a design fault.

Day 22: As the days tick over it becomes obvious we are not going to make landfall before Christmas. In hindsight we should have left the Canaries a few days earlier in the last week of November - about the same time as the ARC in fact. This spurs

Pacific Voyager's **downwind sail arrangement**

Sandra on to make a Christmas pudding, Christmas decorations, blow up balloons, and gift wrap my presents. We are greeted by a rain squall in the morning - I get soaked hand steering in the blustery conditions. As the squall approaches we can see a column of water coming towards us.

A flying fish actually flies through the hatch and lands on Sandra's pillow - the resulting scream can be heard for miles - not sure if it was Sandra or the flying fish. After 20 odd days of intensive reading we are looking forward to our landfall - we need to do something else. The thought of walking more than a few metres and sleeping on a steady bed is incredibly appealing. Both of us continue to have back aches due to the constant rocking. I try strapping a book to my back to give it support (I should try a corset next time). Otherwise we have not had any medical issues - we are quite fit and healthy breathing the fresh sea air.

Day 23: On my morning inspection I see no ships, but I do see a few storm petrels circling around *Pacific Voyager*. As I critically consider every aspect of the boat, I visualise the forces being transmitted through the structure. My biggest concern is the self-steering shaft which attracts a huge sideways force as the stern yaws across its course. I find three flying fish on the deck which Sandra cooks following a recipe from our Mediterranean seafood book. She soaks them in lemon juice, then pops them in the frying pan with a tablespoon of olive oil, tops this with sliced potatoes, onions, rosemary, thyme, salt and pepper - puts the lid on to act as a mini oven and cooks the dish slowly. The extra effort pays off - they are delicious.

Squalls: As we approach Antigua we pass through a squall belt - it is one squall after the other. The squalls are quite distinctive, looking like nuclear mushrooms. If we see a squall approach I hand steer because the sudden gusts of wind are often too much for the self-steering gear (perhaps we should have used the autopilot). I try to steer away, but it is difficult to determine their course and I am sure I steer into them as many times as I steer away from them. The leading edge of a squall is like a wall of water advancing towards us. When it is about ten metres away I first feel a gust of wind which is quickly followed by heavy rain. The power surge is tremendous, it is like being back on my motor bike opening up after rounding a corner.

As a squall approaches the wind shifts and increases by 10 to 15 knots which is okay, but we are always concerned it will be more. Squalls at night are the worst,

Rory hand-steering in a squall

because we cannot see them coming - oh to have radar. When we are hit by a squall in the middle of the night I rely on the wind instruments to give me wind speed and direction, so I can steer an effective course and avoid a gybe (even though we have preventers). In these situations wheelhouse steering would be ideal.

Day 24: Christmas Day - we both leave out our socks at the end of the bunk and Santa fills them with presents in the morning. We receive Christmas greeting on the SSB, but we cannot respond - very frustrating. In keeping with the Christmas spirit we have mince pies for breakfast while we open our presents. Christmas dinner is a tin of turkey, tinned petits pois, rosti potatoes, gravy and stuffing - and later when we have space - Sandra's home-made Christmas pudding with UHT long life whipped cream, and a mug of ground coffee. Although we miss the company of family and friends to share Christmas dinner with, it is a novelty to have Christmas at sea.

Day 25: Boxing Day - about fifty miles out from making our landfall I feel it is prudent to check our position with our Zeiss sextant. The Zeiss is a pleasure to use, all the parts move easily and it feels like the well made precision instrument it is. I know I should use the sextant more often, because I always have to re-learn the calculations each time I reduce a sight. I take a sight at midday to calculate our latitude and an afternoon sight to get a feel for our longitude. I assume my sights are accurate to plus-minus 10 miles - this puts us near our GPS position.

Day 26: Landfall - there is a great feeling of anticipation and excitement gradually building up as our landfall approaches. As luck would have it, we make our landfall at night. I confirm our position from a light on the headland overlooking English Harbour. As we prefer not to enter unknown ports at night, we heave-to until daylight - really pleased we have empirically proved the world is round!

Further Readings:

Radio France International, 42 Avenue Coriolis, 31057 Toulouse Cedex, France
Gibb, Jane., *Reluctant Cook*, Adlard Coles Nautical
Davidson, Alan., *Mediterranean Seafood*
Hammick, Anne., and Heath, Nicholas., *Atlantic Islands*, RCC. Pilotage Foundation

13 *Antigua*

Columbus came in search of gold and spices - we are searching for sun and reggae. Our plan is to port hop down the Leeward and Windward Islands from Antigua to Grenada and enjoy the Caribbean culture.

Geography: The West Indies extends in a great broken arc from the Peninsula of Yucatan almost to the mouth of the Orinoco and forms a gigantic breakwater separating the Atlantic Ocean from the Caribbean Sea and the Gulf of Mexico. The western wing of the island arc is commonly called the Greater Antilles; Cuba, Jamaica, Hispaniola [Haiti] and Puerto Rico. While the eastern wing is called the Lesser Antilles, comprising the Leeward Islands and Windward Islands.

It was on Columbus' second voyage of discovery that he took a more southerly route and discovered most of the islands in the Eastern Caribbean. The first island was sighted on a Sunday, hence he named it *'Dominica'*. Sailing north he landed on an island he called *'Marie-Galante'*, named after his ship the *'Gallant Santa Maria.'*

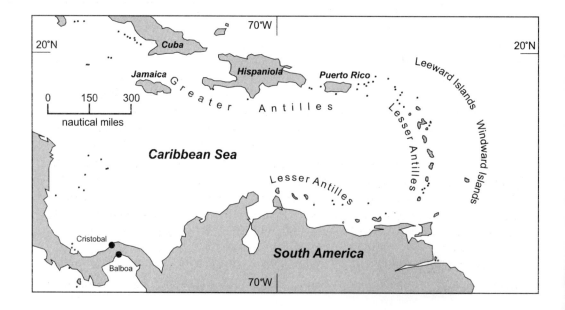

Continuing north he sighted and named; Guadeloupe, Montserrat, Antigua, Redonda, Nevis, St Kitts, St Eustatius and Saba, before heading west for the Virgin Islands. He named Antigua, '*Santa Maria de la Antigua*,' after the painting of the Virgin Mary in the Seville Cathedral.

Dominica, Martinique, St Lucia, St Vincent and Grenada are commonly called the Windward Islands because they are closer to the prevailing easterly winds than the Leeward Islands, which are further west. The Leeward Islands include; the Virgin Islands, St Kitts, Nevis, Antigua, Montserrat, Guadeloupe and Iles Des Saintes.

Besides location, the island groups are different in other ways. The Windward Islands, for example, are more mountainous, volcanic in origin and very picturesque. Climatically they are warm and wet, receiving much heavier rainfall than the Leeward Islands. The north-eastern or windward side of the windward islands are drenched with rains and

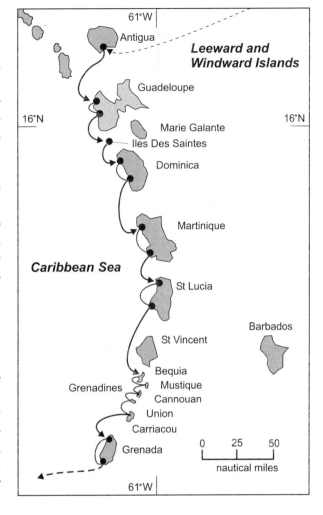

heavily wooded, making them almost uninhabitable. The population is therefore concentrated on the drier, sheltered western sides.

I have always wondered why Columbus named the Caribbean Islands the West Indies, when in fact they are nowhere near India. This embarrassing blunder occurred because Columbus thought he had discovered India, the land of spices and gold for which the Spanish were searching. Despite the significance of his journeys, Columbus never realised he had discovered a New World, but always thought they were islands off the coast of East Asia. It is a consequence of his geographical disorientation that these people are called *West Indians*. At the time there were two measurements for the circumference of the Earth - Eratosthenes of Alexandria (24,000 miles), and Strabo (18,000 miles). Columbus believed the smaller and less accurate figure, and consequently he was 6,000 miles short of Cathay. In fact, he was lucky the American continent was in between to break his journey.

After Columbus' discoveries the Spaniards quickly occupied these islands, and they remained a Spanish preserve throughout the sixteenth century. The British,

French, Dutch and Danish interlopers followed later, as their might and influence in Europe increased.

Our time in the Caribbean turns into a *'flying visit'* to over 20 of these islands in four months. We explore most of the islands from Antigua to Grenada, together with the Dutch ABC's and San Blas islands before reaching the Panama Canal.

Sugar: As the Caribbean developed, so sugar became its white gold. In 1674 Sir Christopher Codrington established the first commercial sugar plantation on Antigua. Its success was soon followed by others and, at its height, there were 150 profitable sugar mills dotted around Antigua. The sugar production was labour intensive, because the sugar cane had to be crushed immediately after cutting to prevent it being spoilt, and the plantations had to be large scale to warrant the cost of having a crushing mill on site. The sugar industry was supported by cheap slave labour from Africa, and protective tariffs in England which maintained a high sugar price. The sugar industry eventually went into decline when its three protective pillars were removed: slavery was abolished in Britain in 1834 (France in 1848), sugar beet started to be grown in Europe, and the sugar markets were opened up to free trade. This, in turn, caused the sugar price to plummet, which precipitated the collapse of the sugar estates in the Caribbean.

Slavery brought about 10 million Africans to the Americas - about 4 million to the Caribbean Islands alone. A shipping triangle was established where ships would leave Britain with trinkets and muskets to barter for slaves in Africa. The slaves were then taken to the new world, and the ships would return to England loaded with sugar, molasses and rum.

Forts: The sugar crop made the Caribbean Islands, in general, and Antigua in particular, a very valuable country. It is hard to believe today that Antigua was considered more valuable to Britain than its 13 North American colonies, together with Canada and India. This white gold was subsequently to lead to the imperial wars of the late 17th and 18th centuries - for this reason the islands are dotted with strategically positioned forts.

Caribbean post card of the traditional sugar cane cutters

The English built two naval bases in the Caribbean; Port Royal in Jamaica and English Harbour in Antigua. Antigua was the centre of the British colonial administration for the Leeward Islands, ranging from the British Virgin Islands (BVI's) in the west to Dominica in the south. And English Harbour, with its naturally protected anchorage, became the dockyard for the British Navy and the head quarters of the British East Caribbean fleet. Here they were able to maintain their ships near their area of naval operation. While the French, on the other hand, preferred to send their ships back to France for repair and maintenance during the hurricane season.

27th December (Monday) - English Harbour: What a beautifully calm and peaceful morning to make our landfall. As the sun rises we cautiously enter English Harbour, which is packed solid with yachts. We look for an empty space to drop our hook. We have completed our first ocean crossing in 26 days. It is now time to celebrate. I note in the log book: *07:00 safely anchored in English Harbour.* As we look around we see golden sandy beaches fringed by gently swaying palm trees. We cannot believe the tranquillity after all the constant motion across the Atlantic.

After covering the mainsail and bagging the genoa we relax in the cockpit. A great feeling of contentment and personal satisfaction swells over us, although it is not something to shout about because all the other cruisers in the anchorage have also sailed across the Atlantic. I look around the boat at all the equipment that has functioned well. Once we left port the self-steering did all the work. I have read about people having to hand-steer across the oceans. The Hiscocks in Wanderer III actually hand-steered all the way round the world. I am so pleased with our self-steering that I lean over and kiss it - others may kiss the ground, but I feel the self-steering is healthier and also it is more accessible at the time!

Squall: With our Avon Redcrest dinghy inflated and launched, we are about to fit the 2 hp Suzuki outboard when we notice a squall rolling down the hillside, so we decide to wait until it passes. The rain is a pleasant relief in the humid conditions so we sit in the cockpit and let the rain run down our faces. But our tranquillity is suddenly shattered by a strong gust of wind which surprisingly picks up the dinghy and throws it into our Aerogen wind generator. In horror we watch broken blades go flying in different directions as the dinghy gives a whoosh and collapses. Stunned, this is not the Caribbean welcome we were expecting, we stare at the remains of the dinghy and wind generator in disbelief. The dinghy is cut in half and only two blades are left on the wind generator which looks like a boxer after his teeth have been knocked out.

What else can we do but forget about going ashore and have a very early sundowner and sleep. The following day is spent patching the dinghy and finally we go ashore on the third day.

29th December (Wednesday) - Mail: After checking-in with the authorities who are conveniently placed in Nelson's Dockyard we go straight to the *poste restante* to collect our mail. *"What's your name?"* the lady asks at the post office. *"Burke."* "Oh yes there are three letters for you."* Surprisingly the postmistress prides herself on knowing the names on all the letters and how many there are for each person - what a great service. Can you imagine the Royal Mail doing that?!

After changing our money we go in search of fresh fruit and vegetables, *'Tinned everything'* was taking its toll on us. Is this the start of the dreaded scurvy, or lead poisoning? Shocked at the prices, which are typically a £1 a lb, and poor quality - a medium sized cabbage, for example costs £4, four times the UK price - we buy only what we need for dinner tonight.

Nelson's Dockyard is named after the great man himself - Lord Nelson who commanded HMS *Boreas* in this area of the Caribbean. He also watered his ships here in 1805 before continuing his transatlantic search for Admiral Villeneuve and

Rory in front of Nelson's dockyard

the French fleet. He finally found them and the Spanish fleet in Cadiz, which shortly afterwards lead to the historic Battle of Trafalgar.

Nelson's Dockyard has been restored to its original condition to become one of Antigua's main tourist attractions. There are a number of historical museums interspersed between the bakery, the rigger's workshop and the sail loft. I remember seeing a photograph of the Hiscocks laying out their sails in an unused building - it is now a thriving restaurant. The renovated facades give an aura of history about the place.

31st December (Friday) - New Year's Eve: It is happy hour - *"Twofors"* - from 20:00 to 22:00 at the Copper and Lumber Store (now a pub). Like bees to a honey pot all the yachties appear to catch up on the latest gossip. By 23:00 we are both worn out - we have been drinking copiously, talking verbosely, and dancing energetically. As we leave the dinghy dock to go back to *Pacific Voyager* others are just arriving for the action. Bob on *Emma Louise* arrives with his family. We all watch in amazement as a drunk Frenchman climbs into Bob's dinghy and tries to start the outboard. Bob cannot believe his dinghy is being stolen before his very own eyes. Pat, his wife, restrains him *"It's okay he's drunk."* The Frenchman tries another dinghy and, as he climbs over he falls head first over the side. As we all rush forward to help what we fear is a drowning man - he miraculously stands up - the water is only two foot deep!! Back on board we battle to stay awake until midnight to see the harbour light up with fireworks.

2nd January (Sunday) - Steel Band: One of the highlights of English Harbour on a Sunday afternoon is to visit Shirley Heights and be entertained by a local steel band. Walking up the 1000 foot hill is quite a strain on the calf muscles after 26 immobile days at sea. However, the rhythm of the steel band's reggae and the outstanding views make the effort worthwhile. It is amazing what they can do with a few old oil drums. The steel drum, called a pan, is a uniquely Trinidadian invention. It has its origins in the 1940s when aspiring musicians took discarded oil drums and hammered out the bottoms. Meanwhile in Jamaica, reggae was being derived from a blend of ska, blues, calypso and rock.

Shirley Heights: The construction of the fortifications overlooking English Harbour began in 1781 under General Sir Thomas Shirley, who was governor of the Leeward Islands. The fortifications at Shirley Heights consisted of a blockhouse, barracks, magazines, stables, cisterns, platform

Steel band at Shirley Heights - Anyone for Reggae?

for four cannons on the gun emplacements and ordnance buildings - these are now a restaurant. In those days, there must have been a feeling of anticipation with the gun batteries of Fort Berkeley and Fort Shirley strategically positioned to protect the harbour from a surprise attack by the French.

3rd January (Monday) - Caribs: Our evening stroll along Galleon Beach ends up in a tropical-looking bar for a beer. The barman who is a Carib tells us he is not happy about the Europeans invading the islands. Sandra whispers in my ear *"He must have forgotten it was originally the Caribs who invaded the Arawaks."*

The Caribbean was originally settled by the Arawaks 2000 years ago - they comprised of a group of South American tribes migrating north from the Orinoco

basin. They were a well-organised, artistic, gentle and peaceful society. The men fished, hunted and farmed, while the artistic women made red clay pots, which they often engraved.

Classic view from Shirley Heights overlooking English Harbour

The Caribs arrived much later - about 1200 AD. They were warring tribes also from South America and also migrated up through the islands. They drove off or killed the Arawak men and enslaved the Arawak women, reputedly eating the flesh of their victims. The Caribs call themselves *'Kalinas'*, which evolved through Spanish, French and English into the present day name - *'Carib.'* Interestingly the word *'cannibal'* is derived from *'caribal'* or *'Carib.'* The Caribs were hunters and gatherers who defended their lands and kept the Europeans at bay for more than a century.

4th January (Tuesday) - Green Flash: We are invited to a cottage on Galleon's Beach to have a sundowner and see the green flash. *"The what???"* I ask. We have never heard of such a thing but, sure enough, as the sun dips below the horizon, there is a green flash. *"Wow, that's worth another drink*!!!"

Apparently the green flash has been known about for years - Jules Verne in 1882 refers to it in his book *Le Rayon-Vert*. The physics of this phenomena are quite straight forward. The rising or setting sun appears as a spectrum of light from red and yellow to blue and green. The red sun disappears first, followed by its refracted or bent rays. The yellows and orange are absorbed by the ozone and vanish. The blues, indigos and violets should be last, but they get scattered by the atmosphere (one of the reasons the sky is blue, otherwise we would see a blue flash). So the last piece of colour from the sun that is seen is the surviving emerald green - the green flash. The elusive green flash is so seldom seen that it creates a mystic curiosity. There are plenty of limiting factors: the conditions must be clear, with no cloud on the horizon - smoke or haze will stop the event in its tracks. And to be alert is vital because the green flash only lasts a fraction of a second - one blink of an eye lid and it will be missed.

There is an old Scottish legend - someone who has seen the green flash is incapable of being deceived. It enables them to see closely into their own heart and to read the thoughts of others - a bottle of Scotch probably helps as well.

Departure: After two weeks in Antigua recovering from our Atlantic crossing we feel it is time to move on to the next island - Guadeloupe. There is much to explore and experience, and little time if we are to catch the tradewinds and weather window in the Pacific.

Further Reading:

Marshall, Michael., *A Cruising Guide to the Caribbean*
Time Life International, *Recipes - The Cooking of the Caribbean Islands*

14 *Guadeloupe and Iles des Saintes*

The Caribbean Islands are conveniently spaced for day hops, with fresh easterly winds between the islands to fill our sails. There are plenty of sheltered bays and anchorages on the western side of the islands to protect us from the prevailing winds and ocean swells. Our plan is to port hop down the Leeward and Windward Islands from Antigua to Grenada.

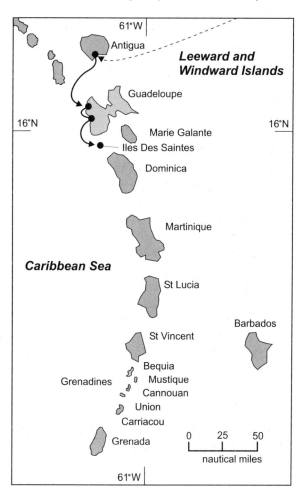

9th January (Sunday): Our so called early start - we are up at 06:15, but it takes over two hours to pack everything away - finally departing at 08:30. After stopping for just two weeks in Antigua the log has fouled up again, so we look to the GPS for our speed. Halfway across, a school of pilot whales accompany us for a wonderful five minutes. They must be looking at us watching them as they keep station. They are close enough for us to clearly distinguish their round noses. With a good 20 knots of wind all the way across, we sail into Deshaies Bay at 16:00, and anchor near the beach in 4.4 metres of water.

Deshaies is a very attractive bay frequented by many of the cruising yachts sailing between the islands. Scanning the shore with our 12x50 binoculars we notice an outstanding church surrounded by French colonial style cottages, tempting us to go ashore and explore, but it will have to wait for morning. We opt for a quiet night on-board.

Guadeloupe postcard of a local shop

Guadeloupe was named by Columbus in 1493. Prior to his voyage of exploration he had made a pilgrimage to the monastery in Estremadura in Spain, where he had spent a long time praying in front of the statue of the Virgin of Guadeloupe. The monks asked him to name an island after their monastery.

It is hard to believe that in 1763, at the Treaty of Paris, France relinquished its claims to its provinces in Canada for butterfly-shaped Guadeloupe. But that was when the sugar industry in the Caribbean was thriving, and Canada was considered a cold expanse of dense forest.

10th January (Monday): There are rain showers in the morning so I catch up with some items on my endless list of jobs. Sandra has been pestering me to fix the galley spot light's corroded switch. I hot wire the connection and switch it separately. In the afternoon the weather has improved so we launch the dinghy and motor ashore. As we pull our dinghy up the beach we are surprised to find a water tap conveniently positioned, supplying mountain fresh water of much better quality than Antigua, and it is free.

After leaving the officialdom of Antigua we welcome the laissez-faire approach of Guadeloupe. The customs office consists of an unlocked room where we can help ourselves to a declaration form and fill it in if we want to. There is no one to help us because the French obviously place no importance on this bureaucracy, although they appreciate that other Caribbean islands do.

It is only when we come ashore that we realise how lush and green the vegetation really is, much more so than Antigua which is only 50 miles away. This must be because of the higher mountains, a feature usually associated with the Windward Islands. Besides having good drinking water, the French islands also make excellent French bread (or baguettes) for five francs (US $1 = 5 fr.), which we buy by the armful. Unable to resist, I discretely start nibbling at them. Back on board, we eat what is left with cheese and Spanish wine.

After a wine-induced kip, we motor over to our neighbour, Paul on *Albatross*, and interview him for our book. He has been cruising the Caribbean for years. With all the newer yachts bristling with electronics, it is refreshing to meet Paul who can survive with only a few basic instruments. *"If my log fails I can still tell if I am doing a 100 or 120 miles a day, quite accurately."* As a German, Paul says he has no problem swapping books written in English, but the war books are depressing because the Germans are always losing!!!

13th January (Thursday): Off again, but this time we sail close to the coast to marvel at the colourful Caribbean houses dotted amongst the prolific tropical vegetation. Although the west coast is protected from the easterly tradewinds, some sneaky squalls still manage to worm their way through and hurtle down the ravines. One 40 knot squall catches us as we approach our next anchorage. Over canvassed, spilling wind, we hold on as we tack towards the anchorage. These conditions remind us of the Canaries, but with such dense vegetation we would have expected the gusts to have been less severe.

14th January (Friday) - Pigeon Island: The first snorkelling adventure of our trip is at Jacques Cousteau's marine sanctuary around Pigeon Island. Full of expectation, we take our dinghy and motor the short distance to Pigeon Island and find a protected cove to snorkel around. Initially we are more concerned about our snorkelling techniques than to notice the tropical fish swimming with us, and the 26 different types of coral they have catalogued here. But, as our confidence develops, so we can marvel at the beauty of this undersea world.

Jacques Cousteau is well known for his underwater marine programmes, but he should also be acknowledged for co-inventing the scuba gear; the self-contained underwater breathing apparatus that allows divers to explore the hidden underwater world.

When we come to leave, our grapnel anchor has fouled a rock. Fortunately we are only in 3 metres of water so we can retrieve it by hand, but it makes me think a house brick, or a rock, would have been a better throw away anchor.

As we motor back to *Pacific Voyager* in our dinghy, we pass a man standing on his transom signalling for a lift ashore. His dinghy has been stolen so many times that he now swims out to his anchored boat with his clothes wrapped in a plastic bag. We take him ashore, then stroll along the beach, and buy some tasty looking doughnuts to eat later. *Emma Louise* sails into the anchorage and joins us for an afternoon Caribbean tea. Instead of tea we have rum punches with the fresh doughnuts.

15th January (Saturday): Kim and Jane on *Rival Chief* (a Rival 34), sail into the anchorage in the late afternoon and invite us over for dinner. Jane rows over to collect us as we have packed our dinghy away in preparation for

Caribbean sailing - ready for another squall

an early start tomorrow. Jane used to row for Cambridge University so we are in good hands. Kim is a qualified surveyor and, over dinner, he tells us about his final year university project, developing astrological tables. Kim feels it would be quite straight forward to publish a 50 year nautical almanac. I hope he does it soon because to buy the almanac every year is expensive. Kim balances his job and lifestyle, by surveying in the North Sea during the northern hemisphere summer, then sailing in the South Pacific during the southern hemisphere summer. (We often read about Kim's exploits in Yachting Monthly).

Braai on the beach with Kim and Jane (*Rival Chief*)

16th January (Sunday) - Iles des Saintes: As we approach the narrow channel between Guadeloupe and the Saints, the wind increases to a boisterous 35 knots - on the nose of course. Unable to make a direct course we have to put in a few exciting tacks. The seas have built up to a cheeky, short, steep chop - this is Caribbean sailing at its most exhilarating. As I helm in the open cockpit, getting soaked from the continuous spray which dries off just-in-time for the next dousing, I am left with a salt crust on my face which cracks every time I blink. We experience additional excitement as a breaking wave catches the bow and washes the anchor locker lid overboard. Okay, so I should have clamped it down, but at least it is tied on.

Naval Battle: Iles Des Saintes is well remembered by the British for Rodney's battle with the French in 1782. This was when the British fleet of 35 ships of the line first used the tactic of breaking the French line of battle. This tactic was successfully used again by Nelson at Trafalgar in 1805.

We anchor in a small sheltered bay below Fort Josephine. In the evening its braai (BBQ) time on the beach with Kim and Jane *(Rival Chief)*. Away from the crowds on a calm, warm, balmy evening, we feel at one with nature - this is what life is about.

Inside Fort Josephine

Panoramic view from Fort Josephine

Commanding view from Fort Napoleon   **The moat of Fort Napoleon**

The sound of the surf can be heard gently breaking on the beach, followed by the tinkering of stones as the water runs back. This is a one of those idyllic anchorages we often dream about.

17th January (Monday): After breakfast, a group of us gather on the beach to scramble up the hillside to Fort Josephine. The fort is derelict, but there are panoramic views over the bays and we can see another fort on the main island, appropriately named, Fort Napoleon. How romantic to have Fort Josephine and Fort Napoleon facing each other - only the French would do that.

18th January (Tuesday): Sail over to the main port, Bourg des Saintes, to buy some very expensive provisions. The town was originally settled by French fisherman who built their small cottages, which are now painted white with red roofs, trimmed with pastel painted ginger-bread type carvings. The cottages are surrounded by gardens of brilliantly colourful flowering plants - like a chocolate box setting - just waiting to be photographed.

In the heat of the midday sun we hike up the hill to Fort Napoleon, which was built in the mid 19th century, and also has commanding views of the approaches. The two forts are strategically positioned to place any attacking force at a distinct disadvantage.

19th January (Wednesday): With an early start we sail between the mountainous islands which are covered in a thick lush forest. We are surprised to see a scar on the side of an otherwise beautiful landscape. Looking through the binoculars we are shocked to see it is a rubbish tip. *"You won't believe the rubbish we took ashore yesterday, is being dumped right back in the sea again!!!"* As we make our way to Dominica, our parting sight of Iles des Saintes are white fridges, black tyres, and a rainbow of coloured plastic bags.

Further Reading:

Marshall, Michael., *A Cruising Guide to the Caribbean*
www.caribbean-beat.com

15 Dominica

Dominica is the first of the Windward Islands. The islands are coming thick and fast now. We have not read up on Dominica other than to identify we should make for Prince Rupert Bay in the north of the island and expect to be welcomed by some boat boys.

19th January (Wednesday): And, sure enough, after a robust sail to Dominica as we approach Prince Rupert Bay we encounter our first experience with the infamous *Boat Boys*. They have two settings on their 40 hp outboards, tick over and full wick - so they are either stopped dead in their tracks or racing to their next destination. They race everywhere - race out to meet us and engage business - race to buy fruit and vegetables for us - then race back to our yacht. This must be the height of free enterprise and customer service. The boat boys probably get better prices for fruit and vegetables as they have all the contacts ashore, so it is almost compulsory to use them. Our boat boy is called Jack and he is very helpful and polite - in complete contrast to the boat boys' reputation.

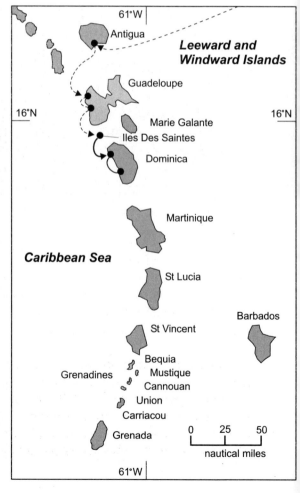

In fact Dominica is a misunderstood country. As a tourist destination it is poorly marketed internationally, consequently it has one of the least developed tourist industries in the Caribbean. But for those who make the effort to come here, this is an island bequeathed by nature with a rich, aesthetically enchanting geographical legacy, making it an ideal destination for the eco-tourist.

Dominica has towering green mountains, covered in dense tropical forests, deep valleys and countless streams, providing magnificent scenic views. Agriculture is the mainstay of the island's economy with bananas being the main crop, followed by coconuts.

Fort Shirley: In the late afternoon we motor over in our dinghy to explore Fort Shirley which guards the north entrance to Prince Rupert Bay. When the 1763 Treaty of Paris transferred Dominica to the UK, the British engineers were quick to build up their defences and naval facilities. The fort was built to protect the Royal Navy when they anchored to collect fresh water from the Indian River. Dominica was subsequently recaptured by the French, but lost again to Britain after the Battle of the Saintes and the Treaty of Versailles. The last British garrison abandoned the fort in 1854 and left it to the

Fort Shirley guarding Prince Rupert Bay

mercy of the luxuriant forest which quickly spread and engulfed the massive walls and ramparts cut from volcanic rock.

From 1983, a small team of masons and woodcutters worked for ten years to recapture the fortress from the forest and turn the area into an open air museum. The military complex locked in the forest, consists of seven batteries, seven cisterns, powder magazines, ordinance storehouses, officers' quarters and barracks for 500 men.

Looking down from the parapet we can see the newly built visitors centre and quay where the cruise ships berth. They have been constructed on the site of the old military jetty and dockyard. It is a somewhat artificial arrangement away from the local town (Portsmouth) which is completely run down. When the cruise ships dock the passengers walk from their ship directly to Fort Shirley - have a look around - then buy tee-shirts and gifts before sailing off to the next port.

20th January (Thursday) - Indian River: We employ Jack to take us up the Indian River for EC $20 - we could have taken our own dinghy, but we felt this is one of his perks. Jack collects us in his boat and slowly motors to the mouth of the Indian River. To our surprise and pleasure he turns off the outboard and quietly rows the rest of the way up the river. We enter a tunnel of greenery formed by the overhanging vegetation and their reflections; it is quiet and peaceful under its canopy. The trunks of the tall swamp bloodwood trees rise out of the shallow river, and the giant bwa mang trees arch overhead displaying their sculptured buttresses growing along the water's edge.

We feel close to raw primordial nature as we catch glimpses of green herons and kingfishers hunting for fish, together with hummingbirds, red-necked pigeons and egrets - not to mention the vast number of red fresh-water crabs crawling along the river banks.

This used to be the main highway for the Caribs travelling from their villages to the sea, but now it seems to be used exclusively by the tourists. The river meanders through swamps and marsh lands before silently entering a clearing where we disembark and wander around a plantation. Jack encourages us to pick bananas, grapefruit and breadfruit. After several hours we return to *Pacific Voyager* laden with *'fruits of the Caribbean.'*

Banana Boat: A cargo ship anchors in the middle of the bay, it is here to collect bananas. Soon large green stalks of bananas start appearing on the shore, ready to be transported by lighter to the cargo ship. This should keep the boat boys busy for a couple of days.

Bananas form the backbone of Dominica's economy. They were first introduced to the Caribbean by the Spanish who brought them over from Indonesia. As the demand for

Left: Rory, his rucksack laden with fruit from the orchard

Below: Jack rows us up the Indian River

Caribbean sugar declined, so the plantations were used to grow bananas. We are advised that a bright yellow banana might look appealing, but it will taste much better when it has a light sprinkling of brown speckles on its skin. The speckles are a sign of ripeness and not a sign the fruit is going off. It is best to allow bananas to ripen at room temperature, never in the refrigerator. A sprinkling of lemon juice will stop the banana from *browning* after peeling and slicing.

A Boat Boy carrying Dominica's yellow gold - from a tourist brochure

Anchorage Hotel: Continue sailing down the coast - we reach the Anchorage Hotel by late afternoon. *"I wonder if we'll be approached by the boat boys, or have they knocked off for the day?"* No sooner had I spoken, than they are racing out to us at full wick. They offer to take our line ashore and tie it to a tree so that we can moor stern-to. For this service they want EC $10. However, our latest guide book says it will be EC $5, so we tell them and they immediately reduce their rate to EC $5. (We are not sure if we incurred their wrath, because as we pull in the stern rope when we are leaving there is a porcupine spine poking through the rope. Fortunately I notice it before impaling myself).

21st January (Friday) - Trafalgar Falls: Join a few other cruisers from the Anchorage Hotel for a trip to the Trafalgar Falls. As we enter the bus, we confirm with the driver that the price will be EC $20 each, but halfway along the driver tries his luck and decides he is a taxi and now wants to charge US $20 each. With safety in our numbers, he sensibly backs down. However, his driving is not so sensible - driving like the clappers he continuously overtakes on blind corners as the narrow road zigzags its way up through the hills, flanked by dizzy drops into emerald-coated valleys below.

Anchorage Hotel - *Pacific Voyager* **moored stern-to on the narrow shelf**

Left: Rory relaxing at Trafalgar Falls
Above: Shopping at the Roseau market

The mountain peaks are cloaked in cloud most of the time, which makes rain a near certainty. Dominica's mountains are covered by a true rain forest which forms one of the finest examples of a prime oceanic rainforest in the Western Hemisphere. All this daily rain forms gentle streams, which combine forces to create larger rivers and hanging waterfalls, that hurtle over cliff edges and thunder into the valleys below.

Access to Dominica's hidden secret is finally traversed by a footpath which cuts through the thick, green, sub-tropical vegetation. The path is bordered by ferns, flowering ginger, lilies, orchids, and a canopy of trees and vines which filter the sunlight and turn the clearings into lush green townships. It is a short steep walk, through the rain forest, scrambling over the bolder strewn ravines to the waterfall. Trafalgar Falls and the hot water pools are conveniently located for alternate dipping. As we bath in a cascade of hot sulphur water we give ourselves up to Trafalgar's medical powers.

22nd January (Saturday) - Roseau: Take a bus from the Anchorage Hotel into Roseau, the capital. Roseau's market offers excellent value for their locally grown fruits and vegetables, particularly bananas and grapefruits. We even buy a whole stalk of bananas for less than a pound. While we are in the market, no sooner have I turned my back and Sandra gets accosted by a dirty old bugger who tries to kiss her. The local people are extremely embarrassed and angry by this and shoo him off. A local girl then escorts Sandra around the market and organises even better prices, and some extra juicy papayas.

Walking back from the market we stop at a local cafe to quench our thirst. Sandra chats to a group of young people sitting next to us. It is interesting to hear

Left: Dominica's youth chat to us about their future on the island

Below: Local bus - decorated Caribbean style

their thoughts about life, and what work they hope to do in Dominica. The country's future is, after all, in their hands.

On the bus back to the Anchorage Hotel we are crammed in like sardines with reggae blaring in our ears, but for EC $1 we cannot complain. I have a case of rum on my knee, so it will be rum punches all round for sundowners, as we watch for the green flash.

23rd January (Sunday):
Back in Roseau we watch the locals playing the national game of cricket in the central park - these are budding Windies in the making. We then stroll through the botanical gardens and cannot resist taking a photograph of this flamboyantly decorated bus. This symbolises the typical Caribbean way of expression.

For our last evening in Dominica we invite our neighbours, Helen and Neil (*Alexandra Louise*), over for a rum sundowner. Now that we have a case of it we can afford to be generous. They have sailed over with the ARC and are now meeting the NARC's!!! The NARCs are the non-ARCs, and they only have one rule - there are no rules!

Further Reading:

Shepard, Reba., *Banana Cookbook*
Marshall, Michael., *A Cruising Guide to the Caribbean*

Martinique

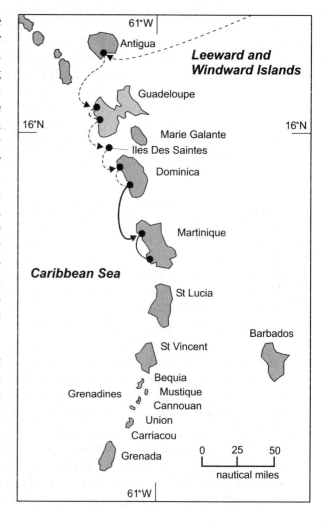

Log book: chart 371, Martinique (scale 1:79,700). After another robust inter-island sail, Martinique's dominating volcano, Mt. Pelle at 4430 feet, guides us in. Columbus made his landfall at Martinique in 1502, but it was not settled by the French until 1675. It was later captured by the British in 1762, but then exchanged with Guadeloupe for the French provinces in Canada at the Treaty of Paris. Empress *'Not Tonight Josephine'* was born here in 1763. After Guadeloupe and Iles des Saintes, Martinique is the third of the French islands we visit in the Caribbean.

Saint Pierre: Anchor off Saint Pierre, then row ashore. It is not a very attractive town, although there are colourful bougainvillaeas galore, with palms and shrubs lining the esplanade. We visit the old prison where a black slave miraculously survived the 1902

Leeward and Windward Islands map labels:
61°W
Antigua
Guadeloupe
16°N
Marie Galante
Iles Des Saintes
Dominica
Martinique
Caribbean Sea
St Lucia
Barbados
St Vincent
Bequia
Grenadines
Mustique
Cannouan
Union
Carriacou
Grenada
0   25   50
nautical miles
61°W

Above: Saint-Pierre is not a very attractive town
Left: Rory sleeps while Sandra visits the Gauguin museum

volcanic eruption, and also visit Gauguin's Museum of Art (little did we know that we would later visit the islands in the Marquesas that influenced many of his impressionist paintings).

Although the volcano looks peaceful now, in 1902 it violently spewed out incandescent gas, hot ash, and lava which overwhelmed the local town of Saint Pierre below it, killing 40,000 people. The Caribbean Islands are mostly of volcanic origin, which has been evident recently with eruptions at Soufriere (1979) and Montserrat (1997).

24th January (Monday): Sailing South, we pass Fort de France which looks a bit over crowded and too busy for us, however, the next bay, Grand Anse Bay, looks like a more peaceful setting. Feeling energetic we row ashore in our dinghy and lock the Avon to the quay. Feeling even more energetic we walk round the town and over the headland to the next bay - Petite Anse d'Arlet. It is all very pretty with picturesque market stalls, quaint brick houses and shutter-type wood panelling, quaker style. Dark clouds give us a few minutes warning to find cover - then, whoosh, a rain squall buckets down. And, as quickly as it comes, it goes.

At the dock we prepare to row back to *Pacific Voyager*, but I cannot unlock the padlock which is securing the dinghy to the quay. I struggle with the lock for over five minutes, cursing myself for putting us in this annoying situation. When another dinghy comes ashore, Sandra, in her best French, asks the Swiss owner of the dinghy if he would please take her out to our yacht to get an adjustable spanner so that we can slacken off the bull dog clips securing the lock.

The Swiss chap willingly takes Sandra to our boat and she returns a few minutes later with the spanner in hand. Sandra returns the keys so I try the lock just on the off chance - IT OPENS ! *"Don't let him see it,"* Sandra pleads. I wait a few moments, then cast off. Thinking the excitement is over for today I take in the views as Sandra

The quaint houses in picturesque Petit Anse d'Arlet

rows. But something is not quite right - our boat does not seem to be where I am expecting to see it. I check my bearings, perhaps I am disorientated, but no. *"I'm sure we were nearer that yacht. We seem to have moved."* As we get closer I am now convinced we have dragged and what is more, *"Our anchor buoy's missing."* I can see the concern rise on Sandra's face as she rows a little quicker. Back on board, I look around, *"Hey Sandra we're ADRIFT."* Fortunately it is calm, otherwise *Pacific Voyager* would have been well on her way to Panama by now. Although we have 30 metres of chain out in 8 meters of water, the squall that passed over an hour ago has dragged *Pacific Voyager* into deep water and the anchor chain is hanging vertically off the bow.

Pulling the anchor up is quite a strain with all our chain hanging vertically off the bow. Eventually, with the anchor up, we motor around the headland and anchor for the night off Petite Anse d'Arlet in 4 metres, with 20 metres of chain out at 5:1 ratio, just to be on the safe side. This is a lovely spot which prompts Sandra into an artistic frenzy; out come her art materials from their airtight waterproof Tupperware containers. They have not seen the light of day since Dittisham.

Sandra sketching the church and the rainbow at Petite Anse d'Arlet

It is a spectacular evening as we settle down in the cockpit with a sundowner to watch the sun's shimmering disk kiss the glassy surface of the sea. As darkness descends on us, the early evening street lights create smooth amber reflections which bounce across the water towards us. As a side show, fish spring into life jumping in and out of the water in a mad frenzy. We listen to Donovan singing *Catch the Wind*. As the moon rises it sends beams of light shimmering and dancing across the water, creating a marble like floor over the calm anchorage. It is all so heavenly tranquil.

26th January (Tuesday) - Diamond Rock: Away by 07:30, our earliest so far in the Caribbean. As we leave Martinique we sail past Diamond Rock, which at 176 metres high is a haven for sea birds. The weather is settled so we are able to safely get in close and marvel at the tenacity of the 120 British marines who in 1804 (one year before the battle of Trafalgar), hauled a cannon and equipment up an almost vertical rock face, and called it HMS 'Diamond Rock.' For 17

Pacific Voyager **sails close to HMS** *Diamond Rock* **as we leave Martinique**

months they caused havoc with the French shipping trying to navigate the inside passage to Fort de France. Eventually the French found a weak link - they cut loose a skiff loaded with rum. Unable to resist, the British sailors captured the rum and that night got completely drunk, which allowed the French to retake the rock.

As Martinique fades into the distance our breakfast on the run consists of baguettes and cheese - delicious - as we munch our way to St Lucia.

Further Reading:

Marshall, Michael., *A Cruising Guide to the Caribbean*, Adlard Coles

17 St Lucia

St Lucia receives frequent coverage in the yachting magazines because the ARC finishes their trans-Atlantic rally at the Rodney Bay marina. We are intrigued to see why the ARC moved here from Barbados.

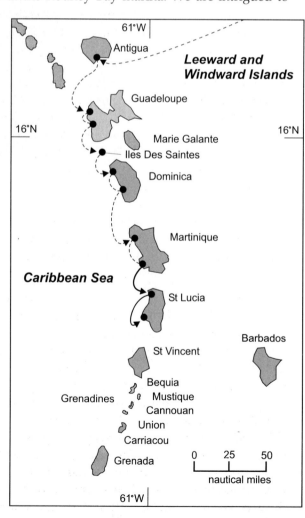

St Lucia (Helen of the West): As we sail into Rodney Bay we spot the orange and yellow hull of *Aethelwyn*. We have not seen them since Cadiz. "*Ahoy Aethelwyn.*" Tony explains the layout of the inner harbour, where we should anchor and where we should check-in. The entrance fee costs EC $30 (about £7) which is not too bad, but the custom officer copies the details from the ship's papers letter by letter - this takes forever (I should have fallen asleep as I did in M'diq).

The Rodney Bay anchorage is overlooked by, yet another, **Pigeon Island**, the 17th century haunt of pirates and largest bay on the island. In 1782 the bay harboured Admiral Rodney's fleet which defeated Admiral de Grasse at the battle of the Saintes, and cost the French the Caribbean. Ashore there are remnants of the old British

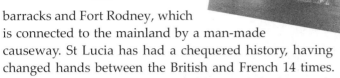

barracks and Fort Rodney, which is connected to the mainland by a man-made causeway. St Lucia has had a chequered history, having changed hands between the British and French 14 times.

LPG: After checking-in we walk round the marina facilities to see what else is available. Since our memorable snorkelling experience at Jacques Cousteau's Marine Sanctuary we feel we need better snorkelling equipment, but the prices here are twice the Westmarine catalogue price, which is off-putting. We decide to just buy propane.

The propane refilling station is conveniently located beside the marina. First thing in the morning we drop our gas bottles off, and collect them after they have been filled in the afternoon. I am not sure if we caught the staff on a particularly bad day, but they have a very unpleasant attitude and, when Sandra questions why they have over-filled our bottles in a hot climate (something Calor Gas strongly recommends against in their booklet), they tell Sandra, *"You're wasting our time!!"* A week later, when I change the gas bottle, we have a strange problem. When I connect the bottle and press the gas knob a strong hiss of gas comes out. I switch it off but the hiss continues. I notice when I turn the gas off at the bottle, the pressure in the pipe actually increases!!! After what seems like a very long time (in reality only a few seconds) the gas runs out. Perhaps some of the liquid gas got into the line and expanded?

Sadly, contrary to the ARC's survey, we find the people working in Rodney Bay marina are quite indifferent to the tourists. Dominica, with the least developed tourist industry, has been the friendliest Caribbean Island so far.

27th January (Thursday) - Wedding: Feeling energetic we walk along the headland on the north side of the bay to the Pigeon Island National Park. The ruins of old fortifications remind us of the importance of these islands in years gone by. A European couple are having their wedding photographs taken in typical wedding poses amongst the tropical surroundings. She is dressed in white, he is wearing a morning suit, there is a horse and carriage, a best man, a photographer - but no one else - no relations, no friends, no screaming kids. *"Where are your friends?"* I shout over as they are preparing for another photograph. *"They're all in England!!"* they reply. *"Would you like us to join you to make a crowd?"* They decline our generous offer! (Some months later we saw a TV programme which explained this strange but popular phenomena. The idea is, that instead of having a reception in the UK and an overseas honeymoon costing a fortune, the couple fly off to a romantic tropical island in the Caribbean, get married and have their honeymoon without the expense of a reception. But unfortunately without their family and friends).

Taking the mini-bus into town - the deafening sound of reggae pulsating every bone in our bodies

28th January (Friday) - Castries: A local mini-bus takes us into Castries, the capital of St Lucia, for EC $5 each. The driver's favourite reggae music is blasting away in our ears, the base pounding so much it actually gives my back a pulsating massage. Conversation is almost impossible, and the driving is so frightening that even Evil Knevil would have been concerned. When we arrive safely at Castries, and ease ourselves out of the bus, we thank God for organising the traffic so that the driver could overtake on blind corners - I can understand now why the Pope kisses the ground.

Caribbean drivers tend to either drive dangerously fast or dangerously slow. It is impossible to tell what they are thinking. For no apparent reason they may decide to switch lanes, or stop in the middle of the road to have a chat with a friend, or abruptly accelerate and overtake on the inside of a blind corner.

Many of the taxis' exhausts pump out black smoke as the engines gives their all. I dread to think about the condition of their brakes and steering. The continuous sounding of the horn is not always meant to be a warning either, it could be a joyous announcement of their presence. From their driving antics I can see they would probably do very well stock-car racing.

Cathedral: The Cathedral of the *Immaculate Conception* forms one side of Columbus Square in the old centre of Castries. The building has a sombre grey stone exterior with a faded red tin roof, but the interior reveals a joyful splurge of colour and inspiration. It surprises us to see statues of Jesus as a black person - we have been conditioned to think of him only as a white European.

Library: On the west side of the square is St Lucia's National Library, a grand old building with stately columns. It looks like a building which should contain huge amounts of knowledge and, sure enough, the library prides itself on a collection

of antique maps of the island and historical information. But we are after a UK paper to catch up on world events. Great, we find one copy of *The Economist.* This is the first international newspaper we have read since leaving Gibraltar.

Rory about to munch a pastry from the bakery in Castries

29th January (Saturday) - Breadfruit: I have always wondered what bread fruit looks and tastes like. After all, this was what HMS *Bounty* was carrying when the crew mutinied and ended up in Pitcairn. Sandra buys a large breadfruit in the market We will cook it tonight when three ex-marines; Kevin, Lev and John (*Suedama - Nicholson 32*) come over for dinner. Later, Sandra cooks the breadfruit as chips served with vegetarian sosamix burgers and Heinz tomato sauce. As the three social athletes are salivating to the smell of Sandra's tasty cooking I interview them for our cruising book.

1st February (Tuesday) - Marigot Bay: Up anchor and have an exhilarating sail down the coast, past the entrance of the main port of Castries, and past a massive oil tank farm which looks like the main supply for the Caribbean. Marigot Bay is soon upon us. It is a deep inlet with steep sides covered in lush vegetation, a classic hurricane hole. Legend says that an entire English naval fleet hid in the inner harbour from the pursuing French warships. This marine cul-de-sac is well known as the location for the 1967 film, Doctor Doolittle, which starred Rex Harrison. We anchor on the starboard side close to a palm fringed beach and a tropical looking restaurant appropriately called *Doolittles*. The inner harbour has a Moorings yacht chartering base which is always a good sign that it will be a safe port.

30th January (Sunday): In the morning a young local chap, on a broken surfboard, paddles over to sell fruit. The fruit looks precariously balanced - one wave and it could all roll off. We feel this spirit of free enterprise should be encouraged, so we buy some fruit before he loses the lot.

Later that afternoon I call to Sandra, *"We have uninvited company on board,"* - Larry the lizard. He probably arrived on the fruit we just bought. There are quite a few annoying flies buzzing around, so I swat some for Larry. I place them on top of an upturned bucket - Larry sneaks up and zaps them with his tongue at lightening speed. We video the kill, thinking we can slow it down like some wild life programme. *"I wonder if he can kill all the flies around the place???"* He must have heard me because the next time we look over, he has gone.

2nd February (Wednesday) - Dinghy Stolen: After a sundowner, followed by burger and chips at Doolittle's bar with John and Linda (Carter 39), we walk back to the dinghy dock to find their dinghy is missing. It is about eleven o'clock in the evening and very dark, almost pitch black. John organises a boat boy to motor him round the anchorage and marina to look for the dinghy. They soon find it tied to a yacht. When asked why they took the dinghy, the woman replies that, when she came to the jetty, their dinghy was missing so she assumed that John had taken hers by mistake. *"And why didn't you return it when you found your dinghy?"* The amusing side is that, as she unties John's Avon Redstart she also unties their own Avon, and the skipper, seeing his dinghy drifting away, jumps in to retrieve it.

Back on board their Carter 39, having an, *'Avon welcome back drink,'* they tell us about their trip to Soufriere. *"Be careful if you go to Soufriere - we were conned. A little child ran up to me with arms out stretched, so I automatically picked her up. The next thing I was pestered for hours by the mother to give money to look after the child."*

Sailing past the Pitons in the morning sun - shortly followed by a drenching squall

4th February (Tuesday) - Pitons: Although Soufriere Bay and the Pitons (twin peaks), sound attractive from the tourist brochures, we have now been put off by all the stories of the pestering locals. This also applies to anchoring under the Pitons (Petit Piton rising 2400 ft. and Gross Piton rising 2600 ft.), where apparently the yachts moor stern-to which will mean the boat boys will be there wanting to take the lines ashore. "*I wonder if the locals realise that when they con one tourist, they lose ten more potential paying visitors.*"

Looking at the charts we plan our next leg south to St Vincent, but St Vincent also has a reputation for pestering boat boy. "*If we leave really early we should be able to make Bequia before nightfall and miss St Vincent completely.*"

5th February (Saturday): Up really early to give us sufficient time to reach Bequia in daylight. Our parting sight of St Lucia are the impressive Pitons; first in the brilliance of the morning sun, followed only a few minutes later by a drenching during our first squall of the day.

Further Reading:

Marshall, Michael., *A Cruising Guide to the Caribbean*, Adlard Coles
Calor Gas., *LPG for the Bluewater Yachtsman*
Macmillan Press, *The Cooking of the Caribbean Islands*

18 Bequia, Mustique, Grenadines

5th February (Saturday): Log book: Imray chart, Lesser Antilles - Martinique to Trinidad. We have a really early start and pass the towering peaks of the Pitons

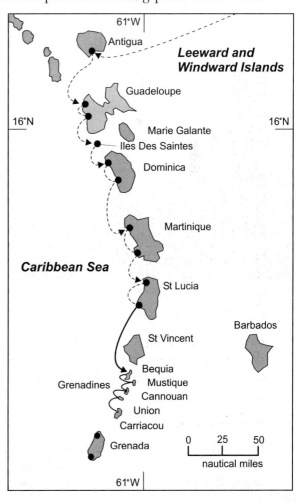

around first light as we encounter our first squall. There is good wind strength most of the way. At one point off St Vincent the wind freshens to 45 knots while we are reaching. For some reason it does not seem that strong and we are able to keep all our sails up, as we cream along. The wind drops later in the afternoon so we motor sail to keep our average speed up as we want to make Bequia before dark.

Bequia: The light is fading as we enter Admiralty Bay; another popular international yachting haven and, of course, it is packed. There is no way we can get close to the small town, so we anchor in 6 metres at the back of the fleet opposite Princess Margaret's Beach.

6th February (Sunday): After a reasonable lie-in we motor to a dinghy dock outside the gingerbread house and walk into town to check-in (fee is EC $20). The town has a relaxed atmosphere

Tough life - Rory relaxes at the dinghy dock in front of the *Gingerbread Cottage*

Sandra checking out the vegetables at the local beach-side stall

as we walk past waterfront cafes all looking very *'cafe society'*, but when we get to the small vegetable market we are put off by the expensive prices and the clouds of flies all over the produce. However, there is a hardware store where I buy a length of timber, at a reasonable price, for one of my many jobs.

Bequia is a popular destination with cruisers and tourists, as we gather from the crowded anchorage and packed cafes. This volume of boats has encouraged some enterprising entrepreneurs to market their goods and services directly to the cruisers. There is a water taxi ferrying people around, a barge supplying fresh water, a floating laundry service and even a floating vegetable shop and delicatessen. Many sailors rave about Bequia, but it is too busy for us - we prefer the quieter anchorages.

8th February (Tuesday) - Whale Island: Up anchor and sail to an abandoned whaling station at Petit Nevis. Foolishly, we tow the dinghy, which decides to flip over as we beat into 20 to 25 knots of wind. Fortunately, we are able to recover it without damaging the painter. After anchoring we row ashore to explore the old whaling station and its disused equipment. Looking at the blubber boiling pots we can visualise the work that went into whaling.

Exploring a very windy Whale Island

View from the lookout on Whale Island

In the past, when a whale was sighted from the lookouts on the coast, two, open, whaler-boats manned by six hardy men would sail or row in the direction being indicated by flashing mirror signals from the lookouts. They would come up directly behind the whale's tail, move alongside the body - then zap - in would go the harpoons mortally wounding the whale. The whale would later be towed to a small inlet where it would be cut up for food for the locals, and boiled for its oil. The stench of cooking whale meat in vast cauldrons is reported to be overpowering. The shallow water and the beach would have been a mass of huge bones. As recently as the 1960s cruisers would have seen the whalers still using the old methods of oil extraction.

9th February (Wednesday): Mustique is only a short island hop away. After a quiet sail we anchor off Basil's Bar, in Britannia Bay - another crowded anchorage. Although we are on the leeward side of the island there is a constant swell creating breaking waves on the beach - all very attractive, but will make going ashore in the dinghy a challenge.

Mustique is said to be the island of the rich and famous, so we are intrigued to visit the place where they play - names like Mick Jagger, David Bowie, Raquel Welch and Princess Margaret spring to mind. Colin Tenant (Lord Glenconner) bought the island and developed it into a very special place for relaxation and reflection. There are about 60 houses dotted around the island in picturesque locations.

Rory and a Mule but nowhere to go

10th February (Thursday): Up early to look around the island. We consider hiring the local mode of transport, called a *mule*, which looks like a golf cart, and can be hired for EC $70 a day. *"But the island is not that big, let's walk."*

As we stride along the wide verges, next to the narrow roads, everything is exceptionally clean and tidy. All the houses, gardens, roads and verges are immaculately kept; a complete contrast to the other Caribbean islands. The island is now privately owned by the Mustique Trading Company and it is their responsibility to keep the island looking pristine. There is a small airstrip for light planes flying in from Barbados. *"So this is where they land."* And the recently renovated 18th century Cotton House is now a restaurant and hotel with small guest houses.

Generally having a nosey around, we head towards Mick Jagger's house and then, would you believe it, there he is mowing the lawn!!! I wave and shout out, *"Hi Mick"*. He looks up and calls us over for a beer - I wish!!! I feel a close affinity with Jagger and the Stones. I have enjoyed their music since the 60s, so I am intrigued to see Mick's house. We think it is in the north east corner, but do not see any house names which give it away, like; *Honky Tonk Woman*, or *Satisfaction*.

Sandra reading in the shade on a deserted beach

Beach: As we walk around the northern part of the island we come across a deserted tropical beach and decide to spend the afternoon here. The beaches on Mustique have plenty of attractive picnic spots, with wooden tables and thatched umbrellas offering much needed and appreciated shade.

Later in the afternoon an American couple come strolling along the edge of the surf sipping champagne. As they walk back, thinking he might be a movie producer or some sort of American tycoon, I knock up a conversation with them, and we end up with an invitation for dinner. They have rented a house called *Sapphire* with another couple for a week. After a tasty dinner they offer us their spare bedroom for the night. *"Thanks, we'll certainly take a shower,"* makes a change from a bucket of cold water. *"But we would rather get back to our boat."* We explain that cruisers very rarely leave their boats for the night just in case there is a problem.

Most of the houses on the islands are available for holiday rentals at reasonable rates, which includes a cook and a gardener. According to the Sapphire's visitors book, the previous week's guests were, Brooke Shields and Andre Aggassi.

11th February (Friday): Today we decide to walk round the south end of the island where Princess Margaret's house is located, but it is not possible to actually see the house from below the towering cliffs. In 1960, the then owner of the island, Colin Tenant, presented Princess Margaret with a wedding gift of a 10 acre plot perched on the southern corner. As we wander back to the town we speak to a musician who has just had afternoon tea with Princess Margaret. Sandra is green with envy - greener than the *green flash.*

Back in town we find a local store which sells beers for EC $3 We have a couple then stroll down to Basil's Bar where it is EC $6 a beer. The famous Basil's Bar is

perched on stilts above the pounding surf, an ideal setting for a fresh seafood lunch.

Ambling along the front we watch local fishermen repairing their fishing nets. I take an excellent photograph which we later

Fishermen - Britannia Bay anchorage in the background. We used this photograph on the back cover of *Managing Your Bluewater Cruise*

Our peaceful anchorage in Corbay

include on the back cover of our book *Managing Your Bluewater Cruise*. They are selling superb fresh shellfish, so we buy two large crayfish for EC $6 / lb, which we will grill later for dinner, served with lemon, salad and chips.

Back in the breezy anchorage the Avon Redseal dinghy flips over yet again with the Suzuki outboard on the transom. We rush into another first aid operation, *"I'm sure this will shorten the life of the outboard."* Our frustration is eased witnessing one of the most elusive wonders of the ocean world. Magically as the last of the sun disappears over the horizon like a blazing globe of mercury, there is a green flash of light - stunningly bright and shamrock-green. Just the right memory with which to leave Mustique.

14th February (Monday) - Cannouan Island (Corbay): It is St Valentines Day and Sandra demands roses and extra kisses. Valentines Day is all about roses - apparently in Greek mythology the goddess Chloris came upon a beautiful dead nymph and turned her into a flower to which Aphrodite donated beauty, brilliance, joy and charm, while Dionysus added fragrance. Zephyrus, the west wind, obligingly blew away the clouds so Apollo could bathe the flower in the sun, and the rose was then given to Eros, the god of love, who named it the *Queen of Flowers*.

We listen to the 08:30 net on 4483 Khz before setting off. After the hustle and bustle of the large busy anchorages of Admiralty Bay and Britannia Bay, we head for the quiet, secluded anchorage of Corbay in Cannouan. Although there is room for two or three yachts to anchor, we are on our own most of the time. For a few days we totally relax and enjoy our own company. I swim a couple of times a day to clean the hull while Sandra catches up on her canvas work, making courtesy flags for Panama, Grenada and Galapagos, and a sail bag to replace the one which was blown over the side and sank.

A visiting yacht gives us a huge chunk from a large fish they have just caught. Sandra cuts it up into steaks and grills some of it for dinner. The rest she marinates with lemon juice, a splash of wine, a dash of Worcestershire sauce, onion and tomatoes. Now it will keep for the following day's breakfast, lunch and dinner. After this over indulgence we will not need to eat fish again for another month.

Being away from the crowds we make the most our own company. The slow rhythm of our life means that we can relax, read, write letters, write our books, and even play chess.

Rory playing chess

22nd February (Tuesday): Having spent the past few days snorkelling we are now ready to explore the island. Taking with us walking boots, rucksacks, hats, a lunch of cheese, fruit and crackers, and water to drink, we are off. We first bush walk over a headland and along to the next beach until we find an overgrown track

Ruins of a hurricane damaged Anglican church - Sunday service cancelled

leading up into the forest - obviously not many people walk here now. After a few miles we come across a disused cotton estate and an old stone Anglican church which was damaged by a hurricane in 1921. The buildings are half derelict and the once proud

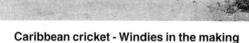

Caribbean cricket - Windies in the making

church now stands in ruins. *"This must have been a thriving community at one time."* Sadly the cotton plantations are no more and it looks like nobody has thought of anything to replace them with - not even bananas!

Our walk takes us across to the east coast, where there are stunning views of the rugged cliffs which are taking a battering from the Atlantic rollers. In Charlestown we buy a coke. We are parched walking in the heat and fancy something with a kick in it. The centre of attraction in the village is the cricket ground, which has seen better days. Cricket is quite topical at the moment, as the English team are touring the Windies - and England have just lost again!!!

23rd February (Wednesday) - Mayero Island: Reluctantly we leave our idyllic anchorage for Mayero Island and anchor in Salt Whistle Bay. It has clear water, white sand, and is referred to in the tourist brochures as a *Caribbean dream beach come true*. On the beach we are approached by a hawker selling colourful tie-dye tee-shirts. The popular theme seems to be images of the island and colourful parrots.

Above: View of Horse-Shoe Reef, Tobago Cays from Mayero Island

Right: Mayero Island - *"Sandra would you like a parrot tee-shirt?"*

The island has spectacular views looking over to the famous Tobago Cays. From our vantage point we map out a clear route to the Horseshoe reef by observing the turquoise shades of the crystal clear water.

24th February (Thursday) - Tobago Cays: Sandra is really looking forward to experiencing the Cays after all the positive reports we have heard. Up early to motor the short distance to the Horseshoe Reef - the Mecca for snorkelling. The Cays are packed with anchored yachts. They must also have heard about the snorkelling. Although the reef protects the snorkellers from the Atlantic rollers, the tradewinds still blow, unrestrained, at a healthy 25 knots. We anchor in 4 metres of water, then row ashore to nearby Jamesby Island. The island consists of just a small sandy beach which soon gets unbearably busy as crowds of tourists are ferried over. This is not the tranquillity we are looking for.

I notice a tender stop in front of our boat and tilt up the outboard. *"I bet he's wrapped his prop on our tripping line."* I am concerned he might cut it. When he comes ashore to pick up his guests, I ask him what happened. *"No problem,"* he replies, which gives me increased cause for alarm. We row back and examine the line. Sure enough the outer braid has been cut through close to the buoy. Fortunately we only have to shorten the line by 1 metre.

Jamesby Island before the hordes of tourists arrive

Union Island - Rory studying nursery sharks as they swim in a shallow pool outside a restaurant

Palm Island: Leaving the Cays much earlier than planned, we take a short cut through the reef to arrive at yet another Palm Island. This island has been developed, by John Caldwell, from a mosquito infested island to a small paradise. John Caldwell is well known for his book *Desperate Voyage*. Palm Island is widely advertised in America as a tourist destination - we are not that impressed - the beach is stony, and the bay is only suitable for a day anchorage.

Union Island: Motor the short distance over to Clifton Harbour, the official check-out port, before sailing on to Grenada. The anchorage is busy and uninviting. If there was no requirement to check-out we would have sailed on immediately. We have this uneasy feeling about the place which is soon confirmed when a Moorings charter yacht picks up our tripping buoy.

The next day we row ashore and tie up at an old quay where there are a number of other dinghies. The customs office is located at Clifton airport, which is a short walk from the harbour. The airport was built in 1993 and is surrounded by lush green grass - a complete contrast to the nearby town. After checking-out, we get back to find a group of boat boys waiting by our dinghy aggressively demanding money. *"My friend, we have been looking after your dinghy."* I leave Sandra to talk her way out of this one as I find these chaps extremely arrogant and annoying. I mentally cross Clifton off the cruising map.

26th February (Saturday): It is a short sail from Clifton to Frigate Island which is opposite the quiet gentle village of Ashton. At last we find a peaceful anchorage away from the pestering boat boys.

28th February (Sunday): After a couple of days catching-up on life I finish reading James Mitchener's *Caribbean*, while Sandra finishes *A Passage to India* (I know which way we will be going home). We sail around the coast to Chatham Bay to see its famous flock of pelicans. There are six other yachts in this large bay which is walled in by mountainous cliffs. As we anchor, there are eight large billed pelicans sitting majestically on a rocky outcrop looking as if they are taking no notice of the world around them, but when there is a slight movement in the water they explode into flight. Every so often as a welcome gust of wind ripples across the bay, the anchored yachts immediately swing in line with military precision - the gusts purge the stagnant air leaving the bay refreshed. Sandra swims ashore to where a local chap is carving a model of an old man from white cedarwood. He has already completed a parrot, several fish pendants and bangles, together with bracelets made from coral. He charges US $10 for a small fish and $20 for larger items. His wife has been making tie-dye shirts with screen prints of the Caribbean and Union Island. These she strings across from branch to branch to dry in the sun.

As a treat for afternoon tea, Sandra makes *Betty Crocker* fudge brownies and flapjacks à la sesame seed. Sundowners tonight are made from rum, lime, sugar and lemonade. Dinner is a lentil loaf, with carrots and potatoes, and dessert is banana ambrosia.

Sandy Island taken by Sandra swimming in the water

1st March (Tuesday) - Carriacou (Chatham to Tyrrel Bay): On the way to Tyrrel Bay we pass Sandy Island and try to replicate the photo that Michael Marshall has in his Caribbean cruising guide, page 123. Sandra jumps in the water with her waterproof Minolta camera while I motor into position.

We anchor in Tyrrel Bay where we meet John (UK) and Betty (Trinidad) who live on their yacht *Kellydown*. John is a construction engineer building a jetty at the head of the Bay. Sundowner time - we have a delicious rum punch with grenadine syrup, followed by onion quiche, pasta with pasta sauce, coleslaw, sprouting mung beans and toasted pumpkin seeds. John tells us about the mangrove swamps in the north corner of Tyrrel Bay which are a recommended hurricane hole. *"We'll have a look at that tomorrow as we leave."*

2nd March (Wednesday) - Mangrove: As we depart for Grenada we motor around the channel in the mangrove swamp. The forest swamps form an important part of the marine ecosystem. The mangroves shed their leaves, forming a nutrient compost (this is what smells). This nutrient is an important component of the food chain, providing food for a large number of creatures. The mangroves survive in tidal areas where their roots are not covered continuously by the sea so enabling the roots which stick up from the mud to breathe. These fibrous roots act as a giant filter trapping silt and preventing it from being carried out to sea. This makes the mangrove a great coastal builder extending its own environment seawards. As the land becomes too shallow for the mangrove, other plants take over, and so the mangrove moves seawards. Without mangrove forests there would be much more coastal erosion.

We have finally reached the end of the labyrinth of the Grenadine Islands, inlets, swamps, and dream islands. Now we are ready to sail to the last of the Windward Islands - Grenada.

Further Reading:

Marshall, Michael., *A Cruising Guide to the Caribbean*, Adlard Coles

19   *Grenada*

Grenada was named by Spanish sailors after Granada, the province of their homeland. Grenada is the last of the Windward Islands, and is known as the *Spice Island* of the Caribbean, because it is the leading producer of nutmeg, mace, cinnamon, ginger and cloves. However, its recent claim to fame was the 1983 military takeover with the assistance of Cuban troops - this was closely followed by an American invasion returning the country to democracy.

2nd March (Wednesday): As we approach the coast of Grenada in the blazing afternoon sun and a gentle 15 knot breeze, the beauty of the thick vegetation and outstanding red blossom encourages us to follow the coast as close as possible. There are many partly hidden houses peeping through the lush tropical forest. This fertile and colourful coastline is the best scenery we have seen in the Caribbean.

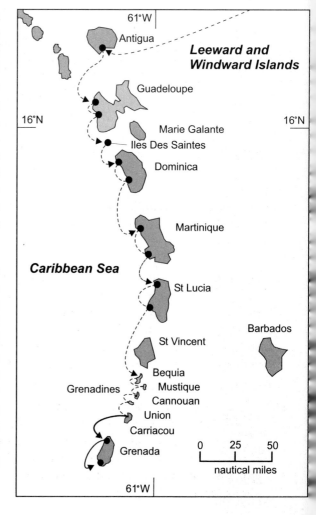

We are accompanied by a local fishing boat, the lads have erected a plastic sheet acting as a sail to propel them downwind. The race is neck and neck. In the late afternoon we are attracted to the beautiful bay of Halifax Harbour and decide to anchor for the evening, sharing this secure inlet with two other cruising yachts.

The steep wooded slopes of lush vegetation surround us, portraying an almost over-powering greenness. Before dark we row ashore for a short walk to stretch our legs. A local chap with a Rastafarian hair style is getting ready to have his evening wash and, as we row back, we notice he is rubbing himself with leaves from a nearby tree. "*Is that how he dries himself and gets the salt off?*"

Later in the evening we begin to notice an unpleasant smell. The next morning the cause of the smell becomes obvious - we are anchored beneath a waste disposal site. "*Let's get out here.*" It is unbelievable that they would use such an exquisite bay to dispose of their waste.

St Georges Harbour - yacht club and anchorage to the right

3rd March (Thursday) - Grenada Yacht Club: Continue our cruise down the coast to Saint George's the capital and its main port. Fort George, built in 1705, overlooks the entrance of the harbour. We anchor near the Grenada yacht club which is located on a prominent point looking over a protected lagoon to the right of the main harbour. The yacht club charges EC $1 for a shower and EC $2.75 for a cold *'Carib'* beer - so we can be sparkling clean as we sup our sundowner on the colonial terrace while looking for the green flash. I buy their club burgee and send it to our yacht club in Porthmadog. The yacht club also sells fresh water at a reasonable price - five cents a gallon (this compares to 30 cents a gallon elsewhere in Grenada), but then we do have to lug the jerry cans down a steep hill to the jetty (a trolley would have been useful). After making a few trips we have full tanks, and longer arms! Our diesel bunkers have lasted since the Canaries, which is a measure of our fuel consumption. There is an inviting fuel jetty near the anchorage, so we motor over to fill up. This should last us through to Panama.

4th March (Friday): Grenada is one of the better ports to stock-up in the Caribbean. There is a great fish market where we buy smoked marlin and some freshly caught local fish. On to the vegetable market - although the vegetables are a little pricey it seems the more we buy the more leverage we have to bargain. Up the hill, past Barclays bank and on the way to the British High Commission, we find a host of small interesting shops selling everything we need for provisioning, including Grenada's famous spices.

Rory with a sack-full of letters from the *poste restante*

7th March (Monday): Cricket: The locals were all smiles when the Windies beat England at cricket a few days ago, but today they have long gloomy faces. They were bowled out, and we won. I always knew the Windies enjoyed their cricket, but here we are seeing cricket as part of their culture like rugby is to the Springboks and the All Blacks.

Mail: After collecting a huge bundle of letters from the *poste restante,* we find a quiet spot in the corner of the cockpit to read them. Our friends are now writing to our agent, who has sent all our mail to Grenada in one big envelope. Some letters are nearly six months old - it is like receiving a time capsule of messages. I have noticed how our friends say they envy our cruising lifestyle in the sun, idyllic anchorages, sundowners, and snorkelling, in reality it is not quite like that all the time. In our letters we have started to write and tell them we do like to hear about the British weather, and we do miss the music in the Irish pubs, the TV, the *Economist,* and the facilities of Western living.

Most things are expensive in the Caribbean compared with Europe, but sending mail is reasonable so we grab this opportunity to catch up with all our letter writing. We spend a couple of days writing nearly 100 airmail letters. (We are to later find out that most of them were never received. We can only assume that the stamps were removed from the letters. Our mistake was not to insist they frank the stamps in front of us).

Mail Order: When we broke our Aerogen wind generator blades in Antigua we ordered a new set of blades right away as we had on board the manufacturers catalogue with part numbers and prices, and were able to send a cheque with the order. Now in Grenada, two months later, their parcel is awaiting our collection.

10th March (Thursday) - Newspapers: The British Consulate is up the hill in the centre of the town. We are pleased to see they keep a few past copies of the Times for visitors to read. Although we have been listening to the BBC World Service to keep us up to date, we still like to browse through the UK newspapers - this is one of the luxuries we miss. (This turns out to be the last UK newspapers we will read until we arrive in New Zealand).

Travel Visas: Back on board we consider our next port of call "*Let's go to Venezuela.*" Great idea until we find out about their visa requirements from a travel agent.

We just had to take this photograph of a policeman controlling the traffic at a not very busy, three way junction

Before we arrive we have to buy an entry visa at US $30 per person. We also have to fax our port of arrival for permission to enter, another US $20 for the fax. Once we arrive at Margarita, the harbour duty is US $100 and, as the officials are positioned at opposite ends of the town, so we are more or less obliged to use a local agent to check us in and out, costing a further US $30 per vessel. *"I think we will give Venezuela a miss."*

Venezuela means little Venice; the Spanish gave this appealing name to the coastal towns around Lake Maracaibo, before extending it to the whole country. They also spawned the legend of eldorado, a small gold mining village from the days of the Conquistadors, which lured men to South America. Although eldorado proved to be a myth, the idea persisted. Nowadays, with diesel at 20 cents a gallon, Venezuela attracts yachts with large bunkers to fill up for a year or so!

"What about sailing to Columbia?" We check the visa requirements with the travel agent and, would you believe it, we have to go to Venezuela to get the visa!!! This is all becoming too difficult. (However, friends of ours did sail to Cartagena without a visa and a local agent handled all the paperwork for just $60 per yacht).

11th March (Friday) *Sherpa Bill* moors beside us. Their yacht is well known for the Spitfire canopy over the companionway - hence their nickname, Biggles. After interviewing Bill and Hazel (also OCC members) for our book, they join us for sundowners and dinner. Sundowners consist of rum punch with orange and pineapple juice, a dash of Angostura bitters and grated nutmeg, and nibbles of spicy curry flavoured popcorn. The next morning, to our surprise, they actually sail Biggles off their anchorage and out through a narrow channel - you will not find us doing that.

12th March (Saturday) - Secret Harbour: Sail around to Secret Harbour which really is a yachtsman's haven - we could have spent the whole season there. Of all the harbours and anchorages we visit in the Caribbean, Secret Harbour and Hogs Island seem to be the most welcoming and friendly. Their relatively safe location is a great playground for children to play together, which gives the parents time to relax and socialize.

Now we have been cruising for nearly a year in Europe and the Caribbean we feel we are in the main stream of bluewater cruisers. When we approach a new anchorage we almost always know someone from a previous encounter. It is

We dinghy to Hog Island for a picnic, flea-market and treasures of the bilge sale

intriguing how we are continually leap frogging past each other, only to meet again hundreds, sometimes thousands of miles away. This time it is Bob and Delores (*Summer Wind*) who we first met at Sagres, and last saw in Gibraltar. They have already sailed around the world, and are now doing an Atlantic circuit for fun. We sail in company around to Secret Harbour. Bob is not happy with their anchorage, so I row his dinghy while he sounds the bottom with his lead line, which is armed with a chunk of soap to sample the bottom.

14th March (Monday) - Trinidad: Another trans-Atlantic reunion is with Robyn and Phil (*Wisecat*), who we met in Arrecife, but only now do we get a chance to interview them for our book. They have been cruising for ten years in their cat, and will be returning to Australia, with a much larger family than when they started. They give us many interesting comments on how to bring up children on a small boat - not for our personal information, but for our cruising book. (At the time we thought ten years was far too long to spend cruising around the world but, as it turns out, our circumnavigation will be longer!!).

A few of the cruisers have just returned from the Trinidad carnival which occurs this time every year and is the oldest surviving carnival in the world. Over a rum sundowner we watch a video of the event. It looks spectacular, a cocktail of colour, people dressed in lavish costumes, and enormous puppets parading and jiving to the calypso music echoing from the steel bands.

15th March (Tuesday): *"Let's drive round the island."* In the morning we join a group of cruisers for a mini bus day trip around the spice island. We heard about the trip yesterday on the morning cruisers net and signed up immediately.

They start with a conducted tour of a working sugar cane processing plant - one step away from rum! The rum industry grew on the back of the sugar cane industry. After cutting the cane it is gathered and transported to the mills to squeeze out the sugar rich juices. The extract is then boiled up in large copper bottomed pans to reduce the water content. As the extract is cooled, the sugar crystallises on the surface. Successive boiling produces more sugar, leaving behind a thick sweet sludge with a high sugar content - called molasses. By adding water and yeast, the sugar in the molasses is fermented into alcohol. This weak alcoholic fluid is distilled, the alcohol is boiled off and the vapours collected and cooled, producing a clear fluid with a high alcoholic content - called rum!!! This is called strong white rum and has a sharp taste. To obtain a smoother flavour it is matured in oak barrels, taking up the caramel colour of dark rum.

They advise us that the next time we scan the shimmering rim of the sun for a rare glimpse of the mysterious green flash, that this atmospheric phenomenon is easier to view if our glass is topped up with rum. Their rums are appropriately called - Fort rum, Bounty rum, and Buccaneer rum. Traditional rum punch (from tourist guide book): Take a handful of ice cubes, a generous measure of dark rum, a squeeze of juice from a slice of fresh lime and add sugar to taste. Top up the glass with orange juice and grate a little fresh nutmeg on top and garnish with a slice of fresh lime or a cherry - cheers!

Loofah: The driver suddenly stops the minibus and reverses back. "*Do you know where a loofah comes from*?" he asks. We all look at each other to see who will win the mystery prize. Meanwhile the driver jumps out of the bus and pulls down a dark brown looking pod from a tree and peels it back to reveal - voilà - a loofah!

As he is running out of time, the driver stops at the Concord Falls car park giving us only 30 minutes to fast walk there and back. Grenada really is agriculturally prolific and, on the foray up into the rain forest, we understand why it is called *Spice Island*. Everywhere we look we see spices in abundance. One section of the path is covered by a thick carpet of **nutmegs**. It is amazing to see the nutmegs just lying on the ground where they have fallen, and just for the taking - we all return with pockets bulging.

Nutmegs can be used in a multitude of recipes and, in particular, to our delight, add a great flavour when grated on top of rum punch. The nutmeg is surrounded by a layer of mace, which turns yellow as it dries and is a wonderful flavouring in sauces and other culinary delights.

17th March (Thursday) - Check-out: Bob and Delores join us on the walk over the hill to Prickly Bay to check-out. It is a really hot and humid day. We arrive to find the officer having his hair cut. Slightly disgruntled, he tells us we should have bought our yachts over to Prickly Bay. This would have been a long sail out of our way. Fortunately Sandra sweet talks him while he is having his hair cut. This does the trick, and he then proceeds to make up his own clearance forms. (Later we meet some cruisers who were forced to sail their boat around to Prickly bay before they were allowed to check-out. I hope they find this chap another job soon before he gives Grenada's tourist industry a bad name).

Weather Forecast: As we prepare to leave for Panama, listening to the weather forecasts becomes important again. The two main forecasts we listen to are; Herb (*Southbound II*) on 12,359 Khz at 20:00 GMT operating out of Bermuda (now Canada), and covering weather for the Atlantic. And Dave (*Misteen*) on 8104 Khz operating out of Trinidad, and covering the Caribbean. Our departing forecast for our cruising area is 20 knots out of the east - just right for a comfortable passage.

Further Reading:

Marshall, Michael., *A Cruising Guide to the Caribbean*, Adlard Coles

20 *Dutch Antilles ABC's*

Now that we have cruised most of the Leeward and Windward Islands it is time to make our passage across the Caribbean Sea to the Panama Canal. The plan is to sail from Grenada directly to the Panama Canal but, our plan are to change as we approach the Dutch Antilles.

17th March (Thursday): Log book: chart 4402, Caribbean Sea (scale 1: 2,750,000). With a good forecast of 20 knots out of the east we set sail from Grenada on St Patrick's Day. *Pacific Voyager* is hoping this robust breeze will carry us around the top of South America to Panama. On our first day at sea, food is the furthest from our minds as we regain our sea legs and get back into our stride again. This is our first overnight passage since landfall in the Caribbean nearly three months ago.

19th March (Saturday): Pole out the jib to starboard with the whisker pole, and the genoa to port through a block on the end of the boom - *Pacific Voyager* feels more balanced with this arrangement, there is less rolling. Progressively we pass north of the Venezuelan islands we would have loved to have visited; Los Testigos, Isla de Margarita, Isla La Blanquilla, Isla Orchila and Los Roques.

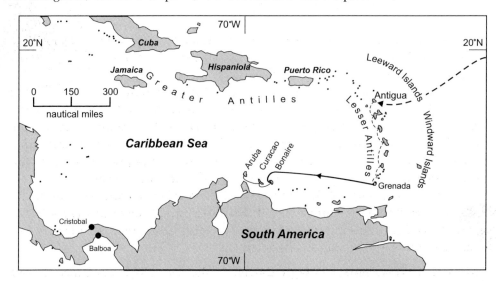

20th March (Sunday): Herb (*Southbound 11*) 12,359 Khz in Bermuda and David (*Misteen*) 8104 Khz in Trinidad both give us detailed weather forecasts. Today they forecast 40 + knots for the north coast of South America and particularly off Colombia. Although we can happily sail through a gale, we feel it prudent to look into stopping somewhere to let the strong winds pass. A quick check of the chart indicates that we can make Bonaire before dark - a decision is made, we alter course.

Bonaire: The Dutch Antilles consists of Aruba, Curacao and Bonaire - hence they are called the ABC's. Our decision to alter course could not have been better timed, as it is just a case of changing direction without needing to tack back. About 13:00 we sight land and sail past a rocky headland a few hours later. Making good progress down Bonaire's rugged coast, it looks like we will make port before dark but, as we pass the next headland, the wind shifts and increases to 25 knots on the nose. Our efforts to tack against it are hopeless. *"We're not going to make it. We either have to heave-to for the night, or turn back and anchor where we saw those mooring buoys."*

We turn back to have a closer look at three unused mooring buoys we passed earlier. Then, on the VHF radio we hear, *"Pacific Voyager - Pacific Voyager."* It is someone ashore. The caller suggests we pick up one of the buoys as this area is a diving sanctuary and our anchor could damage the coral - we take his advice.

21st March (Monday) - Curacao: Set off early and have a brisk sail over to Curacao, with following winds and a following sea. We approach Spanish Waters cautiously as we do not have a chart. The water is crystal clear so the rocks can be seen quite clearly. As we make our way up the coast we identify the fuel tanks which are the only clue to the entrance. Spanish Waters is an amazingly large natural harbour with the narrowest of entrances - less then 50 metres across in one place.

"NEELEEN"

Ralph & Kathleen Neeley

Once through the entrance we request directions on the VHF from anyone who may be listening. Kathleen off *Neeleen* immediately responds and gives us clear directions. When we later pop over to thank Kathleen we are surprised to find her confined to a wheel chair! Kathleen is a polio victim who has been an invalid for many years. They had their yacht specially built in New Zealand with a gantry aft to lift and lower Kathleen into the dinghy, and below deck the floor has been arranged for Kathleen to move round in her wheelchair. We are very impressed at how they have overcome a disability that would have kept most people ashore.

All the cruisers frequent **Serifundys** which is an informal yacht club beside the anchorage. Serifundys is extremely well organised with plenty of cold beers, books to swap, washing machines and LPG refilling. They even organise a free bus to take the cruisers to the local supermarkets when they need to shop.

23rd March (Wednesday) - Magic Castle: At the Serifundys' bar I meet a well

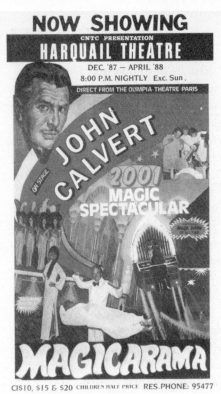

All John's stage props are stowed in Magic Castle's hold

Geraldina Mook

Geraldina, who is also a model, shows us around the distillery

dressed gentleman. I say, "*Hello.*" We shake hands - I look down and my watch has gone!!! This well dressed gentleman turns out to be John Calvert, a magician, who lives with his wife Tammy on their 60 foot yacht *Magic Castle*. They have built their yacht to be their mobile home and working base. Their hold contains all their stage props for their magic show. Seeing John's set-up fires my imagination. We should try and do the same - not magic shows - but book publishing (see *Sustainable Cruising*, page 277).

24th March (Thursday) - Ansell Brewery: The cruisers at Serifundys' organise a trip to Ansell's brewery - this is one of those fun trips. Ansell are proud that they are the only brewery in the world that uses distilled sea water to brew their beer. At the end of the tour we do plenty of sampling to see if we can taste the sea water.

After the brewery visit we now seek more entertainment - as luck would have it the brewery is near to the Curacao Liqueur distillery. This is where they make interesting coloured and flavoured liqueurs from ingredients such as orange skins. Geraldina, our hostess, who is also a beautiful model, guides us through their selection.

Now for something to eat. I spoil Sandra with a meal at Burger King. After many months at sea on ships stores we are surprised how delicious junk food can taste - no please do not quote me on this.

25th March (Friday) - Buy Equipment: We purchase some marine equipment from a dealer called Imca (Marine Technical Trading - Brakkeput Aruba 23, Curacao NA). He is able to import almost anything at a good price. We can now tick off from our wish list: Caribe RIB dinghy (made in Venezuela), 8 hp Yamaha outboard, Panasonic handheld VHF, Yaesu SSB, safety strobes, and blue Sunbrela marine canvas to cover the dinghy.

Martin in his workshop - OCC Port Officer for Curacao

Martin (Electrical Connections) is a good example of a British expat who sailed from the UK many years ago and got stuck in Curacao. He now services electrical equipment on visiting yachts. Email: thomson_neall_martin@hotmail.com.

Bob finding our oil leak. Sandra is impressed with Bob's working clothes

1st April (Good Friday) - Oil Leak: Hot cross bun day and oil leak. There has been an annoying oil leak from somewhere under the engine for some time, but I cannot work-out where it is coming from. This is the kind of challenge that Bob (*Emma Louise*) enjoys. As we run the engine Bob traces the oil leak back bit by bit to the oil pressure sensor. The next day I take the bus to the Perkins agent. Unfortunately they cannot replace the part, but they do have a blank. The leaking oil pressure sensor is used to switch on the exciter field on the alternator only when the engine pressure is up; this way there is no additional alternator load on start-up. I fit the blank and rewire the alternator - this does the trick - no more oil leaks.

3rd April (Easter Sunday) - Dry Food: Gabi off *James Cook* shows us how to dry - anything from bananas and apples to mushrooms and carrots. She chops them into thin slices and places them on a grid in the sun, turning them over regularly. We successfully try this method with mushrooms, although they can also be dried in a brown paper bag in the sun. Drying food is an interesting option for us, especially as our fridge is not working.

15th April (Saturday): At last we drag ourselves away from the vibrant social life of Spanish Waters for the tranquillity of the San Blas Islands - or so we think. With a good long range forecast from Herb we are off. As we motor out of Spanish Waters I notice the Perkins temperature gauge is a little higher than before. I check the exhaust. The water is coming through, although perhaps a little less than before. I am concerned but keen to get going. Halfway between Curacao to Aruba we encounter head winds and, unbelievably, Herb forecasts more strong winds off the coast of South America. "*Let's pull into Aruba and wait for a better forecast.*"

16th April (Sunday) - Aruba: As we approach Oranjestad, Aruba's main port, we have difficulty finding the entrance through the reef, so we radio for advice. The harbour master responds and sends a boat to guide us in. I am concerned there will be a charge. "*There's no charge we just want to get you in safely.*" We later find out that a yacht went aground on the reef a couple of weeks ago, so they obviously do not want that to happen again to another visiting yacht. They lead us to a dock. "*Sorry we can't give you a berth, they are all full.*" They arc all so polite. We have never been treated so well in the Caribbean. Even the immigration and custom officers drive to the harbour to see us. Grenada, please take note!

Buzzed by pelicans alongside the quay

Engine Temperature: I am now very concerned about the engine temperature. It is much higher than before. I check all the potential problem areas; the fresh water jacket is okay, and there is water being pumped through to the exhaust - perhaps not as much as before. I check the seacock - water fountains in. I check the raw water pump - it is flowing through, but maybe not as forcefully as the seacock. Sensing a problem I check the flow at the oil cooler and eventually find coral growing in the inlet pipe which has narrowed the bore - problem identified. I chip away at the coral totally surprised that such a thing could happen.

17th April (Sunday) - Weather Forecast: Besides walking round the town our main focus is on gathering weather information as we are keen to push-on to Panama. The quay we are moored alongside is adjacent to where the visiting cruise liners berth. *"They must have the latest weather forecasting equipment."* I go on board *Song of Norway* and ask them for the weather information. I am disappointed to find they only have a simple weather teleprinter. We continue gathering weather information from Herb and *Misteen*, and also hear from Colin and Marianne (*Ketchup II*) that they have just had 50 knot winds off the coast of Colombia, and have broken their boom as they broached in 15 foot seas.

18th April (Monday): As the days press on we begin to accept that the coast of South America always seems to attract strong winds. *"I think we'll have to accept we are going to get 40 knots and get on with it."* Hanging around for the perfect weather can be very frustrating. Although the winds may be strong, at least we will have a following wind, sea and current which should give us a fast passage.

21 San Blas Islands

18th April (Monday): With Herb's weather forecast of 35/40 knots off the South American coast of Colombia, we are ready to do battle with the elements. Apparently the north coast of Colombia is renown for pirates, high winds, big seas and the American Coastguard. Jimmy Cornell, *Ocean Cruising Routes*, "*... a very rough passage, confirmed by the fact that many experienced sailors described their passage across the Caribbean Sea as the roughest part of their voyage round the world.*" Not very encouraging reading. Our plan is to sail from Aruba to the San Blas, arcing around Colombia about 60 miles offshore to avoid a counter current and also keep clear of any pirates!!!

Log book: chart 4402 Caribbean Sea (scale 1:2,750,000). The wind increases soon after we leave Aruba. We reef down the head sail to the storm jib and triple reef the main - if anything we are under powered, but comfortable, much more comfortable than on the Atlantic trip.

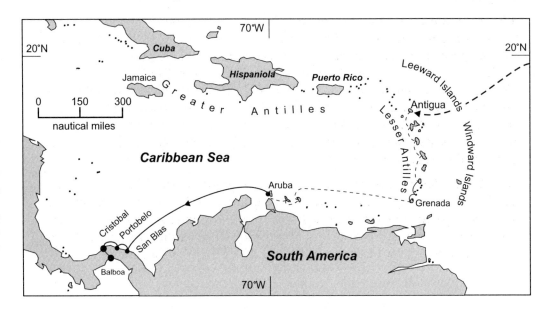

Self-Steering: With the prospect of 35 to 40 knots and a following sea I am concerned about the Hydrovane, so I (foolishly) removed the rudder and wind vane before we left Aruba. I have always felt the Hydrovane's rudder is in an exposed position, although ours has never been damaged, and I have never heard of one being damaged. The Neco autopilot has always given us good service. It has a more secure arrangement than the Hydrovane, with its drive attached directly to the rudder quadrant. The Neco's electronics steer a more accurate course than the Hydrovane. The only problem with the Neco is that we have to run the engine for an hour every four hours to power the batteries.

Neco autopilot controls

Now that we are totally dependant on the Neco autopilot - it stops!!! I cannot believe it and now I have no back-up as the Hydrovane is disconnected. My mind races through the consequences - at worst we are going to have to hand steer for five days. I inspect the wiring connections. I inspect the switches. I inspect the fuses - and then suddenly it starts to work again. I do not know what I did, but boy am I relieved.

During this passage the winds are generally 30 knots out of the east with periods of 35 knots, gusting up to 45 knots. *Pacific Voyager* with her long fin and skeg is directionally stable down the face of the following seas. Even though some of the standing waves look like they are going to break all over us, we only catch the top of a few. When I am below, I always know when some spray flies into the cockpit as it generates a scream from Sandra sun bathing in her favourite spot at the back of the cockpit. After learning to sail in the UK I still find it odd to only be wearing my underpants and sun hat in gale force conditions.

Pirates: We have heard stories about pirates and drug running off the coast of Colombia. When a plane flies over us we wonder if we are being monitored by the US anti-drug surveillance - the last thing we need is to be boarded and searched. Apparently they are known for leaving boats in a mess and, seeing how tightly packed our lockers are, the mess would be horrendous.

After two days of strong winds, following currents and consistent seas, we are making good progress - we are more than halfway and *Pacific Voyager* is handling the following seas very well. The wind is progressively easing, until it dies away completely. With less than 50 miles to go we are left with the choice of either motoring or spending another night at sea. *"Let's motor so we can enjoy waking up in a calm protected anchorage."*

22nd April (Friday) - San Blas: The Holandes Cays are a 7 mile necklace of low-lying coral atolls with golden sandy beaches, swaying coconut palms and protected anchorages, which can only be approached through narrow passages in the reefs. This string of atolls used to be called the San Blas Islands, but are now called collectively the Kuna Yala - *'Home of the Kuna Indians.'*

A smudge on the horizon steadily grows into palm fronds streaming like flags in the breeze, as we make our landfall. I call a few times on the VHF requesting local knowledge. *Mountain Oyster* responds and gives us good directions to enter the pass into the protected anchorage, where we anchor amongst seven other yachts. We feel safe and snug as we listen to distant surf pounding on the outer reef - this is the last sound we hear as we drift off to sleep.

The San Blas islands come as a welcome change from the overcrowded anchorages and commercialism of the Caribbean Islands. The Kuna Indians are very welcoming when approached, otherwise they are reserved and keep a respectful distance - no pestering boat boys here. These are truly the paradise islands of Panama.

The Kuna Indians lead simple lives; the men grow crops, fish from their dugout canoes, and gather coconuts, while the women folk attend to their homes and embroider molas. These traditional Kuna Indian embroideries are their main *'dollar'* earning cash crop, which they sell to the visiting yachts.

Mola: A mola is created from many layers of rectangular colourful cotton material, laid on top of each other and cut into to produce a huge variety of patterns and designs. Each raw edge is turned under and neatly stitched to prevent fraying. It is a similar process to an applique, but in reverse. The more layers and colours, the more intricate the design, and the more expensive the molas become. The molas were traditionally used as the front and back panels on blouses worn by the Kuna women, but now they are sold to the tourists as individual panels or made up into useful items such as tee-shirts, hats and bags.

The cruising women cannot resist buying molas; it is not a case of can I buy one, but how many??? *"They'll make lovely birthday presents."* At first we are only going to buy one, then a short list develops of presents for relations and friends. In the village the molas are displayed like tea towels hanging on a washing line - we buy two at $20 each. As we leave another lady beckons us to see her molas inside her house on her washing line - all very discrete. We buy another four molas including a mola of a baby parrot for Dominique, our god daughter. By the time we leave the San Blas, Sandra has spent over $400 on molas!

The molas we keep for ourselves, Sandra makes up into decorative covers for our cushions and a shoulder bag. The designs look as exotic as the Kuna Indians themselves - a truly exquisite souvenir to take home, and easier to pack than our Moroccan carpet.

Molas from the Kuna Indians in Panama

24th April (Sunday) - Plank: After breakfast we are keen to explore the small uninhabited island we are anchored beside. We motor over in our new Caribe RIB dinghy - stepping ashore the only foot prints in the sand are ours. The tide mark is littered with fallen palm trees, palm fronds, driftwood, flotsam and brightly coloured plastic bags and packaging. At least the driftwood has the romantic appeal of something that has floated around the oceans for miles and has been naturally aged over the years, but the plastic items are an unwanted example of uncontrolled industrial pollution and the throw-away society. About halfway around the island I find a plank of wood, *"I've been looking for a plank to hold our jerry cans on deck since Southampton."* I pick up the plank and carry it back to the dinghy like some timber kleptomaniac.

A stingray glides over the shallow sand - its implausible disk shaped body clearly visible through the transparent sea. Multitudes of small crabs are combing the beach, popping in and out of their homes in the sand. As we reach the end of this natural nature reserve, I take a few classic tropical photographs for our book, with palm trees in the foreground and our yacht foreshortened in the distance.

Children: Sandra is a big hit with the children - she chats to them and gives them sweets. And good news about free sweets travels fast! They are obviously not worried about taking sweets from strangers here. We even have an eleven year old boy called Albertino paddle over in his dugout canoe surreptitiously to say hello. Sandra joins Albertino in his dugout canoe just long enough for me to take a photograph of this hair-raising experience. *"It feels like I'm sitting on a wobbly jelly fish,"* Sandra bravely screams.

Kids being kids in the remote San Blas Islands!

The Kuna Indians make paddling their dugouts look very easy. These dugout canoes, or cayuka, are made from a hollowed out log. I remember seeing in Malawi, an African knee deep in wood shavings as he hollowed out a tree trunk to three fingers thick, and carved the high prow into a point to break the waves.

Sandra and Alberto in his dugout canoe

Not only do the Kuna Indians think nothing of paddling these unstable crafts, but they also sail and motor them as well. Everyday we see them use the natural power of the wind to sail across to the island they use for cultivating their crops. On their way back, they exchange and barter their fresh avocados, limes, green peppers and tomatoes for our rice, sugar, flour, fish hooks and petrol for their outboards. One of our deals includes two large lobsters and a crab for half a can of petrol.

Snorkelling: The crystal clear water gives me the opportunity to clean all the barnacles off the hull. The prop was vibrating a little as we motored in. I have visions of it being completely covered in barnacles, but it is only the boss that is covered with a few barnacles and none on the blades. While I am underwater with my scraper I check around the rudder, bottom of the keel, scuppers, and all the skin fittings.

Below: Trading with the Kuna Indians
Right: This is the result - dinner!

Left: Herb and Nancy *(Red Shoes)* interview us for Yachting Monthly

Below: Nancy's photograph is printed in Yachting Monthly

Meanwhile Sandra is snorkelling with her friends Dale and Nigel (*Kieren*). There is plenty of sea life around - Sandra sees a three foot barracuda quietly watching them from a distance, and a stingray majestically swirling towards her like a flying saucer. Nigel suddenly stands up then ducks down, again and again. "*What's up Nigel????*" "*I've lost my front tooth!*" Then up he comes with tooth in hand. As luck would have it, it landed on his fin!

28th April (Thursday): Looking through the binoculars Sandra says, "*There's a yacht motoring into the anchorage. Its name is Red Shoes.*"

"*That name rings a bell - yes it's Herb and Nancy who write for Yachting Monthly. Call them on 72 and invite them over.*" The next day Herb and Nancy join us for lunch and interview us for their Yachting Monthly bluewater letter.

Night Glasses: It is a pitch black night. "*They're taking a risk,*" I thought as we watch a set of navigation lights from a yacht as it enters the anchorage. The next day we meet them - Mark and Catherine off *Inamorata* (Hans Christian 42). Not only are they familiar with the area, but they were using night glasses. Mark informs us, "*You can actually see the palm trees with them even though there's not a flicker of light.*" Mark's bag of toys also includes an ultrasonic link to his headphones, so he can listen to his ship's stereo while he motors around the anchorage, and a poison dart blow-pipe kit from the Orinoco in Venezuela. Mark invites us to practice blowing his darts into a polystyrene bulls eye.

31st April (Saturday) - Pig Braai: "*Would you like to join us for a pig roast?*" asks Catherine. All the cruisers get together and buy a pig for $75 from the Kuna Indians. The pig is delivered ready for Catherine to stuff with onions, breadcrumbs, plums, mangoes, sage, rosemary and thyme. Then she wraps the whole thing in tin foil. Our job is to collect coconut husks, driftwood and anything that will burn from one

Fetching coconut husks for the fire

of the uninhabited islands and motor it over in our dinghy to where other cruisers are digging a deep hole for the fire. Herb and Nancy bring a metal pole (an antenna in its previous life) from *Red Shoes* to skewer the beast, and make a manual rotisserie. Soon the pig is roasting nicely - a pig-watch is organised while we sup an early sundowner and consider how this scene would fit into *Lord of the Flies*.

Several hours later, we all tuck into the most fantastic tropical feast of roast suckling pig, and a wide range of vegetables, salads and home made breads, that everyone has contributed to.

The pig braai is the perfect climax to a wonderful week in the San Blas. As we literally drag ourselves away to Portobelo, we leave with a mind full of memories and a sack full of molas.

Left: Preparing the pig rotisserie
Below: All the cruisers gather around for the party

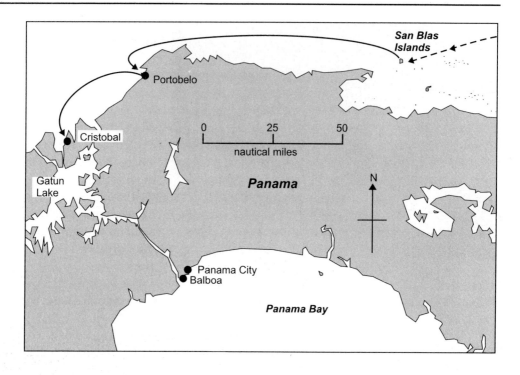

1st May (Sunday) - San Blas to Portobelo: Log book: chart 396, Barramquilla to Miskito Bank (scale 1:1,000,000). Just as it is getting dark we make our departure - we have really left it too late, because if we have any problems it will be dark before we clear the reef. I watch the echo sounder very closely as we navigate through the reef and it is not until we get into deeper water that we can relax. We tack out to give us sea room from the reefs along the coast - there are no navigation lights around here.

"*Portobelo - where have I have heard that name before?*" I know it is a street market in London. Yes, but Portobelo also used to be the capital port of the Spanish Main. Portobelo means beautiful port, so named by Columbus on his fourth voyage to the Caribbean. When the Spanish plundered the Inca's riches in Peru, a stream of booty flowed north across the isthmus to Portobelo where it was stored before its journey to Europe. In those days, these waters were full of privateers always looking for an opportunity to raid any unprotected treasure ships. In 1671 Henry Morgan stole a whole year's supply of treasure from Portobelo, and then went on to ransack Panama City with his 37 galleons and 2,000 men.

2nd May (Monday) - Portobelo: As we motor sail up the estuary we first see the old Spanish gun battery on the left side of the channel. These gun ports have a commanding view of the channel. In 1595, during Sir Francis Drake's last attempt to plunder Spanish treasure, the cannon fire would have bombarded his ships. Drake later died from yellow fever and his body was buried at sea just off the entrance to this beautiful harbour. But in 1739, Admiral Vernon's British forces were more successful, and went on to overrun the port.

Left: Portobelo guns peaking over the ramparts

Below: Portobelo's ruined fortifications

Anchoring near the old town, we go ashore to explore the ruined fortifications. The original cannons peak above the ramparts of the fort, remind us of the hidden secrets they harbour.

Portobelo is uncomfortably humid this evening - there is not even the faintest breath of wind. And, of course without wind our windchute is useless. This is when we need an electric fan blowing down on our faces. Instead we sleep in the cockpit to get some relief. Tomorrow we will continue along the coast to one of the greatest engineering projects of the 20th century - the *'Panama Canal'*.

22 Panama Canal

The Panama Canal is one of the principal crossroads of the maritime world and an incredible feat of engineering. Our plan is to sail to Cristobal, transit the Panama Canal to Balboa, then enter the Pacific Ocean. As the cyclone season in the Pacific has already finished, we are keen to push on to the Galapagos Archipelago and the other Pacific Islands. There have been many different stories about the bureaucratic requirements to transit the canal so we are not sure what to expect.

History: The history of the Panama Canal and the concept of a canal across the isthmus dates back to the Spanish Empire:

1534: Charles 1 of Spain ordered a survey of a possible canal route across the isthmus of Panama, to carry Inca gold and silver from Peru to the Caribbean side for transhipment to Spain.

1855: The California gold rush encouraged the building of a railway across the isthmus of Panama. This was the preferred route to the west coast, rather than the long and dangerous wagon-route across America.

1880: After their success building the Suez Canal, the French started building the Panama Canal following the route of the railway line but, after 20 years, they had only excavated two fifths of the canal. Tropical diseases extracted a terrible toll on the labour force - 20,000 died. And when the financial company went into bankruptcy, Ferdinand de Lesseps finally accepted defeat.

1903: The Republic of Panama originally broke away from Colombia (with USA backing) to build the Panama Canal. America leased the canal zone in perpetuity, a ribbon of territory across the isthmus. At that time the canal involved the construction of the largest dam ever excavated, the largest canal locks ever built and the largest gates ever swung.

1914: After 20 years of French construction, followed by 10 years of American construction, the canal was finally opened in 1914.

1999 (31st December): Panama Canal handed over to Panama.

The opening of the Suez Canal followed by the Panama Canal completely re-orientated the trade routes of the world. For the bluewater cruisers the Panama Canal enables them to circumnavigate without having to lock horns with the Roaring Forties and the Cape of Storms.

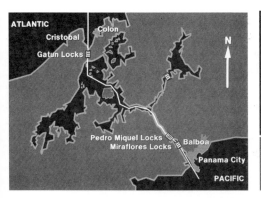

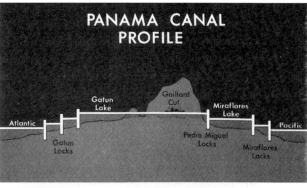

The Panama Canal has also influenced international ship design, creating what are known as Panamax ships - less than 1000 foot long, and 100 foot wide. The QE2 is a good example of a liner which was especially designed to use the canal.

3rd May (Tuesday) - Portobelo to Cristobal: As we approach the entrance to the Panama Canal there is shipping everywhere - a real hive of activity. Over the breakwater there are masses of ships anchored, a dramatic contrast from a few dugout canoes in the San Blas to one of the busiest shipping ports in the world.

We motor down the channel keeping well over to the side. I recognise all types of commercial ships; reefers probably carrying fruit, container ships packed high with containers and offshore drilling vessels which are a maze of piping.

As we approach the yacht anchorage area called the *Flats,* we recognise *Alexandra Louise,* we last saw Helen and Neil at the Anchorage Hotel in Dominica. We call them up on the VHF and Helen invites us over for dinner to compare notes.

Irish Passport: Once anchored we decide to use our old Avon Redseal dinghy with the Suzuki outboard instead of our brand new Caribe RIB, as we are concerned about it being stolen. Conveniently, the immigration department have a temporary office at the Panama Canal Yacht Club. The yacht club is located up an inlet near the *Flats* - it would be a long row, but it is a comfortable motor in our dinghy.

No visa is required for Sandra's British passport, but a US $10 visa is required for my Irish passport - so there is some benefit in being British after all. The Immigration Officer gives us a map of the town which indicates the location of the officials we must visit to organise our transit of the canal. He can also organise additional line handlers for us at US $40 each per transit, but this will not be necessary as we intend to swap line handling with other cruisers. Finally the immigration officer advises, for our safety, not to walk the streets outside the canal

zone, particularly at night - rather to take a taxi between shops. This may appear extravagant, but at US $1 per trip it is a cheap personal safety precaution. Gone are the days of the old canal zone when it was an Edwardian traveller's paradise.

Officials: We walk into town to start the application process to transit the canal. An official asks me to list the last four ports we have visited - with dates!!! As I am cursing myself for not bringing the log book, he can see I am struggling so completes the form for me!!! *"You must have been to Aruba a month ago, and Grenada a couple of weeks before that? "Oh yes,"* I reply.

Next he asks us to fill in a Handline Lockage Request. Then he asks,

"Do you have fenders?" - "Yes."

"Do you have four 125 foot lines?" - "Yes."

"Do you have four line handlers and Master on board?" - "Yes."

"Are you able to anchor?" - "Yes."

"Can your yacht make 5 knots?" - "Yes."

He then discusses the different configurations in the dock:

"Centre of lock, okay - plenty of work for line handlers."

"Centre of lock nested with other yachts, okay - again plenty of work for line handlers."

"Alongside a tug - best because you simply secure yourself to the tug."

"Alongside the sidewall of the lock - not advised as the spreaders could knock against the dockside if the boats rock."

"Please sign here," and he pushes the blue form in front of me. *"We now need to measure your yacht. When will it be convenient?"*

"Any time."

The official makes a phone call and everything is organised for the next morning.

4th May (Wednesday) - Admeasurement: The admeasurer is ferried over in a tug which towers over our deck. I am surprised to see an young, attractive, uniformed lady jump down. Being the perfect gentleman, I hold the other end of her measuring tape while she measures widths and lengths of the boat; then she goes below and spends ten minutes banging on her calculator to give us a measurement of 14 tons. Later we hear from our friends that they were also measured at 14 tons - so why all the palaver? For this admeasurement we pay $130.

But that is the only expensive part, because the transit costs $2 per ton, therefore our fee is only $28 - what a pleasure! And this includes a pilot to guide us through the locks. (Note: they have since changed the fee structure. Budget $500 for a 40 foot yacht).

Admeasurer calculating our tonnage in *Pacific Voyager's* saloon

Banking: A one dollar taxi ride takes us to the Chase Manhattan Bank. Up to now we have been using our Eurocheques and interbank transfers to change money, but the Eurocheques are not supported in Panama, and the interbank transfers take a week, so we thought we would use my Access Mastercard to draw some money. The bank teller says they can cash up to $500 per day. *"Great - $500 will do me fine."* They take my card and return a few minutes later with apologies that they have been instructed to withdraw the card!!!

The last time we used the credit card was in the Canaries to buy anchor chain (remember the chain that parted). I posted Access a cheque for £70, with a covering letter. They replied to the letter and debited my current account but, as it turns out, they did not credit my Access account. (Later, when we arrive in Balboa there are two letters from Access waiting for us, demanding payment within 14 days regardless of the fact that we had advised them that correspondence could take a couple of months to reach us while we are travelling).

Penniless, we order an interbank transfer and hold off buying provisions for a couple of weeks. (After many letters, Access finally acknowledged their mistake, but the compensation for their incompetence, and our inconvenience, is much less than we expected. We now have a Visa card!!!).

5th May (Thursday) - Oil slick: Awake to a colourful sea with a kaleidoscope of colours as the sun's rays are refracted by - oh no - our fascination soon turns to horror as we realise this is another oil slick! A quick look over the side confirms the worst - more oil stains on the side of the hull and dinghy. It turns out that an operator at the oil terminal beside us left a valve open and pumped out oil for over an hour. Fine for commercial vessels, but for yachts it not only looks disgusting, but can damage the gelcoat. The oil gets everywhere, particularly from the dinghy and ropes when we bring them on board.

Panama Canal - *Pacific Voyager* **covered by an another oil slick**

Brenda (*Ashymakaihken*) rows over to say she is collecting claims from the yachts for the oil slick damage. Here is ours:

APSA, Pacific Voyager, Pier No. 16A
Colon, Panama

Dear Sir,

While my yacht, *Pacific Voyager*, a British registered vessel was anchored in the Flats, we sustained oil damage to our yacht and tender resulting from your oil spillage. We were advised that the oil spillage of 1153 barrels was caused by the incorrect shore valve being open while pumping. We therefore hold your company responsible for the negligence of your operators and make the following claim to address the damage to our yacht.

Surveyor to advise scope of repair	300
Damage to boot topping and topsides	2500
Damage to tender	100
Damage to warps	100
Management fee to plan and coordinate	500
Re-survey	150
Total claim	US $3650

We reserve the right to extend this claim further at a future date.

Yours faithfully, Rory Burke, Captain (As we go to print, no reply so far).

Cigars being made in the *Free Zone*

9th May (Monday) - Free Zone: Every morning at 08:00 there is a cruisers net on the VHF. Today they announce information about a company offering to buy booze from the *Free Zone*, clear it and deliver it to the yacht club for $12. *"What is the Free Zone?"* This is a duty free shopping area, or shop window for South America. Retail buyers come from all over South America to see what is available. We take a taxi to the *Free Zone*. This is an excellent opportunity for us to buy two sets of good snorkelling gear at a reasonable price - fins $47 and goggles $35. At a cigar shop Sandra is mesmerised by the way they roll their cigars. I would love to buy a box, but we do not smoke. Instead we buy a few cases of grog in a wine shop. By 18:00 it is all delivered to the yacht club for just $12.

8th May (Sunday) - Army Brunch: A few days ago on the morning net it was announced that a minibus will come to the yacht club to take cruisers to the American Army base for the weekly Sunday brunch. *"Please put our names down on the list."* So today we are off to chow all we can eat for $8! The spread includes; all the breakfast cereals that go snap, crackle and pop; all the meats that can be roasted, a garden of vegetables; and all the desserts and cheeses we could possibly glutton ourselves on. Needles to say everyone tries to eat half their body weight and returns completely bloated. Thank you American tax payer!

Yacht Club: The Panama Canal Yacht Club in Cristobal is air-conditioned and, with beer at $3 a jug, a good time can be had by all. We pop round for a beer most days, except the day they have a general election, as the bar is closed - surely the very day people need a drink!

9th May (Monday) - Panama City: Up early to take the bus into Panama City. While I am looking for the girl on the tourist brochure, Sandra is looking for thread for her canvas work. (Unfortunately the thread we buy in Panama has too high a cotton content, so after two seasons in the UV it deteriorates. This is particularly noticeable on the dinghy cover, where the panels are coming apart).

In the main shopping area they have a strange custom, the shop assistants stand outside their shops and clap their hands to entice people inside. The first time this attracts our attention, but when we realise they are clapping their hands all the time we ignore them - like everyone else!

Panamanian girl in tourist brochure

10th May (Tuesday) - Supermarket: Sandra and Catherine (*Inamorata*) take a taxi to the El Ray supermarket, which has a wide selection of produce at European prices. They return laden with bags of stores to keep us going across the Pacific.

12th May (Thursday) - Transit: Log book: chart 1299, Panama Canal (scale 1:50,000). With extra food and beer on board, together with our three additional line handlers; Lance, a German tourist, Mark and Catherine (*Inamorata*), and their cat *Half-Hitch*, we are ready to go. Mark used to be in the Merchant Navy so he busies himself organising the four mooring ropes. He clears a space and snakes them out for quick

Half-Hitch *(Inamorata)* on rat-catching duties

Catherine and Mark *(Inamorata)* help us transit the canal

Entering Gatun's first lock - following a Panamax car-carrier, which completely fills the lock

deployment. Our pilot is eventually ferried over at 11:00 - three hours late. His name is Hannibal and he is impeccably dressed - dripping with gold. One gets the impression that this job is just a stepping stone to higher positions come the revolution!!!

Hannibal checks out the boat; crew, ropes, sufficient fuel, and beers. *"Your beers are warm - I'll organise some ice."* On Hannibal's instructions we up anchor and motor slowly up the channel towards Gatun Lock. Hannibal has his own handheld VHF radio to contact the Canal Authority. There is constant communication about who we are sharing the lock with and where we are to be positioned. It seems there was a plan, but these plans change as the day progresses. Today we are positioned behind a Panamax car-carrier which completely fills the width of the lock. Hannibal is continually instructing me on boat position, boat speed and how to approach the lock. He is very caring about our boat and crew.

Two hours later we follow the car-carrier into the first of the three Gatun Locks, along with Helen and Neil (*Alexandra Louise*) and a tug. The tug moors alongside the wall, *Alexandra Louise* moors alongside the tug, then we in turn moor alongside *Alexandra Louise*.

Everything goes okay as the water floods in, and we rise up inside the lock. But, just as we are relaxing thinking there is nothing to this Panama Canal transit, the car carrier in front of us decides not to wait for the motorised mules to

The Panamax car-carrier starts motoring out of the lock which sends a wall of water towards us

pull it out - it starts its propellers in the lock. Yes in the lock! A wall of water comes back towards us. *Pacific Voyager* is all over the place, with the lines taking the strain in the swirling currents. As the car ferry leaves the lock, so the water settles down, and we motor to the next lock - for a repeat performance!!

Sandra makes tuna mayonnaise sandwiches for lunch, which we wash down with plenty of cold beers, that have been sitting in a large sack of ice. Over lunch Hannibal tells us about the history of the canal. It took seven years to dig the Culebra Cut (renamed the Gaillard Cut after the engineer responsible for this section). It formed the principle excavation of the whole canal project as the canal builders faced their most difficult challenge, carving eight miles through rock and shale. They excavated and moved enough rock to build the equivalent of 28 pyramids in Egypt. Each transit of the canal uses some 52 million US gallons of water through the 18 foot culverts. This is enough water to supply a city of 250,000 people for a day. By a quirk of geography, the isthmus of Panama lies west to east, not north to south as you would expect from the alignment of the continents. Consequently when Balboa crossed the isthmus with his conquistadors in 1513 (six years before Magellan), he named the Pacific Ocean, the *South Sea*. Not to be outdone I tell Hannibal we also have canals like this in Birmingham - perhaps not so big, but he does not need to know that!

With the hand-over of the Panama Canal, the Canal Authority has a challenging future. They need to be entrepreneurial and innovative to be competitive in an ever changing market: transcontinental pipelines will reduce the oil tanker tonnage; containerisation offers the possibility of railing the containers; and the new breed of cruise liners are actually bigger than the Panamax, so they cannot use the canal. I ask an American what he thinks would happen if the canal is ever closed for some reason. He replies, "*Nothing will happen for a few weeks while the politicians talk. Then there will be chaos for a few weeks while the disaster recovery planning kicks in. Then they will rail all the containers from San Francisco to Galveston, and not use the canal again. And yachts will be trucked across on a low-loader - it's only 50 miles.*"

It takes a few hours to pass through Gatun's three locks, and rise up 85 feet to Gatun Lake, a man-made fresh water lake. Gatun Lake is 148 sq. miles, and provides water and electricity for the people of Panama. Because we were late leaving Cristobal, we do not have sufficient time to motor to Balboa

Gatun Lake - navigating through the sunken forest

before dark, so Hannibal instructs us to pick up a mooring for the night. After a refreshing swim and wash in the fresh water lake, Sandra cooks a scrumptious dinner of chicken, rice and salad, and after several bottles of red wine we all settle down for the night.

13th May (Friday): *"Oh no! It's Friday the 13th."* Not a good day to be negotiating the Panama Canal!! At 06:30 a ship's horn announces the arrival of our new pilot for the second day. Carlos introduces himself, then checks over the boat and we are away by 06:45. Carlos directs me to a 21 mile short-cut through the old forest which was flooded when they made the lake. Many of the tree trunks are still sticking up on either side of the narrow channel. It is a weird feeling knowing this was a forest 100 years ago. We make good progress across the forest with the unexpected bonus

of our cooling system being flushed through with fresh water.

At Gaillard Cut the mountains rise up steeply on either side, giving a feel for the enormity of the excavation. The canal's width has since been increased in stages. In fact they are still blasting it - we hear a warning siren - then boom, and a geyser of water erupts close by.

Pedro Miguel Lock: The arrangement this time is centre lock on our own with a bulk carrier behind us. A shout makes us look up, as four monkey's fists come flying over. We attach our four, 125 foot lines, which are then hauled ashore and made fast to a bollard. We then tension up and centre ourselves in the middle of the lock and, as the water level goes down, so we let out the lines - this is where the longest lengths of rope are required. Everything goes smoothly and we motor out of the lock.

Above: Pedro Miguel locks - middle lock position, with a bulk carrier behind us

Right: Young, attractive line handlers at the ready

As we pass the Pedro Miguel marina we can see a number of yachts which have stopped over to haul-out and antifoul before entering the Pacific. This is a secure location away from the cities, but the hassle is they now have to organise two lots of line handlers.

Miraflores Locks: Entering the last double lock, our position is controlled by four geriatric line handlers who are walking too slowly for us to keep steerage. This would not normally be a problem, but this section is where the fresh water from Gatun Lake mixes with the salt water from the Pacific, creating turbulent eddies and whirl pools which spin us sideways in the lock! But, as we are only 35 foot long in a 100 foot wide lock, why worry? With the opening of the last lock, so we enter the Pacific, and another ocean for us to explore. There is something special about crossing an isthmus to another ocean and, even more so, when a single lock gate opens up the other half of the world.

With the opening of a single lock gate - so we enter the other half of the world

Further Reading:

www.canalmuseum.com

Passing the Bridge of the Americas - leaving the West behind!

23 Ecuador

As we enter the great Pacific Ocean, the largest ocean by far, "*What route should we take?*" We definitely want to follow in the footsteps of Charles Darwin, so the Galapagos Archipelago is a must. And all the cruisers seem to go to Tahiti, it appears to be the central crossroads of the Pacific. With Galapagos and Tahiti anchoring our route, how should we travel between them? Our options are; a northern route to Tahiti via the Marquesas and the Tuamotu Archipelago, or a southern route to Tahiti via Easter Island and Pitcairn. Unfortunately Robinson Crusoe Island, named after Daniel Defoe's book, is too far south to be considered.

Easter Island, famous for its statues standing guard like lonely sentinels, and Pitcairn Island, famous for the mutiny on the HMS *Bounty* in 1789, are historically unique. But, if they are so popular, why are most of the cruisers sailing the northern

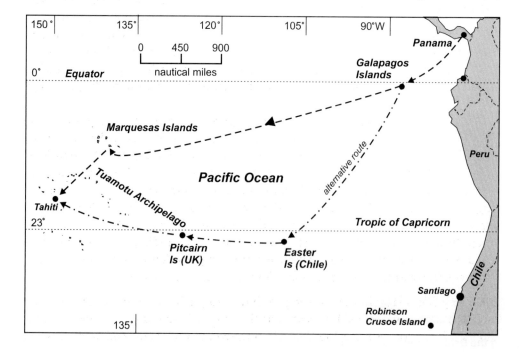

route via the Marquesas? The answer is that both Easter Island and Pitcairn Island have exposed anchorages. Even after making the effort to sail to them, it may be necessary to wait for settled conditions, and once ashore the visit may be for just a few hours as the weather could rapidly deteriorate. We decide to take the risk adverse route via the Marquesas and the Tuamotus to Tahiti.

Magellan: The Pacific Ocean was named by Ferdinand Magellan, in 1519, after navigating the Magellan Straits. To his officers he said, *"Gentlemen, we are now steering into waters where no ship has sailed before. May we always find them as peaceful as they are this morning. In this hope I shall name this sea the Mar Pacifico."*

The Pacific Ocean consists of some 25,000 islands rising from the surface of the deepest ocean. Some of the islands are atolls, which look like a scattered necklace of islets encircling a lagoon, while others are the remnants of ancient volcanos poking their heads above the crystal clear waters, and capped with white clouds. The Pacific Ocean covers a third of the globe; it has the deepest trench off the Philippine coast where the sea bed plummets to 11,000 meters; there are some 2,000 languages spoken here, 700 in New Guinea alone, and we are hoping to get by with only English, French and Spanish.

Balboa yacht club (since burnt down)

23rd May (Tuesday) - Las Pearlas: Log book: chart 1300, Approaches to Panama (scale 1:150,000). Las Pearlas were first claimed by Balboa for Spain in 1513. It is thought that the famous 31 carat Peregrina pearl worn by England's Mary Tudor probably came from one of the Islands.

Yachts en route to the South Pacific often stop at one of these islands for their final preparations. So after a short stopover at Balboa for our final shop, we sail to Las Pearlas Archipelago which is only 35 miles away. After the day's sail we anchor for the night in a sheltered bay at Contadora Island to double-check *Pacific Voyager* before departing across the Pacific.

The hills are so green, and the atmosphere so humid, that we feel the photosynthesis is about to become audible. The tranquil blue skies we had yesterday morning become increasingly obscured by ominous menacing cloud formations. Sure enough, it pours down overnight. In the squalls, *Pacific Voyager* bucks and rears as if she is in a rodeo. When it rains in this part of the world - it really rains. A huge thunderstorm brings torrential rains - we have not experienced rain this heavy before. It is literally bucketing down and, of course, the rain finds more places to weep through in our cabin. We are now on drip-watch, finding leaks everywhere - leaks we never knew we had. The leaks are compounded by the humidity that threatens to cover the boat in mould. However, there is a bonus!

24th May (Tuesday): In the morning we have caught 100 litres of water, our main tank and jerry cans are overflowing, and the dinghy is full of rain water - time for our first bath since leaving the UK!!! Feeling wonderfully refreshed, and with full

Las Pearlas - First bath since leaving the UK - sorry no photo of Sandra!

tanks, lockers bursting with provisions, and gear checked, we are now physically and mentally ready for the Pacific Ocean. Leaving Las Pearlas by the south passage between Santa Catalina and Isla Chapera, it is approximately 1,200 miles to the Galapagos Archipelago so, with good winds, the passage should take about 10 days.

Our start is rather uncomfortable, with torrential rain and cross seas. As we beat to windward in lumpy seas, we are both feeling queasy - perhaps sailing is not so great after all. We have little energy to do anything and *Pacific Voyager* looks a mess. It feels damp. It is damp. And Sandra is running out of dry tea towels to catch the drips. This could turn into an endurance test. With the boat pitching and rolling the crazy motion is threatening to knock the life out of the fruit and vegetables in our small hammock over the galley. If the skins get damaged the fruit will go off quicker.

It is surprising how much flotsam there is floating around in the water; tree trunks, branches and all sorts of industrial waste. Log Book 21:00 - *sailing through squalls all day. Humid below with all the hatches closed, makes our night watch very unpleasant.*

25th May (Wednesday): The wind has eased to the awkward speed of 20 to 25 knots on the nose. It is awkward because at 20 knots the genny is powering away, but at 25 knots it is overpowered. We can only reef down to our no.2 jib as we are not carrying a no.1 jib. *Pacific Voyager* needs the headsail power to beat to windward, so we hang on the genoa. Under normal circumstances this would be annoying, but with head winds and the Humboldt current pushing us north, forward progress seems impossible - it is a real challenge. After what we thought was a good 24 hours beating to windward - 12 hours on one tack and 12 hours on the other tack - we are almost back to the same position we were the day before. I can feel a twinge of desperation swell up inside me, *"We could be here forever at this rate!"*

Our options are to either tack north with the Humboldt current and risk missing the Galapagos Islands as we continue on to the Marquesas, or tack south east to Ecuador where the Humboldt current is weaker, gain more south, then tack westwards where the northerly current is narrower and the wind more likely to be favourable. As we are really keen to see the Galapagos Islands we tack south east.

Booby: A booby lands on the foredeck. *"Sandra we have company."* The booby preens itself on the bouncing pulpit where it balances for an incredible 24 hours - most of the time on only one leg. Boobies are aptly named because they look clumsy for a bird - birds are generally graceful. I read that the term booby-trap was derived from the simple trap the sailors used to set to catch the booby, a noose with a piece of food inside. Sandra in her true hospitable fashion tries to feed the booby with some tinned tuna. Initially the booby seems tempted by Sandra's offerings, but then it decides to leave its previous meal on the genoa, flies off and circles the boat. To our horror it tries to land on the wind speed anemometer on the top of the mast. Its weight could easily break the delicate instrument. At this point we start shouting and waving our arms to frighten it off. It gets the message and leaves us.

Booby on the bouncing foredeck

30th May (Monday) - Shipping Lane: The seas are calmer now and the skies are clearing. After seeing absolutely nothing for days everything happens at once. First we spot a baby shark as we change the genoa; then we spot a school of whales 300 meters away, and then a huge container ship appears bearing down on us. Sandra radios to the container ship (*Futuro*) on the VHF. They have seen us and will steer clear if necessary. Then we spot another two ships *Sea Hunter* and *Gongodilla* and, with darkness approaching, we can see a long line of navigation lights, one ship after the other stretching into the distance. *"Where are they all coming from?"* Sandra asks. I check the chart, there is nothing special about this area, we are in the middle

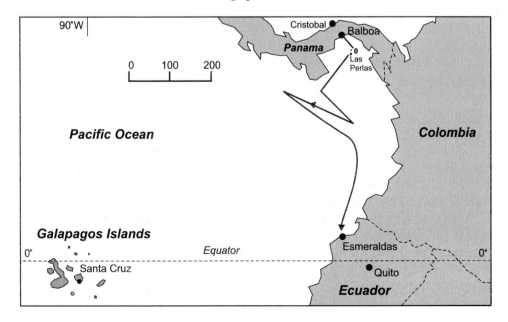

of nowhere, and then it dawns on me. *"Yes of course we are crossing the main shipping route from Panama to South America."* It is like a maritime M1. Tacking away brings us back into the cruising isolation we prefer.

Diesel: To improve our performance against the Humboldt current and our tacking angle, we have been motor-sailing and have now used up much of our valuable diesel. I check our engine hours since leaving Panama and calculate our consumption at 3 litres per hour. *Pacific Voyager* will have to ras (replenish at sea) soon, or bunker. "*I wonder if we can pop-in somewhere for fuel?*" I check our large scale chart of South America - West Coast (scale 1:1,394,000), which only shows one port in our area - Esmeraldas. Although we do not have the appropriate harbour charts or cruising pilots, we decide to try and buy fuel at Esmeraldas. This will at least give us the option of motoring all the way to the Galapagos if necessary, rather that than to become one of Jimmy Cornell's statistics!!

1st June (Wednesday): As we approach the coast of Ecuador, we can see a number of oil tankers moored offshore. *"They must have single point moorings - so there should be deep water here."* (At the time we were not aware this oil terminal is at the end of the trans-Andean pipeline, and is the main oil terminal for this part of South America).

08:00, as we approach Esmeraldas a speed boat with two fisherman on board come over to say hello; they make a cigarette sign, then go on their way. *"What does that mean?"* We are a little nervous, Esmeraldas is well off the cruising route. What sort of a reception will we receive?

Approaching Esmeraldas' harbour slowly, we are closely watching the echo sounder. I have no idea what the harbour layout is like, but I feel if there are oil tankers around then it should have commercial port facilities. Two local chaps are fishing from a dugout canoe as we pass a channel marker. Sandra shouts over to them in Spanish, *"¿Dónde puedo comprar diesel por favor?"* (Where can I buy diesel please?). One of them points to the entrance of the harbour. *"Gracias."* (Thank you). Continuing on towards the entrance we can see what looks like a fuel barge on the port side and what appears to be the customs building to starboard - we make straight for the fuel barge.

Alongside the fuel barge we are greeted in Spanish by a chap who looks like the manager. Now Sandra's Spanish comes into its own, *"Buenos días senor. Puede ayudarme? Necesito diesel, por favor."* (Good day sir. Can you help me? I need diesel, please).

"Si, Si."

"¿Cuánto cuesta?" (How much is it?).

"2000 sucres."

"¿Aceptan tarjeta dinero americano?" (Will you accept American dollars?).

"No." We are mystified - everyone accepts American dollars! And of course we have not got a credit card any more.

"¿Hay algún banco cerca dónde se pueda cambiar dinero?" (Is there a bank that changes money near here?).

He points towards the town to indicate the direction for the bank. It is about a four kilometres walk. I feel a little uneasy about leaving the boat, but it looks safe enough tied to the fuel barge in an isolated corner of the harbour, and there is a security fence around the compound. Nipping into a port to bunker is one thing, but to take a stroll around the town may be an issue with the immigration officer.

With *Pacific Voyager* locked up and our boots on, we prepare for a long walk, but feel a twinge of excitement at the prospect of seeing a new town. As we walk past the office, the manager calls us over and offers to take us into town in his pick-up truck. He drives along a dirt road passing scores of local fishermen maintaining their small boats and nets. The inner harbour looks grubby, there are no other yachts. It looks a bit like the squalid *graveyard* corner of the harbour in Gibraltar.

There is a wide dual carriageway running through the centre of the town, with trees lining the central reservation. The layout is well planned and obviously built during a former period of prosperity. But there is little traffic now and the town is generally run down and untidy. A far cry from the time when Esmeraldas was a busy port used by the Spanish conquistadors opening up Ecuador.

The manager takes us to a shop which sells plastic containers. We buy four, 20 litre containers, which will increase our range by 120 miles. I would have bought more if I thought there was room to lash them on the side deck. They are rectangular which will store better than the round containers we bought in Panama.

As we drive back towards the harbour Sandra asks the manager, "*¿Perdone, dónde esta el banco?*" (*Excuse me, where is the bank?*).

"*Si, dinero americano, está bien.*" (*American dollars are okay*), he replies. I wonder what made him change his mind. Probably best not to ask. By the roadside there are a few small kiosks selling food. We stop to stock up on some local produce; bread, cakes and fresh fruit.

Back at the fuel barge we take on 70 gallons of diesel at US $1 per gallon ($1.50 a gallon in Panama). Great, now we feel comfortable. It is a pity we cannot hold a tonne of fuel (next boat!). As soon as the diesel cans are stowed away we cast off and depart from Esmeraldas without a backward glance. There is not another yacht in sight and we feel we are pushing our luck in the wrong place. But with full bunkers and some fresh cakes we are leaving with relieved smiles on our faces.

Further Reading:

Hemming, John., *The Conquest of the Incas*
www.ecuador.org
www.lonelyplanet.com

24 *Galapagos Islands*

Since leaving Esmeraldas we have made excellent progress in the right direction! We could happily motor sail all the way to the Galapagos if necessary, now that we have plenty of fuel on board. The bread and flat cakes I bought from the street trader in Esmeraldas are excellent - really tasty. I wish I had bought more now as the sea is a bit bouncy for Sandra to cook.

4th June (Saturday): Log book: chart 4811, Mexico to Ecuador (scale 1:3,500,000). Change headsail from genoa to no.2 jib as the wind picks up. During the early hours of the morning we can see lots of flying fish jumping in our phosphoresce and, sure enough, daylight reveals 12 flying fish and a couple of squid on the deck. We even have one flying fish in the cockpit.

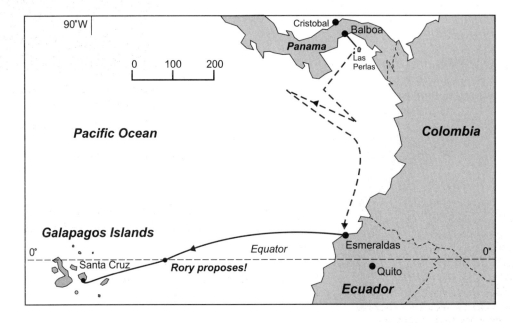

Try increasing watches to 6 hours to give the person below nearly a normal night's kip. The cold north-flowing Humboldt current is lowering the temperature even though we are near the equator - Sandra has started to use a blanket at night to keep warm. As we progress westwards we can tell from our drift that the Humboldt current is getting weaker.

Sandra makes bread and scones, which I top with Heinz baked beans for breakfast (only 50 tins left). Dinner is mash potatoes (from a packet), courgettes and a tin of ham. Sandra notices a small cockroach in the galley. Where did that come from???

I finish reading *The Life of JF Kennedy* - I feel I now know more about the American political system. My next book is Columbus' four journeys, which of course I should have read in the Caribbean. Meanwhile Sandra is reading about the life of Charles Darwin. The conditions are rough and bouncy, which makes our movements slow and awkward - we do not feel like doing anything more energetic than reading.

7th June (Tuesday) - Crossing the Equator: Log book: chart 1375, Galapagos Islands (scale 1:750,000). As we sail further south the sun climbs a little higher each day, and the north star a little lower. A feeling of anticipation grows as *Pacific Voyager* draws closer to the equator. It is traditional to ask Neptune's permission to cross the equator, so Sandra dresses up as a mermaid (*Aqua Sandra*), and I dress up as Neptune (*Neptune Rory*). Fortunately this event occurs in the afternoon so we can video the action. On the GPS we watch our position slowly change, *"Nearly there, where's the line on the sea???"*

Sandra asks permission, *"Oh Neptune Rory please may I cross the equator and be accepted into the southern hemisphere - and please don't make me do something horrible."*

I reply, *"Oh Aqua Sandra according to the ancient Order of the Deep you must pay homage and be initiated before you can enter the southern hemisphere."*

Aqua Sandra asking permission to cross the equator

"Oh Neptune Rory I hope my initiation will be a pleasant one."

"Oh Aqua Sandra according to Michael Palin you must eat a bowl of ...."

"Oh no ...."

I am so impressed by Aqua Sandra's attire and beauty, that I get down on bended knee clutching my trident and propose.

"Oh Aqua Sandra will you marry me?"

"Oh Neptune Rory I accept - what about my engagement ring?"

Neptune Rory just before he proposes

"I haven't got one."
"I want a ring," demanded Aqua Sandra.
"What about a monel split pin?"
"That'll do perfectly thank you."

8th June (Wednesday): Beating into 25 knots of choppy seas - we both feel punch drunk. Our bodies are exhausted, and now the SE winds are tracking through south to SW - we could be headed again!!! This is becoming a real challenge. During the day two pilot whales come close to have a look at us. Dinner at 18:00 is tinned tuna and potato salad in a plastic bowl - followed by half a bar of chocolate.

9th June (Thursday) - Fishing Boat: A day out from the Galapagos, we see a fishing junk approaching us. There is Chinese-type lettering on the side. We pass in front of them, then they change course towards us. After all the talk about pirates we get this uncomfortable feeling as they edge closer, which is sad really, because they only want to come over and say hello and wave - we wave back and they leave.

See more small cockroaches on board - we are not alone any more. Must have picked them up in Panama, or Esmeraldas, while we were alongside. *"They must be breeding - how are we going to get rid of them???"*

On the SSB we speak to Helen (*Alexandra Louise*). They are already in the Galapagos. She warns us about the strange setup between the custom officer and harbour master in Academy Bay. *"Don't check-in to the custom officer, because he will charge you $100, better to check-in to the harbour master who doesn't charge. But, be careful, as Neil has already spent a couple of hours in jail while the customs and harbour master argued between themselves over finances."*

10th June (Friday): 07:30 - Sandra awakes to the most beautiful sight of Santa Cruz and Santa Fe. It is one of those perfect mornings, the blue South Pacific is twinkling under the gentle breeze, the air is crystal clear, perfect visibility, blue skies, and just sufficient breeze to fill our sails. What a wonderful way to end our trip after all the trouble we have had getting here. It has taken us 17 days to do a 10 day trip - people who left after us got good winds and are already in the Galapagos.

A school of dolphins arrive, looking like torpedoes of phosphoresce gliding along effortlessly with us, crossing under our bow from one side to the other. With our cruising speed of 5 knots and their cruising speed of 20 knots, they have full control. This is a spectacular greeting to the Galapagos Islands and hopefully an indication of more to come.

Sandra speaks to Brenda on the VHF - Brenda warns us, *"Try and get in before the weekend otherwise the officials may charge you overtime."* On goes the engine to make sure we arrive early afternoon.

A couple of hours later we motor into Academy Bay (Santa Cruz), and look for a suitable spot to anchor. Several yachts are anchored in the harbour full of charter boats and fishing vessels. Finding a gap, we anchor in 7 metres of water. The holding feels good, but the bay is open to an uncomfortable swell so, like most of the other vessels, we use a kedge anchor from the stern to swing the bow into the swell.

Harbour Master - Check-in: Hurriedly we pump up our dinghy and motor ashore to check-in with the harbour master before closing time. Our meeting with him is very cordial - he is accompanied by his wife Martha who translates English to Spanish, and back to English for us. The harbour master tells us to have nothing to do with the immigration department, "*They want to charge you $50 to check-in and $50 to check-out, they are crooks. I will give you clearance.*" And the

Sandra stepping ashore at the dinghy dock near the harbour master's office

harbour master only charges us $75 harbour dues to anchor for five days! His charges seem inconsistent, because last week Helen and Neil (*Alexandra Louise*) paid $65 for 7 days, and as we leave Ken and Gret *'Old Timers'* only pay $35 to stay for 4 days - both bigger boats than ours!!! And for some reason a singlehander is allowed to stay as long as he wants - for nothing!!!

When the harbour master has completed filling in his forms from our ship's papers he says he will keep our ship's papers for us in his safe. I wish I had taken photocopies as this leaves me with an uneasy feeling for the rest of the week.

History: The Galapagos Islands were first discovered by the Bishop of Panama, Tomas de Berlanga, in 1535, when he anchored here in search of water. "*It seems as though God had showered stones,*" said the Bishop about the desolate landscape of Batolome Island. The profusion of wildlife we are aware of today must have then been masked by the stark volcanic landscape.

The Galapagos Islands began their rise from the sea about five million years ago. The islands lie near the junction of three of the earth's tectonic plates, and are moving slowly south east over a hot spot, which feeds fiery magma to the volcanoes on the western islands of Fernandina and Isabella. The eastern islands are older and colder and, for the most part - inactive.

In the 17th and 18th centuries buccaneers, whalers, and sealers used to anchor in the Galapagos. During that time they filled their holds and decks with more than 150,000 giant tortoises. These tasty provisions could live for a year or more without food and water in the ship's holds. This devastated the population of these animals and, consequently, some species are now extinct. It was these tortoises (Galapagos in Spanish) that gave their name to the islands. Ecuador, which derives its name from the equator, annexed the Galapagos Islands in 1832 and, in 1959, declared most of the islands a national park.

Although the Galapagos Islands straddle the equator with its warm waters, they are also washed by the cold Humboldt current from the Antarctic, which sweeps north and westward loaded with nutrients. Riding such ocean rivers aboard rafts of vegetation, ancestors of many of the Galapagos' uniquely adapted species probably arrived from mainland South America 600 miles away.

El Nino: We glibly talk about the El Nino changing European weather but, here in the Galapagos, the warm El Nino current can be devastating. Most fish live in a narrow band of temperature around five degrees centigrade - so when the water warms up they have to go deeper in search of cooler water. If the creatures feeding on these fish cannot dive so deep, this breaks the food chain leading to starvation.

Charles Darwin fixed the Galapagos Islands on the map of human imagination after his five year circumnavigation aboard HMS *Beagle* (1832 - 1836). Contrary to popular myth, Darwin had no sudden flash of inspiration during the voyage, but his observations of animals and plants, most famously in the Galapagos, became the hard evidence to support his later theories.

Young Darwin the naturalist

Darwin said of the Galapagos, *"I never dreamed that islands...... most of them in sight of each other, formed of precisely the same rocks would have 13 different species of finches. Each with a different beak suited to the different food."* Darwin concluded that the finches must have had a common ancestor. The findings from the expedition eventually resulted in his theory of evolution. *"Both in space and time, we seem to be brought somewhat nearer to that great fact - that mystery of mysteries - the first appearance of new beings on this earth."* Charles Darwin, *The Voyage of the Beagle*, published in 1860.

Charles Darwin, the father of evolution

Although Darwin's theory of evolution was the corner stone of modern day thinking, when the *Origin of the Species* was first published in 1860, he became the 19th century's most controversial naturalist.

I have always been interested in the evolution of man ever since I attended a lecture on Charles Darwin the *'Shropshire Lad'*, while I was at Oswestry boarding school. The lecture inspired me to visit many of the key archeological sites; the Neander valley (*Neanderthal man*) in Germany, the Cro-Magon hotel (*Cro-Magon man*) in France, and the Sterfontien caves (*Australopithecus Africanus*) in Southern Africa.

11th June (Saturday) - Darwin Institute: The research institute in the Galapagos is named after the great man himself. The Darwin Institute is a twenty minute walk from the dinghy dock. As we walk along the main street, we are surprised to see how many of the shops have the distinctive WWF (World Wildlife Fund) symbol in their window. To be a true eco-tourist we need the panda symbol on our tee-shirts.

The Darwin Institute consists of a number of buildings connected by a decked walkway over the undergrowth, giving an elevated perspective of the terrain. The museum displays are very dated by present day international standards. But as it has the distinction of being at the heart of the development of the theory of evolution,

Brenda, Ashley and Sandra on Darwin Institute's raised walkway

this adds a historical perspective other museums will never achieve. The Darwin Institute is a very special and unique place in its own right - a mecca of evolution.

The Darwin Institute is engaged in preserving the fauna and flora of the islands, as they are under threat from the recent boom in eco-tourists and the increase in local population. This has forced the environmentalists to limit access to the islands which are now a designated world heritage site. The islands are a national park and the seas around them a marine reserve, therefore visitors permits are require.

There seems to be a tortoise breeding programme at the Institute as a number of tortoises have been separated by age into different pens. There are also a few giant tortoises in another location where we can walk into the enclosure. Their massive shell bound bodies and short stubby legs make them appear awkward as they amble along. Apparently their sight and hearing are impaired, enabling us to get quite close to them - although I am sure the tortoises must be used to the 60,000 visitors that pass through the Institute annually. One of the striking features of the Galapagos is that all the animals seem unafraid of humans.

Left: Rory helping a tortoise keep cool with a hosing down

Below: Sandra and Brenda talking to the tortoises

Above: A truck takes us to the lava tunnels

Right: Sandra collecting fruit from the orchard

12th June (Sunday) - Lava Tunnels: Jimmy Perez, who owns the Salymon restaurant, organises a trip for us to see the lava tunnels for US $8 each. The tour guides take us in a farm truck out of town, along a dirt track which winds its way up the side of the volcano. We disembark at a farm where they encourage us to collect oranges, passion fruit and avocados from their orchard - we fill our bags and hats with them. They then lead us to the crater rim, which gives us stunning panoramic views of the island.

I had never heard of lava tunnels before. These lava tunnels were formed when the volcano was active. The molten lava would flow like a river, and a tunnel would form around the lava river as the outer skin solidified. The volcanic Hawaiian Islands are similarly constructed with lava tunnels and moonscape lava fields. The tunnel we walk through is over one km long. We are greeted by a number of troglodyte tortoise skeletons by the entrance - this was obviously their home at some time.

Left: Entering the one km lava tunnel

Below: The final resting place for these troglodyte tortoises. They must have purposefully come here to die

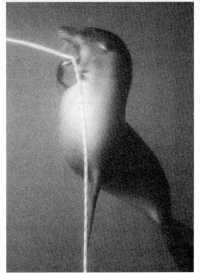

Above: Scene out of Sea Hunt - the seals playing around us
Top Right: Rory swimming with the seals as they frolic around us
Bottom Right: One seal tugs on the rope attached to an empty coke bottle!

13th June (Monday) - Sea Lions: We hear about the possibility of swimming with the sea lions and sharks - Sandra is not so sure about the sharks. Six of us, plus snorkelling gear, lifejackets, cameras and water bottles, pile into our Caribe dinghy. It is a tight fit but the Caribe dinghy feels secure as we motor out to the island at the mouth of Academy Bay.

At Isla Caamano's beach, we anchor about 50 metres off in 5 metres of water. There are plenty of seals on the beach - the sight of some big buggers makes me think we are making a serious life-threatening mistake. As we are preparing to snorkel, the first sea lion pups start to arrive. They swim so close to the dinghy I can reach out and stroke them, tickling their backs as they arch over.

As we ease into the water, we are not quite sure how we will be accepted, but true to form the sea lions just want to play, frolic and clown around with us. A popular toy for them is a plastic coke bottle tied on the end of a line - this soon attracts their attention, and they start playing with the rope, biting and tugging as a puppy dog would do.

The seal's curiosity gets the better of them as they egg each other on - getting nearer and nearer to us as we swim amongst them, but always just too far for us to reach out and touch them in the water. However, one of them courageously inches forward trying to nibble Sandra's fins, then tries to nibble on her camera as she is taking a shot. Sandra tells me later, *"I could feel its whiskers actually tickling my hand!!!"*

Ashore the sea lions look ungainly shuffling along the beach, but in the sea they are in their element, effortlessly diving, gliding and performing acrobatics - they even mimic us as we roll over in the water. We feel privileged to swim with the seals and have a very warm feeling being so close and intimate with these creatures in the wild. This kind of experience does not really happen at home - try and get close to a fox or badger. But at sea, we have been approached by porpoises, stingrays, whales and now the seals . It is amazing how they let us get so close to them.

Left: Sandra cannot be tempted to swim with the black tipped sharks

Right: Male frigate ready for courtship - inflates his stoplight red sac to attract the female

Frigate Birds and Sharks: On the way back we explore an inlet which leads into a narrow canyon running parallel with the shoreline. The frigate birds are nesting in the cliffs, while the sharks are breeding in the water. The frigate birds courtship is a sight to see. The males are perched amid the intended nesting sites in the shrubs, and inflate their stoplight red sacs to catch the eyes of females cruising overhead.

Up the inlet there are a few local lads swimming with some **black tipped sharks**. *"They must be mad,"* Sandra exclaims - but they assure us it is quite safe to swim with these reef sharks - even though this is where they breed!! Swimming with them out in the bay is one thing, but surely the sharks must feel trapped in such a confined space - we are happy to sit this one out.

Marine Iguanas: Motoring on in the dinghy we come across marine iguanas looking like they have come from the beginning of time itself. The marine iguanas would fit well into Jurassic Park, which is still in our minds having recently seen the film in Gibraltar and read the book on passage.

Darwin was intrigued by the iguanas - he had never seen a lizard that was at home in the sea, which is not surprising as the marine iguana in the Galapagos is the only one of its kind in the world - lizards are otherwise exclusively land reptiles. The marine iguanas feed underwater on seaweed but, because they are cold-blooded, they have to keep coming out of the water to heat up in the sun.

The marine iguanas follow a daily routine that maintains their body temperature at an efficient level. At dawn they assemble at the top of the lava ridges and lie broadside to the rising sun to absorb as much heat as possible. Basking in the sun like living solar panels, can bring their body temperature up to 36 Centigrade. As the sun rises and gets hotter so they rotate the narrowest part of their body to face the sun - thus reducing their heat intake. They have no sweat glands and therefore no means to cool their bodies, other than having a swim. This clearly shows how they have evolved to adapt and survive in their unique surroundings.

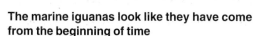

The marine iguanas look like they have come from the beginning of time

The marine iguanas regularly dive down to 12 meters for up to 30 minutes. During Darwin's visit, a sailor on the HMS *Beagle,* as an experiment, tied a heavy weight to a marine iguana, sank it and found that it was still alive an hour later.

The classic tourist photograph is to see the marine iguanas clinging like limpets to the rocks among the surging waves, with their crest of scales running along their backs. It makes the tourists feel like they are stepping back 200 million years when the marine iguana represented the pinnacle of evolution.

14th June (Tuesday) - Buying Diesel: We hear that the harbour master charges $2 a gallon for diesel, yet it is only 67 cents at the petrol station. Ashley (*Ashymakaihken*) and myself naturally feel we should support free enterprise and buy diesel at the lower price from the petrol station. Loading all our empty jerry cans into our dinghies we motor ashore and hire a truck for $2 to take us to the petrol station, where they fill the jerry cans with diesel. Then we drive back to the harbour, and are in the process of unloading the jerry cans when we are approached by a uniformed officer, who says the harbour master would like to see us immediately. *"Please tell him we are busy, but we will be over to see him as soon as possible."*

We finish unloading the jerry cans then take them back to our boats and return with Sandra and Brenda. On mass we go to see the harbour master, who keeps us waiting outside his office for nearly an hour. We notice the petrol station manager come and go. The harbour master and his wife then call us into the office where we sit in front of a large desk facing them, feeling like naughty school kids - here comes the interrogation.

"Welcome, is everything all right?" Martha asks.

"Yes thank you," we all reply together.

"Is there anything you need?"

"No thank you."

"When are you planning to leave?" And so continues a very pleasant and courteous conversation about every topic under the sun - except diesel.

15th June (Wednesday) - Pelican: There are plenty of pelicans flying around the harbour. I am not sure if they are expecting to be fed, but they regularly fly over and perch on the outboard on our dinghy, which is generally lying astern on a short painter. I am dying to get a picture of one perched on the outboard motor, but they always fly off as soon as I get the camera out. I do not have the patience to hide and wait like a real ornithologist.

Pelican launching itself from our outboard - my best shot!

Right: Jan tries on my Panama Hat - she looks much sexier wearing it than I do.

Left: Market day - our last opportunity to stock up for our trip to the Marquesas

17th June (Friday) - Panama Hat: On one of our walks through the town I notice a shop selling Panama hats, *"I wish I had bought one in Panama."*
"Why not buy one here?" Sandra suggests.
"But it's not the same - okay then."

These famous Panama hats are made from the leaves of the toquill palm. The leaves are shredded to form a straw, which are then plaited by hand to make the practical Panama hat. Some even fold flat for ease of stowage.

18th June (Saturday) - Market Day: This is our last opportunity to stock up on fresh fruit before we depart for the Marquesas. We buy stalk a of bananas for $5. Although some of the food is shipped in from Quito, the local farms supply freshly picked oranges, pawpaws, passion fruit, avocados and even live chickens.

Ode to Galapagos:

Together we drank the natural wonders of Academy Bay
Together we swam and played with the inquisitive sea lions
Together we studied every smile of the giant tortoises and marine iguanas
And together we weighed anchor and bid Darwin's Galapagos a fond farewell

Further Reading:

Stephenson, Marylee., *Galapagos Islands: The Essential Handbook for Exploring, Enjoying and Understanding Darwin's Enchanted Islands*
Stanley, David., *South Pacific Handbook,* Moon Publications
Palin, Michael., *Around the World in Eighty Days,* BBC
www.wwf.org
www.mountaineersbooks.org

25

Pacific Ocean

Day 1 [18th June (Saturday)]: As we clear Academy Bay, we feel elated and enlightened by our experiences in the Galapagos, and once more wish we could have spent longer exploring the islands, especially after the epic trip we had to get here. Our plan is to sail to Hiva Oa in the Marquesas, this is to be our longest leg by far at 3,000 miles but, with a following current and consistent tradewinds, we are hoping our passage will be less than 30 days.

Day 2 [19th June (Sunday)]: Awake to find the solar panel has packed up. I check the electrical supply with my AVO back to the wire leading from the panel - nothing. I suspect the problem must be in the panel itself, so I decide to leave further investigation until we reach a calm anchorage in the Marquesas.

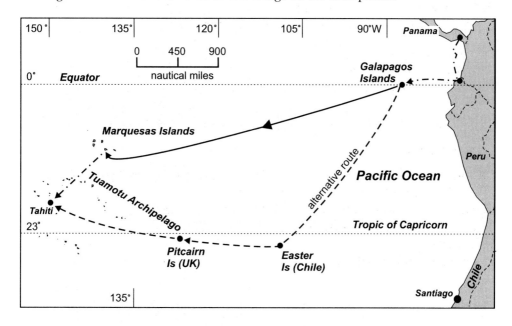

Typical Day: Life at sea has its own rhythm of eating, drinking, reading, sleeping, watch-keeping and sail inspection, with the odd moment of sail handling, GPS navigation, and maintenance thrown in for variety. Our typical day on the Pacific leg starts in the morning with a cup of tea - we are Poms after all. Then we inspect the rig and sails for any sign of damage, and adjust the sheets to suit the wind speed and

Wing-on-wing, **our typical downwind sailing arrangement**

wind angle - we are usually under canvassed having reefed down the night before. With 3,000 miles to our landfall the sails are the prime mover and the key to a successful passage. It is essential to be consistently vigilant. Every time we come on deck we cast our eyes over the sails looking for any telltale signs of trouble. Surprisingly all our repairs have occurred in light airs when the sails flog and whip; not in heavy weather when we would assume the sails were under greater strain.

Our electrical supply is our next consideration. Now that our normally reliable solar panel has packed up, we are reliant on the wind generator and alternator. The wind generator is least effective downwind as the relative wind speed is reduced. This only leaves our engine alternator which we run most mornings for an hour or so to top up the batteries. At night we always sail with the 5 watt anchor light on, but switch everything else off to reduce our power load. We even use the cabin's paraffin oil lamps in the evening as an alternative source of light.

Meals are planned around daylight. Being so near the tropics there are approximately 12 hours day and 12 hours night. Breakfast at first light consists of fruit, cereal and toast. Our main meal is at lunch time followed by a small cooked meal for dinner before it gets dark.

Safety Harness: Our unwritten rule is that the person on watch always wears a harness at night and even during the day if necessary, particularly during rough weather. As we enter the cockpit we clip-on, and advise the other person below if we are going on deck, even if we have to wake them up. At night we also wear a safety strobe light on an armband, or around our neck - the piercing strobe can be seen for miles.

GPS: Instead of going through the palaver of taking two sights a day with the sextant, we take the easy option and note our position with the GPS in the morning and again in the evening. However, there is a problem with our GPS, it is displaying double our speed - a speedy 10 knots, instead of our normal sedentary 5 knots.

Also the memory battery has failed, which would not normally be a problem if the GPS is left on, but as we want to save power, we only switch the GPS on when we want to take a reading. Annoyingly, this means we have to reset it each time, and our concern is that it could pack-up altogether. (Later in New Zealand we have a new internal battery replaced by the manufacturers).

SSB: We are in regular radio contact with a few other yachts crossing the Pacific. The SSB is our only means of communication for weather and position reporting, which is why it is so important as a safety factor to stay in contact. The routine is; say hi, give our position, discuss weather conditions, and exchange information. Sometimes we have a quiz to break the monotony. The SSB channels in the Pacific are quiet - it is as if we have the airways to ourselves, unlike the Atlantic which was a babble of conversations.

BBC: We can only read so much and then we want some other form of entertainment. Our options are to either listen to music cassettes, CDs or the BBC World service. If the other person is bopeep we use headphones. We have worked out the GMT schedule of our favourite BBC programmes, and plan our day accordingly, either listening to them live, or recording them to listen to later on our lengthy night watches.

Flying Fish: Frequently we watch schools of flying fish take flight from beneath our bow wave, bearing off to the side, skimming over the waves and contouring

Sandra collecting flying fish for breakfast from our side deck

like cruise missiles. The changing shape of the marine landscape reminds us of the African safaris we have enjoyed - the fleeing flying fish could almost be a herd of Springbok scampering across the landscape.

Day 5 [22nd June (Wednesday)]: Not a good start to the shortest day on our longest passage. After a night of light winds, we go on deck at sunrise to discover that dreaded sight again - the genoa has blown out along the foot panel - this is the Atlantic saga *déjà vu*. Out comes the Reads Sailmaker as we get cracking on a familiar repair. Thankfully the seas are less rolly than the Atlantic.

Day 8 [26th June (Sunday)]: Turn our clocks back an hour as we move into the next time zone - one hour every 15 degrees of longitude. Our morning inspection reveals breakfast on the side deck - Sandra finds the gunwale covered in flying fish. With twin headsails set and good winds we are recording daily runs between

120 and 135 miles, or approximately two degrees. I suspect we may be getting an extra nudge from a following current.

Bananas: As expected the stalk of bananas we bought in the Galapagos are all ripening at once. In about a weeks time they will all be *'frot'*. I like eating bananas, but a stalk over a week is an impossible challenge - I feel a bit like *'Cool Hand Luke'* (who ate over 50 eggs in one go). Cooking them offers the possibility of confusing my stomach into thinking it is eating something else. Sandra's recipes include: banana bread, banana cake, flambé bananas, banana crumble and cream, bacon and banana butties, and banana curries. Sandra even tries cutting them up into slithers and drying them under the spray hood.

Sinking: This passage is not only crossing the largest ocean in the world, but it is also crossing one of the most remote areas in the world. Few ships pass this way, and no airlines transverse our sailing route. There have been several famous sinkings which have occurred in these waters; the Robertsons (1972), the Baileys (1973), and the Butlers (1989), to name a few. Steve Callahan, in Cruising World, December 1995, wrote an intriguing article about how each of these survivors in their liferafts could have made landfall within a couple of weeks if they could have made just one knot, 30 degrees either side of the prevailing wind.

Day 9 [27th June (Monday)]: During the night the genoa blows out again along the bottom seam. With so much practice, our routine of clamping down the sewing machine on the saloon table is getting quicker and more efficient with each repair. I unpick the stitches with the seam ripper, while Sandra cuts out a new patch. I am sure all these repairs are self-defeating because, with each repair, the patch itself is adding weight in the foot, and its inertia makes the flogging worse. We should really have a new panel or, better, a new sail. It takes one hour to do two metres of repair, so the eight metre panel takes all morning.

Day 11 [29th June (Wednesday)]: Over the SSB radio we hear of a cruiser who shortly after leaving the Galapagos, was hauling in a large fish without wearing his fishing gloves and cut his thumb to the bone on the line. Fortunately they were only a day out of the Galapagos, so they returned to Academy Bay for treatment. This incident reinforces the isolation of the ocean and how vulnerable we are, and the need for good SSB communication.

Our worst accident happens when I notice the genoa's pole is at an odd angle. Instead of being nearly horizontal it is dipping down almost into the sea. Closer inspection reveals the topping lift has parted. As we lower the sails, I foolishly unhook the inboard end of the pole - big mistake. The pole whips round and falls down, giving my forehead a glancing blow. As we stow the pole I can feel blood running down my face. I put my hand on my forehead, half expecting to find a big hole there but, fortunately, it is only a small cut but is bleeding profusely. After stowing the pole Sandra immediately gives me first-aid, while I lie down and ponder how fortunate I am.

Day 12 [30th June (Thursday)]: Wind increases to 30 knots ESE, clear skies, course 227 magnetic. Make our best day's run ever - 160 miles, with triple reefed main, and boomed out genny. However, the downside is that it is uncomfortable as we are bouncing and rolling all over the place.

Charts: Before we left Panama we procured all the charts through to New Zealand - or we thought we had. I now notice there is a gap of

Using the boom as a pole to hold out the headsail

about fifty miles between adjoining charts in the middle of the Pacific Ocean. Even though there is no land within a thousand miles, as we enter this no-mans land it feels a little like falling off the end of the known world. But I assure myself this is how Magellan, Drake and Cook would have sailed all the time.

Day 14 [2nd July (Saturday)]: HALFWAY - what sort of a celebration shall we have today? 1490 miles to go. If we can make 120 miles per day we will arrive in time for Bastille Day on 14th July. The natural world assumes a far greater significance out here in the Pacific - the sky and the sea are watched closely for impending changes.

Day 15 [3rd July (Sunday)]: Oh no, the genoa rips again. This is ridiculous, we must buy a new sail. We have two squalls in the morning - we must be passing through a squall belt. In front of the squalls there is a rainbow so close and brilliant we can almost reach out and touch it. *"Where's our pot of gold??"*

During my night watch I spot two lights on the horizon - is it two ships? No, it turns out to be two bright stars. Then at 02:45 a strong light appears on the horizon and floods the horizon with 3 layers of light. I do not believe in UFO's, but strange things seem to be happening on my watch as I look for traffic. Then I spot a ship on the horizon - our first sighting in two weeks. I monitor its course, but after several minutes it has gone and we are on our own again.

Day 16 [4th July (Monday)]: American Independence Day - but no Americans to celebrate with. I change the camping gas bottle. We are averaging 1 kg per week on passage, down from 1.5 kg per week while at anchor. I always write on a piece of paper beside the bottle the date I start it so that I can keep track of our consumption. I record the Battle of Britain from the BBC World service and will listen to it during my night watch using the headphones.

SSB: Speak twice a day to Ashley and Brenda on the SSB. They are sailing to the Les Gambier from the Galapagos (they have already been to the Marquesas on a previous trip round the world). We are on divergent courses, getting further away from each other. As normal we note each others position, but as I plot Ashley's progress I notice their position is close to a big mooring buoy symbol on my chart. *"Ashley, have you seen that large mooring buoy you are passing?"* *"No - wait one,"* he replies and gets out his chart. A couple of minutes later, *"It's not on my chart."* I am surprised that Ashley only navigates to a GPS waypoint. He checks the chart at the beginning of the passage, then puts it away. The reason I am surprised is that we are still using the GPS as a position fixing tool, and not a course steering tool.

Day 18 [6th July (Wednesday)]: It is my birthday - I am 42. It is amazing to think my last birthday was in Portugal, half a world away. I receive birthday wishes on the SSB from the other yachts we are in contact with, and Sandra spoils me with a bag full of presents wrapped in the newspaper we were using to keep the potatoes fresh.

SSB: On this leg our SSB has really come into its own. Miles Smeeton wrote a book about the sea being his *Floating Village,* we feel exactly the same as we communicate with a number of other yachts on the SSB. By coincidence we are all planning to arrive in Tahiti around the same time so we arrange to meet, and as most of us have not seen each other in person before, we decide to draw caricatures based only on the sound of our voices. On the SSB we hear Chris on *Freya* - he is sailing from Easter Island to Pitcairn Island. We will be interested to hear how easy it is to get ashore there.

The squalls in the Pacific have more sting than the Atlantic with gusts up to 45 knots ahead of a wall of rain. When we are hit by unseen squalls we rush on deck to either hand steer, use the Neco autopilot, reef - or try and do all three simultaneously.

A Japanese ship passes quite closely so we call them up on the VHF. They reply, *"No speak English."* At least we know someone is on watch and courteous enough to reply.

During the night the stars stand-out brightly like pin cushions against a pitch black backdrop - no industrial pollution, or city lights here!

Day 22 [10th July (Sunday)]: Log book: *130 degrees west of Greenwich.* Only 9 degrees to go the Marquesas. The apparent wind increases to 35 knots, we are creaming along at six knots, but the Hydrovane battles with *Pacific Voyager's* yawing - it is steering an anti-submarine "S" course. With the two headsails up, wing-on-wing, the course yaws to starboard - backs the jib - then the course yaws to port - and backs the other jib. I notice one of the hanks has been pulled off the genoa while it was backed. I switch to the Neco autopilot to bring our course under control (in hindsight we could have also put out short warps as tracking devices).
Job list:

- Letter to Apelco again about the battery failing
- Check gooseneck bolt, movement seems excessive
- Lubricate jib halyard top pulley
- Deck light not working
- Waterproof the sprayhood

Day 25 [13th July (Wednesday)]: Speak to Howard (*Alliance*) on the SSB. "*G'day. Do yourself a favour mate and go to Fatu Hiva first, and anchor in the Bay of Virgins. It is a spectacular bay, the locals are very friendly and they have great pamplemousse.*"

Fatu Hiva is also the island where, in the 1930s, Thor Heyderdahl spent a year conducting his research on how the Polynesians live in the bush. Later, he wrote up about his findings in his book, *Fatu Hiva Back to Nature*. Although Fatu Hiva is not a port of entry it makes sense to visit the Bay of Virgins first because, to sail back from Hiva Oa (the nearest port of entry), would be a beat against the tradewinds. I alter course for Fatu Hiva.

Day 26 [14th July (Thursday)] - Bastille Day: I plot the GPS position on the chart, then excitedly I tell Sandra, "*We may see land later this afternoon.*" Having navigated across the Pacific Ocean on GPS alone I feel uneasy about sailing through the night without checking our position the conventional way, so out comes the sextant, almanac and sight reduction tables. This is the first time the sextant has been used since our landfall in the Caribbean over six months ago. I take a midday sight and an afternoon sight, I then spend an hour trying to remember the calculations. The sights are close enough to confirm the GPS's position. On an ocean passage accuracy of +/- 5 miles on latitude and +/- 10 miles on longitude is sufficient in good visibility to make a landfall. I always wish I could dispense with the yearly almanac and our six volumes of sight reduction tables, and adopt a much simpler method - it would at least give us more space below.

Landfall: Late in the afternoon, in the setting sun, we can just make out the cloud capped, towering mountains of Fatu Hiva, appearing pale blue against the horizon. We sail for a few more hours then heave-to for the night.

Landfall late in the evening, after 26 days at sea

Right: Fatu Hiva- our most incredible landfall ever!

Below: Sandra on the foredeck - as we approach Fatu Hiva so the true scale of the mountains become apparent and even more spectacular

Day 27 [15th July (Friday)]: At first light we continue sailing, making for Point Teae at the southern end of Fatu Hiva. The rays of sun light up the east side of the towering volcanic mountains, revealing deep crevasses and sharp shadows. As we approach the land the wind dies completely. With the engine on tick-over we slowly motor up towards the Bay of Virgins, on the west side of the island, where all the anchorages are protected from the tradewinds. With an incredible feeling of elation and contentment that, after 27 days at sea, the longest leg of our circumnavigation is complete, we look forward to sleeping in a calm, sheltered anchorage tonight.

Further Reading:

Heyderdahl, Thor., *Fatu Hiva Back to Nature*, 1974
Robertsons, *117 Days Adrift*
Blewitt, Mary., *Celestial Navigation for Yachtsmen*
Callahan, Steve., *Proactive Emergency Craft*, Cruising World, December 1995, p.64

26 *Marquesas*

After 27 days at sea Fatu Hiva is the most spectacular landfall we have ever made. The enormous towering mountains are a welcoming beacon guiding us in. Our plan is to spend a couple of weeks doing nothing, recovering from our marathon time at sea, then cruise to a few of the other islands in the Marquesas group. The Marquesas were first sighted by the Spaniard Menadione in 1595, and named Las Marquesas after his patron, the Marquis of Mendoza.

Thor Heyderdahl who went native for a year on Fatu Hiva, wrote, "..... *the large island rose from the sea, as if dripping wet with white surf pouring from its coral reef. Mountains wilder than sharks teeth bit into the trade-wind clouds of the blue sky."*

Even **Paul Theroux** has been here. *"The Marquesas had the reputation for being the most beautiful islands on the face of the earth. Because of their steep cliffs, poor anchorages and few good harbours, only a handful of yachts call there. (And we are fortunate to be one of them).*

15th July (Friday) - Bay of Virgins (Baie Hanavave): It is nearly 12:00 by the time we anchor in the Bay of Virgins. Although the anchorage is protected from the prevailing tradewinds, we are still open to swells from the west, and it is very rolly at the moment. Once anchored we sit on the coachroof and savour the sights and sounds of the anchorage. *Pacific Voyager* has never been anchored so close to such impressive mountains. Their steep slopes clothed in thick tropical vegetation, rise almost vertically out of the sea - we

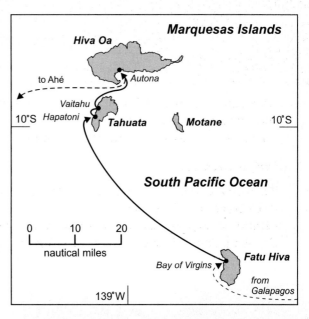

Bay of Virgins - its impressive natural rock tikis guarding the bay

Pacific Voyager, **dwarfed by the Bay of Virgins towering mountains**

literally have to tilt our heads right back to see the tops. The scenery is spectacular, I have not seen mountains this stunning since trekking in the Himalayas. The skyline is a profusion of protruding rock formations which the locals call tikis (Gods).

Our breakfast was delayed while we motored up the coast, so we are now famished. Sandra produces a meal of tinned ham, fried potatoes, and a bottle of wine. It is wolfed down followed by a very deep contented sleep.

Barnacles: Rising refreshed from my slumber some hours later, I pump up the dinghy, launch it and survey the hull which has just carried us 3,000 miles across the Pacific. I am expecting to see a few goose barnacles under the transom, as there were when we arrived in the Caribbean, but I am shocked to see the bow looking like a relief map of the moon. Our hull is a complete ecosystem with all forms of marine life and barnacles looking like mini volcanoes which have formed in the bow wave. It is going to take me weeks to remove them.

Barnacles growing up the bow, looking like a relief map of the moon

Rory filling jerry cans from a tap at the top of the slipway

16th July (Saturday) - Motor ashore in our dinghy to a slipway which is tucked into the left hand corner of the bay. As we approach I can see there is a swell breaking. *"We'll need to be quick to get the dinghy up the ramp before the next wave."* We hold back and pick our moment in between waves.

There is a public water tap at the top of the slipway - it could not be more conveniently positioned. Our water tank level is low after our long passage, so I immediately fill a few of our jerry cans just in case we have to leave in a hurry - this is our risk management in action.

Looking around, a narrow belt of vegetation dotted with houses lines the shore then, behind this, more houses are scattered amongst the vegetation, before a path ascends the mountain into a lush valley proudly guarded by the natural rock tikis.

After many inactive weeks we feel we need to have a good walk to stretch our legs, so we stroll through the village towards the valley leading up into the mountains. The French government have built a concrete road running through the middle of the village, and a storm water drainage system to ensure the fast runoff from the mountains does not cause flooding. This is sound engineering typical of the French Islands. The houses are simply built by western standards and are partly hidden behind lush tropical vegetation. The gardens around the houses are like a menagerie with pigs, hens, goats, dogs and cats. Many of the front doors of the houses are open so we sneak a few glances and notice that inside the houses their furnishings are very scant - concrete floors, foam mattress, a table, a few chairs, small cooker and a few shelves. I am surprised to see in one house a TV connected to a 12 volt battery. *"I wonder how they charge their batteries?"* Then I notice power lines leading up the mountain, *"They must have a hydroelectric scheme."*

Concrete road up through the centre of the village

Chris and Magnus on *Akhnaten* (28 foot sloop)

Akhnaten: On the way back to *Pacific Voyager* we visit the only other yacht in the anchorage, Chris and Magnus on *Akhnaten* (28 foot sloop), from Sweden. They are on a mission, following in the footsteps of Thor Heyderdahl - their hero. They have already sailed to Easter Island en route to Fatu Hiva, and their next port of call is Raroia atoll in the Tuamotus. Thor Heyderdahl has put a number of places on the map of human exploration: Easter Island, where he researched the manufacture of the stone statues; Fatu Hiva where he spent a year going native; and Raroia, where in 1947, his *Kon-Tiki* (Sun God) raft was wrecked on the reef after he had sailed it from South America in 101 days - this proved his theory, that it was possible the ancient Peruvians could have sailed the Pacific.

At 28 feet *Akhnaten* is really cramped and pushed for space. It makes *Pacific Voyager* seem voluminous by comparison. To increase their space below the lads removed their toilet, and now use a *'bucket and chuck-it method.'* Sandra is horrified when I suggest we could do the same!

Solar Panel: Back on board my first job is to check the solar panel which packed-up soon after leaving the Galapagos. I remove the panel from its mountings and see the problem immediately; the electrical connection under the panel has corroded through. Luckily it is a simple job to fit new connectors.

Handheld VHF: Going through the panic bags I am shocked to find the Panasonic handheld VHF's batteries are flat, particularly as this is our emergency communication equipment for the liferaft. (I have since read that NiCad batteries discharge at 3% per day so, after 27 days, it is understandable they could be discharged. However, we now have a XM2000 handheld VHF which we left charged while we travelled overseas for nine months and returned to find it still working. We have also added a mini solar battery charger to one of the panic bags.)

Akhnaten's **sketch of the Bay of Virgins for our visitor's book**

Social gathering outside the church, after Sunday mass

17th July (Sunday): 07:30 row ashore to attend Sunday mass, dressing as smartly as we can, but this is not a patch on the locals' Sunday Best. The ladies wear colourful dresses and most of the men are wearing dark suits. As a fashion designer, Sandra is intrigued by the flamboyance and the originality of their Pacific designs.

There is only one Catholic priest to cover a number of islands, and therefore he has to rotate his visits, probably linking in with the inter-island ferry. He is not in Fatu Hiva at the moment, so today's mass is given by the chief of the island. The congregation's singing is wonderfully powerful, their Polynesian voices are naturally melodic as they sing in harmonious unison. This is the joyful Pacific way of worshipping God. Even though there are only 12 rows of seats in the church they have loudspeakers blasting away to help force their message home. I recognise the Lord's pray and join in, but they say the pray in one breath - I am gasping halfway.

Religious buildings, priests, rites and taboos have always held a central place in Polynesian community life. Hence, the European missionaries found them an easy target, converting their worship to a new Christian God.

After the service the congregation meet outside the church - this is our opportunity to chat with the local people. Sandra is making good headway talking in French and, the next thing I notice, deals are being done. Money has limited value here as there are no shops - they therefore prefer to trade. They ask if we have watches, fish-hooks, perfumes, clothes, waterproofs, ropes, tools, whiskey, and even bullets. In exchange they can trade fruit, carvings of tikis, engraved bowls, and even live pigs.

And, as for the children, they love the most simple things; balloons, coloured pencils and especially bonbons! If only we had known we would have brought more items to swap and give as presents.

Tattoos: We meet Monsieur Tattoo who has an amazing number of tattoos on his body and is also an expert wood carver. After some discussion in French we swap a Stanley hammer and a kettle for three tiki carvings. He also has some finely-carved bowls, but he wants US $100 each. If he does not sell them here he plans to take them to Tahiti on the next ferry.

Bay of Virgins - Sandra walking through the lush tropical undergrowth

18th July (Monday) - Walk: Chris and Magnus told us they trekked from the Bay of Virgins to Omoa, bought some French bread, and trekked back in a day. We do not really want to walk that far, but a walk up into the mountains sounds appealing. Gathering our walking boots, rucksack, packed lunch, water and camera, we are ready for a day's hike. The road through the village soon peters out into a walking track winding its way up the mountain. It is relatively easy going underfoot, and exhilarating as we take deep breaths and fill our lungs with totally unpolluted mountain fresh air. There is plenty of shade from the trees so it is not too hot, but our legs are taking strain; they are not used to this type of strenuous exercise.

Where the track crosses a mountain stream we stop for a rest, it looks cool and inviting. As we listen to the soothing sound of running water we can hear the rustle of lizards and the buzz of insects in the lush vegetation. I am about to take off my boots when a mosquito appears. Out comes the insect repellent to spray our exposed legs and arms. "*That should keep the little buggers away.*" But then another mosquito appears, and another and another. "*Let's get out of here.*"

On the way back down the mountain, we come across hundreds of fallen mangoes littering the ground. Sandra suggests, "*They look okay - why don't we collect some and make a mango crumble??*" Fortunately we have a half empty rucksack with us. Sandra later bakes a tasty mango crumble served with tinned cream. The rest we crush into a breakfast drink, and even use some to make mango chutney. "*This is healthy living.*"

19th July (Tuesday) - Shells: In the afternoon Chris (*Akhnaten*) swims over and introduces Sandra to shell collecting - this is to change Sandra's *raison d'être*. They swim off to snorkel in the corner of the bay. An hour later Sandra returns clutching a hump-backed cowrie - this is to be the first of many shells Sandra is to find in the Pacific. I can see from her expression that snorkelling has taken on a whole new meaning; in fact '*bluewater cruising,*' has taken on a whole new meaning.

Tahuata - a beautiful rainbow welcomes us as a squall rolls down the valley

24th July (Sunday) - Tahuata: After a week relaxing in the Bay of Virgins we have recovered from our 27 day epic, and are ready to move on to the next island - Tahuata. The winds are reasonably fresh between the islands - it reminds us of the Caribbean, As we cruise up the west side of Tahuata, we are attracted to the crescent-shaped bay of Hapatoni, which has a distinctive church near the shoreline, and appears to be a protected anchorage.

25th July (Monday): After a hearty breakfast we row ashore and land on a sandy beach near several houses. By coincidence, this is near the place where the early European explorers first met Polynesian people in the late 1500s - some 400 years ago. Changing our reef-walkers for walking boots, we wander over to an elderly lady standing in her garden, to say hello, and ask directions. She immediately calls her grandson to climb up their pawpaw tree and pick two healthy pawpaws for us. We are touched by her spontaneous generosity. Rummaging in our rucksack we search for something to give her in return. All we have is a packet of powdered fruit juice. She accepts it with a smile.

The pawpaw (or papaya) is a tropical fruit which grows in clusters near the top of a 25 foot tree. The taste is cloyingly sweet, occasionally offset by a slight acidity and a pronounced musky flavour. Best eaten raw, it is customary to serve it with a few drops of lemon or lime juice. The seeds are said to contain an enzyme like pepsin, and are chewed to aid digestion.

Pacific Voyager **anchored in front of Joan of Arc's church**

Hapatoni is a small exquisite village nestled at the foot of a valley, surrounded on three sides by steep mountains. In a large garden to the south of the village is the picturesque, Joan of Arc's church which attracted us here yesterday afternoon. Close up the church is even more impressive. It has a towering steeple, flanked by a red tin roof, and has been built using volcanic rock, both on the exterior and interior. The volcanic rock artistically complements the tongue-and-grove timber panelling, carved doors, and stained-glass windows. The Protestant church on the other side of the village, by contrast, looks like a run down tin shack - I know which God I would prefer to be praying to!

As we explore the small village we come across a copra drying shed. Copra is the name for chunks of coconut meat which are air-dried in racks. Once dried, the copra is shipped to a processing plant to extract the coconut oil which is used in the manufacture of soap, margarine and nitroglycerine, amongst other things. The stench of copra as it decays has a cloying odour which we notice hangs around the drying racks.

Copra drying shed - copra is the backbone of the economy

We understand the French government heavily subsidise the copra crop by giving the local growers an artificially high price. This makes it profitable for local people to harvest the copra, which in turn keeps them gainfully employed and the island's economy ticking over.

On the way back to the beach we pass a newly built house. An elderly man is sitting on the veranda watching the world go by. He introduces us to his two adult sons who want to practice their English. Sandra gets chatting as she normally does and, to our surprise, the father asks for a bottle of whisky. Unable to fulfil his request but with true British hospitality, Sandra invites the sons on board for a cup of tea and cake. On *Pacific Voyager*, while Sandra prepares the nibbles, I ask them if they would like to write something in our visitors book. They are reluctant at first, but when I suggest something like a drawing of a butterfly, which the groovy lad has tattooed on his chest, they grab the pencils and - voilà - a butterfly and horse (horses roam wild here). While we are sipping our tea a wasp flies into the cockpit. The butterfly-man reaches out and squashes the wasp with his hands. Sandra looks at me, as if to say I should do the same - forget it!!

Tattoo: The art of tattooing originated in Polynesia and the tattooed image was originally used to portray the story about the person's background. Needless to say tattooing was banned by the Catholic missionaries. But in French Polynesia today it is still a popular art-form decorating various parts of the body. Some of the

Butterfly man and **Elie** aboard **Pacific Voyager** and their drawings for our visitors book

islanders wearing traditional body tattoos of their cannibal ancestors. Sandra having also seen many of the Marquesian women with neat bracelet and anklet tattoos, that are more like a fashion statement, has been talking about having a tattoo around her ankle and now she is intrigued by the beautiful butterfly tattoo. I can see what she is thinking of suggesting. *"Do you really want someone to puncture your flesh, give you extreme pain and insert a pigment to colour your skin that cannot easily be removed?"* This successfully puts Sandra off and she decides just to admire the art instead.

26th July (Tuesday) - Vaitahu: Up anchor and sail northwards to the next bay - Vaitahu. There are several yachts anchored in the bay; this is where we meet Tim (*Casimer* - Saga 40). He has sailed down from Hiva Oa, with a few other yachts, to spend a couple of days visiting Tahuata. They had to escape from Atuona's harbour when the anchorage became untenable - there were standing waves rolling through the harbour. This is a surprise to us, as we did not experience any unsettled weather in Fatu Hiva.

27th July (Wednesday) - Hiva Oa: We join a small fleet of cruisers who are sailing the 15 miles back to Atuona (Hiva Oa). Tim on *Casimer* arrives first, anchors, and hitches a lift into town before the shops close. He returns hugging a large sack full of French bread, which he shares with the other cruisers.

28th July (Friday): Up early and hitch a lift into Atuona which is only a few miles from the harbour. This is where I test out my theory that we do not need to register our yacht, but we do need to have a ship's data sheet. I have made up a document which contains all the information the authorities are looking for. At the police station the officer copies the information he wants and returns the document. *"Merci Monsieur."* He then tells us something like, *"Bon, vous resterai ici en Polynesia Française pour trente jours et c'est non necessaire payer un bond. Merci beaucoup."* (Which means, *"Good, you can stay 30 days in French Polynesia without having to pay a bond. Thank you."*)

Gauguin: Paul Gauguin the famous French impressionist painter retreated from civilization to the sanctuary of the Marquesas for the latter part of his life. He came to live in Atuona in 1901, after briefly working on the construction of the Panama Canal, presumably to top up his coffers. This remote corner of French Polynesia must have been where Gauguin was influenced by the exuberance of the Pacific's people, scenery, mood,

Paul Gauguin's grave on top of the hill and looking out to sea

and colours. His striking images of Polynesian women rank amongst the most beautiful paintings in the art world.

It is unbearably hot as we walk up the steep hill leading to Gauguin's grave. About halfway up mercifully there is a tap under a large tree. We do not have a drink so much as take a shower. I just fill my hat with water and put it on my head - the water trickles down my face and under my tee-shirt - what relief - sheer luxury. It is a few more minutes walk to the graveyard, and a quick search reveals Gauguin's prominent resting-place facing out to sea. There is something respectful and personal about visiting a famous person's grave - in this case its remoteness and isolation adds to the intrigue.

Food: Back down the hill we go shopping for some crunchy French bread. To our surprise the shop also sells tinned butter and processed cheese at reasonable prices. *"They must be subsidised by the New Zealand and Australian governments."* I buy as many tins and packets as my rucksack will hold - I literally sweep my arm across the shelf loading up my shopping basket. The tinned butter (500g) and processed cheese are both manufactured to keep reasonably well in the tropics without refrigeration. Now we can eat the French way - a crusty baguette smeared with New Zealand butter, a slab of Australian cheese, all washed down with a bottle of wine from Panama!

29th July (Friday) - Petroglyphs: These islands hold many hidden treasures behind tangled vines and lush vegetation. The petroglyphs, or prehistoric rock carvings, are evidence of an early Polynesian culture. Following the directions in David Stanley's guide book, we trek up the steep hillside through the undergrowth. It is excruciatingly hot and humid and, after our past experience, we have plastered ourselves with insect repellent to keep away the mosquitos and no-see-ums, which I am sure are hovering around every corner, ready to hound us. The effort is worth it. In the cool shadows of the tall trees, we eventually reach a huge bolder, behind which we find a gallery of chiselled rock carvings partly hidden by a complex web of vegetation. Over eons of time the elements have weathered away the fine details of the petroglyphs, but we can still identify the faint outlines of fish, birds and turtles. David Stanley, *South Pacific Handbook*, '*Turtles, a favourite food of the gods, were often offered to them on the marae,*" and, the petroglyphs are an, "*.... evocative reminder of a vanished civilization.*'

Pirogues: On this balmy afternoon in the anchorage I hear a distinctive whoosh nearby - I look out to see several pirogues gliding swiftly past. The rowers are training for an inter-island race. I am surprised to see girls paddling alongside males with iron-man physique. Surely the females will be a handicap? But the sight of the girls' bulging arm muscles answers my question. These pirogues are so named because the speed at which they travel is reminiscent of fire. The design has been developed from the early Polynesian war canoes which where used to explore the Pacific. The Polynesians were subjected to famines of devastating proportions, so they frequently had to travel in search of food and new lands, hence the increase of inter-island wars.

Sadly it is time to leave the beautiful islands of the Marquesas

30th July (Saturday): Unfortunately it is time to move on once more so, laden with a sack full of French bread wrapped in our vinegar-soaked tea-towels, we depart these fabled islands for the *Dangerous Archipelago*.

Further Reading:

Hiscock, Eric., *Around the World in Wanderer 111*, Adlard Coles, 1991
Heyerdahl, Thor., *The Kon-Tiki Expedition*, Flamingo, 1948
Heyerdahl, Thor., *Fatu-Hiva: Back to Nature*
Birkett, Dea., *Serpent in Paradise*, Picador
Smeeton, Miles and Beryl., *The Sea is Our Village*
Stanley, David., *South Pacific Handbook*

27 Tuamotu Archipelago

Between the Marquesas and Tahiti lie a vast expanse of atolls - 78 in all. They stretch for 700 miles from Rangiroa in the northwest to the infamous Moruroa Atoll (also spelt Mururoa) in the southeast. The Tuamotus were first sighted and named the *Dangerous Archipelago* by Bougainville in 1767 (the first Frenchman to sail round the world, a year after Wallis visited Polynesia, but a year before Cook). In the late 1940s the Tuamotus were brought into the world's limelight by Thor Heyerdahl's *Kon-Tiki* expedition across the Pacific which ended on Raroia reef and, more recently, by the French for their ongoing nuclear testing on Moruroa Atoll.

Sailing to Raroia atoll, where the *Kon-Tiki* raft landed, sounds like a good idea until we check the chart 4607, Southeast Polynesia (1:3,500,00). Raroia is well off our direct route to Tahiti. Instead we opt to make for a more direct route which will pass close to Takaroa atoll.

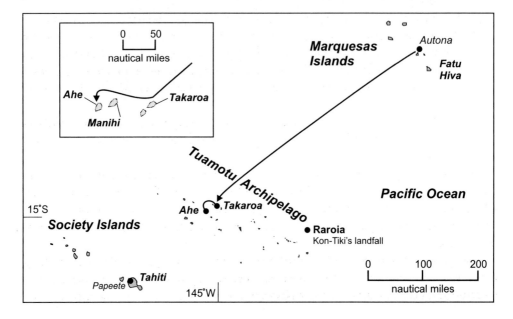

Atolls: The word atoll is probably derived from the Maldivian word *'to close'* or *'unite a horseshoe.'* During Charles Darwin's famous journey around the world (circa 1835), while he was developing his *theory of evolution*, in his spare time he also proposed a *theory of atoll formation.* At the time, it was thought that coral grew at the bottom of the sea bed, and succeeding generations grew on top. Darwin proposed that coral does not grow on the sea-bed, but grows near the surface where the sea temperature is warmer and the sunlight brighter; and that atolls are formed on volcano crater rims, as they subside, or as the sea level rises.

Darwin's theory has prevailed. We now know that although coral may look like plants and trees, it is actually a living animal that grows into massive colonies. In order to form, coral needs sun, clear water and sea temperatures of about 20 degrees centigrade. Around the world, coral grows between 35 degrees north and 32 degrees south. A reef is formed by polyps extracting calcium carbonate from the seawater and depositing it in its skeletons. Coral polyps are living creatures no larger than the size of pinheads but, in their countless millions over eons of time, they have laid the foundations and, with their skeletons, built-up the great barrier reefs.

Coral grows best on the windward side of an atoll where the ocean currents bring abundant nutrients to the polyps, encouraging prolific growth. The opposite happens on the leeward side, where the coral dies and gaps appear in the coral reefs, conveniently forming passes for navigation. (Most of the atolls we visit have a pass on their western side; Ahe, Tahiti, Huahine, Tahaa, Bora Bora and Maupihaa).

Global Warming: The UN summit on global warming has confirmed that *'man has had a hand in the world's increase in temperature'.* Global warming is causing a number of changes which could effect the bluewater cruiser:

- Hotter temperatures will expand the oceans, melt the glaciers, thus raising the sea level (estimate 1 metre in the next 100 years). This will particularly affect atolls, like the Maldives, where the coral is dead and cannot grow to accommodate the rising sea level.
- Hotter temperatures will increase the scale and frequency of tropical storms.
- As the sea temperature rises above 22 centigrade the coral expels the symbiotic algae that inhabits the coral polyp tissue. The coral is dependent on these algae to provide nutrients to survive, and give the coral its colour. Therefore if the sea temperature does not drop the coral will die - called *'bleaching.'*
- As the coral dies, so it becomes a mass of unsightly grey rubble; cruisers who want to snorkel around the brightly coloured reefs, and will turn away in dismay.

The evidence of global warming is very concerning - just consider the coral reefs to be like canaries in a coal mine. With 30% of coral reefs already lost, and another 20% at risk in the next decade, it is a sign that something is very wrong with the oceans when a large part of the most diverse ecosystem on the planet simply tips over and dies.

Dangerous Archipelago: Up until recently these low lying atolls with nothing more than trees marking their existence, were widely avoided by yachtsmen; they were not called the ***Dangerous Archipelago*** for nothing. But, with the introduction of GPS, an accurate landfall at a waypoint by the entrance to the passes can now be safely made (bearing in mind some of the charts where surveyed years ago and are reported to be a mile or two out of position).

30th July (Saturday): Leave Atuona at 15:30 with good winds. During the night there are some strong squalls of 25-30 knots, just when we do not want them. It is very rolly and uncomfortable, and neither of us are feeling our best. The good winds hold for a couple of days before they die away completely. Should we motor or wait for wind? We opt to wait.

2nd August (Tuesday): Our log reads only 25 miles run since yesterday - our worst ever day's run. Weather fluky all day - showers, squalls, with calms in between. Although there is little wind we are still making an average of 1 knot progress - there must be a current carrying us in the right direction. Over the SSB we hear of other cruisers experiencing strong winds of 50 knots on the way to Rarotonga. "*I wonder if we'll be next?*"

3rd August (Wednesday): I wake up to find the sails backed - we are going nowhere. It is dead calm. The sea is completely flat. Surprisingly there is no residual swell like we experienced in the Atlantic. "*It's quieter than being at anchor!*" I even get my computer out - a first for us at sea. But even with the slight motion, the sails flog and, would you believe it, the genoa gets another split on the bottom seam. Log book: chart 998, South Pacific Ocean (Archipel Des Tuamotu) (1:75,000). We ask ourselves again should we motor the remaining 80 miles to Takaroa or just wait? It is so flat and comfortable we decide once more to wait for the wind. We eat well on this calm sea: pasta salad for lunch, whiskey sundowners, oyster dip with spicy chips for pre-dinner nibbles, tuna risotto for dinner, followed by rum truffles.

5th August (Friday): It is still dead calm. "*We've waited long enough - let's motor. At least we can arrive at Takaroa at first light.*" However before we sight land the wind picks up and we enjoy good winds and great sailing at last. From about 5 miles out we sight the tops of the palm trees on Takaroa - if you know they are there it seems to help.

The wind continues to rise as we approach Passe Teauonae. At the entrance we hold back and scan the channel which looks very rough and choppy. The wind is blowing towards the pier we are thinking of mooring against. We do not feel happy about making an approach through the narrow pass to the lagoon. At the moment it is safe for us to wait outside the reef, because the freshening wind is blowing offshore.

I consider anchoring in close, but I do not like the look of the coral bottom and, if the wind shifts during the night, it will back us onto the reef and put us onto a lee shore. That could be more exciting than we want, particularly as there will almost certainly be no lights to give us a relative bearing. Jacob Roggeveen, the Dutch explorer, wrecked one of his ships on Takaroa in 1722. I do not wish to join them in Davy Jones' locker.

"*I think we should push on to the next atoll - this doesn't look inviting.*" As we drift away from Takaroa, we hoist a storm jib to give the Neco autopilot steerage. During the night the wind continues to rise to over 40 knots, making a shrieking wail through the rigging. As the night progresses I can see we are going too fast and will either have to miss the next two atolls or tack around them in the middle of the night. I expect there will be no navigation lights on the atolls, not even lights from dwellings (in hindsight we should have heaved-to until daylight).

Manihi: I navigate north around Manihi during the night. It is a balancing act - I do not want to get too far offshore and have a long tack back or, conversely, get too near the island and run the risk of going aground. I keep an eye on the depth - this is where radar and night glasses would have come in really handy. We are confident of our GPS position which I checked at Takaroa, but I certainly would be very concerned about running a DR under these conditions.

6th August (Saturday): Once clear of Manihi we heave-to until first light then tack the short distance towards Ahe. This is the first time we have needed to wear our Henri Lloyds heavy-weather gear since leaving Gibraltar!!! They really do offer excellent protection against the elements from the cold winds and driving spray as we beat into the weather.

Log book: chart 1175, Plans in the Archipel Des Tuamotus (scale 1:10,000). The chart shows one entrance in detail - Passe Reianui but, as we sail down the coastline, there are no navigation marks to confirm the entrance. We come to what looks like a pass at the correct GPS waypoint but, just to be sure, we continue down the coast a little distance then back track.

The water is flowing out of Ahe's lagoon through the pass at an alarming rate; the sea is bubbling and swirling as we edge in closer. *"I wonder if the current is influenced by the tide - I'll call up on 16 to see if there are any yachts inside."* Bill and Cathleen on *Sea Dabbs* (Crealock 34) respond. After checking their cruising pilot they reply, *"Slack water is 3 to 4 hours after moonrise."*

"When's moonrise?" We hang around the entrance of Ahe going through our almanac, but need not have bothered because the water is continually flowing out. No, this is not some freak of nature, but simply due to the Pacific rollers pounding into the lagoon on the windward eastern side and flowing out of the narrow pass on the western side.

With the Perkins on full wick, we can only manage to inch up the 300 metre-long pass. I take transit bearings on the vegetation to monitor our progress - is it worth it? Yes, our persistence pays off and eventually as the lagoon opens up so the current eases and we make better progress.

Ahe - with the engine at full wick we inch up the pass against the outgoing current

The lagoon opens up into what we think will be a protected area, but now we are exposed to the full force of the wind again, and the seas are very short and sharp. The bow is riding the waves nicely until there are two together - the bow comes straight down off the first wave and buries its nose into the second wave - all over poor Sandra who is on the foredeck hoisting the jib at the time.

Once inside the lagoon we expected to see some indication of life. Surprisingly there is nothing to be seen except for some wooden posts poking out of the water. The atoll looks deceptively small on the Admiralty chart - the entrance is in detail but nothing else. We thought all our problems would be over once inside the pass, but now we do not know which way to turn. "*Call* Sea Dabbs *again.*" They tell us to turn right and follow the coastline until we reach the harbour. (In hindsight we should really have bought a cruising pilot like *Charlie's Charts* and not relied solely on the Admiralty charts).

We tack towards a pole sticking out of the water - to our surprise it is marking a coral head!!!! This is the first time we have been inside an atoll. How can paradise be such a minefield of coral heads? They lurk just under the surface ready to tear our boat apart. Naively we thought the atoll would be a large protected sandy lagoon like we had seen in tourist brochures, but now this tropical lagoon is taking on a different appearance. It takes us over an hour of motor sailing to reach Ahe's only harbour, Tenukupara, avoiding numerous coral heads and buoys along the way. Later we find out these buoys are part of the black pearl industry.

Through a narrow entrance in the coral breakwater, we motor into Tenukupara's harbour which offers protection from all wind directions. It all looks very attractive with turquoise water, white sandy beaches, and motus decked with palm trees, vividly green in the morning sunshine.

There are three other yachts in the snug harbour. After anchoring Willy (*Legolas*) rows over and invites us to his boat for coffee. I bring something stronger as we feel we need it. After an hour or so we return to *Pacific Voyager* to have our traditional settling-in meal. This time it is tinned turkey, stuffing and smash from a packet, tinned peas, gravy, tinned peaches and cream and, of course, a bottle of red wine, followed by the sleep of the dead.

7th August (Sunday): After a good night's sleep and a hearty breakfast we row over in our dinghy to the concrete quay and tie alongside - our first time ashore in eight days. The quay is solidly constructed which makes Ahe one of the easiest anchorages to get ashore. The small town consists of several crisscrossing

Pacific Voyager anchored in Ahe

The solidly constructed quay makes Ahe one of the easiest anchorages to get ashore

streets - French town planning in evidence. Small wooden houses are dotted amongst the coconut trees - all very colourful, neat and tidy, some even have fences surrounding a green lawn. Many have solar panels which the French government supplied to every household; apparently the missing panels may have been sold to visiting yachtsmen - but no-one offered us any. Although the buildings may look basic they all seem to house a television, video, gas stove and a fridge.

Within a few minutes we have walked through the town and into a forest of palm trees which cover the rest of the motu. This area is not so clean and tidy with rubbish strewn everywhere - the San Blas islands were much neater. The coconut plantations are alive with red hermit crabs - most trees have bright metal bands fitted to prevent the crabs climbing up. The thought of meeting one of these crabs in the dark makes me shiver - if their pincer can break into a coconut, what chance does my big toe have? Further on several children are feeding a pig coconut husks - I suppose pigs will eat anything. Sandra plays the *Pied Piper* again as these inquisitive children follow her around the atoll - I suspect they think their may be sweets on offer. Not to be outdone, the pig follows as well!

Back at the harbour, there are more children playing. A small fishing boat, moored alongside the quay makes a convenient diving platform for them. They climb up onto the gunwale and jump as high as they can into the air - then make the biggest splash possible as they crash into the water, screaming at the top of their voices. And they seem to be able to do this continuously, never running out of energy.

Above: Porky the pig even eats coconuts husks!

Right: The fishing boat makes an ideal diving platform for the children

Searching for tiny shells on the beach, while the waves pound the reef

Voilà - Willy and Hilde use the tiny shells they found to make this beautiful page for our visitors book

8th August (Monday): Willy and Hilde (*Legolas*) join us for a walk around the atoll. The seas are still pounding the reef while we collect the minutest of shells from the beach. Later Willy and Hilde surprise us with a beautifully designed page for our visitors book made from these tiny shells.

Ahe's church is the most outstanding building on the atoll and inside it is decorated with masses of small shells just like the ones we found on the beach. Strings of shells are strewn from wall to wall, there are all sorts of religious shell artifacts and even a shell chandelier!

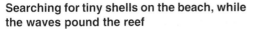

On our walk we meet a local girl, Annalie, and stop to chat, learning some new French words in the process. She shows the girls how to wear a *Tiare* flower behind their ears, as is the Polynesian custom, wearing it either on the left if they are available, or the right side if married. (The problem is Sandra cannot remember which way round to wear them!)

Annalie shows the girls how to wear a *Tiare* flower behind their left ear - but does this mean they are available?

9th August (Tuesday) - Black Pearls: Ari is the chief of the atoll. He speaks excellent English and tells us about the black pearl industry. Thinking rum would be an acceptable trade, we suggest swapping a bottle for a black pearl. This is actually the worst thing we can offer because the islanders want to try and stop drinking completely on the atolls. He politely declines. (We later meet a cruiser who bought a black pearl for US $20. We are then sorry we did not place more importance on buying one in Ahe, as this is, after all, where they are cultivated).

Ari explains how the black pearls are seeded and harvested in a controlled production process. After two years the oysters are taken out of the sea and opened with surgical precision; a snippet of mantle tissue and a nucleus are inserted into

Ahe's charming church, a peaceful setting away from the hustle and bustle. What hustle and bustle?

The interior is decorated with tiny shells from the beach

each shell. They are then put back in the water for another three years for the mantle tissue to form a sac where nacre (the pearl substance that coats the nucleus to produce a pearl) is generated and gives them their black lustre. The sale of the black pearls enables the local people to finance themselves in what would otherwise be a subsistence existence.

10th August (Wednesday): The past few days have been grey and overcast, and today is no exception. The unsettled weather continues with lashing rain. The benefit of all this rain of course, is that our water tank is full; a consideration here because the only water available ashore is ground water, which is not recommended for drinking. My turn to make breakfast - my speciality - baked beans on toast.

Jobs: I make a start on removing the barnacles that have grown on the hull since we left the Marquesas. The water is murky due to the unsettled weather. Willy comes over and helps to clean off the barnacles. He is a great diver and does this sort of thing for fun. Now we have a clean hull, however the freeboard still has oil stains from Panama 4000 miles ago!

While Willy is diving he notices that our anchor chain is wrapped around a coral head, thus shortening our scope. We unwind it and set a second anchor to limit our swinging. Willy tells me about a problem they had when they arrived in Ahe. *"We anchored in 20 metres of water while we went snorkelling. The*

Looking over towards our anchorage at Ahe

coral heads were outstanding - up to 6 meters high. Everything was fine until the wind shifted and we had to leave quickly as our rudder was grounding on the coral. Then we found the chain had wrapped itself around a coral head. Fortunately I had scuba-diving equipment and was able to unwrap the chain. But now I had another problem. Once the chain was freed I had to nip up on to Legolas *quickly, get my gear off and pull up the chain while Hilde tried to hold the boat in position. It was a terrifying experience, as we could have lost everything."*

11th August (Thursday): A wonderful calm day - is the storm over? We are still getting conflicting reports about the weather on the SSB - the whole area is unsettled.

After the gale we have been through we are keen to check the rigging and fittings for any telltale signs of failure, and today is the first opportunity to go up the mast in calm conditions. Sandra prepares herself with protective clothing, while I prepare the bosun's chair and harness. I haul Sandra up on the Gibb brake winch, which is

View from *Pacific Voyager's* mast while Sandra checks the rigging

connected to the bosun's chair, about two metres at a time, and then take up the slack on the jib halyard winch which is attached directly to Sandra's safety harness. The wire rope on the bosun's chair passes through a block shackled to the masthead, while the jib's halyard passes over a block in the masthead - we feel this is the safest arrangement. Sandra inspects all the masthead fittings - everything is okay.

Later in the afternoon, Sandra has the sewing machine mounted on the table - this means business. The genoa needs attention again, a never ending task. It is definitely on its lasts legs. We must have a new one cut in New Zealand. The no.2 jib also needs attention, two eyes need replacing. The eyelet-kit we bought in Salcombe, has certainly paid its way. Sandra's last job is to re-seal the sprayhood. This should stop the odd drip that comes through the material. The spray hood is another candidate for replacement in New Zealand.

Dinner is a paella made with rice, garlic sausage and peas, followed by peaches in sherry and tinned cream. How many more tins?!

12th August (Friday): Another grey overcast day, with intermittent squalls. Sandra tackles the major task of sorting the food lockers and repacks the pilot berth. At last a bit of space. We have definitely overstocked on tinned and dried food. Our meals are now focused on trying to use up a few rusty tins we have found. Lunch today is tinned sweet corn and butter bean casserole, tinned pineapple and cream.

Sandra washes the seat covers, curtains, lee-cloths and ceilings with the excess water we are catching. Since Panama, mildew has been a problem. I suspect it was the heavy rain and humid conditions in Las Pearlas that started it. Sandra applies a second coat of Fabseal on the sprayhood - it seems much better - even though another squall hits us before it has a chance to dry.

Hilde (*Legolas*) rows over with a gift of slices of fried coconut some sprinkled with sugar, some with salt , and also a *fea*, a *Polynesian doughnut* in the shape of a figure-of-eight, which she bought in the village - delicious!

13th August (Saturday): The unsettled weather continues - another session working on the sails. But the highlight of the day is the inter-island cargo boat which arrives in the early morning. The arrival of the boat seems to be the main attraction of the week as, what appears to be the whole community, is down on the dock even if only to look and wave. During most of the morning the locals are busy unloading provisions; food, bedding and building material. (We are to see this on all the atolls and islands we visit when the inter-island boat comes in). With this regular link to Tahiti and the outside world, their remote location does not seem so cut off. They are probably just one step away from internet shopping. The cargo boat leaves by midday for another island, as it weaves its way through the archipelago of atolls.

Dinner is sweet and sour tinned spam (I bet Monty Python never had it cooked this way), with boiled rice and, for dessert, grilled marshmallows and cream.

14th August (Sunday): The weather reports are still confusing, even from Arnold on 8815 Khz USB. However, we feel conditions are improving and it should be okay

We later get to meet Arnold in the Ponsonby Yacht Club in New Zealand

for our two day trip to Tahiti - we decide to leave. We need an early start to give us time to sail between the atolls of Rangiroa and Arutua before nightfall. The lagoon is quite choppy as *Sea Dabbs* and ourselves zigzag our way round the coral heads which, this time, can be clearly seen through the crystal clear water. As we approach the pass, heavy choppy overfalls develop with boiling seas and confused breaking waves, but with a six knot current we are not in the pass for long - we literally pop out of Ahe like the proverbial cork out of a champagne bottle.

Further Reading:

Stanley, David., *South Pacific Handbook*, Moon Publications
Darwin, Charles., *The Structure and Distribution of Coral Reefs*, Third edition
Lucas, Alan., *Cruising in Tropical Waters and Coral*, Stanford Maritime
Charlie's Charts, Cruising Pilot for the Pacific Islands, USA

28 Tahiti and Moorea

Tahiti is the maritime hub of the Pacific, the capital of French Polynesia and the *Pearl of the Pacific*. All the cruisers seem to call here whichever route they take across the Pacific. Our plan is to sail from Ahe to Tahiti and meet up with friends who have taken different routes across the Pacific Ocean.

14th August (Sunday): Once clear of Ahe, *Sea Dabbs* and ourselves make good progress, about 6 knots in a steady 25 knots of wind. Removing the barnacles from the hull has definitely helped our speed. Most of our time is spent below as we are catching the odd wave into the cockpit from a lumpy sea leftover from the gale. The direct route to Tahiti takes us between two atolls - Rangiroa and Arutua - which are 80 miles away. We would like to sight them before nightfall.

The fresh winds continue all day and we feel relieved when we sight Arutua just before sunset. Now we can relax about our position, which is bang in between the

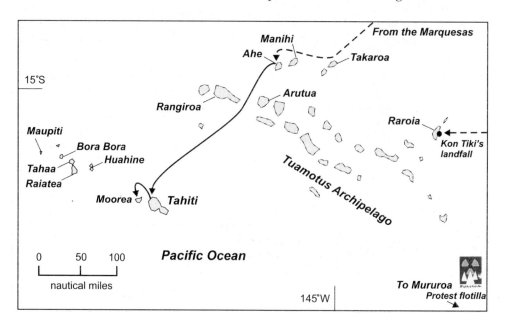

two atolls, thanks to our incredibly accurate GPS. However, at 20:00 hours it is action stations - we are hit by a squall. The wind speed suddenly increases from a steady 20 knots, to a gusty 35 knots. We quickly reef as we are not sure how long the squall will last - if only we had radar. Concerned about *Sea Dabbs*, who are ahead of us, we call them on the VHF to warn them of the squall. 30 minutes later they call back to say they have also been hit by the same squall.

15th August (Monday): The wind continues to push us along at a healthy pace, but it is easing, from 20/25 knots ESE yesterday, to 15/20 knots ESE today. Although this slows our progress, it does make our passage more comfortable.

16th August (Tuesday): 03:00, from about 30 miles out we start to see the welcoming loom of Point Venus' light, piercing through the darkness. And then, at first light, the beautiful towering mountain of Tahiti appears before us as a navigator's beacon guiding us in.

Captain Cook: The Society Islands were named by Captain Cook after the Royal Society in London, that sponsored his expedition to observe the *transit of Venus* across the sun. As we round Point Venus, we are reminded of the camp Captain Cook established there in 1769 to make his observation. The transit of Venus was important, because it enabled astronomers to calculate the distance from the earth to the sun, known as the **Astronomical Unit** (AU). If this distance is accurately known then the distance to the stars can also be calculated by parallax, using the earth-sun-earth distance (2xAU) as the base of the triangle. It was thought that this information could improve their astro-navigation - calculating longitude was still a problem. Although, as it turns out, the best solution using John Harrison's chronometers was well known by the Admiralty.

Halley (of Halley's Comet fame) claimed that the distance to the sun could be calculated accurately by observing the transit of Venus from a number of locations on earth. Kepler's Laws of Planetary Motion, and Newton's Law of Gravitation, predicted there would be a transit in 1761 and 1769, and then not for another 120 years. The observation of the transit in 1761 had not been successful for a number of reasons, cloud over the observation site in St Helena being one of them. This meant the transit in 1769 would be the astronomers last chance for 120 years.

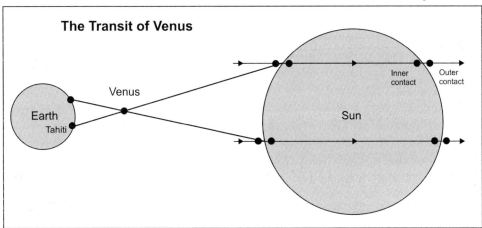

The Transit of Venus

To increase the accuracy of the transit, the observations on earth needed to be as far away from each other as possible. This would increase the base of the spherical triangle, and hence increase the accuracy of the parallax. It was therefore suggested, that one of the observations should be in the South Pacific. The Admiralty supported the project because this expedition covertly gave them the opportunity to look for the Southern Continent, *Terra Australis Incognita*, without upsetting the French or the Dutch.

Captain James Cook

Cook observed the transit by noting the times of the outer and inner contact, as Venus moved across the face of the sun. Cooks observations were then used with other observations to calculate the Astronomical Unit. After the transit Cook opened his sealed orders which instructed him to proceed southwards to 40 South, then westward to look for the Southern Continent until he reached the eastern side of the land (New Zealand), discovered by Abel Tasman in 1642.

Some 20 years later, in 1789, Point Venus was also the place where Captain Bligh collected breadfruit trees for shipment on HMS *Bounty*. He intended taking the trees to the Caribbean, to feed the slaves, not as it turned out, to feed the mutineers in Pitcairn.

Tahiti is at the centre of the Polynesian triangle. It was from this triangle that previous generations of Polynesian voyagers set off to Easter Island in the east, Hawaii in the north and New Zealand in the southwest; hundreds of years before European explorers such as Abel Tasman and Captain Cook knew of the existence of these Oceanic Islands. If you ask these enigmatic people where they originally came from, like the tropic bird, their voyaging ancestors came from a land far beyond the horizon.

Tahiti: Log book: chart 1382, Approaches to Tahiti and Moorea (scale 1:100,000). Tahiti is completely surrounded by a barrier reef. We are making for the Passe De Papeete on the northwest side which should be easy to find. It is after all, the main port of the Pacific. Once through the pass we consider mooring stern-to near the centre of town, but our friends are anchored at Maeve Beach which is further up the channel on the other side of the runway, so we continue on.

Opposite Maeve Beach the water is crystal clear, enabling us to see all the coral heads!!!! We anchor in four metres of water. Then it is coffee and chocolate chip cookies all round as our friends motor over in their dinghies to catch up on each other's long trek across the Pacific.

In the afternoon we take our dinghy over to the marina where we have to pay US $6 for its security. After a short wait we take *le truck*, at $1.40 each, into town. The brightly painted *le truck* has a simple but comfortable bench seat - it is all very clean and functional. As we rock and roll into Papeete (more sedately than in the Caribbean), we occasionally catch glimpses of the peak clad in lush tropical vegetation reaching all the way up to the top, from the palm lined sandy beaches below, near where we are anchored.

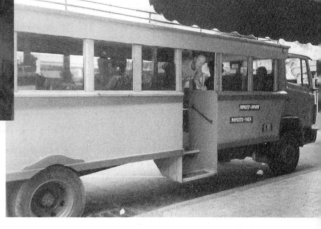

***Le truck* - travelling French Polynesian style**

Tahiti conjures up in our minds romance and a poetic way of life, with the scent of tropical flowers. So the hustle and bustle of a thriving city comes as a shock to our system. The slow pace of life at sea has accentuated our senses, and they are now being overpowered on our first day ashore. The speed of the traffic is dazzling and the noise of the traffic is deafening. As the cars zoom past we are really careful to look both ways many times before crossing the road. Our sense of timing needs to be re-calibrated. Papeete, the largest city in Polynesia has been influenced by modern day living. The stress of work seems to have made the people a little more serious than their smiling and relaxed cousins on the other islands but then, this is a city after all.

Mail: With great expectations we walk directly to the *poste restante*. This is our first mail collection since Panama (three months ago). We had heard that the post office only keeps mail for six weeks, so we wrote informing them we would be arriving in August and to please keep our mail. I give the lady at the counter our passports to check for our mail. She looks through the B's and says they have returned my letters. *"What!!!"* They have been returned because I did not arrive within six weeks of the first letter being received.

"What about the letter I sent you," I ask.

"Yes we have received it," she answers, proudly showing it to me. But obviously they have not taken any notice of its contents - I am furious. We ask to speak to the post master, and so ensues further discussion. I try to explain that when people sail across the Pacific Ocean they do not know exactly when they will arrive and, further, they do not know exactly when people will write to them - we are not clairvoyant. If they want to be the hub of the Pacific this is not the way to treat their clients. He says he is following his instructions. *"Whose instructions?"* *"The President's."* *"Right we'll go and see him."*

For some reason they had not returned Sandra's mail - Sandra receives ten letters. And, for this incompetent service, would you believe they want to charge us for keeping the mail, and the charge is more than the cost of the original stamps for sending the letters from overseas. They wisely decide not to pursue this!!!

So off we go looking for the President at the Presidential office - he is not there. We walk to the Presidential residency - he is away. So we eventually see the Minister of Transport instead. He listens politely and says we should convey our message to the President in writing. We write to President Du Government, BP 2551, Papeete, outlining our problem but, to this day, we have never received a reply.

We talk to other cruisers about their post, some have used the harbour master's office without having their mail returned. Tim (*Casimer*) says, "*There was a large pile of mail chucked in the corner which they invited me to look through.*" So the moral is to use the harbour master in Tahiti, but use *poste restante* in Gibraltar.

Newspaper: To cheer ourselves up we go in search for the British Consulate to read some UK newspapers. The honorary British Consulate works for Avis car hire.

"*Are you the British Consulate?*" we ask the chap at the Avis desk.

"*Yes, what's the problem?*" the consulate replies with a slight frown.

"*Have you got any British newspapers?*" we enquire.

"*What?*" he responds in astonishment, obviously expecting something more problematic.

"*Have you got any British newspapers we can read? We want to find out what's happening in the world.*" It turns out he does not have any British newspapers but, instead, he organises a 25 kg sack of freshly picked oranges at a really good price (48,000 Poly Franc, or $1.70 per kilo).

Market: Now for the central market - Sandra has the urge to buy something. The market is a mixture of food and handicraft. We are more interested in the latter, as we will shop at the Euromache for food on the way back to Maeve Beach. Sandra is immediately drawn to the pareos. I am sure she is thinking about how she can justify buying as many pareos as she did molas in the San Blas. There are hundreds of them for sale, the choice of design and colours are incredible, prices range from US $10 to US $30 depending on the fabric and intricacies of design.

Pareos or sarongs are a diaphanous wrap, made from a large rectangular piece of cotton, rayon or silk fabric. The fabric is dyed into bright vibrant colours, and printed with beautiful images of tropical flowers and Polynesian designs. They are

comfortable and cool to wear in the extreme heat. It makes them the most practical of all garments in the tropics - just wrap and tie around your body in a whole host of different ways. Sandra buys only one pareo in the market at $10. As she is eyeing-up the grass

Papeete market - Sandra looking at pareos

skirts, we exchange glances - now that would be going a bit too far. There is also a vast selection of tropical shells for sale, most of which we recognise from our snorkelling sessions and many of which we already have; cowries, murexes, conchs and augers.

Black Pearls: As we wander round the shops, our attention is drawn to the black pearls in a jeweller's shop window - beautifully presented, mounted in either gold or silver clasps. They are definitely the gem of the Pacific and a quality souvenir. We should have bought one in Ahe where they are cultivated. It would have been a more meaningful purchase, and considerably less expensive.

Back at the anchorage, dinner is on *Ashymakaihken*. Brenda produces a wonderful feast of roast lamb and pork with potatoes, onions, broccoli, carrots and tomatoes, followed by Camembert and olives. Dessert is apricot and apple crumble, washed down with rum punch. Early night 09:45, as we all feel really zonked-out. Immediately my head hits the pillow, I am dead to the world. I even sleep through a torrential downpour which fills all our strategically positioned buckets.

17th August (Wednesday): Feel like a slow day to recover and do nothing - perhaps write a couple of letters and do the odd job. In the afternoon Sandra goes snorkelling with Helen and Neil (*Alexandra Louise*) to explore Tahiti's reefs.

After a refreshing hot water shower, we are ready for our guests; Helen and Neil come over for dinner. As we settle down to eat, Ashley and Brenda (*Ashymakaihken*) also join us, soon followed by Chris (*Freya*), and Debbie (*Ngataki*). Fortunately, we have sufficient food for our extended guest list. For starters we have deep fried prawn crackers and, to drink, rum punch with peach juice, water, lime, Angostura bitters, sugar and ice. Sandra has made an extra large lasagna, which she serves with fresh French bread, olives and salad. *Pacific Voyager* has never had so many people on board at one time for a meal. This dinner turns out to be the first meeting of the voices we heard on the SSB, while we were crossing the Pacific and, needless to say, our caricatures are completely wrong.

19th August (Friday) - Moorea: After four busy days in Papeete it is time to sail to Moorea. There is little wind so we motor the 20 miles between the islands. The mountains on Moorea seem more weathered and craggy than Tahiti. As we motor past the outer edge of the reef surrounding Moorea, we look over the side and, to our amazement, we can clearly see the bottom in 25 metres of crystal clear water. Disbelieving the depth, I confirm it on both echo sounders.

Rory using an umbrella to protect himself from the sun - we desperately need a bimini

Pacific Voyager anchored in the tranquillity of Opunohu Bay

On Moorea there are two bays that are popular with cruising yachts; Cooks Bay and Opunohu Bay. *"Let's try Opunohu Bay first."* After motoring in through Passe Tareu, we take a left turn and anchor in four metres of water in bleached white sand - not a coral head in sight. After the hectic buzz of Tahiti, Moorea offers the more natural South Pacific tranquillity, ambience and quality of life we prefer.

Happy Hour: Once safely anchored in Opunohu Bay, we are eager to explore the anchorage in our dinghy. Chart 1436, Plans in Moorea (scale 1:30,000), shows a channel between the two bays which wanders out near the reef. But we decide to look for a shorter route, not appreciating that the forest of small coral heads would be so extensive. It may be shorter, but it is really slow going as we weave through the chicane of bommies. Eventually we clear the area of coral heads into the deeper water of Cooks Bay.

As we motor towards the anchorage, we pass one of the super luxury sailing holiday cruise ships which caters for the young at heart. They are enjoying every conceivable type of water sport from a floating platform. At the head of the bay we find a number of yachts we recognise. Our friends tell us we are in luck - it is happy hour tonight at the local hotel. How could my Irish blood resist a few beers at a reasonable price?

After a couple of hours, we have had our fill and it is time to motor back to Opunohu Bay, outside the reef this time. This is not as adventurous as it sounds. It

Happy Hour - everyone is dressed in their best going-out clothes

is a calm night with a clear sky and a full moon to guide us. As we motor out towards the pass, we notice the large cruise ship we saw earlier in the day is leaving. We use her lights to guide us through Passe Avaroa. But feeling something is not quite right, we slow down just as we enter shallow water. Suddenly a sandy bottom appears, reflected by the moon's rays. We have entered a forest of coral heads again! I immediately turn the

Left: Notice our newly covered dinghy in the background
Above: Snorkellers return with treasures of the deep

dinghy around and follow the navigation buoys as we should have done in the first place - not cut the corner. Motoring under the moonbeams is magical. All the way to our anchorage, we can clearly see the propeller screwing its way through the water leaving a spiral trial of phosphorescence in our wake.

20th August (Saturday): Baguettes and fried eggs for breakfast - eggs are $3.50 a dozen here, rather than the $5 a dozen in Papeete. Sandra finishes the dinghy cover she started making in Tahiti. It will protect the dinghy from abrasion and UV deterioration. Since Curacao we have been looking at other dinghy covers for ideas, and now Sandra has put her pattern making and sewing skills into practice. Buying 15 metres of Sunbrela in Curacao was a good move, together with shock cord, plastic hooks, leather patches and needles in Salcombe. It has taken Sandra a couple of days in total to cut the pattern and stitch the panels together, but we now feel happier about leaving the dinghy in the sun and alongside a dock.

To cool down, Sandra goes snorkelling with Lane and Sandy (*Mai Tai*), and Brenda (*Ashymakaihken*) to the outer reef, which is only five minutes motoring away. Even though they have to keep looking over their shoulders for sharks, they have a great time enjoying the crystal clear water outside the reef and swimming amongst some huge tropical fish. Moray eels poke their heads out from their protective holes in the rocks, keeping a beady eye on the snorkellers who have invaded their territory and, amongst the rocks, the snorkelling gang find some huge conchs and Pacific top shells, which they bring back to proudly show me.

Easter Island: We hear on the cruiser's net that the Chilean airline is offering a $400, three day round trip from Tahiti to Easter Island, which includes the hotel and meals. The arrangement is that the plane drops the people off at Easter Island on its way to Chile, and collects them on its return leg to Tahiti. At the time $400 each is a bit too much for our budget. (In hindsight, we should have gone, as Easter Island is well off the beaten track and, if you do make the effort to sail there, you are not guaranteed to get ashore, because it has an exposed anchorage. It would have been incredible to have stood beside Easter Island's proud stone statues which stand like lonely sentinels wisely watching the eons of time go by.)

Opunohu Bay's stunning view of Moorea's famous peak

21st August (Sunday): Set off to explore Opunohu Bay in our dinghy - we particularly want to see Robinson Cove, where many classic photographs of Moorea have been taken (see cover of Earl Hinz's *Landfalls of Paradise*). Opunohu Bay offers breathtaking scenery which has been the backdrop of many well known films - Bali Hai in *South Pacific*, and *Mutiny on the Bounty*. This was also a favourite anchorage of the Hiscocks with many photographs in their books to prove it. The anchorage is quite small, with only enough room for two or three yachts. The yachts tend to anchor stern-to in 3 metres of water. Being anchored so close to the shore makes the steeply rising mountains seem even more towering and dramatic.

22nd August (Monday): It pours with rain all night and we catch an amazing 40 litres of water off our awning. The dinghy is also full of water - time for another bath. Sparkling clean we are now ready to exercise our legs. This is our first walk for a while as we have spent all our spare time swimming. The roads, houses and gardens are beautifully picturesque, incredibly neat and spotlessly clean and orderly. It seems there could be a building code that limits the height of the houses to just below the palm tree level. The riot of flora is incredible with hibiscus, Tahiti Tiare, bougainvillaea, gardenias, and frangipani absolutely everywhere, creating a vivid technicolour experience. It is hard to believe the contrast with the other more basic islands. This is one of the visible benefits of French colonisation.

Back on board *Pacific Voyager* we get back to our jobs which include cleaning the hull - the last of the oil stains from Panama has just about gone. Our antifouling from Salcombe is history, but as we are able to regularly dive and scrub the bottom, we can beat the fouling before it has time to develop - and besides it is good exercise.

SSB: Although Cook's Bay and Opunohu Bay are only a couple of miles apart, it is not possible to communicate with our friends in the other bay using the VHF. This is because the mountain between the two valleys blocks the line of sight transmission. However, the obstructing mountain does not prevent SSB communication as it bounces its signal off the ionosphere. Our SSB does not seem to be transmitting as far as it should be, so Ashley (*Ashymakaihken*) brings over a made up antenna and earth for a 12 metre transmission. Our test call is picked up by a Ham operator in America, so obviously there is nothing wrong with our transceiver - it must be our earth plate that needs addressing (we later fit a dynaplate which solves the problem).

Dinner is Sosomix vegetarian burgers, chips and onions with tomato sauce. The Sosomix packets we bought in the UK are nearly finished and, we note for our future planning, that we have not been able to buy any en route. Our evening entertainment is spent on *Ashymakaihken*, watching Ashley and Brenda's video of their visit to Les Gambiers, accompanied with banana spice cake, brandy and coffee. We leave with the impression Les Gambiers is a windswept place.

24th August (Wednesday): Another night of torrential heavy rain, another bath in the dinghy in the morning, but now everything is damp and unpleasant. The dampness is making our clothes smell mouldy - perhaps *Paradise* is not so great after all. We cannot see the sandy bottom any more as the river water has turned the sea a light green-pea-soup colour, with palm fronds, plants and coconuts floating around. But with the heavy rains, the mountains have magically come alive with dramatic waterfalls. I wish we could video it, but our video has packed up. I am sure it was due to the humidity we experienced in Panama.

25th August (Thursday): Out past the reef, we can see the French Navy have eight vessels on manoeuvres (I wonder if they were preparing for the nuclear testing in Mururoa which has yet to be announced. See Mururoa protest in the chapter on New Zealand).

26th August (Friday): More rain during the night, but not sufficient to have a bath in the dinghy this time. We up anchor and motor outside the reef to Cooks Bay, just in time for happy hour. Cooks Bay, named after the great man himself, is another great cruising

Cooks Bay - mirror images reflect on the still water

anchorage. We anchor near a few of our friends, at the head of the inlet, near a jetty and a small supermarket. Being so close to the mountains has the advantage of some spectacular views, but it also means we lose the sun earlier in the afternoon as it dips down behind the mountain.

After a jovial happy hour (or two, or three) at the Bali Hai with a few other cruisers, we all stroll back to the hotel's dinghy dock. Tim's (*Casimer*) dinghy is missing. We motor around the anchorage, searching with our torch along the coastline and fortunately find Tim's dinghy abandoned in the mangrove - but one of the oars has gone, along with a petrol container, and an old pair of shoes. Someone had obviously tried to start the outboard motor, as their rough handling has broken the starting cord. As Tim quickly learns to scull he feels he needs another drink to drown his sorrows. Back on board *Pacific Voyager,* out comes the Jack Iron rum. Tim has already had his push-bike stolen in Cook's Bay when he left it ashore chained to a large tree - unfortunately paradise does have its problems.

30th August (Tuesday): At the small supermarket we buy lamb chops for $8 per kilo and a large frozen chicken for $6. We will have a braai on the transom tonight - it is my turn to burn the food.

The number of yachts in the anchorage are reducing. We get the feeling we are the last of the pack again - turning off the lights. We must get a move-on to be out of the tropics before the cyclone season, and we still have over half the Pacific Ocean to cross and explore.

It is so picturesque here that it encourages Sandra to get out her art box and paint a watercolour of the surrounding mountains. Remember all the art materials she bought before we left England? Well we have almost travelled halfway round the world and she has only opened the box a couple of times. I cannot understand why she gets so upset when I want to get them off the boat because they are taking up valuable space which I can use for my toys!

2nd September (Friday) - Aground: Before departing for Huahine, we motor over to the jetty at the head of Cook's Bay, to top up our water tank from a tap on the quay. This done, we motor slowly across the bay towards Tim to say farewell. About halfway across, the depth alarm sounds, which means there is less than three metres of water. I hesitate, not believing it is so shallow, then we gradually come to a halt - we are aground. It all seems to

Pacific Voyager alongside the quay ready to fill up with water

Left: *Pacific Voyager* aground - cruisers to the rescue. Photograph courtesy of Judy *(Long Passages)*

Below: Still aground! French Navy to the rescue!

happen in slow motion as we motor into a mound of mud and silt. We try to reverse off - no luck. Our predicament soon starts to attract attention; Tim sculls over, Bob (*Long Passages*) motors over in his dinghy, as does Lane (*Mai Tai*), and Peter (*Unicorn*). First they all lash their dinghies to the side of *Pacific Voyager* and all motor together (Tim sculls) - no movement. Then we try everyone standing on the bow to pick the stern up - no movement (but of course we have now added extra weight). Then we try Tim and Lane precariously sitting on the end of the boom, trying to lean the boat over - that does not work either. Bob suggests he takes a halyard and pulls the boat over with his dinghy - I have visions of the mast being pulled out (in hindsight that was probably the best option).

With all the excitement around our boat, we now attract the attention of the French Navy who also decide to join in. The navy motor over in a large inflatable with a 40 hp outboard. They take a line on the stern and give the outboard full wick - nothing happens. They throttle back and reposition the ropes - give it full wick again - this time we slowly ease back - we are afloat! *"Thank you everyone. Now let's get on our way to Huahine before anything else happens."*

Further Reading:
Crawford, Peter., *Nomads of the Wind, A Natural History of Polynesia*, BBC
Stanley, David., *South Pacific Handbook*
www.tahiti-explore.com

29 Huahine and Tahaa

If Huahine and Tahaa are anything like Tahiti and Moorea, then they are worth a visit. Our plan is to sail overnight to Huahine and arrive outside the pass early the following morning.

3rd September (Friday) - Huahine: Log book: chart 1060, Huahine to Maupiti (scale 1:170,000). At 16:00 we join a small fleet of cruisers making their way out to sea for an overnight sail to Huahine. *"What, leave on a Friday???"* After some discussion with Sandra, we decide overnight trips on a Friday are okay. *"It's like weekend sailing."* The sea is exceptionally lumpy - we are not sure what is causing it as the wind is not that strong - maybe we are in an area of cross currents and overfalls. The lumpy sea soon makes us feel queasy and we lose our appetite. It is pitch black with occasional showers. We can clearly see Ashley's strobe piercing through the ink black night. The fleet makes good progress, and arrives outside Huahine's reef just after dawn.

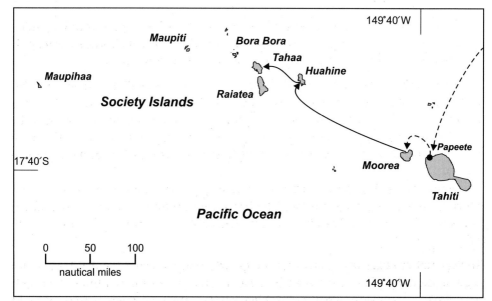

Pacific Voyager sailing to Huahine - photograph taken by Debbie on Ngataki

4th September (Saturday): Once through Passe Avapehi we turn right and wind our way along the channel inside the reef. We are in convoy with *Chase Gallerie* and *Ashymakaihken*. After anchoring in Haapu Bay with a few other yachts, we rest for a while as we feel like we have just walked off a long flight, jet-lagged. We take the dinghy ashore to explore an old marae. This was an ancient meeting place where human sacrifices were supposed to have taken place. The remains are now a weather-worn triangle of stone on a dilapidated oblong structure, with graffiti instead of petroglyphs. Back at the anchorage a busy social life is developing, with sundowners on one boat and dinner on another.

5th September (Sunday): Sandra goes snorkelling with Brenda (*Ashymakaihken*), and Marie (*Chase Gallerie*). Brenda arrives armed with a crowbar, gloves and net bags to hold the shells she hopes to find. Sandra takes them in our dinghy to snorkel out on the distant reef. This is where our powerful outboard comes into its own for exploring those reefs that are miles away from the anchorage. And, the Caribe RIB is an ideal dinghy to snorkel from because it is a very stable platform - almost impossible to capsize.

They have a successful snorkelling session; spotting stingrays half-buried in the sand, finding wonderful shells - cowries, conches, cones and augers, and swimming around some beautiful coral heads. Although the fish are scarce, there are millions of spiny sea urchins with midnight blue centres, clustered in large circles around the rocks, like a protective largaa.

Dinner this evening is at our address: the starter is duck pate with baguettes, the main course is vegetable lasagna and salad, dessert is Hawaiian pineapple crumble, and all washed down as usual with plenty of rum punch.

6th September (Monday): Sandra organises another snorkelling expedition, this time to the reef on the opposite side of the anchorage. Initially, she anchors the dinghy, but then decides to snorkel around it, as the dinghy drifts slowly over the reef. Again they have the most spectacular giant aquarium experience. This time they find zillions of money cowries and the find of the day is a brilliantly white, egg cowrie.

Dinner at Tim's (*Casimer*) address tonight: Tim makes a tuna ratatouille with rice, French baguettes, followed by bread and butter pudding, washed down with a tot of naval rum. The girl who gets Tim cooking for her is going to be really lucky.

7th September (Tuesday): Just as we are getting ready to leave, the Perkins decides to go on the blink. I am concerned because it usually fires-up first time. Leaving it for a while, we consider what the problem can be - then try again. It starts straight

Tim and Sandra relax on a palm tree

away. This is unnerving. (We are later to have the engine completely overhauled in New Zealand. We think the starting problem was caused by the water cooled exhaust manifold leaking water into the head). We motor back along the channel and have a good 23 mile sail across to Tahaa.

Tahaa: With the thunder of surf in our ears we sail through the wide Passe Toahotu, in between two motus, Mahaea and Toahotu. *"Shall we anchor left or right?"* We motor right, then left, then back to the right side again looking for a safe anchorage. *"There's coral all over the place."* Like a dog chasing its tail, we eventually anchor on the right, near *Casimer,* in 4 metres of water and relatively clear of coral heads. I spend the rest of the day working on the engine, changing the engine oil and topping up the hydraulic oil.

7th September (Wednesday): After breakfast we row ashore to the small idyllic looking motu by the entrance - Ile Mahaea. As we wander round the small motu I take some excellent photographs of Sandra and Tim on a sloping palm tree (Tim sailed back the following year and took more photographs which are now included in the RCC Pilotage Foundation, *Pacific Cruisers Guide*). The rest of the day is spent lazing around by the water's edge, and snorkelling.

This is a great place to snorkel. First we swim in the shallow water over a coral garden before the sea bed suddenly descends into a deep valley. As I glide over the edge it feels like I am flying an airship into another world, and I soon forget the sound of my rhythmic breathing through my snorkel. The tropical vegetation above has not prepared me for the splendour of the coral gardens below. I look over to see Sandra swimming

Sandra lies back and thinks of snorkelling

Tim and Sandra lazing at the water's edge - notice our RIB's new cover

through clouds of reef fish that waft over the coral gardens, surging backwards and forwards imitating the fan coral around them. I feel the small fish nibbling at my legs, it is a strange sensation - as I turn to look at them they flit into the protection of a diabolic forest of staghorns. I even see a portly moray eel studying us from the protection of his rocky home. "*Don't worry mate we won't get too close.*"

Back on *Pacific Voyager* we continue our water born activities and clean the hull. If we do this regularly, we catch the green slim before any real growth gets hold and before the barnacles start to grow. It is very tranquil here, although we feel somewhat exposed being so close to the entrance to the pass, but we want to make the most of the stable weather.

8th September (Thursday): At 05:45 - the most spectacular sunrise greets us, capturing the blinding silhouette of the palm trees on the motu and a local fisherman in his dinghy. Both Tim and ourselves up anchor at 09:00 and start motoring slowly around the island. This is a spectacular trip with the sun illuminating the distinct contrasting colours in the water, from the light turquoise in the shallows, to the deep royal blues as the depth increases.

Surprisingly, there are huts built on stilts positioned way out on the reef. They appear to be in a precarious position as the waves pound the reef behind them sending up fountains of spray. As we round the north end of the island we see the incredible view of Bora Bora less than 20 miles away - our next destination.

Swimming *"In an octopus' garden"*. Photographs taken with our Minolta underwater camera

MANAGING YOUR
BLUEWATER
CRUISE

Rory Burke
Sandra Buchanan

Managing Your Bluewater Cruise cover and the photograph from which it was developed

By mid-afternoon we start to look for an anchorage near one of the picturesque motus on the reef. This is not as easy as it sounds; incredibly the sea bed inside the reef rises from a deep 25 metres almost vertically to less than one metre. We do not want to anchor in 25 metres of water, and we need more than one metre - three or four would be minimum. As we continue our search I take a photograph of Sandra standing on the goal-posts to elevate her view - we later use this photograph for the cover of *Managing Your Bluewater Cruise*. Eventually we find a small bench about three metres deep with sufficient room for *Casimer* and ourselves. After anchoring, Tim works on his anchor windlass which is playing up, while we take the dinghy ashore to a small idyllic looking motu.

Mosquito Island: The motu screams, *"South Pacific Idyllic Island,"* with golden sands and lush palm trees swaying in the light breeze. We might even have a swim off the beach. The motu is marked on chart 1103, Tahaa and Raiatea (scale 1:50,000), as Ilot Tautau. As we drag the dinghy up the beach and tie the painter to the nearest palm tree, we notice a mosquito, then another and another. As we look around we are being attacked by squadrons of mosquitos. They are swarming all around us like a black cloud - we take one look at each other, *"Let's get out of here fast."*

Like a video on fast forward, we catapult the dinghy back in the water and zoom off in a desperate attempt to get away from them, but the little buggers are still biting us. What a sight we must have been wildly beating ourselves, as if performing some sacred ritual. As we head back to our boat we pass a *Moorings* charter boat - we are greeted by three chaps, *"We can see we don't need to visit the island."* They tell us they are writing an article for a European yachting magazine about the pleasures of sailing in the Pacific from the Moorings base in Raiatea. We wonder how they will describe the delights of the motu we have just visited??? For us this idyllic anchorage has suddenly lost its appeal.

Looking for a friendlier spot, we motor over to Tapuamu, a small harbour on the island, and tie-up alongside the wharf. I investigate the village shop nearby.

Left: Our windchute ramming air through our cabin

Above: Dinner - two pairs of hopeful eyes look on!!

"Come quick - they're selling cold beers at $1.65 a litre." We also buy a frozen chicken for tonight. Tim and myself down a couple of really cold beers, while Sandra chats to the local chaps in French.

Back on board we invite Tim over for a chicken dinner. After cooking the chicken pieces on our charcoal braai, which is attached to the pushpit, we settle down to our meal in the cockpit. While chomping on a chicken leg I look up to see two pairs of eyes staring at us out of the dark - who is it??? As I peer into the darkness, I see it is only a couple of local dogs looking for scraps. *"Sorry chaps you know chicken bones are not good for you."*

9th September (Friday) - Vanilla Pods: Ernest, one of local chaps Sandra was talking to yesterday at the shop, must have taken a fancy to her, because he arrives at 07:00 on his scooter with a sack full of vegetables, lettuce, cucumbers and pamplemousse, together with a huge bag of vanilla pods from his garden, and then asks Sandra, "*Êtes-vous en menagé?*"

I have always wondered how they put the vanilla flavour in ice cream - this is to be another educational experience. Sandra puts most of the pods in a huge jar of rum, making a vanilla essence and preserving the pods at the same time. And then puts a couple into the sugar bowl to make vanilla sugar - another delicacy, (since then I keep finding what looks like a solidified slug in the sugar).

10th September (Saturday): *Casimer* and ourselves motor out to the reef for the day and anchor in 9 metres of water. This is an ideal spot to relax, snorkel and just potter around. Tim and Sandra go diving and collect 12 juicy mouth-watering clams. I am appalled as Tim accidentally drops one over the side while cleaning them. Later that evening, dinner on *Casimer* consists of superbly cooked clams with garlic and onions in a white wine sauce, followed by chicken in barbecue sauce, mashed potatoes, rice and home grown mung beans and, for dessert, we have Sandra's home made chocolate truffles.

11th September (Sunday) - Haamene Bay: Motor south around the island to Haamene Bay. Although this inlet looks like a perfect anchorage from the chart, in practice the holding is very poor. The bottom appears to be rock and shale - there is no sand or mud for our anchor to bed into. I want to anchor in relatively shallow water so that if the anchor fouls it will be easier to retrieve. Next moment we go aground - déjà vu. We lower the dinghy which is hoisted to the side of *Pacific Voyager* and, without realising it would happen, the reduction in weight floats us off.

Just as it is getting dark, Tim arrives in *Casimer*. A Frenchman calls over and offers him the vacant mooring buoy next to his yacht. I motor over in our dinghy to help Tim take the mooring but, no sooner has he secured the mooring than we hear a hoot from another yacht which is speeding up the inlet, creating a huge breaking bow wave. *"I think he may be staying here."* Tim drops the mooring buoy and slowly eases back, but we get this uneasy feeling about the Frenchman's speed. *"I think he's going to ram us."*

"It doesn't surprise me," said Tim, *"they drive their boats like their cars."* By this time we have cleared the buoy. Just as well as the Frenchman comes racing in. He is going far too fast. Although his wife picks up the buoy, she cannot hold on against their forward momentum. They then proceed to ram their friend's yacht in front of them!!! I am shocked - normally you only experience this type of *"rage"* on the roads.

Sofie's boutique with its beautiful thatch - Polynesian style

12th September (Monday): Our morning walk ashore takes us past Sofie's boutique - a beautiful Polynesian thatched house set in a tropical garden beside the inlet. She is painting impressionist images, similar to Gauguin's, onto silk pareos and other garments. It appears, inspiration has gone full circle - Polynesia influencing Gauguin and now Gauguin's legacy influencing the Polynesian image.

We motor out to the reef for another snorkelling session, then back to Tapuamu harbour again. We would like to sail on to Bora Bora, but there is no wind. We could motor, but do not want to use up our valuable diesel and are not sure if duty free diesel is available at Bora Bora. The full price is not worth thinking about. Back at Tapuamu, I continue working on my book - every time we motor it gives me a days worth of electricity to work on the computer. With French bread, frozen chicken, cold beers and mosquito coils available in the local shop - what more do we need?

Highlight of the week - the inter-island ferry

14th September (Wednesday): Inter-island Ferry: We move inside the small harbour to leave the quay clear for the weekly inter-island ferry to come alongside. As it arrives, so stalls appear from nowhere all around the harbour buildings, selling food, drinks and flowers. The main item of cargo is a Land Rover, which I am sure will be someone's pride and joy as they drive round and round the island's only road!

Our evening walks take us to different corners of the village. Today it is along a tree lined road which circles the island (we should have tried to hire bicycles and toured the whole island). At the end of the bay we see a number of pirogues hanging from their cradles, like America Cup yachts waiting to do service.

Sleep outside in the cockpit tonight because it is so hot, but it starts to rain at 02:00 so we dash inside to suffer the rest of the night in hot, humid conditions.

Left: Tree-lined road around the island
Above: Pirogues hanging in their cradles

Rory cannot believe his luck when we are invited to the island's *beauty contest*

16th September (Friday): The local taxi driver and family are also living on their yacht in the small harbour. I cannot believe my luck when they invite us to the island's *beauty contest* at the community centre. The hall is tropically decorated with flowers and woven crafts, and the tables are laid with Polynesian printed fabric and floral centre pieces. The ladies are wearing beautiful floral crowns, and the young girls are wearing tall tiara-type crowns made of palm leaves. All the locals seem to contribute to the evening's performance be it singing, or dancing, before the main event of the evening - the island's beauty contest. The Polynesian girls are stunning. I can see why the crew on HMS *Bounty* were reluctant to leave French Polynesia.

After the contest, we have a wonderful Polynesian feast of poisson cru (raw fish marinated in lime juice), steak, chips and salad, followed by water melon. Considering this is a small village the place is crowded and the atmosphere is vibrant as the islanders really make the most of the event with true Polynesian enthusiasm.

17th September (Saturday): Having waited five days for the wind, it is now starting to pick up - this could be our window of opportunity. We make a thank you card in French for Mike, Edme and Tevaite, and give them a small present: *Merci beaucoup pour vos hospitalité. Nous avons aimé trés trés beaucoup la fête denier soir. Toujours, Tapuanu et Tahaa sera spécial. Maintenant nous allons à Tonga et après a New Zealand pour décembre et pour six mois, à la fin peut-être deux ans, nous serons en Angleterre. Merci et au revoir. Rory et Sandra.*

With a head full of wonderful memories, we let go the ropes and motor towards the reef, where the coral is shimmering like silk in the sunlight as we sail out through Passe Paipai en route for Bora Bora.

Further Reading:

Stanley, David., *South Pacific Handbook*

30 *Bora Bora*

17th September (Saturday): Log book: chart 1107, Bora Bora (scale 1:25,000). After waiting five days for wind we now have a gentle breeze to blow us across to Bora Bora. 09:00 leave harbour and sail towards the pass accompanied by a number of other yachts who have also been waiting for the wind. Shortly a small armada of cruisers are sailing the 20 miles to Bora Bora.

As we make landfall at the southern end of Bora Bora's reef, we ease around the coast until we reach the only pass - Passe Teavanui. A school of dolphins escorts us through the channel. *"They must be working for the tourist board."* The pass could not be more straight forward, no rocks, and no strong currents. We find a good spot to anchor between the west island, Toopua, and the outer reef. I pick an area which looks free of coral heads and put out three anchors to hold us in position.

Tim *(Casimer),* sailing single-handed, arrives first again and does his usual dash to buy a sack of fresh French bread for his mates, this time from Vaitape the main town on the island. It is our turn to host our neighbours for dinner tonight. I braai filleted mai mai, while Sandra prepares a potato salad, green salad, a lemon meringue pie for dessert, and a rum punch from a packet of grapefruit tang, pineapple juice, rum and water. That night, as we drift off to sleep, we can hear the thunder of the waves pounding on the distant coral reef.

Postcard: Aerial view of Bora Bora showing the pass and Tahaa in the background

18th September (Sunday): According to David Stanley's, *South Pacific Handbook,* this is one of the best snorkelling areas in the world and a shell collector's paradise. Sandra is now hooked into the excitement of finding unusual and native specimens in the water. She has a good mentor - Brenda (*Ashymakaihken*), who is on her third trip round the world. We have a small shell collectors guide, but a larger more detailed handbook would be useful.

Returning from another hard day snorkelling

There are many shells on the shorelines but the best shells are found when snorkelling near the reef. We motor out towards the reef with Brenda and Tim. The flat sandy sea-bed before the reef is the hiding place for a group of stingrays camouflaging themselves in the sand. Nearer the reef, amongst the coral, the water is like a marine motorway with parrot fish, butterfly fish, saddlebacks, tiger fish, and yellow and black striped angel fish all going somewhere. The water is a dazzling kaleidoscope of aquamarines, swarming with amazing, colourful tropical fish; it is so alive it is like jumping into a giant aquarium. In contrast, on the sea-bed, it is as if time has stopped for the sea cucumbers, sea stars and octopuses.

After a refreshing shower back on *Pacific Voyager* Sandra plays scrabble with Brenda and Tim for the grand prize of the *Scrabble Crown*, a cardboard crown Sandra picked up from the Burger King in Gibraltar. This crown has changed hands many times - which just shows how trivial life can get in the tropics!

19th September (Monday): Up at sparrows to motor across to Vaitape in our dinghy with the others. Brenda stays behind to look after the yachts as we have heard there has been a thief operating near the yacht club. The town is a little disappointing as it seems to only consist of Chinese supermarkets and gift shops. Ashley gets his bond returned in-full from Westpac, but Tim loses $75 on his bond through the exchange rate. In Tim's case they changed his money from US dollars to Polynesian Francs, then back again and, after the exchange rate losses and currency fluctuations, Tim is short of $75. He is very unhappy and, not surprisingly, feels the whole bond fiasco is a rip-off.

20th September (Tuesday): Rain, rain and more rain - we catch 80 litres in buckets as the rain pours off the awning. Sandra gets the sewing machine out to do a few canvas jobs. I finish reading one of Hiscock's books that I have borrowed from Tim and Sandra finishes a Clare Francis novel.

Polynesian dancers and a male fire-eater, from tourist brochure

21st September (Wednesday): Up anchor and move to the southern end of the island and re-anchor beside the Bora Bora hotel. After a busy day doing jobs we take our dinghy ashore to see a traditional Polynesian show on the beach at the Bora Bora hotel.

The performers include a dance group of young Polynesian girls wearing coconut bras and grass skirts, a few hunky fire-eaters and a local percussion band. I am quite concerned that the coconuts might pinch the dancing girls' skin, while Sandra and Brenda are really concerned the fire-eaters torch-twirling, sizzling display might singe something important!

After the rhythmic sound of drumming and sensuous dancing, which has probably not changed since the days of Captain Cook, we are all invited to join in, dancing in the sand. The Polynesian dancing involves swinging our arms and legs in and out, using muscle groups that have not been exercised for years, and movements which make us look like a clockwork toy.

22nd September (Thursday): Sandra repairs my shorts which I have worn through. We would normally throw clothes away in this state, but somehow the cruising lifestyle encourages us to make clothes last as long as possible. The salt soon rots away the elastic and the sun bleaches away the colour, so most yachties clothes look as if they have seen better days. Sandra goes to a Polynesian craft evening where the ladies sing and demonstrate their traditional methods of weaving baskets and hats from pandanus.

Brenda, Ashley, Tim and Sandra at the craft show

Sandra bravely feeding the stingrays

Stingrays skim over the sea-bed

23rd September (Friday) - Stingrays: At 09:00 every morning the fire-eaters from the Bora Bora hotel take their guests - mostly Japanese - out to a coral head to feed a school of stingrays. A few cruisers follow their pirogues at a discrete distance so as not to interfere with their entertainment. One of the fire-eaters invites Sandra to feed the stingrays. Sandra very bravely goes forward holding out a piece of raw fish in her hand. There are about twenty stingrays swimming around in a big circle, in 5 foot of water, putting on a wonderful performance. Their disk-shaped bodies skim over the sea bed, then glide through the water like pilots in an underwater air display. One of the stingrays soon spots Sandra's offering and swoops up to take the fish. At this point Sandra takes fright, as she is not expecting the stingray's mouth to be positioned under its body. The stingray also gets a fright and instinctively whips its tail round and catches Sandra's arm. This nasty little scratch swells up and, even though we apply antibiotic cream it takes weeks to heal (as do all cuts in the marine environment).

24th September (Saturday): Over to *Ashymakaihken* to check our charts for the next leg to Maupihaa and Suvarow. There are no photocopy machines available in Bora Bora so it is a case of tracing the one chart I am missing. Just as well I have a packet of tracing paper. Even though I carefully trace all the details I still feel very nervous at the thought of using a traced chart. After rum sundowners there is a big treat tonight; the Bora Bora hotel is showing the video of *Mutiny on the Bounty*. "*Shall I wear my wooden leg, eye patch and parrot.*"

25th September (Sunday): Over on *Casimer* we are looking through Tim's extensive library of cruising books when we spot *South Sea Vagabonds*, by Johnny Wray. This book is about how he built *Ngataki* a 34 foot yacht in 1933 for £11, and cruised her extensively around the South Pacific. As chance would have it Debbie (the new owner of *Ngataki*) has just joined us in the anchorage. Tim is very keen to see *Ngataki* and have his book signed by the owner, so we invite Debbie over for afternoon tea. *Ngataki* is one of the few boats we have seen with galvanised wire rope rigging. When I ask Debbie if the rigging is original, she replies, "*I hope not,*" and chuckles.

26th September (Monday): Hitch into Vaitape to shop in the Chinese supermarket - every respectable town in Polynesia has a Chinese supermarket. The town is fairly quiet, but it has its busy moments when a tourist boat comes in, or an aeroplane lands. The runway was built on a motu by the US forces in 1942; the reef was probably the only flat area they could find. This means all the tourists have a pleasant 20 minute boat ride from the motu over to Vaitape on the central island, a novel way to end a flight, and begin a holiday.

Just outside the town we see a sign *"Bikes For Hire."* We follow the signs to the back of a house where we find two ladies who are not only hiring bikes, but also making pareos. Sandra is intrigued by the simplicity of their manufacturing setup. In large tin pots on a gas stove, they dye large sheets of bleached cloth into bright colours. While still wet, they lay them on the ground, placing palm leaves and various tropical shapes cut in linoleum on top of the cloth, sometimes sprinkling rock salt on it to give a speckled effect, and then the cloth is left to dry in the sun. The result is a beautifully colourful, tropical printed pareo.

27th September (Tuesday): Up at sparrows, hitch into Vaitape again, and hire two bicycles from the ladies to cycle around the island. This is something we should have done on all the islands where they had bicycles for hire. After adjusting saddle heights and checking the brakes and gears - we are away. Sandra has a basket and I have gears!!!! We have a basic map for the island which I have cut from David Stanley's book. It indicates all the tourist spots, such as the second world war gun emplacements which were positioned to defend the harbour pass (circa 1942).

The cycling should be relatively easy as the only road around the island follows the coastline, but this is the first time either of us have cycled in living memory!!! We head for the southern end of the island first where they have the best beaches. We are continually looking up over our left shoulder at the mountain peak, then across to our right towards the reef as the spectacular views are constantly changing around every corner.

At one rest stop I accidentally leave behind my rucksack with my Olympus camera, and only realise my mistake at the next rest stop a few miles further on. I race back at full iron-man speed to find my rucksack still on the bank untouched.

But now I am so knackered, I keel over and it takes me half an hour to recover.

Picturesque Bora Bora, really does live up to the glossy tourist brochures, with beaches of soft white sand, swaying palm trees and shallow lagoons of aquamarine, teaming with hundreds of colourful tropical fish. Cycling around the coast

Stop for a rest at one of the old gun emplacements

also enables us to see a few of the tropical birds; frigate birds, tropic birds and herons.

Sandra is drawn to an art gallery beside the road, which is exhibiting work from various artists, including portraits and landscapes of the area in pencil, water colours and oils. There is also a wonderful framed sketchbook of Jacques Bouillard. He would make rough sketches here in Bora Bora, then finish them

Cycling around Bora Bora

off in his studio in France. Sandra is inspired - it brings out her artistic enthusiasm. I expect she will be opening her art box when we get back.

Our circumnavigation of the island is completed by 15:00. We reward ourselves with a bottle of ice cold beer from a Chinese supermarket. As we return our bikes to the two ladies, Sandra cannot resist the urge to buy one of their $10 pareos she saw being made yesterday.

We consider trekking through the centre of the island, but it looks too strenuous for us. However, we meet David and Hazel (*Mon Tour*) who have also sailed from North Wales. They are as fit as mountain goats, and love to climb anything that is put in front of them. They trekked to the top, and told us it was hard going, even for them, but the views from the top were breath taking.

29th September (Thursday) - Diesel Saga: As a foreign yacht we are entitled to buy duty free diesel which, at less than half the normal price of $1.50 per litre, is a

financial necessity. Sandra begins making enquires about where we can buy diesel. "*Oh it's not available here any more you will have to buy it in Papeete.*" And Papeete is a days sail away. There must be another way. It has been suggested that we can buy duty free diesel

David and Hazel (*MonTour*), looking for another mountain to climb!

from a road tanker, so Sandra makes enquires over the phone. You must appreciate all this is taking place in her schoolgirl French, and from public telephone boxes. After a few phone calls, Sandra eventually gets hold of Mr. Paul on 677049, who says we can buy duty free diesel at 37 cents a litre,

Polynesian phone cards

from his road tanker. After checking the ferry times, we arrange to meet Mr. Paul at the ferry dock when it is free. As Mr. Paul arrives with his road tanker we are ready with all our jerry cans lined up along the dock. Mr. Paul checks our clearance papers which expire tomorrow. He says we can only buy fuel as we leave, so we agree that we will leave Bora Bora straight away - we will do anything to get diesel at duty free prices!!! He is a real *jobs worth*. After filling up we were thinking of anchoring near the Bora Bora yacht club until we hear they charge $28 per night!!! Instead we return to our first anchorage by the pass.

30th September (Friday): As we are about to leave Sandra says, *"We can't leave today - it's Friday."* Superstitious sailors never leave on a Friday and, besides, there is no wind.

3rd October (Monday): There has been no wind for the past few days, but maybe there will be today. Hoping we might find wind further out offshore, we motor out through the pass and wait, but after an hour wallowing in the swell we turn back, and re-anchor in the same spot again.

4th October (Tuesday): Ashley comes over in his dinghy and bangs on the hull.

"I've just heard on the SSB there's a tsunami warning."

"A what?"

"A tsunami - it's a tidal wave."

We try and visualise what this means. Tsunamis are caused by underwater disturbances - an earth quake on the sea-bed. The shock waves travel at frightening speeds with little effect on the deep sea's surface but, as they enter shallow water, enormous standing waves can develop which have been known to wipe out coastal towns and move ships inland. This tsunami is more likely to cause a small tidal surge, so we all make sure we are not positioned over a coral head.

But in the end, this tsunami warning turns out to be a nonevent. However, a year ago a tsunami did hit Rarotonga in the Cook Islands, which almost drained the harbour. A few yachts were subsequently damaged with the incoming surge. This time the harbour master took the tsunami warning seriously and ordered all the yachts out of the harbour - but nothing happened.

5th October (Wednesday): There is a tiny whiff of wind on the surface in the anchorage. I look up at a small cloud capping the peak - it is moving. *"Now's our chance to leave. Let's catch the wind to Maupihaa."*

Further Reading:

Golden Press., *Seashells of the World*
Stanley, David., *South Pacific Handbook*
Alan, Dick., *Off the Beaten Track*

31 *Maupihaa*

Maupihaa is the most westerly atoll in the Society Islands and the most remote - a complete contrast to Bora Bora and Tahiti, which are the tourist Meccas of the South Pacific. Our plan is to sail from Bora Bora to Maupihaa and spend a few days there before sailing on to the Cook Islands. This leg will at least reduce the next hop to Suvarow.

5th October (Wednesday): After one false start due to lack of wind, our second attempt is more successful. Sailing due west with good winds, we sail quite close to the next atoll - Maupiti. Too close really as the reef extends out further than we have allowed for - when we see the waves breaking on the reef we know it is time to bear away.

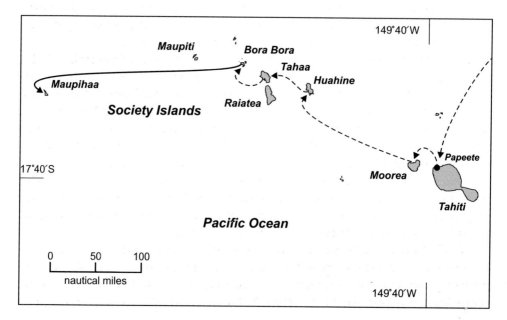

6th October (Thursday): During the night we have a 45 knot squall - it is all hands on deck to drop the main and headsail. The wind continues for sometime so we lie a-hull as we are not sure if it is just a squall, or the beginning of a weather system. After what seems like an eternity, the wind eases and we hoist a reefed mainsail and no.2 jib and hope the rest of the night will be peaceful - it is. The visibility is good as we approach Maupihaa. We are able to identify the tops of the palm trees from about five miles out.

Maupihaa is a coral atoll like the Tuamotus. It consists of a circular reef with a lagoon in the middle, unlike the other Society Islands; Tahiti, Moorea, Huahine, Tahaa, Raiatea and Bora Bora, which all have a mountain or extinct volcano in the middle. As we ease around the atoll there does not appear to be an obvious entrance, no lighthouse, no posts, no buoys, but we know it

Motoring against the fast flowing current into Maupihaa

is here because our friends have already passed through. The sea is crystal clear, like Moorea we can see the bottom in 25 metres of water, and are therefore not too concerned about hitting the reef - this is one of the advantages and safety features of cruising in the tropics.

Eventually we find the entrance - it is very narrow - the French must have blasted the channel through the coral reef. And, as normal, the water is flowing out at a healthy pace, but thankfully not as fast as we experienced in Ahe.

The anchorage with the best protection is on the east side of the atoll, which is on the opposite side from the entrance. Once we clear it, we motor through what looks like a minefield of black pearl pots - similar to Ahe. There are three other yachts in the anchorage, so we look for a suitable spot near to them. There are coral heads (bommies) dotted all over the place - anchoring in coral is always a challenge. Assuming the tradewinds will remain out of the east, we anchor with two bow anchor chains passing either side of a coral head, and another anchor aft, to prevent us backing onto the coral head if the wind direction changes. Once the first anchor is set, I perform the rest of this precision anchoring from the dinghy while Sandra prepares a meal. I even try swimming the fortress anchor into position - the anchor is light enough, but the chain is too heavy for this trick.

Squall: Even in this peaceful anchorage, which can be described with words like *enchanted paradise*, we are still subjected to the occasional squall and, like the ones we have experienced at sea, they hit us unannounced. In fact at sea, if we keep a sharp lookout we can see them coming, but in an enclosed anchorage shrouded by palm trees there is no warning at all. A 40 plus, knot gust shakes the life out of our awning as we swing wildly on the anchor and, just as quickly as it came, everything is peaceful again.

7th October (Friday): It pours during the night and we collect 20 litres of water in a bucket from the awning. This helps to keep our water tanks topped up. Split-pea soup for lunch - Sandra feels she definitely needs a blender. Before we arrive in New Zealand we are trying to use up all our dried food and tinned meats.

Manta Ray: Every afternoon about 16:00 the anchorage is honoured by a visit from a manta ray. Although we can clearly see its fins cutting through the water we cannot get close enough to see it gliding through the water like some marine stealth fighter. We try to predict its route and position the dinghy in the way hoping it will swim underneath us. Leaning over the side with our heads in the water we can clearly see the bottom through our goggles - but no luck, the ray diverts its course, obviously aware of our presence.

8th October (Saturday): During an early morning walk ashore, we see a couple of men building a house, with branches about 25 mm in diameter, which they lash in position. When the island is hit by the occasional, but inevitable, cyclone all these buildings will probably be wiped out, and the residents will either be evacuated or seek protection in the cyclone shelter, which is a concrete building on the motu.

9th October (Sunday): A local person tells us the birds are breeding on one of the motus near the pass. This is an opportunity to see something different, so we motor over and re-anchor. Ashore, as we quietly walk amongst the breeding birds, we are greeted with a cacophony of sound. Very soon we learn how close we can approach them before they fly off. The tropic birds are nesting in the trees, while the boobies (or fou-fous) are nesting mostly on the ground. They are contrasting birds; the tropic birds are small, stunningly white and graceful as they dance above us, while the boobies look motley and act really clumsy for a bird - we even see some of them fly into branches as they take off.

For the early Polynesian travellers, the vision of the tropic bird dancing in the sky indicated they had arrived at their new homeland. The tropic bird, pure white with a streak of red in its tail, embodied the free sprit of their new found life, particularly when it performed its elegant dance of courtship. At the climax of its aerial display, the tropic bird actually flies backwards. Meanwhile the blue footed booby's courtship is a less spectacular slow-motion dance where the male whistles as it lifts up its head, turning one way, then the other. Inspired by the vision of the tropic bird, I can see Sandra is about to burst into her tribal dance routine.

Bird Watching at Night: Ashley and Brenda (*Ashymakaihken*) suggest we go bird watching at night. We are sceptical and would rather have an early night's sleep. However, we join them and set off about 20:00 after dinner and a couple of rum punches - it is pitch black. Ashley is bristling with camera gear, David Attenborough would have been proud of him. Ashley is determined to make the most of this opportunity for some short video sketches he wants to produce. Fortunately it is a calm, still night as we quietly approach the bushes where the birds are nesting. Ashley is in front shining his powerful head torch at the bushes, sweeping back

Boobies nesting in the trees and on the ground

and forth like a Star Wars light-sabre. We think he is crazy because the birds will fly away and so defeat the whole purpose of being here, but no, the birds freeze when the light shines on them. Amazingly, we can actually walk right up to them - almost touch them. The blue footed boobies are the most entertaining. Some are perched on just one leg on a branch, with their heads tucked under their wings - it seems a most precarious position.

This memorable encounter is one of the treasures of our trip - another fascinating interaction with wildlife, on a par with swimming with the sea lions in the Galapagos and the stingrays in Bora Bora. After an hour it is back to *Pacific Voyager* to debrief and eat dessert; pineapple crumble and custard, with a mug of ground coffee and a glass of port.

10th September (Monday): Wake up to complete stillness - the water is as flat as glass, except for the occasional ripple from our hull

Ashley bird watching at night and bristling with camera gear

as we move about. Sandra does a quick pencil sketch to capture the bird islands and their reflection on the lagoon. We have another trip ashore to see the birds again and explore the neighbouring motu. There are two chaps banding the boobies - they tell us that the local people here do not eat the birds, but apparently they do in the Tuamotus and the Marquesas.

For lunch Sandra makes a curry using a tin of corned beef, chilli beans, onions and a packet of chilli sauce - it tastes scrumptiously spicy - we should have done it before. This is now the only way I can eat tinned corned beef - only 30 tins to go!!! More downpours keep our tanks full and gives us extra water for washing. This is a lovely spot listening to the birds beavering away. Their squawking sound is mellowed by the short distance over the water.

12th October (Wednesday): Another lazy day still anchored beside the bird islands. In the afternoon the wind starts to pick up out of the east, and the sea quickly becomes a nasty short steep chop. It soon dawns on us that this strong

Sandra holds the ends of the rope that chafed through on the coral head

breeze could be in for the night and we will be exposed on a lee shore. It would be better to motor back now during daylight to the protected anchorage on the eastern side of the lagoon, while we can still eyeball the coral heads and black pearl pots. With the change in wind direction the load has come off the second anchor. In preparation to leave, I pull this warp in first. To my horror, the rope has chaffed through!!!

Action stations - we quickly get into the dinghy and I search the bottom through my face mask (this is where a moon-pool would come in really handy). Eventually I locate the anchor and can see where the warp has chafed against a coral head. It looks quite deep, maybe seven or eight metres, much deeper than either of us have dived before. I am preparing to trawl with the grapnel when Sandra offers to dive. *"No I'll trawl - it looks too deep to dive,"* but Sandra insists, eager to meet the challenge. I watch Sandra take a few deep breaths, then dive straight down for what seems like ages - then she pops up holding the end of the anchor warp. I grab the rope as Sandra takes an enormous gasp of breath, *"Well done."* I pull in the fortress anchor, really pleased Sandra has recovered it.

We motor back to our original protected anchorage on the east side for a secure nights sleep, followed by a couple of relaxing days while we make plans to leave for Suvarow.

Further Reading:

Stanley, David., *South Pacific Handbook*

Leaving Maupihaa - *Ashymakaihken* ahead of us

32 Suvarow

After six wonderful weeks in the Society Islands it is now time to move on to ensure we leave the tropics before the official onset of the cyclone season. Our original plan was to sail from Maupihaa to Tonga via the Southern Cook Islands, but this year, those cruisers who took a southerly route via Rarotonga, were reporting strong winds (this is the year of the Pacific Storm which became known as the Queen's Birthday storm). A second option is to sail to Aitutaki, which is directly on our route to Tonga, but the entrance to the lagoon is reported to have only 6 feet of water and our draft is more than that, especially the way we are overloaded. A third option is to take a more northerly route and stop off at Suvarow in the Northern Cooks. We are intrigued by the stories we have heard about a New Zealander called Tom Neale who lived on Suvarow for many years, as a sort of modern day castaway, and wrote a book called, *An Island To Ones Own*. This is the romantic option we are looking for.

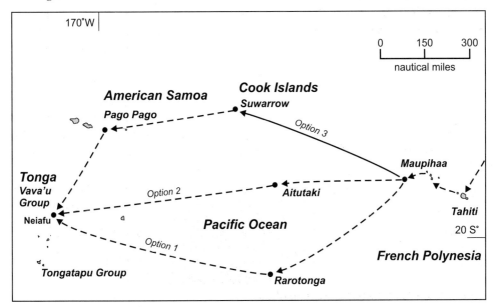

16th October (Sunday): Our departure from Maupihaa is quick - once more we shoot through a narrow pass, as we did from Ahe. There is little wind so we motor for three hours to clear the atoll. Like the tall ships of years gone by we are going to have to wait for the wind.

18th October (Tuesday): The wind is so light and the sea so perfectly calm that we consider using our spinnaker. After a few minutes sorting out the sheets and pole - up she goes and fills - fantastic!!!

Our spinnaker, gives us two knots in calm conditions. A good time for Sandra to read in the shade during her watch

I thought there was no wind, but even the slightest hint of a breeze fills this extremely light material. We are making an amazing 2 knots - 50 miles a day!!! After a reasonable day's performance the wind increases, so we drop the spinnaker for the night. It is very hot below so we sleep in the cockpit, but we are up and down all night putting sails up in the squalls to make the most of the wind, then dropping them in the calms. With our previous sail damage we dare not let the sails flog.

19th October (Wednesday): Only 350 miles to go. The wind is stronger today from the NE and we are sailing at 5 knots with everything up. But the wind does not last and eventually dies in the evening. We then motor for two hours to charge the batteries for the navigation lights. The sunset gives us a green flash, followed by a wonderful moonrise with an incredible red glow - we feel privileged.

20th October (Thursday): We eat the last of the baguettes from Bora Bora. They have lasted well, wrapped in our vinegared tea towels. However, they have become progressively harder, and I become increasingly concerned I might break my teeth. I do not relish the thought of experimenting with our emergency dental kit, especially at sea. The odd squall brings about 18 knots of wind. I steer to make the most of the squalls, some can last as long as 30 minutes. We see the most amazing cloud formation. It is like a giant tube snaking into the distance, looking strangely alien, as if it should be on the Discovery Channel or another planet.

23rd October (Sunday): Suvarow was first sighted by the Russian explorer Mikhail Lazarev in 1814, and named after his ship, the *Suvarow*. (Also spelt Suvarov and Suwarrow). Our first sighting of Suvarow is at the crack of dawn. On the horizon, we notice a small spec, the tops of a few palm trees, about five miles away.

Chart of Suwarrow from Tom Neale's book. He probably knew intimately every grain of sand and every coral head

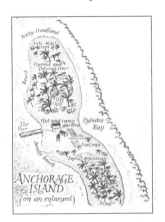

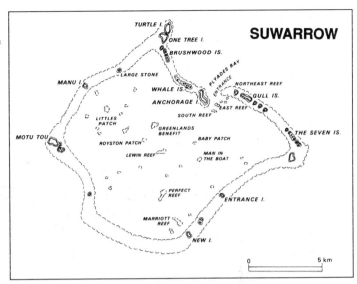

An hour later we enter Suvarow's only pass, which is on the eastern side of the atoll this time. The pass is much wider than Maupihaa and Ahe and we are pleased to see no current flowing. The recommended anchorage is beside Anchorage Island, but looking at the coral bottom through the crystal clear water I can see it is not an ideal anchorage. "*How did it get its name?*" Fortunately for *Ashymakaihken*, with their drop keel, they are able to get in closer to the shore, where there is a clean sandy bottom with good holding. After a couple of attempts we find a narrow strip of sand and are able to set our anchor. The next task is to position our other two anchors to lock *Pacific Voyager* in position. This should prevent her from swinging and wrapping her chain round a coral head, or worse, chafing the anchor warp on the coral (memories of our Maupihaa experience are still fresh in our minds).

Shark: With the anchors safely set a squall arrives. "*This should be a good test of our holding.*" I dive into the water to watch the boat tugging on the anchor chain, transmitting the wind forces to the anchor. While I am checking our anchor arrangement in 12 metres of water I am horrified to see a light grey torpedo shape gliding towards me. My first reaction is to get out of the water fast. "*Don't panic,*" I keep telling myself. As the shark passes underneath me I can see it has a white tip on its fin - this means it is a reef shark and they are supposed to be friendly - who are they kidding and, what is more, how does the shark know it is not dangerous?! I do not take my eyes off the shark as I slowly edge back towards the boarding ladder and climb on board.

While I wait for my pounding heart to calm down I recall John Fairfax's book, *Oars Across the Pacific*, about his rowing venture across the Pacific, and the shark bite he got on his arm from a white tipped shark - mind you he was trying to wrestle with it at the time! He said, "*...he slipped away and before I could blink an eye, had turned on me clamping his mouth at the back of my right upper arm. I felt a searing pain while, with my left hand, I grabbed behind his head, pulling him off and away.....*" (Page 220). Well at least I know what to do in an emergency!

Checking-in at Suvarow's customs - Tangi Jim chops opens a green coconut for us to drink!

I suppose I should take Jacques Cousteau's attitude, as he sees the shark as a creature of perfection, 400 million years in the making. He says the shark provides an essential function for the health of the oceans - they cleanse the sea of the sick, dead and mortally injured. I would like the sharks to know we are both very fit and healthy!!

25th October (Tuesday): After two busy days on board since our landfall we finally row ashore to check-in. We are greeted by Tangi Jim (father), Francis (Tangi Jim's daughter) and Francis' son. Francis seems to be the boss - she invites us to sit under a shaded area and they make polite conversation before asking us to sign their book. Although Suvarow is not an official port of entry, they do stamp our passports. In effect we are asking permission to stay in a marine park. While we are completing the paperwork Tangi Jim chops open a green coconut for us to drink. They are extremely generous considering they have so little. Wow! If only the UK customs could be so welcoming. *"Excuse me sir, would you like a beer while we take down your details???"* (Memories of Portugal come flooding back).

Tangi Jim tells us about how they survive on the island and what they have done to keep it clean and free from flies and pests. They wash their fish in the sea and not near their buildings, they have a flushing toilet and burn all their rubbish. They use plastic to protect the branches of the trees, they plant sprouting coconuts and have made a lovely garden all around their house with a hedge of fragrant frangipani. They have tried growing tomatoes, pawpaws and even Chinese lettuce. They have a clutch of chickens for fresh eggs, and occasionally one for the pot as a special treat on a Sunday and a break from the monotony of the fish and coconuts they eat everyday.

Francis tells us about their experiences with a nosey white tipped shark - it could have been the brother of the one I saw. While they were spear fishing, this shark would actually try and take the fish from the end of their spear gun. The shark must have been attracted by the thrashing of the dying fish and its blood. Naturally this frightens Francis, and after it happens several times - they eventually spear the shark as well.

Tangi Jim, at 69, shows us how to climb a coconut tree

Ashley going native - notice the pandanus rope tied around his feet

We exchange some of our tinned food for six freshly laid eggs and a large breadfruit. Back on board Sandra cuts the breadfruit into quarters and boils it in its skin with onions, garlic, oil and butter - you cannot beat fresh food to keep the scurvy at bay.

26th October (Wednesday): More torrential rain. We are catching the run off by the bucketful - the water tank is overflowing which means plenty of water for washing ourselves and our clothes. Row ashore and Tangi Jim, at 69, shows us how he climbs a coconut tree and brings down their dinner. First he ties his feet loosely together with pandanus leaves so he can hop up the tree, then he takes small hops until he reaches the coconuts - he makes it look so easy. Sandra tries, but only manages one hop before collapsing. We all look away in embarrassment.

Tangi Jim tells us that coconut trees can survive a salt environment and poor sandy soil. Coconuts can float for thousands of miles and are now distributed throughout the Pacific. The tree takes 5 to 6 years to mature, and the coconuts take a year to ripen from flower to nut. While still green, a coconut is at the drinking stage and provides more than a pint of sweet nourishing coconut milk. This should not to be confused with the rancid fluid from the hard ripe coconuts often sold in supermarkets.

We have since heard that coconut milk has many recognised medical applications, for instance, it is used for oral rehydration after severe gastroenteritis. Tangi Jim also explains how to make potchentong, the local bevy. Find a green coconut which is still growing on the tree, and cut a small incision in its base. Under the incision, hang a flask to catch the drips of milk. Leave it for a few hours while the milk ferments. And voilà - it is sundowner time!

Back on board Sandra bakes a breadfruit cheese pie, using a recipe from her Grenadan cook book. By adding a little lemon pepper, the pie is given a delightful tangy taste which helps it go down really well.

27th October (Thursday): Breakfast consists of fried breadfruit, fried eggs, baked beans and brown sauce. Later in the morning while Sandra is reading in the cockpit, she whispers to me, "*Quick look at this.*" I dash up to see two turtles floating by with slow lazy flicks of their front flippers - then one decides to mount the other. Now there are flippers splashing and waving in the air - it all looks very clumsy as the male keeps slipping back into the water. Sandra, the voice of experience says, "*There must be a better way.*" We try to capture this exciting event on film, but they are too quick for us. However, we feel pleased that once again, we are witness to yet another of nature's fascinating events.

I am not sure if turtles lay and hatch their eggs in Suvarow, but this is an event which must be fascinating to witness. Under the cover of darkness, the mother emerges from the sea and crawls up the beach to the soft sand above the high water line and excavates a bowl-shaped cavity with her rear flippers, scooping the sand with remarkable dexterity. Once she starts laying she goes into a trance - I suppose it must be really painful laying 100 eggs the size of golf balls. The mother then fills in the nest, before her laborious journey back to sea, leaving distinctive tracks in the sand - as regular as tank tracks left by a military vehicle.

Unfortunately these eggs are a popular source of food for predators, including some humans, who attribute aphrodisiac qualities to them. Some weeks later the hatchlings will scamper down the beach where they must run the gauntlet of making it into the sea before the sun gets too hot, otherwise they will die of dehydration. It is said that only one in a thousand make it to maturity. But those that survive make magnificent sights for snorkellers and turtle watchers. The adult leather-back can measure up to two metres and weigh almost a tonne.

Turtles are great travellers - they can migrate for thousands of kilometres. Who knows where they go? They have been known to swim for hours without surfacing and can dive to 300 metres. These extraordinary creatures are some of the only remaining marine reptiles and have existed for something like 250 million years, a hundred times longer than humans. They must be doing something right.

28th October (Friday): On our daily walk ashore we wander around to Whale Island which is just north of Anchorage Island. As we pick our way around the shallow pools of water between the motus I nearly walk on a reef shark basking in the sun. I am not sure who gets the biggest fright. I jump a couple of feet in one direction, while the shark darts off zig-zagging in only a few inches of water in the other direction. We are somewhat surprised to see a shark in such shallow water - they will be walking on land next!

Back on board I throw some stale bread over the side and within seconds a few fish start nibbling on the crumbs - then a few bigger fish arrive - and then a shark glides in to investigate! I am beginning to feel I should leave this atoll to the reef sharks.

There are three other yachts in the anchorage. This evening we join Frank and Tracy on *Symphony* for a sundowner and also to interview them for our book. They are heading back from

Sandra walking through a forest of coconut trees

Fiji to Seattle, via Hawaii, and therefore have to beat against the prevailing winds. The constant beating is taking its toll on their boat and its equipment, but after a few days overhauling their systems they are ready to do battle with the elements again. They are also short of diesel, *"I'm sure we can spare 20 litres."*

Tom Neale: Tom Neale lived on Suvarow for many years as a truly modern day Robinson Crusoe. He wrote a book about his experiences there, *'An Island to One's Own'*. This put Suvarow on the bluewater cruisers' map. In his book, Tom described his first thoughts as he arrived at the island, *"... shading my eyes until at last I caught my first glimpse of Suwarrow - the pulsating, creamy foam of the reef thundering before us for miles, and a few clumps of palm trees silhouetted against the blue sky, the clumps widely separated on the islets that dotted an enormous, almost circular stretch of reef."*

"...... then the anchor rattled down. We put a ship's boat overboard and a few minutes later I was wading ashore through the warm, still water towards the blinding white beach."

While I am reading Tom's book, I am also reading another book from the 1950s, *'From Rudders to Udders'* by Jane Taylor. Jane's book is about her trip from England to New Zealand on the yacht *Beyond*. (We later meet Jane in Russell, Bay of Islands). When I read in Jane's book that they sailed to Suvarow, I sit bolt upright as a shudder of recognition runs down my spine. I check Tom's book and, sure enough, Tom also mentions *Beyond* and that it is first yacht to visit the island after he had been there 10 months.

Jane Taylor writes, *"As we entered the lagoon, we saw what appeared to be a naked figure on the reef ...."* [After they anchored] *"... we watched a dinghy being rowed slowly towards us ..."* [In the saloon Jane asked Tom what he would like to drink] *"...I'd really enjoy a nice cup of tea with milk in it for a change."* [Tom said he was] *"... just taking a spell away from the hubbub of civilisation."*

[Jane gave him a glass of rum] *"....his first drink since he arrived on the island ten months ago ..."* [Tom invited everyone for lunch and later Jane sees him] *"....spearing cod and crayfish on the reef with the greatest of ease....."*

Dedication to Tom Neale - the modern day Robinson Crusoe. *'Tom Neale lived his dream on this island.'*

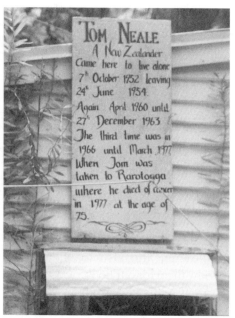

'Tom Neale. A New Zealander came here to live alone 7th October 1952 leaving 24th June 1954. Again April 1960 until 27th December 1963. The third time was in 1966 until March 1977, when Tom was taken to Rarotonga where he died of cancer in 1977 at the age of 75'

Tom Neale, *"I chose to live in the Pacific Islands because life there moves at a slower pace which you feel God must have had in mind originally when he made the sun to keep us warm and provide the fruits of the earth for the taking."*

After Tom Neale left, the Cook Island authorities became worried about Suvarow's sovereignty. Apparently a Scottish yachtsmen lived on Suvarow for a few years, and they were concerned he would claim sovereignty (*What for Scotland?!*). Thus the present family are caretaking the island which is now a national park. While we are chatting with them a cat wanders by. Tangi Jim says it is Tom Neale's. They found it when they first came to the island. It comes close and we can almost sense Tom's spirit of freedom living on in his cat.

As we leave Suvarow it is like finishing a chapter in Gerald Durrell's *'Pattern of Islands'* - an otherwise simple atoll, which has an intriguing modern day history and a strong bond with nature.

Further Reading:

Neale, Tom., *An Island To Oneself* (compulsory reading if you can find it!!!)
Severin, Tim., *The Spice Islands Voyage*, Little Brown
Wallace, Alfred., *The Malay Archipelago*
Taylor, Jane., *Rudders to Udders*, ColCom Press, Red Beach, Orewa, NZ
Fairfax, John, and Cook, Sylvia., *Oars Across the Pacific*, Norton, 1972
Grenada Homemaker's Association, *Grenada Spice Isle Homemakers Cookbook*

33 American Samoa

After the remoteness of the Pacific Islands, and the expensive shops in French Polynesia, we are looking forward to American Samoa with its wide range of products at more reasonable American prices. We certainly need to top-up our diesel bunkers and booze locker.

29th October (Saturday): Leave Suvarow at midday and motor out through the same pass we entered only five days ago. The winds are a healthy 20 knots as we sail around the northern end of the atoll into the deep blue sea. With over 400 miles to go to Pago Pago, we have good winds for the first day, then have to motor on the second day. In the Pacific this year there has been either no wind or storms.

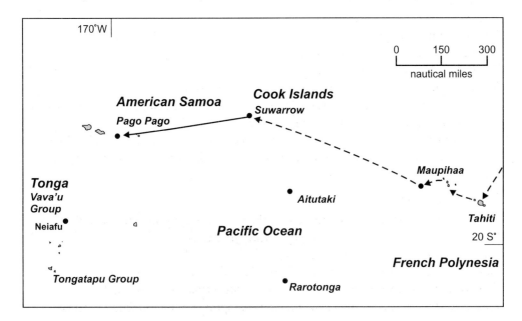

31st October (Monday): We motor all night, making good progress in calm conditions, but the wind continues to allude us. Over the SSB, we hear that the weather fax indicates we are unlikely to find any wind for another couple of days - there are no isobars at all in our area. What shall we do? Motor all the way to Pago Pago? We have sufficient fuel. Or should we wait in this rolly sea for some wind? We discuss our options with Ashley (*Ashymakaihken*) over the SSB.

We opt to motor, but Ashley suggests that they give us a tow and we supply them with fuel as their fuel consumption is much less than ours. We check our GPS co-ordinates and arrange to meet at an agreed waypoint, about five miles equidistant from each other. Sure enough, about an hour later, *Ashymakaihken* appears out of the blue. It always amazes us that there are other vessels out there, just below the horizon, and yet we can go for days or weeks without seeing anything.

Even though the ocean is like glass we decide not to bring the boats alongside as we risk banging the masts against each other. Ashley gets into his dinghy and rows over to collect a few fuel containers and pass us his tow line. Back on board Ashley slowly takes up the slack and the tow begins. We are moving along effortlessly through the water at 4 knots - I thought we might have to hand steer, but the lashed helm works fine in these perfectly calm conditions.

2nd November (Wednesday): After 24 hours of straightforward towing we are making good progress in the right direction and seem to be moving into wind. We hold onto our tow a little longer to see how fickle the wind is. *"The wind seems to be holding, shall we cast-off? Okay, see you in Pago Pago."*

Later in the day we have another Discovery Channel experience - two whales swim alongside us. Sandra has just read, *A Whale for the Killing*, which discusses their intelligence and suggests they are not aggressive, and would not intentionally damage a boat, even when they come near. However, the close proximity of such large mammals still makes me nervous.

Pago Pago: Log book: chart 1730, Samoa Islands (scale 1:446,400). Just as it is getting dark we make landfall. We motor into the harbour and tie-up to the same large mooring buoy as *Ashymakaihken*. The wind is blowing quite strongly now, funnelling between the mountains. After dark, on the VHF, we

Ashymakaihken and *Pacific Voyager* tie up to an enormous mooring buoy in Pago Pago harbour

**The coconut earrings
I secretly buy for
Sandra's birthday**

listen to a nearby yacht concerned about their anchor dragging. They can actually see their position change on their radar screen as they drag.

3rd November (Thursday): Take the dinghy ashore. It is a long walk to the officials' office in the main harbour where we check-in. As we walk into the main harbour, we are surprised to see so many tuna fishing boats, three abreast in some places. But the tuna fishing industry is, after all, the hub of local employment. It is intriguing to see small helicopter decks on top of all the tuna boats' pilot houses. The helicopter pilots are the eyes of the fishing fleet, looking for shoals of tuna. There is one story going around which says, the fishermen leave logs in the sea which create shade for the tuna to shelter under. This seems a tall story, but then I recall the tuna following in our shade on our leg from Cadiz to the Canaries. If this story is true I would be very concerned about these logs left floating around.

After the formalities, we take a leisurely walk to explore the town and see what Sandra can buy. Sandra and Brenda (*Ashymakaihken*) are attracted to shops like bees are to honey - buy, buy, buy. The girls egg each other on, "*I've just bought a shell bracelet,*" "*I've just bought a pareo.*" I secretly buy some coconut earrings for Sandra's 40th birthday, which could happen at sea on passage to New Zealand, so I must be prepared. I saw Brenda buy a pair so I know Sandra will want the same.

The liquor store is conveniently situated near the slipway. The aisles are stocked high with bottles. The price of rum, although not as good as the Caribbean, is much better than French Polynesia. Having decided we would just buy rum, which has become our normal tipple, we purchase six months supply.

8th November (Tuesday): Bacon butties for breakfast. My watch strap breaks. This is the Casio divers' watch I bought in Gibraltar, just over a year ago. I did not envisage needing to carry spare watch straps. I pray it is not going to be one of those days.

There is a plentiful supply of water from a tap on the jetty. I make numerous trips to top up our water tanks with our jerry cans. The Caribe dinghy handles the choppy conditions in the harbour really well. The rigid bow punches through the waves, leaving me completely dry. For the first time we do not fill all our water containers because, even if we spend a week or so in Tonga, we will still have sufficient water for the New Zealand leg. Meanwhile, Sandra is stowing everything in preparation for our next passage.

Weather: Our planned short stopover in Pago Pago to stock-up, is being extended by rough weather. Every morning, from our protected anchorage, we listen to the local weather forecast. It amuses us that the local reports always include an input from a sewage barge which is dumping the island's waste, offshore - I am sure he is taking artistic licence and embellishing the report by adding a few knots to the wind strength and a few feet to the wave height.

We take a bus to the meteorological office at the airport, to see if they have more accurate weather information. This also gives us an opportunity to check-out the local houses. They are mostly a very simple, basic square design, but aesthetically enhanced as they are surrounded by lush vegetation and towering mountains. The houses were probably built in the 60s, when America pumped a lot of money into the country to improve the living standards of the local people.

As we gather all the weather information together, it appears we are in between two weather systems; the winds are easing although large seas are still running, but there is another system on the way - a true definition of a weather window. *"Let's go for it."*

Diesel is available from a garage positioned very close to the slipway, but it is not duty free. Duty free diesel is only available from a road tanker which will drive to the end of the nearby quay. I ring Ben on 633-4101 and agree a price of 81 cents per US gallon, and arrange a time for delivery.

The road tanker arrives a little late so it is a rush to fill all our jerry cans before the light fades. We would prefer to leave in daylight but we want to catch this weather window. By the time we are packed away and motoring out past the harbour it is dark and the wind is freshening - not the best way to begin a passage.

Further Reading:

Mowat, Farley., *A Whale for the Killing,* Pan Books

34 *Tonga*

The Vava'u group of islands in northern Tonga offer some of the best cruising grounds in the Pacific. Our plan is to sail from American Samoa to Tonga and spend a couple of weeks in Vava'u, and then sail on to New Zealand before the cyclone season. It is getting late in the season and a sense of urgency is beginning to develop. As the cyclone season has officially started, 1st November, we should get out of the tropics. We want to sail to Neiafu in the Vava'u group to collect our mail from the *poste restante* but, if the weather conditions are right, we might sail on directly to New Zealand and miss Tonga completely. We can always spend more time in Tonga on our way back to the UK.

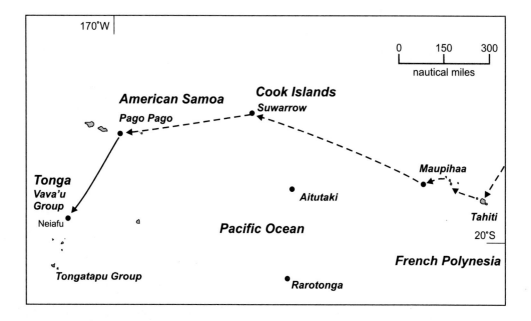

10th November (Thursday): After the rush to leave Pago Pago we are now punching into a healthy 25 knots of wind out of the SW. We can easily make our rhumb line course to Tonga, but are concerned that the wind may shift to the SE and head us, so we are sailing a higher course to give us more options later.

Beating to windward is never comfortable, but with the boat fully loaded her general motion is somewhat subdued - on this heading we have exchanged rolling for pitching. With the side force of the wind on the sails the boat is heeling over in dynamic equilibrium. The bow's fine lines are cutting through the waves and there is no slamming - but there is still plenty of buoyancy in the hull to rise powerfully to the oncoming waves.

Occasionally a rogue wave, foaming white, catches us - there is usually a momentary pause - then a bang as the wave crashes against the freeboard and the full force sends a shudder through the hull and a shower of water across the topsides,

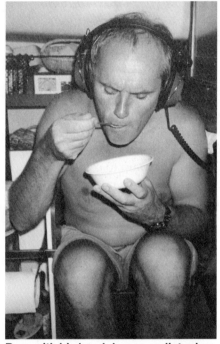

Rory with his headphones on listening to heavy rock

soaking everything in its path. *Pacific Voyager* is in her element. This is probably similar to the Irish Sea conditions she was designed to encounter.

With the decks constantly awash we are on the lookout for drips; the window over the chart table is dripping and so is the saloon hatch. With all the hatches closed the cabin is becoming increasingly, uncomfortably hot and humid - this is where our electrical fans provide some relief. In these conditions, moving on deck requires the tentacles of an octopus. We have progressively reefed down to three reefs in the mainsail, and the no.2 jib.

We are feeling punch drunk from the continuous pounding - there seems to be no relief from the six degrees of motion. The continuous noise is surprisingly loud, considering it is muffled by the packed lockers. Well actually, I have a solution for the noise - I put on my headphones and listen to some heavy music - this is where Led Zeppelin, Queen and the Stones come to my emotional rescue.

Bilge Pump: I bend down to check the bilge - to my horror the deep bilge is full of water, and it is covering the hydraulic motor. *"Where's all the water coming from? And why has the electric bilge pump not come on?"* I switch the electric bilge pump on to manual - the light comes on which indicates it should be working. One of my recurring nightmares is to wake-up and find water sloshing about the floor. This has now turned into a self-fulfilling prophecy. We have not hit anything so the seacocks are an obvious place to start looking for a leak. Sandra checks the forward compartments; speed log, heads and basin, while I check the aft compartments; galley sink, engine cooling, cockpit drains, bilge pump and stern gland - all seem okay. Of course, we have to rummage through the lockers to gain access to the skin fittings - this is when I feel our hull is unnecessarily riddled with holes like a prime Stilton.

By the time we finish checking all the skin fittings, we can see the electric bilge pump is winning - the water level is dropping, but there is still water flowing into the bilge. We check the skin fittings again and eventually trace the inflow of water to the chain locker. In the rush to leave Pago Pago I had forgotten to stuff a rag into the chain hose pipe. Consequently, every time a wave washes over the deck, a cupful of water comes into the chain locker which drains into the bilge. I should add, this is the first windward leg since leaving Panama, 5000 miles away. With the float switch out of action I will now need to check the bilge more frequently.

13th November (Sunday) - International Dateline: As we sail around the world we have crossed a number of artificial lines drawn on the planet. Today it is a big one - the International Dateline. In the author's note we explained how the Greenwich Meridian was established at the 1884 conference in Washington, but for some reason the International Dateline was not defined. One would assume it is on 180 degrees of longitude - making it exactly opposite the Greenwich Meridian. In practice the International Dateline has a zig-zag - countries like Tonga and more recently Kiribati have changed their relative position to the dateline - thus giving it a large eastward bulge.

As we cross the International Dateline, I am trying to work out which way the date should go - is it forwards or backwards? *"Hey Sandra, I think we've just lost a day."* And, sure enough, we have Phileas Fogg's situation in reverse; when he went east about the world he gained a day, while we are going west about the world, we lose a day.

Cyclone: Listening to Arnold's weather net at 08:00 (local time) is the focal point of the morning. It is always intriguing to hear what the other cruisers are up to. Arnold generally starts by reading out the Inter-tropical Convergence Zone (ITCZ). Today his net is to be more eventful - a low which has been stationary west of Fiji for some time is moving south and deepening - it is now classified as a **cyclone.** *"Now what?"* We consider our options. There is no way we wish to go through a cyclone, so we must either try and get into Tonga as soon as possible, sail out of its way, or maybe head back to Pago Pago. We adjust the sails and tighten the sheets, and as if *Pacific Voyager* knows what is expected of her, our speed increases from five knots to six knots - at this pace we should get into Tonga tomorrow evening.

With a cyclone out there, everyone is now glued to their SSB listening for the latest information. As the cyclone continues to move south, we are concerned it could swing towards Tonga and catch us. There are yachts all over the place so someone is going to get nailed. On the SSB we hear conversations between yachts we know - some of the cruisers are positioned right in the path of the cyclone. We can detect the tension and concern in their voices. The skippers have sensibly organised a four hour radio schedule while they go through the motions of preparing their boat and themselves for a storm. I can visualise them securing anything that could move, checking their reefing systems, checking their safety systems and most importantly, encouraging each other.

Tongan stamps of Captain Bligh (HMS *Bounty*) and a turtle

14th November (Monday) - Landfall: It is getting dark as we make our landfall in Tonga. Normally we would heave-to and wait for first light but with the cyclone close-by, we are keen to let it have the ocean to itself. *"It's all yours mate."* We pass through a large entrance between towering rocks into Vava'u and make for the nearest anchorage at Otungake. The Moorings charter company have produced a chart of the area and numbered all the anchorages - this is number 6.

Tonga was visited by Abel Tasman in 1643, and by James Cook in 1773 and 1777. Captain Cook named them the *Friendly Islands*, after the Tongans offered Cook feasts of food and dancing girls. But it has since been suggested that Cook and his crew were probably being lured off their ship so that it could be plundered. However, there must have been a mix up on the Tongan side, as nothing was stolen. Cook presented the Tongan King with a tortoise which was left to wander round the royal garden until it died in 1966, an amazing 200 years later - this really brings history into perspective.

Queen Salote single-handedly elevated Tonga's international presence at Queen Elizabeth's coronation. She caught the imagination of the public, as her open carriage was horse-drawn through the streets of London. And more recently, another famous Tongan, Jonah Lomu, who plays rugby for the All Blacks, will be remembered for crashing through the English defences at the Rugby World Cup.

15th October (Tuesday): After a lazy morning feeling secure and safe from the cyclone, which has now been down graded, we motor to the dock in Neiafu to check-in. Neiafu was originally named Port of Refuge in 1781 by the Spanish Captain, Mourelle, who was en route from Manila to Mexico.

Three Tongan officials arrive - they are like enormous rugby prop forwards. I watch anxiously as the largest official actually jumps down from the dock onto our coachroof - I am sure Nicholson's did not design their boats for such hefty impacts. We have been warned that the officials will confiscate ALL our fruit and vegetables So last night's dinner and this morning's breakfast consumed most of our stock. They are welcome to take the rest - which they do!!! One of the officials takes an interest in my screwdriver which has a translucent yellow handle. *"Can I take this to make a lure?"* *"No I need that for my toolkit."* When they can see they are not going to get any more stuff from us, and we do not have any cold cokes or chocolates, they quickly fill in the forms and leave as daintily as they arrived.

We decide to leave *Pacific Voyager* alongside the wharf while we go ashore to change money, collect our mail, and see the town. There are a few letters waiting for us at the *poste restante*; this is to be our last mail collection until New Zealand.

Handicraft Centre: Surprisingly, Neiafu is a run down looking town, considering this is the capital of the Vava'u group of islands. The most interesting shop is the

Left: Rory checks out Neiafu - pigs in tow
Above: Our coconut *spice* basket!

handicraft centre which Sandra immediately spots. Sandra loves anything that opens and shuts, so when she sees a coconut shoulder bag, which has been cleverly cut, to make two hinged openings, she cannot suppress her instinct to buy, buy, buy.

"What on earth are you going to use that for???" I ask.

"Spices, dear Rory, spices."

Bounty Bar: The Bounty Bar in the centre of town has taken on the roll of an unofficial yacht club, where cruisers meet and information and letters are posted on their notice board. We spoil ourselves with a juicy burger, chips and a bottle of ice cold beer, as we sit on their balcony overlooking the harbour with the yachts anchored below.

After our hearty lunch we tour the town, buy some vegetables from the market and wander back to *Pacific Voyager*. There is a man sitting on the quay beside our boat who greets us on our return. He seems well spoken, but I am a bit taken aback by his attire. He is wearing what looks like a woven floor mat around his waist. I cannot make out if he is a tramp or if this is traditional dress - it looks very clumsy. (We later find out that he was wearing the height of Tongan dress, and he was non-other than the chief of police!!!).

***Pacific Voyager* at Liza Beach, anchorage number 10**

The Tongan women motor over in their boats, to trade their handicraft

Dateline Party: In the evening we have an international dateline party to celebrate the day we lost when we crossed the dateline. We are joined by a few other cruisers including Bob and Judi *(Long Passages)*, and Ozman and Zuhal *(Uzaklar)*. Ozman and Zuhal are the first Turkish couple to attempt to sail around the world and are writing regular articles for a Turkish newspaper. (We have since heard that they have completed their circumnavigation and their yacht is on display in the Istanbul museum!!!). During the party we consume our last bottle of Jack Iron rum from the Caribbean, and consequently most of us proceed to lose another day due to memory loss.

Liza Beach - Anchorage 10: Spend the next ten days wandering from one beautiful anchorage to another. This is a great location to potter around and enjoy doing very little other than reading, writing, snorkelling, and relaxing. It is wonderful to sit at anchor in a secluded bay, all alone except for white sandy beaches and swaying palm trees.

MAF: The Ministry of Agriculture and Fisheries (MAF) in New Zealand have a long list of restricted and prohibited products. Before we left Europe we obtained a list from their embassy in Brussels. The list is somewhat ambiguous and unclear, but to play safe we assume there may be an issue with tinned meats, pasta, rice and coffee. We therefore proceed to either eat or swap all suspect types of food that we have on board. I especially do not look forward to the thought of eating all our remaining tins of corned beef, so when the prospect of swapping them for locally made Tongan handicraft presents itself, we go for it.

Handicraft Trade: There have been a number of places around the world, where local people have come alongside to sell fruit and vegetables - but here in Tonga, they come to sell their handicraft. At anchorage 10, a group of Tongan ladies visit in their open boats. Their boats are full of locally made handicraft consisting of woven baskets, trays, bowls and wooden carvings. One lady is actually making a basket while the others are chatting to us. Over a several days we trade a small flask, glass jar, all our tins of corned beef, bag of couscous, bag of corn meal, jar of instant coffee, packets of powdered milk, packets of cup-a-soup, baking powder,

Karla's village

A young Tongan boy outside his personal hut

stock cubes, barley, oats, popcorn, and pasta for a range of woven baskets and a few wooden carvings. They are very keen to swap their products for food as there is little choice in the shops, but when they see a packet of bow-tie pasta, they laugh. They cannot believe it is actually edible!

20th November (Sunday): The missionaries have done an excellent job of convincing the Tongans that Sundays are only to be used for eating, sleeping, and going to church. Karla who lives in the nearby village, invites Bob and Judi (*Long Passages*) and ourselves to their church for Sunday service. We feel honoured to be asked. The Anglican church is set up in the traditional manner, so every Sunday all the congregation put on their Sunday best and join in the service with forceful enthusiasm.

After the service Karla takes us around her village, where the houses have a basic palm frond thatched roof, and are built with a mixture of timber frames and woven panels (pandanus strips). Karla's family's home seems to have expanded in stages; a separate building to cook using an umu (earth oven), a separate building to eat, and even separate buildings for her boys to sleep in as they reach the age of thirteen. Their furniture is very basic and newspaper covers the walls, but they are happy and proud of what they have.

Far Left: Karla shows us her umu (earth oven)

Left: Karla outside her kitchen with her sons

Kalina shows us her ceremonial wedding wrap - she wants to marry a palangi

Karla invites us into her mother's house where we meet the rest of the family. Karla's mother is a great seamstress and in her simple home she has one valuable asset - an electric sewing machine. This she uses to make the most wonderful creations; dresses, blouses, and skirts for her family and herself.

Karla's sister Kalina, proudly shows us her bridal wedding wrap made from woven flax trimmed with bright coloured wools. (A note for other cruisers - bright coloured balls of wool are very acceptable gifts). She wants to marry a *'palangi'* one day. A palangi (or papalagi - see David Stanley, page 350) is a euphemism for a foreigner or white person - it means sky-buster. There is a Tongan myth that, as Tonga is surrounded by a great ocean, anyone who arrives there must come from the sky.

Feast: To our surprise we are invited to Karla's dining hut to join them for Sunday lunch. As guests, we are asked to sit on the floor in the traditional manner, around the woven dining mat, on which they lay a cotton tablecloth. Kalina sits at the head while the others place before us an enormous number of delectable looking dishes presented in bowls, coconut shells and on banana leaves. This Sunday lunch is more like a Tongan feast with dishes of roast pork, octopus, fish, clams, lobster, crayfish, taro, rice, coconut, banana, cooked papaya with coconut cream, watermelon and to drink, coconut milk and fruit juice. All the baking has been done in Karla's umu except one of the cooked dishes which has been given as a gift. (This is a Tongan tradition, on Sunday everyone cooks one extra dish to give to their immediate neighbour). The family ask us to please eat first with Kalina, which we find a little embarrassing as they just watch and do not eat.

***Pacific Voyager's* bulkhead - Turtle Tapa and wooden carvings from our Tongan friends**

After the huge feast I am half expecting them to bring on the dancing girls !!!!! In Tonga the traditional dancers grease their bodies with coconut oil to which we would be encouraged to stick a few dollar bills as a sign of appreciation. Fortunately we have brought a few gifts of tinned food to give to the family, but then they proceed to give us gifts of tapa cloth which they have made. We are humbled by their generosity.

Tapa cloth is made from the inner bark of the paper mulberry tree, which is soaked and then scraped using shells, and pounded with wooden mallets to soften it. Manioc juice is used to help piece it together and produce a slightly stiff, but pliable paper type fabric. Using red, brown and yellow pigments, they paint and decorate it with traditional Tongan designs. Tapa is used for ceremonial clothing, bedding, room dividers and all sorts of tourist gifts.

21st November (Monday): After two weeks in Vava'u a weather forecasting club is developing. We are all eager for weather information and analysis for our forthcoming trip to New Zealand. (Meanwhile Sandra and Brenda keep disappearing to have a sneaky game of Scrabble.)

Our last purchase of fresh fruit is delivered to *Pacific Voyager*

We are looking for a weather window between the gales and the next cyclone! The consensus is to sneak down the edge of a high and be in NZ before the following front. We have been monitoring the weather faxes from New Zealand and Australia, and I feel I have picked up a trend - the lows are passing over every 8 to 10 days with an associated front followed by a high and settled weather. It is about 1200 miles to New Zealand so, assuming we make at least 100 miles per day, the trip should not be more than 12 days, hopefully less. This means we will catch at least one weather system. As the weather is more likely to be stronger further south, it would therefore be better that we pass a system just south of Tonga which will give us a reasonable chance of reaching New Zealand before the next system.

24th November (Thursday): After only ten days in Tonga, we are preparing to depart. It would be wonderful to explore Tonga's two other groups, Ha'apai and Tongatapu, but that will have to wait for our return trip. As we finally finish checking our gear, a Tongan chap paddles over in his outrigger, dugout canoe, and we buy our last supply of fresh Tongan produce from him.

Further Reading:

Nordhoff, Charles., and **Hall,** Norman James., *Mutiny on the Bounty*
Stanley, David., *South Pacific Handbook*
www.quarantine.govt.nz
www.customs.govt.nz
www.lonelyplanet.com

35 Minerva Reef

With the cyclone season already upon us we are keen to make a quick passage out of the tropics to New Zealand. Our plan is to sail directly from Vava'u (Tonga) to the Bay of Islands (New Zealand). The cruising pilot indicates that, as we approach New Zealand we are likely to experience winds out of the NW, and therefore suggests a curved arc toward Norfolk Island to prevent being headed.

24th November (Thursday): Depart from Vava'u with a good weather forecast, good winds and we make excellent progress. Pass the Ha'apai group to port and also the volcanic island of Tofua. In 1789, Tofua was the island Fletcher Christian intended to paddle to before he was persuaded by his mates to lead the most famous mutiny in the British Navy on HMS *Bounty*. During the mutiny, Captain Bligh and his men were cast off in an open boat. They first rowed ashore to the Ha'apai group, only to be attacked as they put ashore. This was just the start of their problems, they were also attacked when they put ashore in Australia. Their epic voyage would only end safely in the Dutch colony of East Timor, several months later (see *Men Against the Sea*, an excellent read).

25th November (Friday): As we pass Tongatapu, *Pacific Voyager* is sailing well, and the weather forecast is encouraging, so we decide to continue. Every thing looks good for a quick passage to New Zealand. Dinner in the cockpit - chicken noodles out of my plastic dog bowl.

28th November (Monday): Four days into our passage and the weather situation has completely changed - for the worst!!! There are a number of weather forecasts available: Arnold's net, Si-Qui net, a weather fax from Wellington, a weather fax from Darwin and satellite imagery from Jonathan on *Xaxero*. Jonathan is another cruiser on his way south to New Zealand. On board *Xaxero*, Jonathan has written a programme to interpret the signals from the orbiting NOAA satellites. His report is therefore the most accurate because it is not so much a forecast, but an image of what the satellite sees. On the SSB, Jonathan tells us that he saw the last low forming right over him and then it tracked south into a high pressure system. The impact of this low pressure system is compressing the isobars, which in turn is now producing the strong winds and heavy cloud formations the cruisers are experiencing.

South Minerva Reef: A complex weather situation has developed south of us. "*I wish we could pop in somewhere for a few days, to let the weather settle down.*" There is nothing between Tonga and New Zealand, we are in the middle of the Pacific Ocean. "*Well actually there's Minerva reef,*" but we do not have any charts or pilotage details.

Later in the day we speak on the SSB to Bob and Judi on *Long Passages*. "*Where are you?*" "*We're in South Minerva Reef!!!*" They have sensibly pulled into Minerva, for the same reason that we now want to, but they had the foresight to make a sketch of Minerva Reef from a chart on the notice board in the Bounty Bar in Neiafu.

Over the SSB Bob gives me instructions on how to draw South Minerva Reef. "*Set up a 20 by 20 grid and I will give you co-ordinates for the coastline of the reef which looks like a figure of eight on its side.*" With the bottom left corner set as zero X, and zero Y, Bob reads out a series of co-ordinates and I draw the reef. He then gives me a waypoint for the only pass which is located about 10 o'clock on the right circle - from there we will have to eyeball our way in.

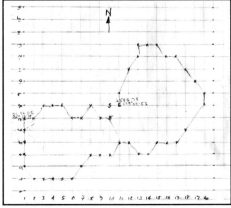

My rough sketch of Minerva Reef and the sketch from Minerva Reef book

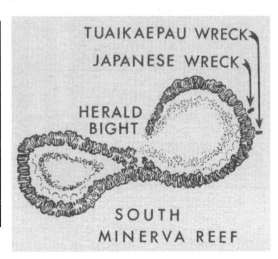

TUAIKAEPAU WRECK

JAPANESE WRECK

HERALD BIGHT

SOUTH MINERVA REEF

South Minerva is named after the whaling ship *Minerva* which ran up on the reef in 1829 - we do not want to rename it *South Pacific Voyager Reef*. South Minerva is a combination of two reefs, each with a seven mile circumference. Even though there is no land on South Minerva, in 1972 a group of right wing American millionaires attempted to seize Minerva and convert it into a taxless utopian state.

South Minerva reef was brought into the limelight when several Tongan sailors were stranded there for fourteen desperate weeks after their ship went on the reef in 1962. They subsequently wrote a book of their experience.

29th November (Tuesday) - Landfall: At 10:00 the GPS indicates we are getting close to our waypoint and I am standing by the shrouds searching for any telltale signs of the reef. South Minerva has no vegetation, no palm trees - nothing. There is only a coral reef which emerges at low water, but is covered at high water. What am I going to see??? As we are still in deep water there is no immediate concern. I see a flash of white. Was that surf? Then I see it again. I shout to Sandra, *"I can see the reef, we must be about three miles away."*

Skirting the northern tip of the reef we get a feel for a safe distance off the breakers, and proceed to our waypoint. There are no markers indicating the pass so we cautiously approach the reef and eyeball our way through, with one eye looking in the crystal clear water for the razor sharp coral, and one eye on the echo sounder watching our depth. To hit a coral head now would be disastrous.

We motor into the lagoon, which is completely surrounded by the reef, a reef that is just a tiny spec in the middle of the Pacific Ocean. It is like entering another world. We motor over towards *Long Passages,* the only other vessel in the lagoon. Bob shouts over, *"We're not happy with this position - we dragged last night."* (For more about their horror story see their web site www.longpassages.org).

"Okay we'll have a look at the bottom near that small rock sticking up." I point to the only prominent bolder of coral on the reef, looking like a mini Table Mountain.

With the depth sounder reading 20 to 30 metres in the centre of the lagoon, it is too deep to anchor, but near the inner edge of the reef the bottom shelves steeply to a shallow sandy ledge of about three to four metres. As we explore the ledge along the east side of the reef, we find what we think is a better location to anchor. The east side of the reef faces the prevailing easterly winds which will blow us away from the reef towards the centre of the lagoon. Although the shallow plateau is deep enough for us to swing on the anchor, we are concerned about dragging back onto the reef if the wind shifts to the west.

We decide to use all of our three anchors; CQR, Bruce and Fortress - this is one of those occasions when we wish we had a few more (we have since bought another two anchors!!!). I position the CQR and Fortress ahead of us about 60 degrees apart, and run the Bruce behind us, down the bank, in case the wind shifts 180 degrees. I note our escape bearing in the log book - 270M.

Anchor Light: There are no lights or land marks to use as reference points, so we ask *Long Passages* to leave their anchor light on at night. Our only warning equipment on board are two echo sounders and a GPS. The echo sounders have upper and lower limits, so they will sound an alarm if we start moving. Although the GPS also has an anchor alarm, it is probably not sufficiently accurate for an anchor watch. If we drag into the lagoon at night I do not fancy wandering around on the GPS alone.

We are the only living souls for miles, in complete isolation on a lonely reef in the middle of the Pacific Ocean. As one roller after another explodes into huge pillars of spume onto the coral reef, we appreciate that this narrow reef is all that protects us from this incredibly powerful ocean. At high tide the water actually covers the reef and it becomes choppy inside the lagoon. When it becomes bouncy at night, it is comforting to look over and see *Long Passages's* light, still bobbing up and down beside us.

30th November (Wednesday): It intrigues me how our life becomes influenced by the tide - at high water we are on anchor watch, but at low water it is generally calm in the lagoon and we go snorkelling. Bob launches his dinghy and motors over, "*Do you guys fancy snorkelling? There was a fishing boat in here when we arrived and they caught lots of big lobsters - maybe they left a few.*"

The reef is absolutely alive with colour and clouds of tropical fish going about their business. This is the best snorkelling we have ever enjoyed. In the azure blue water, we swim through a gigantic coral garden, with deep valleys in between huge coral heads, standing majestically like fairy-tale castles whose soaring towers taper to jewel-encrusted peaks. The coral is illuminated with the spectacular radiance of stained glass windows. Living on the sea-bed are purple and green tube sponges, anemones of every type, impressive giant clams, and small white domes of brain coral which peacefully lie amid the vibrant colours of these hanging gardens in the lagoon. We witness an encyclopedia of tropical fish, from the tiniest reef fish and beautifully patterned angel fish, to the larger parrot fish, snapper and the occasional reef shark. This underwater heaven is better than any 3D IMAX film we have seen. If only we had a professional underwater camera to record this magical valley in the middle of the largest ocean in the world.

After a couple of hours of snorkelling we are ravishingly hungry. Back to *Pacific Voyager* where Sandra makes a paella from dried shrimps (not allowed into New Zealand), dried onions, dried carrots, tinned peas and rice and, for dessert, to use up our powdered egg white, Sandra makes the national dessert of New Zealand, a pavlova.

Pacific Voyager anchored inside South Minerva's featureless reef

1st December (Thursday): The weather is still unsettled. There is an incredible electrical storm during the night - catch 40 litres of fresh water in our buckets. Over the SSB we hear of some cruisers experiencing 45 knots and big seas, and that there are more gales forecast. The rough weather is taking its toll; *Unicorn* (41 foot sloop) has broken its roller-furling forestay, *Quark* (Nic 32) has damaged their forepeak bulkhead, and another yacht has blown out all their sails and are requesting a tow!!! We feel comfortable and snug in our lagoon behind the reef.

Minerva Reef - During low tide we go snorkelling with Bob and Judi (*Long Passages*)

During low tide, Bob and Judi motor over in their dinghy for tea and cake while we discuss the latest weather fax, then go snorkelling in another corner of the lagoon. When we return Sandra makes a fruit cake and chocolate chip cookies. Then it is back to anchor-watch as the tide rises.

2nd December (Friday): The weather prospects are improving - but it is Friday!!! No way will we venture out on a Friday. We sense the weather systems are passing over us. Our weather window of opportunity is approaching. The challenge is to catch the tail-end of the departing low, then the leading edge of the approaching high; motor through the centre of the high, where there is no wind but calm seas, and finally catch the end of the high, and arrive in New Zealand before the next front. As we have a limited motoring range, we have to make the most of the favourable winds.

3rd December (Saturday): Up anchor and we are off retracing our route out through the pass. With full main and genoa set and 25 knots from the north east, we are really gunning it. "*Do you want to share a Stugeron?*" In these rough conditions half a Stugeron helps to limit our seasickness and keep us active. Breakfast is on the run - cheese on toast - wolfed down as we sit wedged in the corner of the cockpit.

4th December (Sunday): After 24 hours of steady wind we can sense its direction is starting to shift and head us. The Hydrovane faithfully tracks the wind round until we are eventually sailing due west. At this point we decide to heave-to and hold our position while the front passes.

Pacific Voyager with its long fin keel, heaves-to nicely just under trysail alone, we do not need to back the headsail to hold the bow off the wind. With this arrangement she holds her position, balanced between fore-reaching and tacking, and comfortably takes the building waves in her stride. It is amazingly peaceful below - a good time to catch up on our kip before the wind shifts sufficiently for us to make our course again.

After 12 hours hove-to I check the wind direction, *"We should be able to start sailing soon. We can just about make our course. Shall we have something to eat before it gets bouncy again?"* Sandra prepares a noodles with chicken stock and dried peas. With some nourishing hot food inside us, we hoist the sails and head for New Zealand once more. With the changing wind direction, the seas have built up very quickly - we are now punching into a choppy cross sea. The sea state is more in keeping with the Irish Sea than here in the middle of the Pacific Ocean.

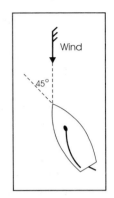

Pacific Voyager's **heave-to arrangement**

6th December (Tuesday): As the clock turns midnight it is Sandra's 40th birthday. *"Happy birthday to you, happy birthday to you, happy birthday dear Sandra, happy birthday to you - I'd love to take you out for dinner, but ....."* I am interrupted by a strong gust - the wind freshens to 25-30 knots, gusting 35 knots. We are over canvassed and the boat is bouncing around too much. So at 00:01 in the morning, on Sandra's 40th birthday, dressed in heavy-weather gear, Sandra is perched on our bouncing foredeck changing the headsail! It takes a long 30 minutes to reef both sails, but now *Pacific Voyager* feels more comfortable, and not so hard pressed, and we can relax knowing the wind-force can increase a little more without us needing to reef again tonight.

Sandra will always remember her 40th birthday as something special. Other men take their girlfriends out for dinner, but Sandra's special treat is a gale on the foredeck of *Pacific Voyager*.

A few hours later, just after sunrise the wind and sea have eased. *"I have some birthday presents for you."* I spoil Sandra with birthday presents from American Samoa - a cassette of their music, two packets of chocolates (Sandra loves chocolates), coconut earrings, a lovely watercolour card by Carla Beauchamp, a pareo from Bora Bora and two tiki carvings from the Marquesas. What more can a birthday girl want???

7th December (Wednesday) - Sails: Beating to windward puts more strain on our sails than sailing downwind, and this leg to New Zealand is our first windward leg for some time. We hear on the SSB of a yacht ahead of us who has actually blown-out all their sails, and is being towed a few hundred miles to New Zealand. *"The tow will probably turn out to be more expensive than a set of new sails."* Smugly, we feel this will never happen to us because our mainsail was new when we left the UK, and although we have repaired the genny a few times, we do have a spare lightweight genoa, and a no.2 jib. But my morning sail inspection reveals extensive sail damage - the genoa's lower luff eye has pulled out and

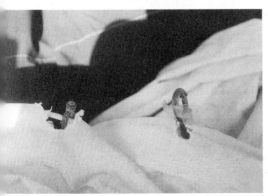

o.2 jib sail damage - the hanks have pulled ut of the eyes

transferred the transverse load to the next hank attached to the forestay. I immediately lash the lower strop to the forestay to transfer the load away from the other hanks. Closer inspection of the luff reveals that some of the other eyes could also pull out if subjected to a high load.

Now, really concerned about our sails, we take a close critical look at the no.2 jib which has not given us any problems and are shocked to find a number of hanks have pulled away from the sail. This is our fault, we left the no.2 jib hanked on to the outer forestay while we used the genoa on the inner forestay - the inner forestay then chafed against the no.2 jib and caused the damage.

Turning our attention to the mainsail, to our horror we notice that most of the plastic hanks holding the sail to the mast are on their last legs - the continuous use since the UK, has worn away the plastic fittings. If one hank was to fail, I am sure the transfer of load would cause the other hanks to fail as well. This would give us a loose luff mainsail!!! We do not have any spare plastic hanks, but we do have a number of small stainless shackles which I fit to the sail's eyes and plastic mast slides.

This close scrutiny reveals that we are also candidates for more sail problems - disasters are often caused by small problems escalating. And if these cruising sails blow out, that only leaves us with a storm jib and trysail.

With all these sail repairs, we have to empty the pilot locker berth to find the sail repair kit - spare eyes, punch and sail-tape - then pack it all away. All done we are ready to go. But now we notice the wind vane's frame has broken again. Back to emptying the pilot berth locker once more, this time to find the spare wind vane.

8th December (Thursday): Today the wind is much calmer at 10 to 15 knots, we are moving into the centre of the high. Have a great day's sailing. Wish it could always be like this. Sandra makes a quick Irish bread recipe. She is using up our tins like crazy; lunch is spaghetti bolognaise with tinned carrots, garlic and onions and tinned green beans on the side - tinned pineapple and tinned cream for dessert. Sandra feels it is getting colder - out come her leggings and sweat shirts. All our warm clothes have been mothballed since Gibraltar - it has been shorts and tee-shirts since then.

As the wind dies we decide to let the seas completely settle down before we start motoring - we do not have sufficient fuel to motor all the way to New Zealand, so we want to make the most of the fuel in calm conditions.

18:00 - the sea is like a mirror. There is no wind and there are just a few small puffy balls of cloud in the blue sky. Our concern now is that the high has split which may let a low in sooner than expected. Looking over the side, I notice millions of jelly fish overtaking us!!! The seas have died down sufficiently for us to start the engine, for what could be a couple of days motoring and make some progress towards New Zealand.

9th December (Friday): After motoring all night, I stop to check the oil and diesel levels. We top up the main diesel tank from the jerry cans lining the side deck. This is not a pleasant operation, and not something I would like to do in rough conditions.

Becalmed - "*Do you have any diesel for sale? I've got a plane to catch in Auckland.*"

I am always concerned about spilling diesel and creating a skating rink.

Later in the afternoon we come across another yacht (Amel 45) - they have already run out of fuel. We motor over to say *"Hi,"* and they shout back, *"Do you have any diesel for sale? I've got a plane to catch in Auckland."* You can never find a garage when you need one! Unfortunately we have no spare diesel. Instead we exchange gifts mid-ocean. We throw them a plastic bag of vegetables, just in case they have to wait a long time for some wind! In return, they throw a plastic bag of books they have read.

We continue motoring for three days in flat calm conditions until we are down to our last 10 gallons of diesel. *"I want to keep our last 10 gallons to motor into Opua when we reach New Zealand."* I turn off the engine - it is absolutely quiet. *Pacific Voyager* is stopped dead in the water - for the next 24 hours we wallow in calm conditions, with 75 miles between us and New Zealand. There are two Taiwanese trawlers in the distance - I call them up on the VHF and ask them for diesel - no response. I do not know how we would have transferred the diesel, but is was worth a try.

11th December (Sunday): The weather forecast indicates the high will continue to split, but the low is going to be weaker than first anticipated. Birds have been flying around us all day - but no albatrosses yet. Now that we are moving south we may see an albatross if we are lucky. They are reported to have a wingspan of five metres, giving them the capability of long-sustained flights. Years ago, seamen believed that the albatross embodied the souls of dead sailors, and it was unlucky to kill one. This was immortalised in the *Rhyme of the Ancient Mariner*, by Samuel Taylor Coleridge. In the southern oceans, albatrosses have been reported to follow ships for weeks - it must take them miles away from their home.

Sandra takes this opportunity to clean all the food lockers, check our supplies, and make walnut fudge brownies from a Betty Crocker packet. Breakfast is grilled spam and baked beans. Lunch is leftovers from last night's dinner of tinned tuna and onions with Bearnaise sauce, tinned carrots and rice - delicious.

12th December (Monday) - Landfall: The winds are better today and we are making good progress. We sight Cape Brett in the late afternoon. *"Is it a cloud or land? Yes it is definitely land. "Yes it's Aotearoa - the Land of the Long White Cloud."* As we inch closer, frustratingly we realise we are not going to make Opua before nightfall - reluctantly we heave-to for the night.

Pacific Voyager **alongside the general store at Opua, New Zealand**

13th December (Tuesday) - Opua: At 04:00, we start the motor - now happy to use our last 10 gallons of diesel. We make good progress for an hour, before we end up punching into 25 knot head winds and rain which slows our progress. "*I wish we had got closer to land yesterday when it was calmer.*" We are accompanied by a flock of gannets diving into the sea like kamikaze pilots - the water surface is thrashed white as they search for fish.

We easily locate the channel markers and motor up the estuary which seems to go on and on. As we pass a line of moored yachts, I see *Blue Moves.* "There's Blue Moves. *We haven't seen Richard since the Canaries.*" We ease over, "*Good-day.*"

"*Good-day, you're just in time for my wedding. We're getting married on Saturday, come and join us. We're having a beach party in English Bay.*"

"*Great we'll see you there. We've got to check-in.*"

Customs: Yesterday, we called the customs on the VHF, to inform them when we would be arriving at Opua. We reach the dock 30 minutes before the officers arrive. Sandra is given a six month visitor's visa on her British passport, while I am only given a three month visa on my Irish passport. It is a wonderful feeling to have completed the first phase of our voyage from the Greenwich Meridian in London to the International Dateline in the South Pacific. Now to explore New Zealand - Sandra wants to meet some real Kiwi blokes.

Further Reading:

Nordhoff, Charles., and **Hall,** Norman James., *Men Against the Sea*
Ruhen, Olaf., *Minerva Reef*, Minerva
Coleridge, Samuel Taylor., *Rhyme of the Ancient Mariner*
www.xaxero.com (Sky-eye Satellite Imagery)

36 New Zealand

After two incredible years, bluewater cruising in the Caribbean and Pacific we are ready for a break, and New Zealand seems like an interesting place to stopover.

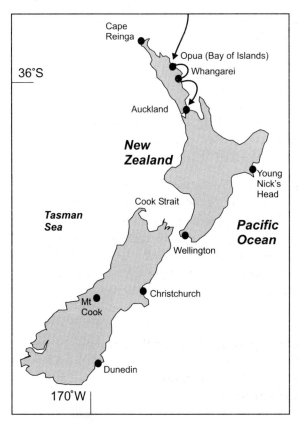

Originally, we thought three years was a long time to spend sailing round the world but, in practice, to meet this schedule we always seem to be rushing from one anchorage to another. There have been numerous places of interest along the way where we would have liked more time to explore. We have literally been dragging ourselves away. The bluewater cruising lifestyle is definitely for us and we are reluctant to give it up in a hurry.

Financially our spending has been within budget and we have sufficient funds to complete our circumnavigation, but the prospect of working for a short while to increase our savings, get back into our professions, and overhaul *Pacific Voyager's* systems sounds appealing.

Motuarohia Island, Bay of Islands

Bay of Islands - Sandra prepares to go hiking

Bay of Islands: Making our landfall in Opua is more by good fortune than design. We had not realised the Bay of Islands is one of the best cruising areas in the world, with plenty of protected anchorages, stunning, picturesque headlands and interesting nature walks, all within a few miles of small harbours to re-victual, buy fuel and LPG, and buy the *Economist* and *Weekly Telegraph* once again. Local facilities include boatyards, yacht clubs, cruiser's nets (VHF 63 and 77), and radio stations providing regular marine weather forecasts.

Breathtaking views at Whangaroa

Stunning view from the Cavalli Islands

Coming ashore at the Cavalli Islands

6th February (Monday) - Waitangi Day: New Zealand's constitution is based on an agreement between the British (pākehā) and the Maori leaders, signed in 1840 at Waitangi in the Bay of Islands. Every year the Governor General and the Prime Minister travel north to Waitangi to celebrate the historic signing of their constitution. It is intriguing to see the contrasting cultures - a 100 man waka (Maori war-canoe), paddling past a modern navy frigate, and the Maori warriors in their traditional battle dress accompanying the Naval cadets marching around the Treaty House lawns.

History: Maori people are descents of the Polynesian explorers who came to New Zealand from the Cook Islands and Tahiti approximately a thousand years ago. They call the Pacific Ocean, *'Moana-nui-a-Kiwa'*, which means, *'The Great Ocean of the Blue Sky'*. And they named New Zealand, *'Aotearoa'*, which means, *'The Land of the Long White Cloud'*. Abel Tasman was the first European to discover New Zealand in 1642. It was initially named *'Statenland'* and later changed to *'New Zealand'* after the Province where the Dutch East India Company had its chamber. It was Captain Cook, in 1769, who literally put New Zealand on the map - his map. He charted and named most of the bays and headlands around the coast, such as; Cook Strait, Mt. Cook, and Young Nick's Head.

Above: Maori Warrior, performing the traditional challenge - courtesy of Warren Jacobs (Al Fresco)

Right: Cook's statue in Gisborne, with Young Nick's head in the background. Nick Young was the first person on Cook's ship to sight New Zealand

Waitangi Day, 100 man Waka and navy frigate in background

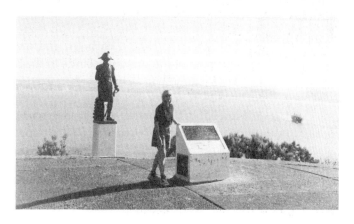

Whangarei: After three months in the Bay of Islands we cruise down the coast to Whangarei, another popular destination with bluewater cruisers. The marina is conveniently situated within a short walking distance from the shops and marine facilities. While we are in Whangarei, *Pacific Voyager* is fortunate to survive horrendous flooding caused by heavy rains and debris, which dams the river up stream - then whoosh - it releases a tremendous amount of pent up energy which flattens many of the piles the yachts are tied up to.

Whangarei marina floods - *Pacific Voyager* makes it into the national paper

Category 1: Shortly after we arrive in New Zealand, the government introduces a law which requires **all departing yachts** to be inspected to category 1. Although it seems like a good idea, the implications for visiting yachts and international treaties are horrendous. We join a number of protesters who are against these draconian regulations, but all our arguments fall on deaf ears. It eventually takes an American yachtsman to leave without an inspection, and be fined NZ $10,000 on his return. After two appeals, the verdict is reversed and the law scrapped.

MORUROA

Mururoa: The announcement by the French government that they will resume nuclear tests at Mururoa sparks a sharp protest from the New Zealand people. The Kiwi's still remember the sinking of the *Rainbow Warrior* in Auckland harbour, and they see these tests as an ecological invasion of the pristine islands in the South Pacific. Hundreds of people crowd together at the Viaduct Basin to give a fleet of yachts a great send off - they are taking the protest to Mururoa atoll itself. This is probably the first time yachts have been used to make a political protest.

During our evening walks around Westhaven Marina, we visit the protest control centre at Ponsonby Yacht Club where they are contacting the yachts by SSB every evening. The French have been using Mururoa since 1966, as a nuclear testing site and they have just about made the atoll completely unsafe for human habitation for the next 100 generations.

Auckland Viaduct - Mururoa protest

America's Cup: After the Mururoa protest the Viaduct Basin is redeveloped for the America's Cup. The Kiwi's have an enviable depth of match racing talent - yacht designers, yacht builders and crews. It is therefore not surprising that they eventually win the America's Cup when they get the right mix of yacht design, crew synergy,

Rainbow Warrior's **propeller overlooking the** *Warrior's* **watery grave**

professional management and team motivation. The TV coverage is excellent. We all become serious armchair sailors, in our case watching the America's Cup on our nine inch Sony TV, in a protected anchorage.

Visiting the America's Cup village is part of the fun - we join thousands of enthusiastic supporters checking out the fleet of Super Yachts, buying souvenirs and relaxing in the cafes, bars and restaurants surrounding the harbour. Over four million people visit the village which is more than the total population of New

Zealand. The racing yachts leave the village every morning to a hero's send off, with the crowds cheering, and fog horns blaring - there is an electric buzz of anticipation. The yachts are accompanied by media helicopters and a fleet of supporting boats thrashing the sea white in their wake.

Black Magic **sailing beside us in the Hauraki Gulf**

Rory going to work in the morning

Employment: Now we are back in a western country, our cash-flow is in a serious tail-spin. What with buying a car and petrol, visiting pubs, eating out at restaurants, together with Sandra's new wardrobe, we need to find employment fast to reverse the cash-flow. Most cruisers are travelling on a tight budget, so settling back into society means it is essential to find work relatively quickly.

To apply for work permits, we need all our personal documents (birth certificates, degrees and certificates of employment etc.), which are hidden away in the attic of our house in Cape Town. Life would be so much easier if we had left them with someone for forwarding. But when we left the UK, we did not intend to work en route. It therefore takes us a few months to get all our documents reissued at source.

New Zealand has a small economy which fortunately for us is experiencing an upturn when we arrive. We initially apply for jobs advertised in the NZ Herald (main newspaper), but make little progress. We then change our approach and offer a product - short courses in project management. But first we have to develop all our business systems from scratch; company name, office, address, telephone, fax, email, letter heads, business cards, VAT registration and lecturing venue - together with marketing the courses and developing lecturing notes. However, once we get going, our short courses are successful, and we also start lecturing part-time in the local technical colleges and universities.

Pacific Voyager: After cruising from Britain and interviewing many cruisers about their boats, we now have a much better idea of what systems we should have on board. The scope of our refurbishment is going to be far more ambitious than our fitting-out in Salcombe car park.

With more funds available we progressively upgrade all *Pacific Voyager's* systems. It is as if we have satisfied our initial whim of cruising and now we are going to plan the next leg in more detail, so that, *Pacific Voyager* will be better equipped, and more comfortable.

Further Reading:

Sinclair, Keith., *A History of New Zealand,* Penguin Books

37 *Sustainable Cruising*

Do we work to live or live to work??? Do we cruise on our savings or cruise on our income??? When we sailed from Britain to New Zealand we lived off our savings - this is obviously not sustainable. To achieve our holy grail - *sustainable cruising* - we have reorganised our work and our boat to give us an income stream while we cruise.

Finding employment along the way is a stop-go situation and not really sustainable cruising. For us, writing books offers the best opportunity, because now our income is generated by our books sales while we cruise. This chapter will discuss how we have setup our boat and reorganised our lifestyle to write our books.

Why Write Books?: In some respects I had already started to walk down this career path before we set off cruising - I had written a book on Project Management which is used by universities and business schools around the world. It was then an obvious step to develop this further to include bluewater cruising books based on our present lifestyle, experiences, and access to cruising information. We also looked into writing short articles for yachting magazines, but did not make any headway there - in fact the closest we got was to be paid US $100 by *Ocean Navigator* for not printing our article!!!

Being interviewed by the BBC

Pacific Voyager's office area with notebook computer, printer, telephone and fax

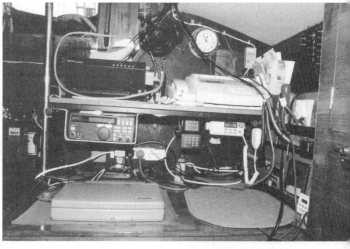

Our Boat: To turn our boat into a writing office we had to make a number of radical changes. Our Nicholson 35 was originally designed as a coastal cruising yacht for the British Isles - she was therefore never really designed for bluewater cruising, and certainly never designed to be a writing office! To become a bluewater cruising yacht our main challenge was to find space to carry sufficient diesel, water, provisions and sailing gear: to become our writing office we needed to add two work stations with 240 volt power supply, together with storage for our reference books and notes. We are fortunate the Nicholson's hull shape will accommodate a 25% increase in displacement without significantly affecting its hydrodynamic performance.

Our Office: By using notebook computers we are able to accommodate two work stations, varying our work position from our bunk, chart table, saloon table to cockpit table. These computer systems are at the heart of our mobile office. Computer technology is the key to our flexibility, so it is essential to continually upgrade our computer systems to keep pace with the latest equipment. When we left the UK we were using an AT 386 lunch-box computer with Word Perfect and Lotus (see page 61). This was soon replaced by two Toshiba Satellite notebooks using Microsoft Office, Pagemaker, Photoshop and Coreldraw, and now we are using a Dell Inspiron to give us a large screen and increased hard drive storage.

We have always used the pilot berth for storage - initially we fitted a lee-cloth across the opening, but now we have subdivided it into three compartments with shelves for our books and notes, and a section for a 12 volt Sony TV and video.

Pilot berth, now converted into a storage area

Rory talking to Janet Murphy of Adlard Coles Nautical, at the London Book Fair, about our book proposal

Electrical Power: While in a marina we obviously use shore power, but the challenge is to be able to continue writing in the picturesque anchorages along the coast. We have a wind generator and solar panels that provide alternative power depending on the weather conditions prevailing at the time, and this is supplemented by the main engine with a 120 amp alternator. The electrical power is stored in two banks of deep cycle batteries, which supply 12 volts through an inverter and 24 UK plug points strategically located on a ring main. To control the electrical systems the power-in and power-out are monitored by an array of instruments.

Communications: This is one of our weakest links - staying in touch while cruising is a real challenge. Our first step is to reduce the need for people to contact us directly. To do this we have appointed a number of agents and distributors around the world - Kelvin Hughes (UK), Sowester (UK), John Wiley (UK), Robert Hale (USA), Technical Books (SA), Kirby (AUS), Addenda (NZ), Publishers Associates (HK), and Pansing Distribution (Singapore). The internet is our main information highway where we can send and receive our mail through our web site.

Book Proposal: The starting point for our books is to formalise our ideas and inspirations into a structured book proposal. This is not only very useful for controlling the development of our books, but essential when talking to publishers.

Nerve centre at Yachting Monthly, talking to a very helpful Paul Gelder about a book review

Southampton Boat Show - book
signing with Julian Van Hasselt on
the Kelvin Hughes stand

Book signing after our presentation at the Madoc
Yacht Club, Porthmadog

Consider the following headings:
a) Brief overview of book.
b) Target market, who will buy our book.
c) Competition and why someone would buy our book in preference to other books in the market.
d) List of chapters with short overview.
e) Book size, number of pages, number of photographs and drawings - this should provide sufficient information to calculate the cost of producing the book, and retail price.
f) Marketing - list magazines for book reviews, and training courses for adoptions.

Production Cycle: We write our books in MS Word, before setting-up the text in Adobe Pagemaker. Photographs are scanned and adjusted in Adobe Photoshop, and diagrams are drawn in Coreldraw. When the book is complete we send the book on CD to a repro-house to run out imposed positives, which we then courier to a printer.

Marketing: Once the book is printed the marketing starts. We usually run-on the cover on 100 gm paper for our distributors to use as an information flyer. We approach yachting magazines and newspapers for book reviews, and radio stations for interviews. We also approach yacht clubs and attend boat shows to make presentations and to do book signings.

With a few more books in the pipeline we hope our writing and publishing will keep our cruising kitty topped up to ensure that our *'Voyage of a lifetime'* takes us a lifetime!!!

Further Reading:

www.bluewater-cruising.com
www.burkepublishing.com

Budget

APPENDIX 1

Two burning questions frequently asked about our bluewater cruising are; *"Did you experience any rough weather*?" and *"How much did it cost*?" To answer these and many other questions, we have included a number of appendices to discuss our yacht, its equipment, and our approach to bluewater cruising.

Budget: At the outset we established a budget to mirror our savings and income. Developing our budget was an iterative process - with each turn of the wheel we converged on a list of expenses that matched our income and savings. It was essential for us to establish a realistic budget so that it could be planned, financed and controlled. We knew if we had blindly gone bluewater cruising without a financial model, we would have run the risk of pecuniary failure and an early end to our trip.

1. Financial Model: There was obviously a trade-off here between what we wanted and what we could afford. To determine the cost of our cruise we developed a simple financial model: the total cost was progressively subdivided into smaller units of expenditure that were easy to identify and estimate. In project management this is known as a **cost breakdown structure**:

1.0.0 Total Bluewater Cruise
    1.1.0 The Yacht
        1.1.1 Yacht
        1.1.2 Travelling Expenses
        1.1.3 Survey
    1.2.0 Equipment
        1.2.1 Coastal Equipment
        1.2.2 Bluewater Equipment
        1.2.3 Wish List
    1.3.0 Annual Expenses
        1.3.1 Living Expenses
        1.3.2 Maintenance, Repairs and Upgrading
        1.3.3 Risk Management

Our level three costs were then subdivided into a list of expense items that have been further developed in the following sections. By using this financial model we were able to identify where the costs occurred and looked for ways of tailoring our expenditure to fit the depth of our pocket.

To complete our bluewater cruise safely and comfortably our yacht needed to be comprehensively fitted out. Our bluewater equipment inventory for budgetary purposes was subdivided into:

- Coastal Equipment Budget
- Bluewater Equipment Budget
- Wish List Budget

Our budget planning was developed in the UK when we were thinking in Sterling. Since then most of our costs have been in US dollars - the universal currency. Where a conversion is required I have assumed $1.5 = £1.

2. Yacht Budget: By monitoring the classified adverts in Yachting Monthly and Yachting World we kept up to date with yacht prices. The budget for our yacht included the following:

Travelling Expenses: This included all the expenses we could incur trying to find a yacht; car expenses, accommodation (B&B), telephone, fax, letters, and emails. Looking for a yacht along the south coast of England incurred mostly car expenses, but if we had looked for a yacht in the Mediterranean or America we would have incurred flying, accommodation, car hire and moving costs.

Survey: In the UK the yacht surveyors have a simple method to calculate the survey costs; the survey fee in pounds is equal to length times beam in feet. A Nicholson 35 is calculated as, 35 x 10 = £350. The surveyor may include personal travelling expenses to the cost if they live a considerable distance from the yacht's location.

Overhaul and Maintenance Expenses: Here, we have included a figure for maintenance because, irrespective of the yacht's age and condition, it would be necessary to check all the yacht's systems to ensure they were working, and in the process bring the maintenance cycle up to date.

Contingency: The contingency allowance is a contribution for yacht procurement negotiation and cost overruns.

Yacht's Budget	Cost
The yacht	$35,000
Travelling expenses to find the yacht	$500
Marine survey	$500
Overhaul and maintenance	$2,000
Contingency	$2,000
Total expenses	**$40,000**

3. Coastal Equipment Budget: After looking at a number of yachts we found that the following equipment inventory was usually found on a yacht fitted out for coastal cruising. If any equipment was missing, damaged, or in need of expensive maintenance, an appropriate amount was deducted from the yacht's typical selling price.

Coastal Equipment	Details	Cost
Hull and deck	Built to Lloyds	
Main engine	Engine hrs - when is next overhaul due?	
Rigging	Age - when will rig need replacing?	
Sails	Condition - when will they need replacing?	
Ground tackle	Windlass and two anchors	
Mooring	Mooring ropes and fenders	
Canvas work	Spray hood and side dodgers	
Interior	Condition of fitting out?	
Galley	Oven and sink arrangement	
Electrical	Charging and batteries	
Plumbing	Fresh water tank, bilge pumps	
Heads	Toilet and basin	
Instruments	Echo sounder, wind, log	
Communication	VHF	
Safety equipment	Liferaft, lifebelts, lifejackets	
Dinghy and outboard	To get ashore	
Spare		
Spare		
Total Budget		

Pacific Voyager: All the coastal equipment in the above list was on *Pacific Voyager* when we bought her. Everything was in good working order, except for the exhaust

system and the oven. We budgeted to repair the exhaust system, and replace the oven.

Pacific Voyager's coastal cruising waterline and bluewater cruising waterline

4. Bluewater Equipment Budget: We defined bluewater equipment as essential equipment required for safety and lifestyle. We did not necessarily expect to find these items on a coastal cruising yacht's inventory. If they were there, we treated them as a bonus and adjusted our budgets accordingly. Our guidelines were established from feedback from bluewater cruisers and international regulations, particularly the ORC category 1 requirements, SOLAS, and the Collision Regulations.

Bluewater Equipment	Details	
Hull	Self-steering gear	
Main engine	Additional tankage	
Rigging	Bosun's chair, cordage	
Sails	Storm and light wind sails	
Ground tackle	Additional anchors and chain	
Dinghy and outboard	To explore the reefs	
Canvas work	Bimini	
Galley	Refrigerator	
Electrical power	120 amp alternator, Wind gen, Solar panel	
Electrical storage	Deep cycle batteries	
Electrical distribution	240 volt inverter	
Plumbing	Two bilge pumps	
Interior	Lee-clothes, secure all lockers	
Ventilation	Fans, wind chute	
Nav	GPS	
Nav	Charts and pilots	
Nav	Sextant, sight reduction tables	
Instruments	Wind speed and direction	
Communication	SSB	
Safety	EPIRB	
Safety	Panic bags	
Heavy weather sailing	Drogue, storm boards	
Emergency	Fire extinguishers, fire blankets	
Medical	First aid kit	
Tools	Workshop, sewing machine	
Spare parts	Offshore kit	
Snorkelling	Snorkelling gear	
Camera gear	Camera, lens, film, video	
Budget		

Pacific Voyager: We have been through four phases of procurement, in the UK, Gibraltar, Caribbean and New Zealand. These were mostly prompted by a requirement for a better lifestyle, for example, SSB to communicate with the other cruisers, and a RIB to explore the reefs.

5. Wish List Budget: These items were not considered essential, but were desirable to enhance our safety and lifestyle. As additional funds became available we considered the following items:

Wish List	Details	Cost
Hull	Autopilot	
Main engine	Alarms	
Deck arrangement	Gantry, goal posts	
Rigging	Running pole, mast steps	
Sails	Second furling headsail	
Anchoring	Additional anchors, second bow roller	
Dinghy	RIB, and spare dinghy	
Galley	Watermaker	
Electrical	Diesel generator	
Plumbing	Hot water, pressurised water system	
Ventilation	Enclose cockpit	
Navigation	Radar	
Communication	Handheld VHF	
Computer	Weather fax, satellite imagery	
Heavy weather	Sea anchor	
Entertainment	TV multi-system and video	
	Diving equipment	
	Bicycles	
	Braai on the pushpit	
	Cockpit table	
Budget		

Pacific Voyager: Over several years we have bought everything on the essential bluewater equipment list and are well into the wish list. Our problem now is that *Pacific Voyager* is bursting at the seams and Sandra wants a bigger boat!

Television and video - now crossed off our wish list

6. Annual Budget: Our annual budget included all the recurring expenses. For convenience these have been subdivided into:
- Living expenses
- Maintenance, repairs and upgrading
- Risk management expenses

7. Living Expenses: Our living expenses included all our day-to-day costs associated with our lifestyle and sailing *Pacific Voyager* - these typically recurred every year. Although some of the individual costs in the table varied from year to year, and place to place, they have been included as a guideline.

	Living Expenses (two people)	Costs
	Main engine running costs	£ 500
	Outboard engine running costs	£ 100
	Rig, sails and canvas	£ 250
	Painting	£ 250
	LPG	£ 200
	Food, household	£2000
	Beverages	£ 250
	Entertainment	£ 250
	Books, stationary, postage, telephone	£ 250
	Mooring, permits, visa	£ 200
	Film	£ 250
	Charts, pilots	£ 250
	Clothes	£ 250
	Travel ashore	£ 250
	Souvenirs	£ 250
	Medical (Doctor, dentist, optician)	£ 500
		£6,000

Pacific Voyager: We have noticed some interesting trade-offs between bluewater cruising and coastal cruising costs. While bluewater cruising we were always at anchor, therefore we had no marina fees but paid a higher insurance premium. By contrast, when coastal cruising we had marina fees, but paid a lower coastal insurance premium.

8. Maintenance, Repairs and Upgrading Budget: Keeping *Pacific Voyager* functioning in the marine environment would always be a continuous battle against the elements. Our rationale was that if we departed with a well-equipped yacht on our three year circumnavigation, we should get back before any major overhauls were necessary. However, as our bluewater cruise extended beyond three years, we needed to budget for some expensive overhauls; main engine, sails, rigging, fridge, anchor chain, electrical systems and canvas work.

Repairs: These are difficult to budget for as they are obviously related to many unknown factors, but we felt a contribution here would at least ensure there was something in the kitty.

An allowance for **new technology** was also included in the budget. As the design and manufacture of equipment is continually improved and upgraded, so older equipment becomes obsolete as spare parts and servicing become more difficult to source. For example, our Decca and Satnav have been replaced by GPS. We also have a handheld GPS as a backup and keep it ready to pop into our panic bag.

Initially we tried to relate these costs as a percentage of the yacht's value, but in reality some of them are actually inversely proportional to the yacht's value. For example, a yacht in poor condition may sell for a lower price, but may require extensive maintenance and upgrading. Finally we opted for a realistic annual contribution to each of these subheadings.

Maintenance, Repairs, Up-grades	Costs
Maintenance	£1000
Repairs	£ 500
Up-grades	£ 500
Contingency	£ 500
Budget	*£2500*

"Fill her up please."

9. Risk Management: We identified a risk as anything that prevented us achieving our objectives. Some risks could be mitigated and passed on to others, for example; we insured against damage to our yacht and to cover hospital fees. Here are our four main identifiable risks:

- **Yacht Insurance:** 3% of insured value for bluewater cruising. However, local cruising was less than 1%.
- **Hospital Insurance:** We budgeted to pay directly for GP, dentist and optometrist, but took out insurance to cover hospital fees.
- **Flight Home:** French Polynesia required cruisers to deposit a bond for each individual on the yacht. The bond was equivalent to the cost of a flight home and was refundable on departure. Whether visiting French Polynesia or not, we felt it was sensible to budget for one trip home per year to see family and friends.
- **Contingency:** This amount covered uncertainties and non-insurable risks.

	Risk Management	Cost
	Yacht insurance	£1000
	Medical insurance	£ 500
	Flight home	£ 500
	Contingency	£ 500
	Budget	*£2500*

10. Total Bluewater Cruising Budget (3 year cruise): Irrespective of these calculations, the more funds available the more one spends. We initially started with £75,000 plus an adjustable mortgage facility, and cut our cloth accordingly. Here is the summary of our original budget.

Item	Total Bluewater Cruising Budget (3 years)	Cost
Yacht	Yacht	£40,000
	Standard equipment	0
Bluewater	Essential equipment	0
	Wish list	0
Annual	Living expenses	£18,000
	Maintenance and repairs	£ 7,500
	Risk Management	£ 7,500
	Contingency	£ 7,000
Total Budget		£80,000

Further Reading:

Burke, Rory and **Buchanan**, Sandra., *Managing Your Bluewater Cruise* (pages 30-39)
Burke, Rory., *Project Management, Planning and Control Techniques*, 3rd Edition, www.project-management-books.com

Yacht Procurement

APPENDIX 2

Trying to value a used yacht is a complex trade-off between;

- yacht design
- size of yacht
- yacht builder
- age of yacht
- yacht specifications
- yacht certification
- workmanship
- materials
- proprietary equipment
- condition of yacht and equipment
- location of yacht
- what the market is prepared to pay.

After looking at several yachts we started to develop a structured checklist to make informed comparisons between different yachts. Our first step was to identify what international standards we should comply with, for example; ORC category 1, SOLAS, and the Collision Regulations. To this we added our personal bluewater lifestyle requirements which we developed from reading cruising books and yachting magazines. The outcome was a unified checklist which we could use for our budget, survey and procurement. (This was further developed en route, after interviewing other cruisers and from our own experiences.)

We subdivided the checklist into five columns; coastal equipment, bluewater equipment, wish list, annual maintenance and survey comments (not shown here). If an item was in need of attention or missing we would assign a cost to bring the equipment up to the required condition. We initially considered items that could fail within three years but, with our extended cruising lifestyle, have now increased this time period to ten years. We did not want to give value to used equipment which could fail en route and may need replacing (particularly as a replacement could be more expensive in a remote location).

The annual cost column identifies recurring maintenance costs, and also considers half-life refits and upgrading. For example, a diesel engine will require annual maintenance, but every five to ten years it will require a major overhaul, and rigging should be replaced every ten to fifteen years.

We have continued to develop our yacht selection checklist. The latest revision is presented here as an example of the one we would use today as we look for a larger yacht to carry Sandra's growing wardrobe and our mobile office!

	Coastal	Bluewater	Wishlist	Annual
Documentation				
Registration				
VAT paid				
Insurance				
Mooring fees				
Marina fees				
As-built drawings				
Construction				
Hull (osmosis)				
Deck				
Keel - ballast				
Skeg - rudder				
Wheelhouse				
Bulkheads				
Engine beds				
Chain plates				
Tankage				
Water				
Watermaker				
Diesel				
Petrol				
LPG				
Deck arrangement				
Spray hood				
Dodger				
Bimini				
Pulpit, pushpit, stanchions				
Goal posts				
Gantry				
Cockpit table				
Steering				
Wheel - linkage				
Emergency tiller				
Self-steering				
Autopilot				

	Coastal	*Bluewater*	*Wishlist*	*Annual*
Main engine				
Engine and gearbox				
Coupling, shaft, propeller				
Engine mountings				
Exhaust system				
Alarms				
Sails and rigging				
Main roller furling				
Headsail roller furling				
Main sail				
Genoa				
Trysail				
Storm jib				
Light weight sail				
Mast, boom, poles				
Winches				
Rigging, standing, running				
Anchoring				
Windlass				
Anchor and chain (1)				
Anchor and chain (2)				
Anchor and chain (3)				
Anchor and chain (4)				
Anchor and chain (5)				
Mooring ropes and fenders				
Mooring cleats and fairleads				
Electrical arrangement				
Shore power charging				
Alternator (high output)				
Wind power				
Solar panel				
Petrol generator				
Switch panel				
Inverter				
240 volt ring main and plugs				

	Coastal	Bluewater	Wish List	Annual
Navigation				
Compass, steering, handheld				
Log				
Echo sounder				
Wind speed, direction				
Charts and pilots				
GPS				
Chronometer				
Barometer				
Radar, reflector				
Sextant and Walker log				
Safety equipment				
Liferaft				
Panic bags				
EPIRB 406				
Harnesses and jack lines				
Lifejackets				
Dan buoy				
Lifebelts				
Lifesling				
Heavy weather sailing				
Storm boards				
Drogue				
Sea anchor				
Communication				
Radio / tape / CD				
VHF, handheld				
SSB				
Weather fax				
TV and video				
Lights				
Interior spots and fluorescent				
Navigation lights				
Deck lights				
Anchor light				
Search light				

	Coastal	Bluewater	Wish List	Annual
Galley				
Oven				
Refrigerator				
Sink				
Fire extinguisher, blanket				
Plumbing				
Heads				
Holding tank				
Shower				
Pressurised water system				
Calorifier, immersion				
Bilge pumps				
Seacocks				
Pipes				
Ventilation				
Fans				
Wind chute				
Dorades				
Hatches				
Heater				
Canvas Work				
Sewing machine				
Cushions, mattresses				
Curtains				
Dinghy and Outboard				
Dinghy				
Outboards				
Davits, outboard hoist				
Snorkelling				
Boarding ladder				
Miscellaneous				
Photography				
Medical kit				
Burglar alarm				
Bicycles				

Yacht and Equipment

This appendix is a description of our yacht and its equipment. *Pacific Voyager* is a Nicholson 35, designed and built by Camper and Nicholson at Gosport in 1975, hull number 114, Lloyds hull release certificate LR 0119/75, British Registration number ON 386839, and Registered Tonnage 10 70/100.

Camper and Nicholson described their yacht as, *".... proven cruising reliability in all conditions."* And Yachting Monthly described her as, *".... the Nicholson 35 is unquestionably one of the all-time classic cruising designs - she is strong and seaworthy with good seagoing accommodation."*

Hull: The hull configuration is a long fin and skeg which gives good directional stability and a secure rudder support. Transverse stability was not an issue in the 70s, probably because, compared to today's standards, the designs where inherently stable with high ballast ratios and narrow beams. Seakeeping is one of the Nicholson's true qualities. Although *Pacific Voyager* pitches and bounces around in heavy seas, she never slams when the bow punches into oncoming waves. It is comforting to know that she will look after us.

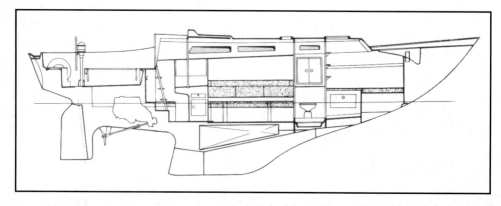

Nicholson 35 profile showing long fin and skeg (MK 2)

Main Engine: Our main engine is a Perkins diesel 4108 lowline (engine number: 108US6752), with a Denison hydraulic transmission (pump and motor). This type of transmission enables the shaft motor to be located remotely from the engine, which means the engine does not need to be lined up to the shaft. We have a two-bladed prop that powers us along comfortably at 5 knots.

Diesel Tank: The diesel tank is positioned under the cockpit sole, aft of the engine. It only holds 35 gallons (160 litres), which may be sufficient for coastal cruising, but for bluewater cruising we added ten (20 litre) jerry cans to give us an additional 200 litres. These are stored in a few places on *Pacific Voyager*; the cockpit locker, cockpit sole and lashed to the guard rails. This gives us a total of 360 litres and a range of about 600 miles, assuming 3 litres per hour at 5 knots. We would prefer to carry sufficient diesel to motor 1000 miles.

Pacific Voyager's **Perkins 4108 lowline engine is shoe-horned under the cockpit**

Steering: Nicholson 35s are fitted with wheel steering on a pedestal at the aft end of the cockpit. Our pedestal includes a Sestral steering compass and night light. The wheel and cockpit coaming seem to be ergonomically designed - I am always able to wedge myself into a comfortable steering position.

Self-Steering: Our Hydrovane self-steering was our unsung hero. The Hydrovane steered *Pacific Voyager* 99% of the time. There were only a few occasions, in rough weather, when the Hydrovane battled to hold its course. During these rare situations we would use the Neco autopilot.

The Hydrovane's Achilles' heel was the design of the wind-vanes. Both cracked at their base, obviously under-designed to accommodate the high shear forces. We have since fitted inner sleeves to strengthen the connections.

Autopilot: Our Neco autopilot has a mechanical drive connected directly to the steering quadrant. It is able to hold a much better course than we can hand-steer. Using the Neco means we need to charge the batteries for an hour every four hours.

The Hydrovane self-steering surrounded by outboards and fenders

Pacific Voyager's **new spray hood, bimini and side panels**

Spray Hood and Bimini: Sandra nursed the original spray hood with a waterproof sealant and made several repairs. In New Zealand we replaced it with a new spray hood, bimini and side panels, enabling us to completely enclose the cockpit and create an extra room. All the panels are zipped, for ease of removal and stowage.

Rigging: *Pacific Voyager* has a sloop rig with two spinnaker poles. The rigging wire was electronically tested by Solent Rigging before we left the UK and given the okay. By the time we reached New Zealand we decided to replace the rigging. We were concerned that our 25% increase in displacement would increase the loading on the rig. We have increased the wire size to 8 mm all round, and insulated the backstay for the SSB. For downwind sailing we have an additional forestay to carry a hank-on genoa. This arrangement works particularly well sailing wing-on-wing. The additional forestay is also used to hank-on the storm jib.

All the halyards and sheets were originally 12 mm braid-on-braid. We have progressively replaced them with 14 mm braid-on-braid for ease of handling. Gybe preventers are fitted port and starboard from the end of the boom to a block on the foredeck cleat. This was a sensible precaution as we were sailing downwind most of the time in the tropics.

Bosun's Chair: We upgraded the original wooden plank seat to a canvas bosun's chair with sides pockets and, as a fixed working platform, fitted two mast steps near the mast head. The brake winch connects to the bosun's chair and the jib halyard connects to the safety harness as a safety back-up (not shown in the photograph). In port, we always checked the rigging after a gale and before a long passage.

Sandra sitting comfortably in the bosun's chair

Sail Plan: Second hand boats always come with a collection of sails - *Pacific Voyager* was no different. We initially removed the old roller furling headsail in preference for hank-on sails. But changing sails on a bouncing foredeck was not fun so, when we arrived in New Zealand we fitted a Profurl B35 roller furling system. Our present sail plan includes:

- Mainsail with 3 slab reefing points (1993)
- Storm trysail in orange (original)
- Genoa 115% with Profurl B35 roller furling (1998)
- Genoa 130% hank-on (original)
- Jib no.2 hank-on (original)
- Storm jib hank-on (original)
- Spinnaker (original)

For the bluewater cruising couple, roller furling sails are obviously the way to go. On our next boat we will not only be looking for a roller furling headsail, but for a roller furling staysail and furling mainsail as well.

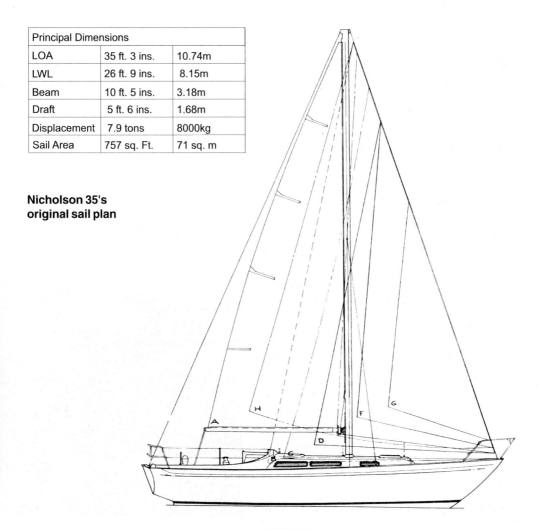

Principal Dimensions		
LOA	35 ft. 3 ins.	10.74m
LWL	26 ft. 9 ins.	8.15m
Beam	10 ft. 5 ins.	3.18m
Draft	5 ft. 6 ins.	1.68m
Displacement	7.9 tons	8000kg
Sail Area	757 sq. Ft.	71 sq. m

**Nicholson 35's
original sail plan**

Interior Arrangement: Although, by today's designs, the Nicholson 35 is a small boat internally, she still manages to absorb all our gear like Dr. Who's *Tardis*. Our continuing improvements have been primarily concerned with increasing our useable storage space and improving their ease of access.

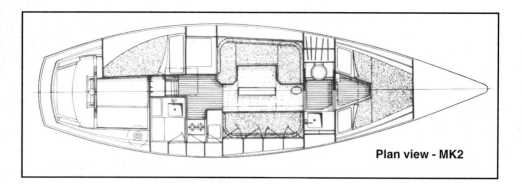

Plan view - MK2

Saloon: The saloon table and seating are the central feature of our cabin. It is the hub of our social life where we have spent many enjoyable dinner parties, getting to know other cruisers - who all have a tale to tell. On passage we dropped the saloon table and inserted the cockpit table to make a double bed. However, in rough weather we reverted to single bunks with lee-cloths to secure us in position.

Cockpit: With our new bimini and cockpit table, the cockpit has become an extra room. This is ideal for a work station, another venue to socialize and great for *al fresco* dining.

Galley: The galley is the centre of Sandra's creative empire. Jamie Oliver's *Puka Tuka* has got nothing on Sandra's scrumptious *Haka Waka Tuka!* Our Plastimo Neptune 2000 oven is on gimbals athwartships and has a fiddle and pot clamps. In rough weather, Sandra is able to soldier on safely with extra long oven gloves and a galley strap. In the event of a capsize the oven is secured to the gimbal mountings with jubilee hose clamps, and the oven door is held closed with preventer clips.

Fridge: Nicholson 35s are fitted with a deep top loading refrigerator which requires *Neanderthal* length arms to reach the bottom. I often see Sandra upended, head first in the fridge searching for something on the bottom.

Sandra in the cockpit eating soup for starters

andra's galley is ablaze with light, as she listens to her
avourite music through her headphones

Galley with hand pump
and fresh water filter

We have replaced the original refrigeration unit with another Danflos pump, but this time fitted a large holding plate.

Sink Area: The galley has a single stainless steel sink which is supplied with hot and cold pressurised water, together with filtered fresh water and a fresh water hand pump. The next refit will include a salt water hand pump.

Calorifier: Our calorifier produces hot water from the main engine's primary cooling jacket. This means after we have motored into an anchorage there is always plenty of hot water for a shower before dinner and enough hot water to clean the plates after yet another culinary delight. The hot shower makes all the difference between camping and leading a normal life.

xtra long oven gloves are a sensible precaution

"Anyone for tea?"

Water: Our 60 gallon (270 litre) water tank is located under the floor below the saloon table. We added a further 200 litres in ten (20 litre) plastic jerry cans, which we stored in the cockpit locker and lashed to the guard rails. This gives us a total of 470 litres which, at a consumption of five to ten litres per day, lasted twice as long as our longest planned trip. We are now considering a watermaker - but will it save space??

Heads: Our Lavac toilet is an excellent piece of equipment. It has a simple vacuum arrangement operated by a Henderson hand pump on the discharge side. The only problem we had was when we upgraded to the Henderson MK5 pump. The choker value kept getting blocked, so we reverted back to our MK1 pump which has flap valves and has never blocked.

Right: Rory filling the water tank

Below left: Port side, toilet and clothes locker

Bottom right: Starboard side, basin and shower attachment

Navigation Area: New technology often makes older electronic instruments obsolete. We started with a Walker Satnav 412 and a Decca navigation unit. Their systems have since been switched off, and the satellites left to burn out as they re-enter the atmosphere. To replace these, we bought an Apelco GLX 1100 GPS

avigation instruments over companionway

from Westmarine who couriered it to us in Gibraltar. As a backup, we now have a handheld Lawrence GlobalNav 200.

Fitted above the companionway we have a set of Autohelm ST50 instruments; speed log, wind speed, wind direction and depth. On passage, the wind direction was invaluable at night when hit by a sudden squall. As we rushed into the cockpit slightly disorientated, the wind direction unit immediately gave us our bearings. In addition, our backup NASA Sting Ray echo-sounder, which has upper and lower limits, was very useful for anchor watch.

Chart Table: The chart table is aft facing, which at first I thought would disorientate us, but Camper and Nicholson have obviously thought this through as it is standard arrangement on many of their yachts. The aft end of the starboard bunk is also the chart table seat, which is not the best arrangement, as at sea the navigator can disturb the sleeping, off-watch person. The chart table is a useful size accommodating a folded Admiralty chart, and deep enough to hold an ocean full of charts. The remainder of our charts are stored in plastic wallets kept under the forepeak bunks.

Sextant: If our electronic equipment failed we had a Zeiss sextant, chronometer, sight reduction tables, and Walker Log as a back-up. I took at least one sight per ocean passage to keep my hand in.

Radar: Radar is on our wish list. We would use radar to warn us of squalls, fog, and to help keep an anchor watch. Our new gantry has a radar mounting so we are ready to go.

Binoculars: We carried two sets of binoculars; a Westmarine 7 x 50 self focusing, and a Pentax 12 x 50. The 7 x 50 were best at sea, while the 12 x 50 were better for inspecting the anchorage from a more stable platform. A more powerful 25 x 50 is on our wish list, as they could be used for bird watching and spotting game etc.

Our chart table - a busy area

Electrical: Our need for electrical power generation, storage and distribution soon outgrew our original coastal cruising equipment. As we progressively added extra circuits to the original 10 circuit breaker switch panel, the wiring became a ball of knitting. Since then we have expanded the switch panel with triple the amount of circuit breakers, switches, volt meters and ammeters. Now we can sit back and accurately monitor the flow of electricity through our system. Our power is supplied by the following:

Pacific Voyager's **wind generator**

Alternator: The original 35 amp automotive alternator and regulator have been replaced with a 120 amp Bosch alternator and a smart regulator to give a higher output.

Petrol Generator: We originally bought a Clarke 600 watt petrol generator. We only used it once in anger in Helford River when we had flattened all the batteries (see page 27). The generator only supplied 8 amps at 12 volts and as we were concerned about carrying extra highly inflammable petrol it had to go.

Wind Generator: Our Aerogen 3 wind generator was initially mounted on a vertical pole bolted to the inside of the cockpit coaming. It was later fitted onto the new gantry. Since then newer technology offering higher output has encouraged us to upgrade to an Air Marine 403.

Solar Panels: In Gibraltar we fitted a Siemens solar panel to the coachroof, just in front of the spray hood. Later we bought a second Siemens solar panel which we attached to the boom when at anchor. Now we are considering a bank of solar panels across the top of the gantry - this should help keep Sandra's fridge cool in the tropics!

Batteries: Our Nicholson was originally fitted with two 90 amp hour lead acid batteries (one starting and one house). In Salcombe we added another four Exide 90 amp hour deep cycle batteries. These have all since been replaced with one 90 amp hour cold cranking automotive battery for starting and four R220 six volt golf cart type deep cycle batteries for bulk storage.

Inverter: In the UK we fitted a Prowatt 800 (800 watts) inverter to supply 240 volts. This was originally to power our computers and my shaver. But with 240 volts available, we have since added a few domestic items we cannot live without, like a food blender, travel iron, hand drill and small battery charger (size; AA, C and D). Sandra now wants a higher powered inverter (1000 watts plus), for a microwave oven and a hair dryer.

Lights: We have progressively improved our interior lighting with eight additional halogen spot lights, two fluorescent tube lights, and numerous small lights for the lockers. Compared to the original incandescent light bulbs, the five watt halogen bulbs give more light for less power - this is obviously a move in the right direction. Sandra's galley is now ablaze with affordable lights and, in our reading corners, we have strategically positioned halogen spot lights.

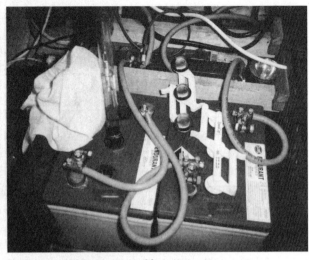

Battery compartment and inverter

It is difficult to gain sufficient light in awkward areas. After struggling with trying to hold torches in my mouth, I eventually fitted a number of self switching dome lights in the engine room and painted the bulkheads white to reflect the light.

Our **anchor light** on the gantry has worked well. It is at a more appropriate height than the mast head anchor light and the bulb is easy to change. At 5 watts, it has a lower impact on the batteries than the 25 watt mast head tricolour.

If our electrical power had failed, we could have used our traditional gimbal mounted **paraffin oil lamps** and lived as they did in the days of sail.

In the cockpit at night, we used an Aquasignal high-powered **spotlight** to illuminate navigational hazards. At anchor, during the night, we always plugged-in the spotlight, just in case we needed to make a hasty departure. Now we are considering a rechargeable spotlight for ease of movement.

Entertainment: Our collection of music systems was rather ad hoc; two Walkmans, a Discman, a Sony radio/tape, a Roberts radio/tape and a Philips car radio/tape stereo. The radios had FM, AM, MW, LW and SW, so we were usually able to find an interesting programme such as BBC World. We tried to restrict our expanding music collection to a box of cassettes and a box of CDs each.

VHF: We had two fixed VHFs, a Navico positioned by the companionway for use in the cockpit, and the other by the chart table. Our XM2000 handheld VHF was especially useful when one of us went ashore. We took it in the dinghy as a safety precaution, when exploring the reefs for example. It was also available to take into the liferaft if necessary.

SSB: We originally bought a Roberts RC818 to receive the SSB channels, but we soon found we were missing out on all the fun and wanted to join in the conversations. Eventually, in the Caribbean we bought a Yaesu transceiver so that we could communicate on the SSB and Ham channels.

The SSB also enabled us to receive weather faxes using *Xaxero's* software. We are now considering buying *Xaxero's* satellite imagery software so that we can actually see what is happening out there.

TV and Video: While we were cruising we did not miss television. In fact most of the islands would not have had coverage and, if they did, the transmission would probably not have been in English. In New Zealand we succumbed to buying a nine inch Sony multi-system TV and Philips video. The TV uses both 12 volt DC and 240 volt AC, while the video uses 240 volts. We find some television programmes help us keep in touch with the rest of the world and the video has enabled us to hire all the films we have missed seeing at the cinema. In New Zealand we especially enjoyed the America's Cup coverage - we all became serious armchair sailors. Our new Dell computer has DVD. This has opened up a new medium for watching movies, and I am sure soon we will be watching television programmes through our computer as well.

Snorkelling: We started our circumnavigation with some old snorkelling gear Sandra had stored in the UK. In the Caribbean we soon realised we needed much better equipment to make the most of snorkelling the coral reefs. We were fortunate to be able to buy good gear at competitive prices in Panama's Free Zone.

Photography: Our outside photographs were taken with an Olympus OM1; our interior photographs with an Olympus Auto Focus with a built-in flash; and our underwater photographs with a Minolta Weathermatic Auto Focus. Originally we took colour prints, but now prefer slides. Slides give a greater depth of colour and have the added advantage that we can use them in our presentations.

Our Panasonic video camera has recorded many memorable events and is particularly good at capturing the motion of the sea. Unfortunately the humidity eventually defeated us as the camera stopped working when some of our film became covered in mould. Next time we need to give more thought to keeping the video camera and video tapes in hermetically sealed boxes.

Anchoring: Anchoring takes on a greater importance for the bluewater cruiser as there are very few marinas on the cruising route and generally the idea is to be located in an idyllic anchorage away from the crowds and at one with nature. Our portfolio of anchor systems grew as we experienced different anchoring conditions and became more aware of the risks. Our anchoring systems include:
- 35 lb CQR with 60 m of 10 mm chain (stowed on the bow ready to go)
- 35 lb CQR with 60 m of 8 mm chain (stowed in the anchor well)
- 33 lb Bruce with 10 m of chain and 40 m of nylon warp (stowed on the pushpit)
- 2 x Fortress with 5 m of chain and 40 m of nylon warp each (dismantled).

Sandra marking the chain with electrical cable ties

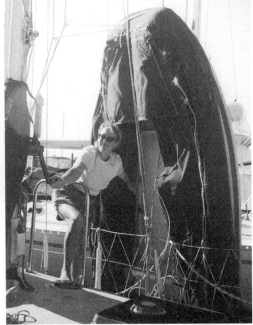

bove: Our dinghy hoisted to the side.
ight: Sandra lowering the dinghy.

Ropes and Fenders: We had a locker full of ropes for every conceivable purpose, together with plenty of anti-chafe plastic tubes and 12 fenders of varying sizes.

Dinghy and Outboard: We initially bought a second-hand Avon Redseal and a new 2 hp Suzuki outboard. The Avon flipped over numerous times. The last straw was when a squall lifted it into the wind generator and broke the blades - it was turning into a liability - it had to go. (Horror story page 99.)

We gave the Avon away and replaced it in Curacao with a Venezuelan-made 9 foot Caribe RIB and 8 hp Yamaha outboard. The Caribe was very robust and could punch into a short chop and still deliver us with dry feet. It was a very stable platform to snorkel from

Above: Our dinghy with wheels

and, with a more powerful outboard, enabled us to explore the reefs.

The RIB with its double bottom, and 8 hp outboard was too heavy to lift, so wheels were essential to pull the dinghy up the beach. On board, we hoisted the dinghy to the side when it was not in use. This was both for security and to limit bottom fouling.

To Sum Up: During our cruise, keeping our gear functioning in the marine environment was a constant challenge - mother nature attacked at every opportunity. And as new technology kept moving the goal posts - we were obliged to buy new gear as the old equipment became obsolete.

Further Reading:

www.longpassages.org (good equipment analysis)
Avon: <stevel@avon-inflatable.com> (Marketing Manager)

APPENDIX

4

Safety Equipment

Safety of life at sea is well supported by a number of international standards; SOLAS, Collision Regulations, and ORC Category 1. We used these regulations as guidelines for our safety equipment selection and installation.

Safety Harness: Man overboard was probably our greatest risk - the chance of not being recovered did not bear thinking about. We therefore took every precaution to prevent either of us falling overboard in the first instance. We wore Kim safety harnesses with a long and a short safety line connected to a Gibb carabiner (the type which prevents accidental opening). At night we also carried a personal strobe light.

In rough conditions, as we entered the cockpit, we hooked-on to one of a number of strategically positioned 'U' bolts. When we had to go on deck, we hooked-on to the jack stay, running fore and aft, along the side-deck.

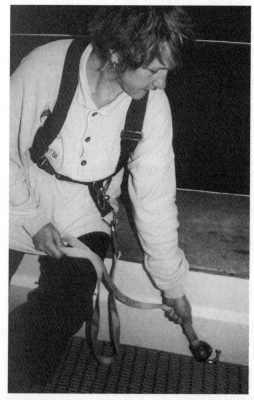

Sandra wearing her safety harness in the cockpit

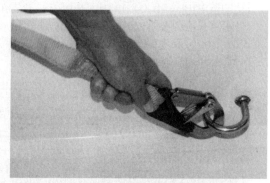

Gibb carabiner - the type which prevents accidental opening

Lifejacket: We had personal self-inflatable Crewsaver lifejackets that we could attach to our Henri Lloyd's heavy weather gear. Our Henri Lloyd jackets had a built-in harness. In the dinghy, we kept two kapok waistcoat type buoyancy aids.

MOB (Man Over Board): If someone had fallen overboard we would then have moved to our next line of defence, which comprised of:
- A throwing line
- Lifebelts with floating lights
- A Dan Buoy with a flag and floating light
- A GPS with *'event'* button to return to the MOB position
- A recovery lifesling.

Liferaft: Our inflatable liferaft was a 6 man RFD liferaft packed in a valise. It was stored in the aft cockpit locker where it was protected from the elements and ready for quick deployment.

Inside the liferaft we had a short term survival kit which comprised of: seasick pills, headache pills, one litre can of water, small calibrated mug, hand flares, space blanket, foot pump, sea anchor and two Mars bars.

FD liferaft packed in a valise, stored in the aft locker ady for deployment

Panic Bags: We supplemented the liferaft's small survival kit with a number of panic bags. We used the ex-MOD flare containers with a lanyard on the body, not on the screw cap. The more we thought about the purpose of the panic bags, the more gear we wanted to include in them. We prioritised the panic bags so that in an emergency and with limited time, we could take the most important bags first. To quantify our needs, we subdivided our survival into time phases. It is interesting to note how our perceived needs changed with each phase:

Phase 1: Send MAYDAY if yacht is about to sink.

Phase 2: Immediate survival - transfer from yacht to liferaft. Operate EPIRB.

Phase 3: Short term survival - first 72 hours (Pacific Storm rescue period).

Phase 4: Medium term survival - one to four weeks (survive on our own supplies). Try and contact any passing ship using our handheld VHF.

Phase 5: Long term survival - one to three months (survive on our own resources, fishing and catching rain water). After the first few weeks the bottom of the liferaft will progressively foul and attract fish. Ocean currents could hopefully take the liferaft into shipping lanes, and eventually make landfall.

Sandra packing our old 121.5 EPIRB into an ex-MOD flare container which we used as a panic bag

Panic Bag 1: We considered this to be the primary panic bag that would help us survive the first 72 hours in the liferaft. It held our 406 EPIRB, handheld VHF and spare batteries, waterproof torch and spare batteries, heliograph, space blanket, basic first-aid kit, basic liferaft repair kit, non-thirst provoking rations such as; glucose sweets, crystalized ginger, ginger biscuits and one litre of water.

Panic Bag 2: Contained: Flares, smoke, dye marker, a welding glove to hold the flares.

Panic Bag 3: Contained: Food for the first four weeks, can opener, Swiss army knife. The food consisted typically of tins and packets of baked beans, sardines, fruit, corned beef, sweet biscuits, savoury crackers and energy food bars. This food was rotated with the ship's stores to remove food with old use by dates.

Panic Bag 4: Contained: Liferaft repair kit (puncture kit and plugs) and gear to help us survive indefinitely; fishing line and hooks (glove to hold fishing line), fish knife in sheath, chopping block, and plastic sheet for catching rainwater.

Panic Bag 5: (Kept below beside chart table.) Contained: Important documents; ship's papers, passports, credit cards, address book, notebook and pen (to write best selling survival story to finance our next boat), hand compass, first-aid kit and survival handbook.

Panic Bag 6: Contained: Clothes to keep us warm and protected from the elements; sweaters, sweat pants, gloves, hats, scarf, cotton long-sleeve shirt, cotton long trousers, sun hat, sun cream (factor 15) and sunglasses.

Water: Our 20 litre water containers would float if slightly under-filled. We planned to grab as many as we could and always kept short lanyards permanently attached to them.

Extra Items: By the chart table, we kept a list to remind us of useful items to grab if we had the time and presence of mind;

- Chart of area and log book
- Dinghy foot pump (to fit liferaft)
- Bailer and sponges
- Waterproofs
- Sea anchor
- Paddle
- Dan buoy and broom sticks which could make a short mast
- Light material for sail (spinnaker)
- Mini solar panel and rechargeable batteries for the VHF and torch
- Lanyards
- Buckets
- Tupperware containers and polythene bags for watertight storage
- Folding umbrella to catch rain water and protect from sun
- Spear gun to catch fish.

406 EPIRB by the companionway ready for activation

RIB: The possibility of not being rescued early on and being in the liferaft for several months is reinforced by reading *'117 Days Adrift'* and *'The Spirit of Rose Noelle.'* It therefore makes sense to try to grab not only the liferaft, but the dinghy as well. On long passages, our Caribe dinghy was partly deflated and lashed down on the foredeck. We needed just a few minutes to pump up the dinghy and make it ready for deployment.

With a working 406 EPIRB, a SAR plane is likely to be only a day away, closely followed by a surface rescue. Note Bullimore's rescue by the Australian Navy in the roaring forties. The EPIRB is really our only effective means of communicating our distress, for that reason we also kept our old 121.5 EPIRB.

SAR: After seeing the film *'Castaway'* where Tom Hanks was stranded on an uninhabited desert island, it crossed my mind to consider what we would need to be able to survive if we found ourselves in similar circumstances - no it will not happen to us!

Further Reading:

Robertson, Dougal., *Survive The Savage Sea*
Bailey, Maurice., *117 Days Adrift*
Callahan, Steve., *Proactive Emergency Craft*, Cruising World, December 1995, p.64
Glennie, John., and **Phare,** Jane., *The Spirit of Rose-Noelle*

APPENDIX 5

Heavy Weather Tactics

By the law of chance, it was inevitable that we were going to encounter heavy weather during our bluewater cruise. In this appendix, we highlight examples of the gear we had on board and discuss our storm tactics. (For more detail see our book, *Managing Your Bluewater Cruise*, pages 264-281).

With only two of us on board, we preferred to adopt 'static' heavy weather tactics that did not involve us having to hand steer the boat. Tactics that allowed us to retreat to the safety and protection of the cabin below. Our options were:

- Lying a-hull
- Heaving-to
- Motor into the sea
- Deploy a drogue from the stern
- Deploy a sea anchor from the bow.

Lying a-hull: *Pacific Voyager* naturally lies a-hull to the oncoming weather. As a short term tactic at night we have used this arrangement when hit by a sudden squall. We would drop the sails, tie them off, and retreat below while the squall blew over. If the squall was the beginning of a storm, then lying a-hull gave us time to gather our thoughts, and consider our options. The findings from the 1979 Fastnet Race indicated that a yacht risks capsize if it is caught beam-on to a breaking wave, with a wave height greater than the yacht's beam. Therefore heaving-to appears to be the safer option as the wave height increases.

Hoisting *Pacific Voyager's* trysail - note how it fits within the area supported by the lower shrouds

Heaving-to: *Pacific Voyager* heaves-to nicely under triple reef main or trysail alone. With the helm lashed over, she would fore-reach into the wind and hold her position comfortably, while we were securely snug below.

Motor: Motoring slowly into the sea, or '*dodging*', is the preferred heavy weather tactic used by fishing vessels. They use minimum speed to maintain steerage and the course can be controlled by the autopilot. The bow presents the strongest and narrowest part of the boat to the oncoming seas. If a wave breaks over the bow it will run along the deck without threatening to capsize her. Note: A yacht's longitudinal stability is much greater than her transverse stability.

Drogue: Deploying a drogue over the stern is an active tactic which can be used as a tracking device to reduce yawing to keep the stern into the breaking waves and act as a sea brake to slow the yacht down. Reduced speed will limit the bow's tendency to dig-in and broach leading to a capsize or pitch-pole.

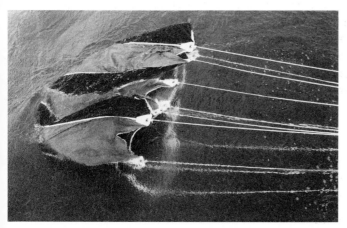

Sea anchor: Our 15 foot diameter sea anchor is deployed over the bow, and inflates like a parachute to keep the bow pointing into the weather, and hold our position. With 100 metres of 16 mm nylon rope, the elasticity in the rope will absorb the surges, as the sea anchor moves within the waves' orbital velocities.

Pacific Voyager's Sea anchor deployed over the bow

Capsize: In the event of a capsize, knockdown, broach, or pitch-pole, we have fitted lee-cloths and safety straps to secure us in our bunks. Our lockers and heavy items, such as the oven and large batteries, are secured to prevent movement. In the event of a capsize we do not want to fly across the cabin, and conversely do not want anything to fly across and hit us.

Further Reading:

Burke, Rory and **Buchanan,** Sandra., *Managing Your Bluewater Cruise*
Mundle, Rob., *Fatal Storm*, Adlard Coles, 1999
Coles, Adlard., *Heavy Weather Sailing*, Adlard Coles Nautical

APPENDIX 6

Disaster Recovery

A cruising disaster may be defined as an event that prevents a yacht providing critical functions for a period of time and could result in significant loss or damage to the yacht and/or the lives of its crew. Our risk management analysis identified a number of risks which could not be eliminated or deflected through insurance. Our disaster recovery plan is the ultimate contingency for the ultimate unplanned catastrophe. Our safety equipment appendix focused on our personal safety, by contrast this appendix on disaster recovery focuses on the yacht's safety.

Damage Control Kit: Our damage control kit is kept in a handy place, separate from our tool kits and panic bags. In an emergency this small tool kit has the appropriate tools we need to address the following:
  - Seacock failure
  - Rig failure
  - Steering failure - emergency tiller.

Right: The emergency tiller fits directly onto the rudder shaft

Below: Bungs are kept by the seacocks in case of failure

Seacocks: I have two recurring nightmares; seeing water rising about the sole boards and losing the rig. On the way to Tonga when we saw water rising in the bilge (see page 254), we immediately checked the seacocks. We know where all the seacocks are positioned, so can instinctively go directly to them. All our underwater skin fittings are protected with a seacock which can be shut off. In the event of the seacock itself being damaged, we keep a tapered bung tied to the seacock to ram into the hole.

Rig Failure: My other nightmare - losing the rig. If we were to lose the rig, the disaster recovery bag contains a hefty pair of wire cutters to cut it and a pair of pliers to disconnect the rigging screws. Although we would want to ditch the rig as quickly as possible to prevent it damaging the hull, at the same time we would want to salvage the poles for a jury rig.

Removing the log for a split second produces a fountain of water. Imagine what a hole in the hull would be like.

Steering Failure: If the steering linkage were to fail, we would use our emergency tiller which connects directly to the rudder shaft. In addition we have the Hydrovane self-steering which has its own rudder.

Further Reading:

Burke, Rory., *Project Management Planning and Control Techniques*
Burke, Rory., *Disaster Recovery at Sea (Using Risk management Techniques)*

APPENDIX 7 *Toolkit*

Our tools, spare parts, consumables and materials grew from a couple of tool-boxes, to one or more tool boxes per trade. Subdividing our toolkits this way meant we could easily find our tools and generally only needed to use one tool-box per job.

During our fitting out in Salcombe we purchased all the tools and spare parts we thought we would need during our cruise. If we needed a tool we would rather buy it than borrow. We assumed if we needed it once there was a good chance we would need it again. We also bought tools and spare parts for jobs we knew we could not do ourselves, but felt that if we had the gear on board at least it was available for an expert to use.

We bought all the offshore maintenance kits the equipment manufacturers recommended, plus the spare parts we might have needed over the next three years, especially the parts to be changed regularly such as fuel and oil filters. We realised that spare parts for certain equipment would not be readily available on the cruising route, in some cases we bought more than one - if it had failed once it could fail again, or we might accidentally drop it in the bilge. After cruising for many years, our spare parts locker has also grown exponentially.

As gear is improved and updated, the old model becomes obsolete and the spares are not readily available - another reason to buy extra spares. We had this problem with the Henderson MK1 hand pump on our Lavac toilet. When we left the UK, we bought a couple of kits, only to find a few years later we could no longer buy them. The pump had been superseded by the MK5. We decided to upgrade to the new MK5 pump for which spare parts were available. Soon afterwards the choke value blocked. Unblocking the toilet was not fun. After this happened twice, and the most helpful comment we got from the manufacturer was to change our toilet paper, we decided to change back to the MK1. Fortunately, the MK1 uses the same diaphragm as the MK5 and we could easily cut flap valves from a piece of neoprene rubber (see page 300).

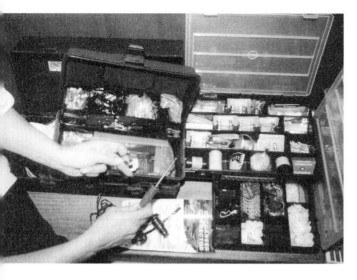

Electrical tool-boxes and electrical spares

Tool-boxes: In Gibraltar we bought a number of cheap plastic tool-boxes for £1.50 each. They were just the right size to fit neatly in the space above our starboard locker. For ease of stowage, we now have more tool-boxes and numerous rectangular, stackable Tupperware boxes. Our subdivision of tools and tool-boxes includes:

- Disaster recovery kit (in pouch kept by the companionway)
- Riggers kit (in leather pouch)
- Tool rack by chart table (most frequently used tools)
- Handy toolkit under chart table
- Electrical tool-box
- Electrical fuse box (contains all the types we have on board)
- Battery box (contains all the types of small batteries we have on board)
- Mechanical tool-box
- Socket sets
- Plumbing tool-box (pump and toilet kits)
- Dinghy and outboard tool-box (including puncture kit and spark plugs)
- Carpentry tool-box
- Rigging tool-box
- Sail repair kit (hanks, eyes, shackles)
- Canvas work box (patches, needles and thread for sewing machine)
- Bosun's kit (palm and whipping twine)
- Individual tools in dedicated area (e.g. the spanner for the LPG bottle)
- Padlock box
- Fastening box
- Stainless steel self-tappers box

Power Tools: With our Prowatt 800 inverter supplying 240 volts we have a number of power tools; sewing machine, hand drill (rechargeable), orbital sander and grindette.

Further Reading:

Burke, Rory and Sandra., Managing Your Bluewater Cruise (pages 302-319)

Insurance

Should we insure our yacht? This may seem a surprising question to the coastal cruiser who pays less than 1% premium, but to bluewater cruisers on a budget, paying 3% premiums could be 25% of their annual budget - a seemingly disproportionately high amount.

We were keen to insure our boat and pass on all our insurable risks, such as losing our yacht, as this represented a fair chunk of our savings. However, trying to establish what information the marine insurance companies were looking for was confusing. After we had set out on our circumnavigation, their intransigence left us with an uneasy feeling that we were not adequately insured even though we had paid our premium.

We started looking for an insurance company at the London boat show. We required information and guidance on the type of cover available and the costs. The insurance brokers were not really interested in offering bluewater cover. This was reflected in their extortionate premium of £2000 for a £30,000 vessel, equivalent to over 6%.

Also, they would only quote after we had bought a yacht. We were concerned that we could buy a yacht, and the insurance premium would turn out to be more than we could afford or worse, buy a yacht that the insurance companies would decline to insure. There were also crew considerations. The insurance companies wanted four competent crew, whereas bluewater cruisers are typically a husband and wife team.

I started to make some headway when I contacted **St Margaret's** insurance, who were brokers for **Lloyd's of London**. They were prepared to adjust their premium depending on the cruising area;

- UK to Canaries 1%
- Atlantic crossing + 0.3%
- Caribbean + 0.2%
- Pacific Ocean + 1%.

St Margaret's asked me to define our route. At the time I was not sure exactly where we would go other than the standard bluewater cruising route. A route I thought they should be familiar with as they were providing cover for other bluewater yachts. Off the top of my head I said, *"We'll go to the Canaries, across the Atlantic to the Caribbean, then through the Panama Canal to the Pacific." "Where in the Pacific?" "I'm not exactly sure yet, but definitely the Galapagos and Tahiti."*

Survey: The next step was to survey the Nicholson 35 in Salcombe. We wanted the survey to comply with St Margaret's requirements. We were surprised when they said they had no requirements, other than the surveyor should be a member of the YBDSA for indemnity purposes, and only required a survey report for their files.

In Gibraltar, when I checked through the small print on our policy for the next leg of our journey, I was shocked to find they had excluded the particular area of the Caribbean I had told them we would be sailing through in order to get to the Panama Canal. We wrote to St Margaret's asking them to change their wording to include our route from Antigua to Panama.

We were surprised when St Margaret's replied saying they required a further 1% increase in premium. Although St Margaret's replied to my letters, they never answered my questions as to why they increased the premium. It was infuriating trying to deal with an insurance company which seemed to be hiding behind their corporate image. Further, they were demanding a reply within 14 days of them sending their letters to us, even though they knew our mail cycle was more like two or three months.

With this unfortunate experience, I am sorry now we did not take out a policy with Pantaenius. I am sure Barrie Sullivan, the managing director of Pantaenius UK, would have been more professional. This impasse was resolved in New Zealand, when we declined further cover with St Margaret's and took out a local policy which was not only more appropriate, but a fraction of the UK premium.

Further Reading:

email: info@ybdsa.co.uk (for the Yacht Builders, Designers, and Surveyors Association)

APPENDIX 9

Medical

The thought of cruising in the tropics is the epitome of a healthy lifestyle: taking in deep breaths of sea air interspersed with plenty of exercise; swimming, snorkelling, walking, sailing and a stress free lifestyle. What more could one ask for?

Checkups: To address the risk of being away from medical facilities, a year before our departure, we had checkups with our local doctor, dentist and optometrist. This was good forward planning as Sandra required a minor operation and it gave her plenty of time to recuperate.

Immunisation: Our doctor had a world wide immunisation chart set out in a matrix format. We told him where we intended to go - he looked along the line - we held out our arms and he started jabbing until it felt like a pin cushion.

First Aid Training: We attended a two day course run by St John's Ambulance. This course gave us a basic understanding of the medical problems facing the  bluewater cruiser and methods of dealing with injuries and infections. It also gave us guidelines to develop our own first aid kit.

First Aid Kit: There were many medical kits on the market which had been compiled by experts and various medical lists in the yachting magazines. We gathered as much information as we could before deciding to subdivide our medical kit into three:
1. Frequently used medication
2. Panic bag (ORC recommendation)
3. Special items not regularly used.

Medical Insurance: We opted for a world wide hospital policy which covered us for serious medical treatment involving operations and hospitalisation. We worked on the premise that we would pay for all minor health care costs, such as visiting the doctor or dentist, but wanted cover for any expensive hospital treatment. While we were in Europe we were covered through the E111 form.

Seasickness: As the sea state increased, we were both affected by the boat's motion which caused a sensory conflict between our inner ear balance and visual perception - seasickness. We tried to stay in the area of least motion - the saloon or cockpit which were nearer the centre of floatation. Although seasickness made us feel lethargic, we soon worked out what we could do to avoid the problem and planned our day accordingly.

On a long passage it was essential to eat something to sustain our energy levels. When feeling queasy we found we could eat or drink the following; noodles cooked in a simple chicken stock, Sandra's home baked fatless fruit cake, tinned pineapples, apples, crystallized ginger, ginger biscuits, ginger or peppermint tea.

We generally wore seasickness prevention wrist bands - just in case they worked! And had Stugeron pills at the ready. We would also keep reminding ourselves what Nelson said, *"It's the first three days that are the worst."*

Further Reading:

First Aid Kit: Yachting World November 1985
First Aid Kit: Cruising World December 1991
Department of Health (UK): *Health Advice to Travellers*
Department of Health (UK): *Immunisation Against Infectious Diseases*
World Health Organisation: *International Medical Guide for Ships (ORC recommended)*
Justins, Douglas and **Berry,** Colin., *First Aid at Sea*, Adlard Coles Nautical

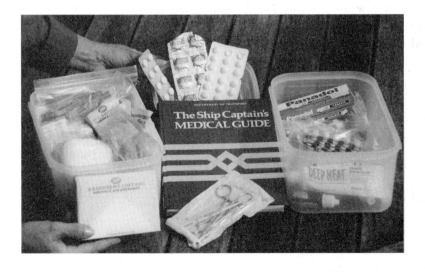

Book List

Abe, Tania., *Maiden Voyage*, Coronet Books
Acton, Shane., *Shrimpy*
Admiralty., *NP136, Ocean Passages of the World*
Alan, Dick., *Off the Beaten Track*
Allcard, Clare., *Living Afloat*, Adlard Coles Nautical
American Boat and Yacht Council., *Standards and Recommendations Practices for Small Craft*
American Bureau of Shipping., *Guide for Building and Classing Offshore Yachts*
Andrews, K. R., *Drake's Voyages*, Weidenfeld and Nicholson
Atwood, E.L, Pengally H.S., *Theoretical Naval Architecture*
Aughton, Peter., *Endeavour*, Windrush Press

Bailey, Maurice and Maralyn., *117 Days Adrift*
Bamford, Don., *Anchoring*
Beilan, Dr. Michael., *Your Offshore Doctor*
Beiser, Arthur., *The Proper Yacht*
Belcher, Bill., *Wind-Vane Self Steering*, Captain Teach Press
Birkett, Dea., *Serpent in Paradise*, Picador
Blewitt, Mary., *Celestial Navigation for Yachtsmen*
Blyth, Sir Chay., *The Impossible Voyage*
British Medical Journal, *ABC of Healthy Travel*
Brotherton, Miner., *The 12 Volt Bible for Boats*, Waterline
Burke, Kathy., *Managing Your Escape*, Seven Sea Press
Burke, Rory and Sandra., *Managing Your Bluewater Cruise*

Calder, Nigel., *Boatowners Mechanical and Electrical Manual*, Adlard Coles Nautical
Caldwell, John., *Desperate Voyage*
Callahan, Steve., *Proactive Emergency Craft*, Cruising World, December 1995, p.64
Calor Gas., *LPG for the Bluewater Yachtsman*, Appleton Park, Slough, SL3 9JG
Charlie's Charts., *Cruising Pilot for the Pacific Islands*
Chichester, Sir Francis., *The Lonely Sea and the Sky*
Childers, Erskine., *Riddle of the Sands*
Churchill, Winston., *Four Volumes of the English Speaking People*
Clark, Miles., *High Endeavours* (about Beryl and Miles Smeeton)
Clay, Warwick., *South Pacific Anchorages*
Cloughley, Maurice., *A World to the West*, David McKay (New York), 1979
Cohen, J., *The Four Voyages of Christopher Columbus*, Penguin, 1969
Coleridge, Samuel Taylor., *Rhyme of the Ancient Mariner*
Coles, Adlard., *Heavy Weather Sailing*, Adlard Coles Nautical

Cooper, Bill and Laurel., *Sell Up and Sail*
Coote, Jack., *Total Loss*
Copeland, Liza., *Just Cruising*
Cornell, Gwenda., *Cruising With Children*, 1992
Cornell, Gwenda., *Pacific Odyssey*, Adlard Coles Nautical
Cornell, Jimmy., *Canary Islands Cruising Guide*, World Cruising Publishing
Cornell, Jimmy., *Modern Ocean Cruising*, Adlard Coles Nautical
Cornell, Jimmy., *World Cruising Handbook*, Adlard Coles Nautical
Cornell, Jimmy., *World Cruising Routes*, Adlard Coles Nautical
Crawford, Peter., *Nomads of the Wind, A Natural History of Polynesia*, BBC
Cunliffe, Tom., *Ocean Sailing*

Darwin, Charles., *The Structure and Distribution of Coral Reefs*
Dashew, Steve and Linda., *Bluewater Handbook a Guide to Cruising Seamanship*
Dashew, Steve and Linda., *Offshore Cruising Encyclopedia*, Beowulf Publishing Group
Davidson, Alan., *Mediterranean Seafood*
Daywood, Richard., *Travellers' Health*, Oxford University press
Defoe, Daniel., *Robinson Crusoe*
Donaldson, Seven., *A Sailor's Guide to Sails*
Duffet, John., *Boatowner's Guide to Modern Maintenance*

Fairfax, John, and **Cook**, Sylvia., *Oars Across the Pacific*, Norton, 1972

Gelder, Paul., *InterSpray's Race Around the World*
Gelder, Paul., *The Loneliest Race*, Adlard Coles Nautical
Gelder, Paul., *Yachting Monthly's Confessions*
Gibb, Jane., *Reluctant Cook*, www.yachthoneyjar.com
Glennie, John., and **Phare,** Jane., *The Spirit of Rose-Noelle*
Golden Press., *Seashells of the World*
Grant, Jim., *Complete Canvasworker's Guide*, International Marine
Gree, Alan., *Anchoring and Mooring Techniques*, Adlard Coles Nautical
Grenada Homemaker's Association, *Grenada Spice Isle Homemakers Cookbook*
Griffith, Bob and Nancy., *Bluewater*, Norton (sail books inc), 1979

Hammick, Anne and **Heath**, Nicholas., *Atlantic Islands*, RCC
Hammick, Anne., *Cruising on a Budget*, Adlard Coles Nautical
Harper Collins, *Flags*
Harris, Mike., *Small Boat Communicate*, (formerly, *Guide to Small Boat Radio*)
Harris, Mike., *The Compass Book*, Paradise Cay
Harris, Mike., *Understanding Weather Fax*
Hawthorn Series, *Irish Farmhouse Cooking*
Hemming, John., *The Conquest of the Incas*
Heyderdahl, Thor., *Art of Easter Island*
Heyderdahl, Thor., *Fatu Hiva Back to Nature*, 1974
Heyderdahl, Thor., *Kon-Tiki Expedition*, Flamingo, 1948
Hill, Annie., *Brazil and Beyond*
Hinz, Earl., *The Complete Book of Anchoring and Mooring*, Cornell Maritime Press

Hinz, Earl., *Understanding Sea Anchors and Drogues*
Hiscock, Eric., *Around the World in Wanderer 111*, Adlard Coles Nautical, 1991
HMSO, *The Ship Captains Medical Guide*
Hood, *Safety Preparations for Cruising*, Waterline
Howard, Jim., *Handbook of Offshore Cruising*, Adlard Coles Nautical
Hughes, Henry., *Immortal Sails*

Innes, Hammond., *The Last Voyage* (of James Cook)

Jones, Tristan., *Yarns*, Adlard Coles Nautical
Junger, Sebastian., *Perfect Storm*

Kanter, Corinne., *The Cruising K.I.S.S. Cookbook; The Keep It Simple System*, 1996
Kemp, Peter., *The Oxford Companion to Ships and the Sea*, Oxford University Press 1988
King, Bill., *Capsize*, Nautical, 1969
Kittow, June., *Favourite Cornish Recipes*
Knox-Johnston, Sir Robin., *A World of My Own*, Cassell

Larsson, Prof and **Eliasson** R., *Principles of Yacht Design,* Adlard Coles Nautical
Leonard, Beth., *Following Seas*
Leonard, Beth., *The Voyagers Handbook: The Essential Guide to Bluewater Cruising*
Lewis, David., *Ice Bird*
Lipe, Karen., *The Book of Boat Canvas*, Seven Seas Press, Camden, ME
Lucas, Alan., *Cruising in Tropical Waters and Coral*, Stanford Maritime
Lucas, Alan., *The Tools and Materials of Boat Building*, Horwitz Publications

Macmillan Press, *The Cooking of the Caribbean Islands*
McLaren, Gavin., *Atlantic Crossing Guide*, RCC Pilotage Foundation
Marchaj, C.A., *Seaworthiness: The Forgotten Factor*, Adlard Coles Nautical
Marshall, Michael., *A Cruising Guide to the Caribbean*, Adlard Coles Nautical
Marshall, Peter., *Around Africa: From the Pillars of Hercules to the Strait of Gibraltar*
Marshall, Peter., *Celtic Gold*
Martin, Colin and **Parker**, Geoffrey., *The Spanish Armada*, Penguin, 1988
Mate, Ferenc., *Best Boats to Build or Buy*
Mate, Ferenc., *Shipshape: The Art of Sailboat Maintenance*
McDavitt, Bob., *Metservice Marine Manual for the South Pacific*
Meisel, Tony., *Nautical Emergencies*, Norton
Merry, Barbara., *Splicing Handbook*
Michener, James., *Tales of the South Pacific*, 1947
Moitessier, Bernard., *Cape Horn, the Logical Route*
Moitessier, Bernard., *The Long Way*
Mowat, Farley., *A Whale for the Killing*, Pan Books
Muir-Bennett, Alison, **Davis**, Clare., *Hitch-Hikers Guide to the Oceans*
Mundle, Rob., *Fatal Storm*
Murdoch Books, *Step-by-Step Moroccan Cook*
Murdoch Books, *Step-by-Step Spanish Cooking*

Neale, Tom., *All in the Same Boat: Family Living Aboard and Cruising*, 1997
Neale, Tom., *An Island To Oneself*
Nicholson, Ian., *Surveying Small Craft*, Adlard Coles Nautical
Nordhoff, Charles, and **Hall**, James., *Men Against the Sea*, Little Brown, 1934
Nordhoff, Charles, and **Hall**, James., *Mutiny on the Bounty*, Little Brown, 1932
Nordhoff, Charles, and **Hall**, James., *Pitcairn's Island*, Little Brown, 1934

O'Brien, Conor., *Across Three Oceans*, Granada
Ogg, Robert D., *Anchors and Anchoring*
ORC, *Category 1 Requirements*, (19 St James Place, London, SW1A 1NN)

Pack, Geoff., *Blue Water Countdown*, Yachting Monthly
Palin, Michael., *Around the World in Eighty Days*, BBC
Pardey, Lin and Larry., *Mediterranean Adventure*
Pardey, Lin and Larry., *The Capable Cruiser*, Norton.
Pardey, Lin and Larry., *The Care and Feeding of the Offshore Crew*, Norton
Pardey, Lin and Larry., *Storm Tactics*
Pastorius, Kay., *Cruising Cuisine: Fresh Food from the Galley*, 1997
Payson, Herb., *Blown Away*
Pocock, Michael., *Pacific Cruising Guide*

Reeds, *Reed's Nautical Almanac*
RCC Pilotage Foundation, *Atlantic, Spain and Portugal*
Roberston, Dougal., *Sea Survival A Manual*
Roberston, Dougal., *Survive the Savage Sea*
Roberts, John., *Fibreglass Boat*
Robinson, Bill., *Cruising the Easy Way*
Rose, Sir Alec., *My Lively Lady*
Ross Institute, *Preservation of Personal Health in Warm Climates*
Ross, Walace C., *Sail Power*
Roth, Hal., *After 50,000 Miles*, Stanford Marine, 1977
Roth, Hal., *Two on a Big Ocean*, 1972
Rousmaniere, John., *Desirable and Undesirable Characteristics of Offshore Yachts*, Norton
Rousmaniere, John., *Fastnet Force 10*
Ruhen, Olaf., *Minerva Reef*, Minerva
RYA, *Yacht Safety - Sail and Power*
Ryan, Rob., *Stay Healthy Abroad*, 1995

Saunder, Mike., *Yacht Joinery and Fitting*, Hollis and Carter
Schlereth, Hewitt., *How to Buy a Sailboat*
Severin, Tim., *The Spice Islands Voyage*, Little Brown
Severin, Tim., *St Brendan Voyage*
Shane, Victor., drag .... data base....
Sheahan, Matthew., *Sailing Rigs and Spars*. Hayness Publishing Group
Shepard, Reba., *Banana Cookbook*
Simpson, Colin., *Lusitania*, Penguin, 1983
Sinclair, Keith., *A History of New Zealand*, Penguin Books

Skoog, Jim., *Cruising in Comfort*
Slocum, Joshua., *Sailing Alone Around the World*
Smeeton, Miles and Beryl., *Once is Enough*
Smeeton, Miles and Beryl., *The Sea was Our Village*
Sobel, Dava., *Longitude*, Fourth Estate, London
Spurr, Daniel., *Upgrading the Cruising Sailboat.*
Stanley, David., *South Pacific Handbook*, Moon Publications
Stanley, Stewart., *In the Empire of Genghis Khan*
Stephenson, Marylee., *Galapagos Islands: The Essential Handbook for Exploring, Enjoying and Understanding Darwin's Enchanted Islands*
Stoddard, Charles., *Cruising the South Seas*, 1987

Taylor, Jane., *From Rudders To Udders*
Tilman, H.W., *Eight Sailing / Mountain Exploration Books*
Theroux, Paul., *Paddling Oceania*
Thomson, George., *Traditional Irish Recipes*
Thornton, Tim., *The Offshore Yacht*, Adlard Coles Nautical
Time Life International, *Recipes - The Cooking of the Caribbean Islands*
Toghill, Jeff., *Boat Owner's Maintenance Manual*, Reed

Ullswater., *Everest*

Vaitses, Allan., *What Shape is She In*
Von Dorn, William., *Oceanography and Seamanship*, Dodd, Mead and Company

Wallace, Alfred., *The Malay Archipelago*
Wiley, Jack., *Canvas and Upholstery Projects for Boats*, TAB Books
Worth, Claud., *Yacht Cruising*

Useful Addresses:

American Boat and Yacht Council, PO Box 806, 190 Ketcham Ave, Amityville, NY 11701
American Bureau of Shipping, ABS House, 1 Frying Pan Alley, London E1 7HR
Adlard Coles Nautical, email: jmurphy@acblack.co.uk
ARC, web: www.worldcruising.com
Avon Inflatables, web: www.avoninflatables.co.uk

BBC, London Calling PO Box 76, Bush House, Strand, London WC2B 4PH
Boat Jumbles, web: www.boatjumbleassociation.co.uk
Bluewater Rallies, web: www.yachtrallies.co.uk
Blue Water Sailing, web: www.bwsailing.com

Calor Gas, www.calorgas.co.uk
Calvert School, 105 Tuscany Road, Baltimore, Maryland 21210
CCA, Ivory House, St Katherine Dock, London E1 9AT, UK
Cruising Association, 1 Northly St, Limehouse Basin, London E14 8BT, England
Cruising Helmsman, email: carolinestrainig@yaffa.com.au
Cruising World, 5 John Clarke Rd, PO Box 3400, New port, RI, 02840-0992

Henri-Lloyd, Smithfold Lane, Warsley, Manchester M38 0GP
Herb Hilenberg, (Ham radio), email: hehilgen@aol.com
Hydrovane, Yacht Equipment, 117 Bramcote Lane, Chilwell, Nothingham NG9 4EU, England

Latitudes & Attitudes, email: editor@latsandatts.net
Lonely Planet, web: www.lonelyplanet.com

Mariner's Library, Sailing Classics, Grafton Books, 8 Grafton Street, London W1X 3LA

National Maritime Museum, www.nmm.ac.uk (at Greenwich)

Ocean Cruising Club (OCC), PO Box 996, Tiptree, Colchester, CO5 9XZ, UK
Ocean Navigator, email: editors@OceanNavigator.com
ORC (category 1), 19 St James Place, London, SW1A 1NN

Radio France International, 42 Avenue Coriolis, 31057 Toulouse Cedex, France
RNLI, email: seasafety@rnli.org.uk
Ross Institute, London School of Hygiene and Tropical Medicine, Keppel Street, London, WC1E 7HT
RYA, RYA House, 2 Romsey Rd, Eastleigh, SO50 9YA

Seven Seas Cruising Association (SSCA), 521 South Andrews Ave, Suit 8, Fort Lauderdale, FL33301, 33301-2844, USA

Yachting Monthly, email: yachting_monthly@ipcmedia.com
Yachting World, email: yachting_world@ipcmedia.com

YBDSA, email: info@ybdsa.co.uk

Westmarine, www.westmarine.com

Xaxero, www.xaxero.com (Sky-eye Satellite Imagery and weather fax)

Index

Managing Your Bluewater Cruise (Preparation Guide)
Rory and Sandra Burke

ISBN 0-473-03822-6

£17.50 (352 pages, 200+ photographs)

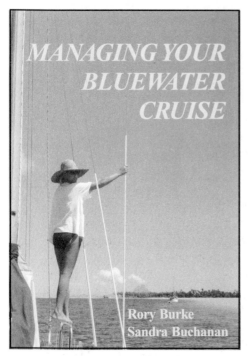

This is a preparation guide for those sailors who are considering bluewater cruising. Thoughts of bluewater cruising keep many of us going through the stresses and frustrations of working life. Yachting magazines and sailing books make excellent bedtime reading where one can drift off to an idyllic anchorage and dream of how life could be. But if you want to bridge the gap between fantasy and reality your bluewater cruise must be **effectively managed**.

Bluewater cruising has all the features of a complex project, requiring effective budgeting, procurement, scope management and time planning. Most importantly it requires effective risk management and disaster recovery for the safety of the crew and integrity of the yacht. This is in addition to the basic navigation and sailing skills you will require to get from A to B.

To establish the required condition (minimum standards), this book works closely with the ORC category 1 requirements, SOLAS and other international regulations. It includes many comments from yacht designers, equipment manufacturers, equipment suppliers, and other bluewater cruisers who are '*out there doing it*'. Where appropriate this information is presented in the form of structured checklists, procedures and cruising tactics.

Bluewater cruising, we discovered, was not just a sailing epic but a completely new lifestyle offering something for everyone. During our cruise we had many wonderful encounters with nature; swimming with the stingrays in Bora Bora, frolicking with the seals in the Galapagos and watching the blue-footed boobies nesting at night in Maupihaa. Our cruise was like a programme out of the History Channel as we followed in the footsteps of the great explorers: Columbus, Drake, Darwin and Cook. It seemed as if history, geography and nature had come alive, it was not a picture in a book any more - we could see it, we could hear it, we could even reach out and touch it. If this is the lifestyle for you, then the next few years could be the **most rewarding period of your life**.

 www.bluewater-cruising.com

visit our website for more information and book reviews

Project Management Planning and Control Techniques
(3rd Edition)
Rory Burke

ISBN: 0-620-23414-8 (Burke Publishing.com)
ISBN: 0-471-98762-X (John Wiley & Sons)
£23.95 (352 pages, 200+ diagrams and tables)

Project Management Planning and Control Techniques (third edition) is designed to take the reader step-by-step through the latest planning and control techniques, particularly those used by the Project Management Software and the Project Management Body of Knowledge (PMBOK).

As a training manual and academic text, this book has been well received by a wide market of users: from university under-graduate and post-graduate degree programmes, to short practical courses and certification for practising managers (PMP). With 75,000 copies printed, this book has established itself internationally as the standard text for project management techniques, and is supported with an Instructor's Manual for lecturers.

Despite the advances in project management software, the project manager still needs to understand the basic principles of project management to apply the software successfully. The text explains the techniques used by the software packages, so that manual calculations can be compared directly with computer algorithms.

Project management techniques are now used outside the traditional project industries, and a *management-by-project* approach has been adopted by many companies in an effort to keep their work packages small and manageable. Could this be - goodbye MBA, hello Project Management?

Fashion Drawing Techniques (A Short Course from Basic Sketches to Portfolio Presentations)

Sandra Burke

ISBN: 0-473-05438-8 (Burke Publishing.com)
(Book size - A4, 256 pages, 250+ photographs and sketches)

Fashion drawing is an integral part of the fashion designer's portfolio of skills, enabling them to develop ideas and communicate on paper. This book will teach you **how to draw** fashion figures and give you an insight into the world of fashion.

The text is set out as a step-by-step learning programme. Starting with basic *'triangle and oval'* figures drawn on a *'ten head'* format, you will quickly progress to adding body shape and clothing and, with a little practise, will soon be able to draw professional fashion figures.

The text is supported with explanatory drawings and photographs. Drawing exercises and worked solutions speedily aid the learning process and promote confidence in drawing.

Once the basic drawing techniques are mastered you will then be encouraged to explore and develop your creative flair and expression, and present your work professionally.

Target market: This book has been written for schools, colleges and university fashion design programmes in Britain, America, Hong Kong, Australia, New Zealand and South Africa. Internationally key people in the fashion industry and education, from designers, illustrators and lecturers, have given their support and input into the writing of this book.

Special mention is given to computer software and CAD, explaining how new technology can be used within the realms of fashion drawing and portfolio presentations.

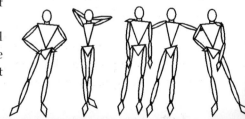

An instructor's manual with additional exercises and worked examples will be available for lecturers, together with internet support.

Disaster Recovery at Sea (Using Risk Management Techniques)

**Disaster
Recovery at Sea**
*(Using Risk
Management
Techniques)*

Rory Burke

Disaster prevention and risk management are new terms to the cruising environment - it is more common to talk about safety of life at sea (SOLAS), heavy weather tactics, fire fighting, and preventative maintenance. However, it is my objective to show how risk management techniques can be effectively applied to the cruising environment.

Cruisers are surrounded by risks. Most of the equipment and gear on our boats could fail and put the safety of the crew and integrity of the boat at risk. In reality it is not possible to respond to every risk - there is simply not the time nor the resources available. Therefore, we need some method of identifying the risks and quantifying their impact, so that we can prioritise our responses and focus our efforts on the most serious risks first.

The text also describes how to implement a **Disaster Recovery Plan,** the ultimate contingency for the ultimate unplanned catastrophe. A disaster may be defined as any event that prevents your boat providing its critical functions for a period of time resulting in significant loss or damage - for example, being dismasted or hitting a partially submerged container.

The practical application of this risk management approach in the marine environment is discussed. A number of real life marine disasters are presented - hopefully we can learn from how others responded.

Bluewater Checklist

**Bluewater
Checklist**

Rory Burke

"Have I forgotten anything?" Know the feeling? Checklists provide an effective management tool to confirm you have everything on board, and that you have completed all your tasks. During our cruise across the Pacific we complied many checklists, proformas, and procedures to control all our activities.

Presented here is a comprehensive portfolio of checklists covering every aspect of bluewater cruising from shopping lists to equipment lists, and safety procedures to maintenance records. Where appropriate, we have included checklists from international institutions (ORC Category 1, SOLAS and RNLI), manufacturers, yachting magazines and other published material.

The perfect checklist for one skipper, may be a clumsy fudge for another skipper. The book includes our personal checklists as well as suggestions from other sources, and many prompts to enable you to develop your own checklist tailored to your yacht, your equipment, and personal preferences.

www.bluewater-cruising.com

visit our website for more information

Rory was educated at Wicklow and Oswestry. He has a MSc in Project Management (Henley), an HND in Naval Architecture (Southampton) and has worked on marine projects in Britain, South Africa, New Zealand and the Middle East.

At the age of forty, having dreamt about bluewater cruising for over twenty years, Rory finally decided to take the plunge. He discovered that the bluewater adventure opened up new opportunities as he visited new countries and met people from other cultures; that history and geography suddenly came alive as he followed in the foot-steps of the great explorers.

The bluewater lifestyle gave him a sense of purpose where he felt he was living life to the full and he had more time for friends and time to write.

Rory is a member of the Madoc Yacht Club (Porthmadog), the Ocean Cruising Club (OCC) and a fellow of the Royal Geographical Society (RGS).

Rory being interviewed by the BBC

Sandra about to go snorkelling with the Galapagos Sharks!?

Sandra has a Master of Design degree from the Royal College of Art and has worked in the fashion industry in Britain, South Africa and New Zealand.

Sandra found the bluewater lifestyle gave her the time to catch up on her reading, writing and experiment in the art of cooking local dishes - from breadfruit to taro and coconuts to bananas. Sandra loved snorkelling in the crystal clear tropical waters and exploring the reefs with all their splendour, wonderful tropical fish and amazing shells - a far cry from the fashion shows of London, New York and Paris.

Rory and Sandra live on their yacht *Pacific Voyager* and are presently cruising the South Pacific. They have organised their yacht to not only provide a comfortable home, but an office where they write their books to achieve sustainable cruising.

Photograph, courtesy of Herb and ncy Payson, Yachting Monthly